Professional Business Writing

Seventh Edition

Elizabeth Kerbey
San Jacinto College Central
Business Office Technology
Pasadena, Texas

Marilyn L. Satterwhite
Business Division
Danville Area Community College
Danville, Illinois

 **Glencoe**
McGraw-Hill

New York, New York   Columbus, Ohio   Woodland Hills, California   Peoria, Illinois

Library of Congress Cataloging-in-Publication Data

Kerbey, Elizabeth.
    Professional business writing/Elizabeth Kerbey, Marilyn L. Satterwhite.—7th ed.
      p.cm.
    Rev. ed. of: Modern business correspondence/Donna C. McComas, Marilyn L.
    Satterwhite. 6th ed. 1993.
    Includes index.
    ISBN 0-07-821165-4 (alk. paper) -- ISBN 0-07-821166-2 (pbk . : alk. paper)
    1. Commercial correspondence. I. Satterwhite, Marilyn L. II. McComas, Donna C.
    Modern business correspondence. III. Title.

    HF5726.M425 2002
    651.7'5—dc21

                           00-060989

Glencoe/McGraw-Hill

A Division of The McGraw·Hill Companies

Printed in the United States of America.

Send all inquiries to:
Glencoe/McGraw-Hill
21600 Oxnard Street, Suite 500
Woodland Hills, CA 91367

ISBN 0-07-821165-4 (Student Text)
ISBN 0-07-821166-2 (Instructor's Annotated Edition)

3 4 5 6 7 8 9 008 05 04

Contents

Contents

Continued

Get ready for an exciting journey into the world of business correspondence through writing—you will be learning about letters, memorandums, and reports. You will also learn the basics of writing appropriate e-mail messages and various other documents.

But first, you will study how a message is developed from correct word choices that make up good sentences, which then become excellent paragraphs. All this will help you compose a message that does its job the first time!

Professional Business Writing will be useful to you on the job and at home as you produce messages that build goodwill and achieve the response you desire from the receiver. When you are ready to begin your job search, the information provided in the last two chapters of this text will be valuable to you as you develop your résumé and get ready for interviewing for a position.

STUDENT TEXT FEATURES

Professional Business Writing uses a variety of text and margin features to present concepts of interest and importance to your study of business writing. The text includes the following features:

The text, which is divided into four parts, contains 20 chapters, each of which opens with an introduction to the concepts and includes Objectives to guide your study of the chapter material.

Concepts and principles of communication are presented individually in the chapters so that you can focus on them selectively, and then see the concepts and principles applied in numerous examples. Key Points draw your attention to concepts or principles of significance that you need to commit to memory.

Checklists are provided for various topics to give you an opportunity to apply the principles to a communication message and then verify your understanding of the principles on the Checklists.

Oops! features provide real-world examples of the misuse of communication. You will be asked to analyze the situation and determine what should have taken place to avoid these poorly communicated messages.

Succeed! features give you an opportunity to analyze, critique, and decide what should be done about a particular situation. You will often be asked to distinguish between words or phrases that sound or look alike or to answer questions about how you should prepare a particular type of message.

CD-ROM references are provided throughout the text to direct you to the accompanying CD-ROM for additional activities.

Internet Activities give you the opportunity to search the World Wide Web to further your knowledge about topics related to the information in the chapters.

Proofreading activities give you a chance to check your understanding of grammar, punctuation, capitalization, and good writing style.

The Summaries describe what you have studied and prepare you to use the chapter information in the Worksheets.

End-of-chapter Worksheets let you check your understanding by answering questions, composing business messages, and completing exercises that relate to the chapter material.

The three appendixes cover Formatting, Interviewing, and Grammar.

COMPONENTS OF THE PROGRAM

Professional Business Writing is a complete, well-rounded program that includes the following components:

- A text-workbook with abundant instructions, examples, exercises, and worksheets for practice. The activities provide you with an opportunity to check your understanding of various concepts presented in the chapters.
- A CD-ROM with additional exercises and activities that relate to the concepts and principles presented in the text. The CD-ROM provides hands-on completion of editing and proofreading exercises, as well as composition of letters, memos, reports, and other documents; it also contains the *Glencoe Interactive Grammar* program for refreshing your grammar skills.

We have enjoyed developing this exciting text and its CD-ROM for you. Good luck in your studies using *Professional Business Writing*.

Elizabeth Kerbey
Marilyn Satterwhite

Acknowledgments

Special thanks go to Patricia A. Massey, College of the Mainland, Texas City, Texas, for her contributions in reviewing and developing various chapter material for this edition. Her contributions have brought timely content to this textbook.

The following educators have contributed significantly to the development of this text with their reviews and valuable comments. We thank them for their input.

Alan Baxter
Technical Career Institutes
New York, New York

Ben DeSure
Duff's Business Institute
Pittsburgh, Pennsylvania

Cora Goodner, CPS
Exxon Mobil Upstream
    Research Co.
Houston, Texas

Carol Jordan
Chemeketa Community College
Salem, Oregon

Joyce Kijowski
Sawyer School
Pittsburgh, Pennsylvania

Marilyn Leonardo
Boyd School
Moon Township, Pennsylvania

Betsy Ray
Indiana Business College
Indianapolis, Indiana

Dean Rehm
Skadron College
San Bernardino, California

Willis S. Vincent
City of Cincinnati
Employment and Training Division
Cincinnati, Ohio

William H. Wray
ECPI Technical College
Roanoke, Virginia

Doris Youngman
Florida Sports and
    Orthopaedic Medicine
Palm Harbor, Florida

Principles of Good Writing

Writing professional correspondence is a multifaceted, or many-sided, challenge. Both planning and composing effective messages require that you put the principles and techniques in Part 1 into practice. At first you will have to use them consciously and with much thought; later (sooner than you think), you will master them and use them with ease.

Every business writer should be able to produce a professional written message that

1. Is structurally complete.
2. Achieves its purpose quickly, clearly, and effectively.

The techniques you will learn in Part 1 will help you write a message that favorably impresses the reader and accomplishes its purpose. You should not expect to master all the techniques at once, but you will quickly see that writing is a combination of things going on at the same time, not a disconnected series of steps to do in a certain order.

Several letters and memos in this book were written by students. If you keep practicing and follow the general suggestions given in Chapters 1 to 6, you will also be able to compose successful letters and memos.

Being proficient in the following topics discussed in the chapters can be valuable to you in your professional and personal writing, as follows:

- Understanding the characteristics of professional writing
- Choosing the right words
- Writing good sentences that comprise good paragraphs
- Building goodwill in messages

All of these features of good writing can be put into practice when you study:

- Chapter 5 to learn how to plan and prepare specific messages, and
- Chapter 6 to begin composing, editing, and proofreading your own writing.

You will realize very quickly that writing follows some definite rules, procedures, and techniques, but it can be fun. Here are the chapters in this part to get you started:

Chapter 1

Characteristics of Professional Business Writing

Additional education is an investment of your time and money, but in what better way can you invest your time and money than in yourself? This course is one of a series of courses designed to provide you with the background and skills needed to succeed in the business world. Business writing is one skill that may be as important as all your other skills combined.

Objectives

After completing this chapter, you should be able to:

- Explain the importance of writing ability.
- Discuss how your communications are your trademark.
- Explain the advantages of written communication.
- Describe the total effect of your message on the reader.
- Identify the six Cs of professional business writing.

THE IMPORTANCE OF WRITING ABILITY

Job skills alone will not ensure your success in business if you lack the ability to communicate with supervisors, customers, and coworkers. Employers want to hire business workers with top skills; consequently, they screen résumés and job application forms for evidence of an applicant's knowledge and experience. More and more frequently, these job application forms include essay-type questions designed to test an applicant's ability to write effectively.

When hiring or promoting, employers will usually choose (from equally qualified candidates) the individual who demonstrates the best skills as a business communicator.

 The ability to communicate effectively with others is repeatedly identified as a top requirement of the successful businessperson.

Communication skills are also most often included on lists of areas in which employees need to improve. Whatever path your career may take, from entry level to the highest executive level, your written communication skills are vital to you. Finding a good job or receiving a promotion may well depend on how fully you have developed these skills.

Communication is a very important part of our world today. You may be a very intelligent person, but if you can't get your ideas across to others, you will be perceived as less intelligent than you are. Ideas are commonplace. The ability to clearly *communicate* ideas to others is rare. Learning to communicate your ideas effectively is what this book is all about.

WRITTEN COMMUNICATIONS—THE LIFELINE OF TODAY'S BUSINESS

You might think that technology would decrease the amount of communication needed. In fact, technology has *increased* the amount of communication because there are so many additional ways to communicate—e-mail, voice mail, cell phones, pagers, fax, Web pages, palm-sized computers, memory aids, and so on. Although technology has increased the methods by which a message can be transmitted, businesspeople have three primary formats for sending and receiving written information:

1. Letters
2. Memos
3. Reports

These forms of communication permit an exchange of:

- Ideas
- Facts or information
- Recommendations
- Proposals

Business writing is functional, useful communication. Without this exchange of information, business as we know it could not exist. Written communication becomes easier when you think of it this way:

 A business message (a letter, memo, or report) is simply a professional business conversation transferred to paper or electronic media.

The impressions customers, clients, and business associates form of you and your organization are important and lasting—and many of these impressions are based solely upon your written documents (or communications).

Goodwill is the favorable image people have of a business. Effective business messages build or retain goodwill, a priceless commodity that is hard-earned and easily lost. A business or an organization can never have too much goodwill. Writers who recognize this purpose of business messages strive to sharpen their *understanding* of *psychology* as well as English composition. Because the exchange of written communication is vital to business and essential for promoting goodwill, the art of producing professional business messages will help ensure your success in business.

YOUR COMMUNICATIONS ARE YOUR TRADEMARK

The memos, letters, and reports you write demonstrate your ability, or lack of ability, to communicate as a professional.

 Whether you like it or not, many people judge your ability and your intelligence by the quality of your writing—which includes the accuracy of your spelling, punctuation, and grammar.

Your written messages are a permanent record of your ability to write. People who read your communications form an opinion of you and your organization. Presenting yourself well in writing means that you will project a favorable image of your organization as well as promote successful business operations both internally and externally.

The techniques presented in this book can also be applied to your personal-business transactions. Everyone must write business messages in dealing with schools, medical facilities, travel agents, government agencies, retailers, banks, insurance companies, and other businesses. Professional business-writing skills assist effective communication in all aspects of life.

ADVANTAGES OF WRITTEN COMMUNICATIONS

The business letter—whether it is sent by the United States Postal Service (USPS) or electronically—has several advantages over other types of business communication. Some of the advantages are listed on the next page.

Succeed!

1-1—Think About Psychology and Message Writing.

How will understanding psychology help you retain goodwill?

Go to Student CD-ROM Activity 1-1.

1. A letter is frequently less expensive than a personal visit or a telephone call.

2. A letter and/or memo will get into an office when a telephone call may not be accepted. (Even the executive who travels a great deal or is too busy to be reached by phone will eventually read his or her mail.)

3. People seem to attach greater importance to a written message than to a phone call.

4. Business correspondence provides documentation (a written record) of a transaction and becomes a document that may be legally acceptable as a binding contract or as evidence in a court of law.

5. Business letters and/or memos are confidential, usually read in private. The reader will most likely be able to concentrate on the message without interruption. Therefore, material that might be unsuitable for a telephone conversation can be communicated in a letter or memo (especially if the envelope is sealed and marked "Confidential" or "Personal"). Remember, however, that if you fax your letter, it may not be confidential depending on the location of the fax machine on the receiving end. Sending the letter via e-mail as an attachment is also not confidential.

6. Statistical or technical data, charts, graphs, diagrams, pictures, and other enclosures can be sent with a letter or memo.

7. A written message is a fast method of sending the same information to a number of individuals and ensuring that all individuals get identical information.

8. Business writing allows you to spend time, as you need it, on the content of your messages and to word them in the most advantageous and persuasive way. A telephone call or personal contact, however carefully planned, is subject to the events of the moment.

1-2—Notifying Attendees of a Meeting. *You have to notify 25 people of a meeting. Would you call them? Why or why not? What would be the best way to notify the people?*

PROFESSIONAL BUSINESS WRITING IS A WRITING-ORIENTED COURSE

Simply watching a tennis match will not teach you how to play tennis, nor will strolling through an art museum teach you to paint pictures. By comparison, reading good business messages or reading about how to write professional business messages won't teach you how to write them.

 To develop your writing ability, you must do two things:

1. Analyze good and bad examples of written messages.
2. Practice writing business letters, memos, and reports.

This course will offer you many opportunities to compose effective business messages in response to realistic communication problems.

THE TOTAL EFFECT ON THE READER

Most people respond favorably to the naturalness, courtesy, friendliness, and sincerity of a message. Picture your reader receiving your communication. Will he or she be receptive to its message? Follow your reader's reactions in reading the message. A reader will stiffen at the sentence:

> *We* give every request full consideration.

but will relax when the sentence is rewritten as:

> *Your* request will be given full and prompt consideration.

> OR We will carefully consider *your* request.

The total effect on the reader determines what his or her reaction will be. Specifically, it determines whether you will get a positive reaction. If your communication does its job properly, you'll be able to answer yes to the following three questions:

1. Will the reader understand the message?
2. Is the tone of the business correspondence positive?
3. Will the letter or memo do its specific job and also build goodwill?

Question 1: Will the Reader Understand the Message?

Writing must be simple if it is to be clear. The simple sentence is the most useful tool in business writing. The **simple sentence** is a single independent clause containing both a subject and a predicate and expressing a complete thought. Resist the temptation to join a single idea to another idea with one of these links: *and, but, nor, or.* To keep your sentences simple, avoid overuse of transitional expressions such as *therefore, moreover, however,* and *accordingly.*

Avoid using complex and vague words. Fancy words won't impress the reader. *Use simple words* your reader will easily understand (without consulting a dictionary) to help the reader quickly grasp your intended meaning. Be correct and natural in your use of words and construction of sentences so that your writing flows smoothly. Your reader will understand you and be grateful to you as well.

 The highest compliment a reader can pay you, the writer, is to say, "Your letter (message) was simple, clear, and easy to read."

Question 2: Is the Tone of the Business Correspondence Positive?

How you say what you have to say may influence your reader just as much as *what* you say. Your letter or memo will appeal to the reader if you:

- Use a conversational, informal writing style.
- Stress positive rather than negative ideas.
- Emphasize a "you" viewpoint throughout the letter or memo.

The friendly tone of your writing should suggest that:

- Your attitude is positive.
- You are interested in the reader.
- You sincerely want to help.

Naturalness, courtesy, friendliness, and sincerity are all essential to achieving a good tone in business writing.

Question 3: Will the Communication Do Its Specific Job and Also Build Goodwill?

The easy readability and friendly tone of your message will attract and impress your reader. In addition, your communication should do both of the following:

1. Accomplish its specific job.
2. Increase goodwill.

One of the main objectives of all business writing is to encourage the reader to react favorably—to build the reader's goodwill toward you and your organization. You can't always do all that the reader wants, but you can almost always convince the reader that you understand his or her problems and that you want to do something about them.

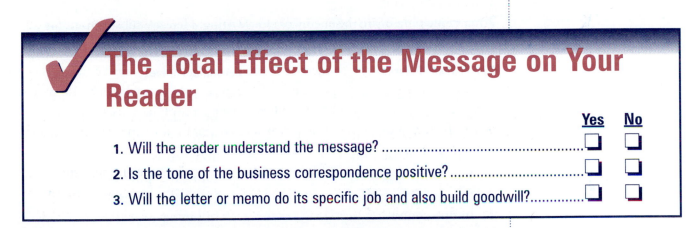

The Total Effect of the Message on Your Reader

	Yes	No
1. Will the reader understand the message?	☐	☐
2. Is the tone of the business correspondence positive?	☐	☐
3. Will the letter or memo do its specific job and also build goodwill?	☐	☐

THE SIX TESTS OF EFFECTIVE CORRESPONDENCE

 Key Point To communicate easily and effectively with your reader, apply the following six "C" principles: (1) courteous, (2) clear, (3) complete, (4) concise, (5) correct, and (6) consistent.

Courteous

Successful writers carefully choose the words they use, avoiding words to which they themselves would react unfavorably. In short, they put themselves in the reader's place by trying out the words on themselves before writing them to others.

Many times you've heard this expression:

 "It's not *what* you say, it's *how* you say it."

The people who read your business messages will judge you and your organization by your friendliness and courtesy. A friendly message is informal and written in a natural, conversational style. A courteous message conserves the reader's time and effort by using words that are easily understood.

Through your writing, project an attitude that focuses on the reader—the *"you" attitude*. Show the reader that you are genuinely interested in communicating. The tone of your message should also show your sincerity and desire to be of service. You should be as helpful, pleasant, and courteous to the reader as possible.

Clear

Clear writing is easy to understand. Clear writing demands short words. Clear writing should leave no doubt in the reader's mind of the shade of meaning that is intended by the writer.

Trite Expressions

Trite, vague phrases are the enemy of clear writing. Here are substitutions for some of these phrases:

Trite or Vague Phrases	Substitute Phrases
acknowledge receipt of	thank you for
at an early date	by Friday, May 2
at the present writing	now
attached please find	attached is
due to the fact that	(omit this phrase)
for your information	(omit this phrase)
in due course	in ten days
in receipt of	thank you for
regarding the matter	(omit this phrase)
regret to inform	(omit this phrase)
this is to acknowledge	thank you for
we are pleased to note	(omit this phrase)

Active and Passive Voice

Active verbs make writing forceful, more concise, and more interesting to read or to hear. Active verbs are verbs used in the *active voice* rather than the *passive voice*.

 active voice   The subject of the sentence *performs the action* described by the verb.
Example: The general <u>manager</u> <u>approved</u> the proposal.

passive voice   The subject *receives the action* described by the verb.

Example: The <u>proposal</u> <u>was approved</u> by the general manager.

The active voice creates the illusion of movement; the passive voice limits movement.

The Participial Phrase

A frequent enemy of forceful writing is the participial phrase. When introduced by such words as *assuring, hoping, believing,* and so on, the participial phrase is the weakest verbal construction in the English language. Compare these two sentences:

> **WEAK:** Assuring us that Plan A was the best deal, the sales associate wrote the order.

> **STRONG:** The sales associate wrote the order as he assured us that Plan A was the best deal.

The most important advantage of clear writing is that it helps the reader to grasp the essential message quickly. Make your writing clear by occasionally using linking words and phrases as transitional devices to join related parts in each message. Preparing a plan or outline will help you organize and present your thoughts clearly. A clear organization and presentation will help reader understanding and retention.

   Writing so that your message can be understood isn't enough— you must write so clearly that your message *cannot* possibly be *misunderstood.*

The keys to clarity (which will be discussed in more detail in later chapters) include:

- Logical arrangement
- Specific terms instead of general ones
- Directness
- Consistency
- Balance
- Comparison and contrast
- Unification

Complete

Completeness is closely related to clarity; a message may be unclear because essential information has been omitted. This request cannot be processed because it is incomplete:

> **INCOMPLETE:** Please send me some paper.

The reader needs to know how much, what size, what type, and other specifications. A good guide for the completeness test is to ask whether your message answers the "five Ws and one H":

 Completeness Test: Who? What? Where? When? Why? How?

When you are replying to an inquiry or request, be thorough in answering all questions asked, and even anticipate the reader's reaction by providing other relevant information.

Writing a complete message will show your genuine interest in the reader and your wish for a favorable reaction. Doing this will also save you the expense and possible embarrassment of a follow-up message.

Concise

Concise doesn't necessarily mean brief or curt. Being concise is saying what you have to say in the fewest possible words—which may mean two words or hundreds. You are concise when you cut down your business correspondence to essentials, stripping it of unnecessary words.

 Concise is not the opposite of long; concise is the opposite of *wordy*.

Teaming up two or more words of the same or similar meaning robs business messages of conciseness. For example:

> We are *grateful* and *appreciative* . . .
>
> We stand *ready, willing,* and *able* to be of *assistance* and *service* . . .
>
> We *look forward* with *anticipation* to . . .

Being concise means saying all that needs to be said and no more. Do not leave out important facts, but do increase communication effectiveness by (1) omitting irrelevant details and (2) providing complete, pertinent information with few words.

Correct

Spelling and typographical errors reflect in a negative way on you and your organization. You must be sure that the information in your message is correct. Even a small error in a date or an amount or an identifying number may result in loss of time, money, or goodwill—or all three. Verifying facts and paying attention to accuracy of details is time well spent.

Reasons for errors fall into two categories:

1. **Typographical.** Wrong letters, extra words, words left out, errors in spacing.
2. **Failure to check reference sources.** Misspelled words and names; errors in word selection, dates and figures, capitalization, and punctuation; and incomplete information.

1-1:

BE CAREFUL WHEN WORDS LOOK QUITE SIMILAR.

Sentence from an actual fundraising letter: "Encourage your friends to reserve your table during your assigned shirt so you can be their server."

Consistent

Your message needs to be checked for consistency before it is sent. Sue Camp, in *Developing Proofreading and Editing Skills,* lists four types of inconsistencies in business messages.

1. **Treating similar things differently.** Examples of treating similar things differently include indenting some paragraphs in a letter but not all, separating parts of a phone number with periods in one place and hyphens in another, and using different courtesy titles for the same person.

2. **Conveying unintentional bias.** Examples of unintentional bias would include not listing names in alphabetical order and putting a courtesy title with some names and not others.

3. **Making a sequencing error.** The order may not seem logical when items are not listed in a chronological or numeric order.

4. **Overlooking contradictions.** Contradictions would include math calculations that are not correct, and facts and dates (day of week and date do not agree) that are incorrect.

Most consistency errors are not noted until the second reading of a document.

Chapter 6 and Appendix C will help you check each message to ensure that it is correct.

1-2:
OVERLOOKING INACCURACIES AND CONTRADICTIONS.
Sentence from an actual letter: *"You paid $130 of your $150 bill, which leaves an unpaid balance of $10."*

THE IMPACT OF A UNIFIED MESSAGE

As you write, don't think in terms of the parts of your message or of each principle. Think of the overall effect of the whole message. Be aware, however, that overlooking even one quality that is important to the reader may weaken or destroy the effectiveness of your message.

You should take time not only to determine the important points to include and the best method of organizing and presenting them but also to review and improve what you have written. The reader's positive response will prove your success. When you succeed, you will know that you understand how to make a good impression and promote goodwill through effective business letters and memos.

Go to Student CD-ROM Activity 1-2.

SUMMARY

When the message you write passes the six tests of effective business writing, you will have reached your goals of informing, persuading, and positively influencing the reader.

The techniques of composing business messages discussed in this text will clear up misconceptions and help you to produce letters, memos, and reports that achieve their purpose. Remember that your business messages are your trademark. Your ability to write effective business messages will be one of your best skills for future success.

Name _____ Date _____

WHAT'S WRONG WITH THESE?

On the lines below, write what is wrong with the following sentences:

1. This is to acknowledge that we are in receipt of a copy of your order.

_____
_____
_____
_____

2. Enclosed you will find my check.

_____
_____
_____
_____

WRITING AN ANSWER

3. List six advantages a written business message may have over a personal visit or phone call.

_____
_____
_____
_____
_____
_____
_____
_____

4. Name three ways in which your writing skills can make you valuable to a prospective employer.

_____
_____
_____
_____

Name _____ Date _____

5. Give five techniques you will use to improve the clarity (clearness) of your writing.

_____

_____

_____

_____

_____

_____

6. List the six Cs of effective correspondence.

_____

_____

_____

_____

_____

_____

Applying the six Cs. Each of the following sentences lacks one of the C qualities. On the line provided, write the C quality that is lacking and the word or phrase that improves the italicized word(s).

7. *We are in receipt of* your check for $59.

_____

8. The personnel manager reviews all the impressive résumés and calls *them* for interviews.

_____

9. Please *advise me as to the date on which* you plan to make delivery.

_____

10. We *demand* payment now.

_____

11. The supplementary forms should be mailed in a *seperate* envelope.

_____

12. Please send me *some black computer ribbons.*

_____

Name _____ Date _____

WRITING AN ANSWER (continued)

13. *I am writing to take this opportunity to say* thank you for helping with last week's report to stockholders.

    _____

14. The confirmation of your *accomodations* was mailed this morning.

    _____

15. The usual discount is *6%* but we are offering a special 10 percent discount this month.

    _____

16. The sales representative told my boss that *he* did not have time to attend the training.

    _____

17. The meetings will be on June 4, May 6, and July 9.

    _____

18. Thank you for your Check 877 *in the amount of* $75.

    _____

19. Please call me Monday, January 3. (Note: January 3 is Tuesday)

    _____

Using the Internet

You will need access to the Internet to complete the Internet activity in each chapter. If you are not familiar with the Internet, ask your instructor for help or go to your school library or computer center for help.

Connect to the Internet and follow the steps below to get a list of Internet terms.

a. Type in the Web address (the URL) in the address box of the browser you are using.

b. Type: <http://www.noahsays.com/computers/2.htm.>

c. If you cannot connect to this site, do a search with the word Internet and look for a site that says glossary or terms or definition.

d. Print a copy of the terms.

e. Submit a copy of the terms to your instructor. Retain a copy for your notes to review later.

Chapter 2

Choosing the Right Words

Chapter 1 presented an overview of the principles of writing professional business messages. In this chapter you will begin the actual writing process. You will learn that

- A word can have more than one meaning

- Some words are more appropriate than others

- Incorrect words may cause confusion, and

- Pleasant and positive words produce a better effect on the reader than unpleasant and negative words.

Objectives

After completing this chapter, you should be able to:

- Explain why your reader may interpret your words differently from your intended meaning.
- Find resources to get help in choosing your words.
- Choose simple, concise, appropriate, correct, specific, and positive words.

THE WRITING PROCESS

You might think of writing as a building process. Composing messages requires several overlapping steps.

 Key Point The writing process involves these steps:
- Choosing words and phrases
- Creating sentences from those words and phrases
- Grouping the sentences into paragraphs
- Organizing paragraphs into coherent messages
- Editing and proofreading the messages

These steps represent a simplification of the writing process. We will begin to examine this process by looking at the simplest parts of language—words—and the many ways in which your choice of words affects your communications.

 Key Point The basic tools of writing are words.

THE MEANINGS OF WORDS

A writer must pay attention to the way a word may be interpreted as well as to the dictionary meaning of that word. Compare these sentences:

The speaker has a *loud* voice. The speaker has a *powerful* voice.
We sell *cheap* clothing. We sell *inexpensive* clothing.

How did you react to each sentence? The words *loud* and *powerful* have similar dictionary meanings, but loud sounds noisy whereas powerful seems effective. In the second set of sentences, *cheap* implies poor quality whereas *inexpensive* implies a low price.

 Key Point A word's **connotative meaning** is its subtle, suggestive, and sometimes emotional meaning whereas its **denotative meaning** is its dictionary definition. **Semantics** is the study of word meanings.

The connotative meaning of a word may vary from person to person, and it is difficult to anticipate how different people will react to different words. The writer must therefore try to choose words with positive connotations.

Before we study the ways writers use words in writing messages, let's consider how your mind processes words.

How Your Mind Processes Words

When you read or listen, each word goes into the part of your memory in which your brain has stored all the words you have ever heard or read. Your brain matches each word with the stored words and, based on context, matches the meaning.

Look at the following example of the many meanings for the word *stand*:

> *Stand* up! (move into an upright position)
> We can *stand* only one more day here. (tolerate)
> The organizations *stand* for different causes. (represent)
> Put the books on the *stand*. (a small rack or counter)
> *Stand* trial. (undergo)
> Take a *stand*. (a position or opinion)
> A *stand* of trees (a group or growth)

Your reader or listener will decide what *stand* means based on the context, or the text that accompanies the word.

Getting Help in Choosing Words

Keep in mind that the object is to choose words your reader can easily understand. One way to get help in choosing words is to use a **thesaurus**, a book or electronic resource that provides synonyms. For example, if the word *stand* did not seem to express exactly what you intended, or if you had already used the word in a previous sentence, a thesaurus could provide a substitute word. A thesaurus can also help you choose familiar words that your reader will be more likely to understand.

Remember this principle when you choose words for your writing:

 Use familiar words. Your reader will be more likely to attach your intended meaning to familiar words.

To communicate effectively with your reader, use short words to keep the message readable. Most familiar words are short, one- or two-syllable words. Help your reader understand your writing by using:

- Simple words
- Concise words
- Appropriate words
- Correct words
- Specific words
- Positive words

We will now study each of these categories of words in more detail.

SIMPLE WORDS

Short, familiar words help your reader understand your meaning quickly. More complex words may require the reader to reread or to consult a dictionary. Short words have more force and clarity than long words do. Simple words, however, are not always short. And short words are not always simple. For example, the word *attire* is shorter than the more commonly used and familiar word *clothing*. *Discern* is a shorter word than the more familiar *understand*. As a rule, though, choose a shorter word rather than a longer word unless the longer word expresses the meaning more clearly or naturally.

2-1—Using The Thesaurus *Use the thesaurus of your computer software to find simpler words for* punctilious, gainsay, pragmatic, *and* compendium.

The following example is very difficult to read with its unfamiliar, long words.

> The aggregate cadre would be honored to entertain submissions suggesting improvements to take under advisement for the betterment of our exigency procedures.

The next sentence expresses the same idea. The short or familiar words make the reading much easier.

> Please send your ideas for improving our emergency policy.

 Short, familiar words help your reader understand your meaning quickly.

In the following list, complex words and phrases are given in the first column and a simple translation is given in the second column. You will see many of these complicated words or phrases in business messages; however, strive to use the more familiar substitutes in your correspondence.

Avoid These Complex Words	Use These Simpler Words
approximately	about
are cognizant of	know
ascertain	determine
assistance	help
commence	start
consummate	complete **OR** finish
endeavor	try
expedite	rush
facilitate	help
interrogate	ask
negligible	small **OR** slight
numerous	many
procure	get
pursuant to your request	as you asked
render services	serve
subsequently	later
take under advisement	consider
terminate	end **OR** finish
unexpectedly delayed	delayed
utilize	use

CONCISE WORDS

Use only as many well-chosen words as you need to convey your message. Conciseness helps make your meaning clear and saves the reader time. In addition, your reader may lose interest if the message is wordy.

 Make your messages concise in order to keep your reader's attention.

In the following example, the reader must "wade through" wordiness to get to the point.

> I'm writing in response to your letter of recent date to advise you that the person to whom you referred in your letter, Ms. Lannie Crouch, is no longer employed in our division of the company as of June 30 due to the fact that she was promoted and transferred to New York.

We could eliminate two-thirds of the words of that sentence and state the message concisely as follows:

> You may reach Ms. Lannie Crouch in her new position in our New York office.

Notice that all necessary information remains, and the message is clearer and easier to read.

Time Wasters	Time Savers
at a later time	later
at the present time	now
at this point in time	now
costs a total of $125	costs $125
due to the fact that	because
during the month of February	during February
first and foremost	first
for the purpose of providing	to provide
held a meeting	met
if it meets with your approval	if you approve
in order to	to
in the amount of	for
in the event that	if
in the near future	soon
inasmuch as	since **OR** because
put in an appearance	appeared
until such time as you can	until you can
venture a suggestion	suggest
with the exception of	except

APPROPRIATE WORDS

Trite Expressions, Slang, and Clichés

To write effectively, choose appropriate words and avoid inappropriate words such as (1) trite expressions, slang, and clichés, (2) technical vocabulary or jargon, and (3) biased or gender-specific words.

Avoid overused expressions and slang in your professional business writing. A business message filled with such phrases will not be effective. A few examples of trite expressions and better alternatives are given in the following lists.

Trite Expressions to Avoid	Better Expressions to Use
acknowledge receipt of	thank you for
as per our conversation	as we discussed
in accordance with your request	as you asked
in view of the fact that	because
please do not hesitate to	please
regret to inform you that	am sorry that
take the liberty of sending you	send you
under separate cover	separately
we are in receipt of	we have

 Keep your writing free of clichés and slang expressions.

In addition to sounding unprofessional, clichés and slang expressions such as the following are confusing to readers who are not familiar with such expressions.

Expressions to Avoid	
ballpark figure	light at the end of the tunnel
beat around the bush	needle in a haystack
break the ice	nipped in the bud
by leaps and bounds	play it by ear
draw the line at	put your best foot forward
from A to Z	step in the right direction
give and take	strike while the iron is hot
in a nutshell	think on your feet
it was touch and go	turn the corner
lay your cards on the table	ups and downs
leave no stone unturned	

Because the workplace has become multicultural, writers must also be careful to use words and phrases that people with limited English can understand. For example, compare the expressions *look into*, *look out*, *look up*, and *look over*. The reader whose English is not strong may know what *look* means but get in trouble when *look* is used in a phrase. Or, a reader may understand what *cut* means by itself but *cut* used with another word produces a different meaning. Compare what *cut off*, *cut out*, *cut up*, and *cut down* mean. Be aware of expressions that may be confusing to people whose primary language is not English, such as these:

Irregular Phrases to Avoid	Clearer Words to Use
come up with	suggest or conclude
look it up	find or research
put up with	tolerate
talk it over	discuss

2-1:

AVOID CLICHÉS.

Upon hearing someone say "look it up," a visitor from the Middle East gazed at the ceiling.

Key Point In the increasingly multicultural workplace, you can help your readers understand your messages by using ordinary words.

Technical Vocabulary or Jargon

Many businesses use terminology that is unfamiliar to other people. When you create external messages (ones sent to people outside your company), you must consider your reader's experiences and interests. For example, the utility industry uses terms such as *load factor, Off-Peak Kva, Primary Kva, fixed fuel factor, cogenerator, municipalities, reconcilable fuel,* and *kwh.*

Be sure that you explain unfamiliar words and tell your readers what abbreviations and acronyms mean.

 Key Point Consider your reader's experiences and interests when choosing words.

Biased or Sexist Words	Bias-Free Words
chairman	chair or chairperson
cleaning woman	cleaner or helper
congressman	member of Congress
landlord	owner or manager
mailman	postal worker or mail carrier
mankind	people
manpower	staff, personnel
policeman	police officer
repairman	repair technician
salesman	salesperson or sales representative
spokesman	spokesperson or representative
waitress	server

 Key Point Be sensitive in your writing to the personal feelings of your reader. Choose words that will not offend the reader, whatever his or her heritage, sex, or physical attributes may be.

Bias-Free Words

Be sure to use gender-neutral terms such as *flight attendant* instead of *stewardess.* Avoid references to race, age, and physical characteristics, including handicaps.

In addition to using bias-free nouns like the ones above, writers must also be careful to use gender-neutral pronouns. For example, the statement "A police officer should always display his badge" incorrectly assumes that all police officers are male. Substitute his or her or rewrite the sentence to avoid the biased construction.

A police officer should always display *his or her* badge.
Police officers should always display *their* badges.

 **SUCCEED!**

2-2—Working with Culturally Diverse Others *A visitor from Indonesia doesn't understand what a speaker means by "The Sun Belt." How would you explain this expression to a person from another country?*

Internet Activity

2-2 Search the Internet for Terminology Choose a hobby or sport you are not familiar with, and search the Internet for terminology specific to that hobby. List five words or terms that an "outsider" would find unfamiliar. Suggested search words: *scuba diving, skydiving, stamp collecting, photography, gemology.* Be prepared to submit your list to your instructor.

 *Go to Student CD-ROM Activity 2-1.*

In the second example, notice that the plural construction requires that *badges* be plural as well. Be sure that nouns and corresponding pronouns agree in number (singular or plural). In this badly worded sentence, *Everyone should bring their lunch*, again the two pronouns do not agree in number. *Everyone* means "every single one" and is a singular pronoun. *Their* is a plural pronoun. To remedy this incorrect sentence, you might reword it in one of these ways:

Everyone should bring *his or her* lunch. **OR** Everyone should bring a lunch.

The following pronouns are singular. Be sure to make the other words in your sentence agree with them.

- anybody, anyone, anything
- each, either
- every, everybody, everyone, everything
- neither, nobody, nothing
- somebody, someone, something

CORRECT WORDS

Help your reader understand exactly what you mean. You can do this by using the right word for every circumstance. Words that sound alike but have different meanings and spellings are called **homonyms**—for example, *to, two, too*. **Pseudohomonyms** sound similar but differ in meaning and spelling—*affect* and *effect*, for example. **Antonyms**—such as *hot* and *cold*— have opposite meanings.

Use a dictionary or thesaurus to verify a word's exact meaning or to help you choose the best word. A few words that are easily confused follow.

Often Confused or Misused Words

accept—except	hear—here
access—excess	human—humane
adapt—adept—adopt	imply—infer
addition—edition	its—it's
advice—advise	later—latter
affect—effect	lay—lie
aisle—isle	lead—led
all ready—already	lessen—lesson
altar—alter	loose—lose
among—between	may be—maybe
amount—number	moral—morale
anxious—eager	passed—past
appraise—apprise	patience—patients
bad—badly	personal—personnel
bare—bear	precede—proceed
canvas—canvass	presence—presents
capital—capitol	principal—principle
cereal—serial	quiet—quite

choose—chose	realtor—relator **OR** relater
cite—site—sight	respectfully—respectively
coarse—course	right—write
complement—compliment	stationary—stationery
correspondence—correspondents	suit—suite
council—counsel	than—then
disburse—disperse	their—there—they're
eminent—imminent	to—too—two
farther—further	whose—who's
fewer—less	your—you're
formally—formerly	

 Use correct words to keep your writing professional.

Redundant Expressions

Avoid repetitive or redundant expressions. In the following expressions, omit the italicized words, which are unnecessary.

adequate enough	*final* outcome
attached *hereto*	*free* gift
basic essentials	*honest* truth
close *proximity*	*necessary* prerequisite
combined *together*	open *up*
consensus *of opinion*	postpone *until later*
continue *on*	refer *back*
cooperate *together*	seldom *ever*
end result	*true* facts
exact same	*very* unique
exit *off*	

Nonexistent Words

Careful business writers avoid using words that do not exist. For example:

Nonword	Correct Word
alright	all right
hisself	himself
irregardless	regardless
irrepairable	irreparable
revelant	relevant
your's	yours

Other Incorrect Expressions

In addition to nonexistent words, errors in the use of prepositions, conjunctions, adverbs, adjectives, and articles occur in business writing. The list on the next page contains misused words and phrases.

Incorrect Expressions	Correct Terms or Phrases
and etc.	etc.
anywheres or somewheres	anywhere or somewhere
between us three	among us three
between we two	between us two
between you and I	between you and me
different than	different from
don't have but	have only
eight items or less	eight items or fewer
inside of	inside
like I said	as I said
might of	might have
real pleased	very pleased or really pleased
should of	should have
the reason is because	the reason is that
these kind	this kind OR these kinds
try and	try to
two pair	two pairs
your invited	you're invited
where it's at	where it is

 Writers lose credibility when they use incorrect words or expressions.

SPECIFIC WORDS

You can make your writing more precise by using specific words rather than general words. Specific words present a clear, sharply defined picture in a reader's mind. General words present a hazy, indefinite picture to the reader. For example:

> What do you imagine when you hear the word *car*? Now suppose we say *a blue car*. Has the picture in your mind changed? Let's get more specific—*a metallic-blue Mustang*. How does your image differ from what you thought when we said *car*?

Giving the reader a mental picture of what you describe requires imagination as well as creativity. A thesaurus can help you find just the right word. Sometimes you must use more words to be specific, as illustrated above.

 You can be specific in your writing by limiting your use of extra words that have broad, general meanings. Use more specific words to give your reader an accurate picture.

Whenever you can, supply an exact fact, figure, or description to make your writing concrete and specific. The following examples show how you can replace many general expressions with specific words.

Avoid These General Expressions	Choose These Specific Words
a huge loss	a loss of $3.2 million
an appropriate time	within ten days
fast	in 20 minutes
for the full amount	for $240.02
great month	July profit of $10,000
long way off	1,520 miles
soon	by June 30
substantially	50 percent

You must constantly consider your choice of words in your writing. Write concretely by choosing vivid, image-building words rather than vague, general words.

POSITIVE WORDS

Use positive words to give a pleasant aura to your message. Warm words stimulate a positive reaction from the reader. Positive words, such as the ones listed below, produce a desirable psychological effect on your reader.

Positive Words

advantage	enjoy	progress
agreeable	fortunate	satisfaction
benefit	generous	success
comfortable	pleasure	valuable
encourage	profit	welcome

Here are examples of words that suggest negative ideas.

Negative Words

alleged	inadequate
apology	inconvenience
blame	inferior
broken	insinuation
cannot	loss
carelessness	neglect
claim	problem
complaint	refuse
criticism	regret
defective	sorry
delay	suspicion
discomfort	trouble
dissatisfied	unable
error	unfair
failure	unfavorable
impossible	unfortunate
inability	unwilling

Internet Activity

2-3 Using Specific Words and Phrases

Go to your school's home page to find the exact date and time registration begins next semester. Write a sentence for your instructor giving that information. If your school or college does not provide this information online, choose another nearby college or university. Be specific in your writing—provide the school or college name, as well as the dates.

 **Go to Student CD-ROM Activity 2-2.**

 Key Point The words *neglect, blame,* and *error* do not bring a negative response when you write "We neglected to tell you . . ." or "We take full blame . . ." Yet, when those words are used with *you* or *your,* the recipient may react angrily. For example, "You neglected to . . ." will offend the reader.

✓ Choosing The Right Words Checklist

Your words will convey your intended message if you can answer "yes" to each of these questions:

	Yes	No
1. Did the connotative and denotative meanings of your words convey your thoughts?	❏	❏
2. Did you use familiar, short words?	❏	❏
3. Are your expressions concise—not wordy?	❏	❏
4. Did you avoid overused words, trite expressions, slang, and clichés?	❏	❏
5. Did you consider your reader's background and interests?	❏	❏
6. Are your words gender-neutral and bias-free?	❏	❏
7. Did your pronouns agree in number with the nouns they represent?	❏	❏
8. Did you use your dictionary or thesaurus to verify meanings and spellings?	❏	❏
9. Did you omit unnecessary words such as redundancies?	❏	❏
10. Were you specific in your descriptions?	❏	❏
11. Did you use positive words to add a pleasant aura to your message?	❏	❏
12. Did you avoid using negative words?	❏	❏

SUMMARY

As you begin writing, refer to the lists of words and phrases in this chapter. You will develop good writing skills by paying close attention to the way you express yourself.

Name _____ Date _____

WHAT'S WRONG WITH THESE?

Each of the following expressions or sentences contains a negative, wordy, redundant, biased, or slang expression. In the space provided, indicate what's wrong with each phrase.

1. We regret to inform you that the item is out of stock.

   _____

2. An invoice in the amount of $154.95 is enclosed.

   _____

3. A hostess in a restaurant should always be courteous to diners.

   _____

4. The day was a bummer.

   _____

5. The errors were few in number.

   _____

6. I am sorry to have to inform you that it is our policy that we cannot assume responsibility for loss of items from your car.

   _____

7. Ms. Barker repeated her instructions over and over again.

   _____

8. All businessmen want to look professional.

   _____

9. You neglected to enclose your check.

   _____

10. The purpose of this e-mail is to invite you to our get-together.

    _____

Chapter 2 Worksheet

Name _____ Date _____

WRITING AN ANSWER

Substituting Better Words or Phrases. The italicized words in these sentences include misused words, nonexistent words, and inappropriate expressions. Rewrite each sentence on the line provided, substituting a better word or phrase for the italicized words.

11. The children *were cutting up* in the restaurant.

    _____

    _____

12. Each person should pick up *their* packet before the meeting.

    _____

    _____

13. The *councilor* gave me *advise* on the *amount* of classes I need for my degree.

    _____

    _____

14. Susan and Jerry have the same *identical* mousepads.

    _____

    _____

15. *Like* I said in my recent memo, *your* welcome to attend our staff meeting.

    _____

    _____

16. We will *remunerate* you for your expenses.

    _____

    _____

17. The video was *way cool*.

    _____

    _____

18. If you do not know the date of the incident *off the top of your head*, please *look it up*.

    _____

    _____

Name _____   Date _____

19. *In the event that* I do not *show up,* call my assistant.

_____

_____

20. *Get in touch with* me if I can help you.

_____

_____

21. Everybody should use *their* own judgment.

_____

_____

REWRITING SENTENCES

Precise Word Choices. **These sentences contain vague expressions. Rewrite each sentence to make it more specific. Note: You may assume any information necessary to make the sentences specific.**

22. You should apply for the job as soon as possible.

_____

_____

23. I will arrive at your office at the appointed time.

_____

_____

24. Only a few people attended the monthly meeting.

_____

_____

25. You will receive your scholarship check in the near future.

_____

_____

26. We want to order some pencils.

_____

_____

Name _____ Date _____

LETTER EXERCISE

Circle the correct words in the following letter:

Dear Ms. Sawyer:

In response to your request, I am honored to serve as (chairman, chair) of the speaker committee. My committee has (begun, commenced) scheduling speakers for the next year, and we have (a lot of, seven) speakers committed (all ready, already). Only two asked to be (paid, remunerated); therefore, we will be able to stay within the (ballpark figure, estimate) of $350.

When we (assemble together, meet) next week, we will ask members to (render, give) us their ideas for additional speakers.

If you have (further, farther) suggestions, please (advice, advise).

Sincerely,

Name _____ Date _____

ANALYZE AND WRITE

Avoiding Inappropriate Expressions. Choose one of the following examples.

- What does the cliché *lay all your cards on the table* mean? Write a sentence saying that you want to "lay all your cards on the table" about a situation, but do not use that expression.

  _____

  _____

  _____

  _____

  _____

  _____

- What does *put our heads together* mean? Write a sentence suggesting that you and a coworker put your heads together to work on a problem but avoid the cliché.

  _____

  _____

  _____

  _____

  _____

  _____

Verifying Corporate Names

In addition to using correct words in their business writing, careful writers always verify the spelling, abbreviations, and punctuation of company names. Search the Internet for the official corporate names for five large companies. Suggestions: oil companies, restaurant chains, automobile manufacturers. Because the Internet contains many sites that display incorrect information, you must go to each company's official Website. Print out one page from each site that shows the full official name of the corporation. Write each company's full name on the lines below.

_____

_____

_____

_____

_____

Writing Sentences and Paragraphs

Words alone do not communicate; they must be arranged appropriately.

A good writer:

1. **Constructs sentences by choosing words carefully and organizing those words into complete thoughts.**
2. **Joins sentences to form logical paragraphs.**
3. **Unifies the paragraphs.**

The way you construct your sentences determines the way your reader will interpret your ideas. If you assemble those sentences effectively, you can lead the reader through your ideas. Your goal is to present smoothly flowing ideas to your reader.

CONSTRUCTING SENTENCES

The "rules" for constructing sentences are not so complicated. Of course, you should observe the principles of written English; otherwise, you will distract your reader.

Generally, sentence construction in business writing is more conversational than it is in formal writing. Communication takes place more efficiently when the reader is thinking about *content* rather than the *way* you are presenting your ideas. Follow these nine guidelines for writing effective sentences:

1. Construct each sentence so that it contains one complete thought.
2. Include only one idea in each sentence.
3. Vary the sentence lengths.
4. Write concisely.
5. Use the active voice.
6. Vary sentence structure.
7. Link sentences naturally.
8. Punctuate sentences correctly.
9. Use correct grammar.

1. Construct Each Sentence So That It Contains One Complete Thought

 A *sentence* is a grammatically correct arrangement of a group of words that expresses one complete thought.

If a group of words provides only part of an idea, it is a **sentence fragment**.

> **FRAGMENT:** Because you are a valued customer

> **FRAGMENT:** If you will return the item this week

Each fragment above starts an idea but does not complete the thought. You might finish each sentence this way:

> **COMPLETE SENTENCE:** Because you are a valued customer, we hope that you will visit us soon.

COMPLETE SENTENCE: If you will return the item this week, your November 30 statement will reflect the credit.

Sentence fragments, frequently introduced by prepositions (*with, in,* and so on) or participles (*realizing, looking,* and so on), sometimes appear in conspicuous places that readers notice—as opening or closing ideas. Notice the italicized fragments in the following examples.

WEAK OPENINGS WITH FRAGMENTS:

With reference to your suggestion concerning refunds. Within a week I hope to have a solution to this problem.

Knowing that you expect only the best from your supplier. We offer only high-quality products in our catalog.

You can make these openings acceptable by substituting a comma for the first period. You can make them even better, however, by rewording them and applying some of the principles you learned in Chapter 2.

COMPLETE SENTENCES WITH STRONG OPENINGS:

We welcome your suggestion concerning refunds. Within a week I hope to have a solution to this problem.

You expect only the best from your supplier, and you will find only high-quality products in our catalog.

Notice how much more effective a strong closing is than the following trite expression, which is also a sentence fragment.

WEAK CLOSING: Thanking you in advance for your courtesy and cooperation in this matter.

STRONG CLOSING: We appreciate your cooperation.

Sometimes you may want to use a sentence fragment deliberately—for emphasis. It can express a complete thought if an exclamation point or a question mark follows.

That's right—*lifetime protection!* Worldwide, 24 hours a day. And how?

Tonight! Our special Sundown-to-Sunup 40 Percent-Off Sale—*don't miss it!*

In these examples, sentence fragments make the tone of the message "breezy" and "chatty." This informality may help to quickly establish both friendliness and a feeling of trust in a sales letter or direct mail advertisement. In general business correspondence, however, such informality can be inappropriate because the reader may think that the writer is being sarcastic or insincere.

Use sentence fragments sparingly in most types of business writing. Use fragments only for a clear purpose and when you know that your reader will not consider the fragment a grammatical error or an expression of an insincere attitude.

2. Include Only One Idea in Each Sentence.

Just as sentence fragments do not express one complete thought, sentences that contain more than one idea weaken the message. Too many ideas expressed without a pause tend to run together in the reader's mind.

 Each sentence should convey a single thought.

> **WEAK:** Thank you, Ms. Long, for your May 12 letter endorsing our newsletter and giving us your temporary address, where we will send your next three copies, beginning with the June issue.

In this opening sentence, the writer attempts to do two tasks: to thank the customer for the compliment and to confirm the temporary change of address. Because the two ideas run together in one sentence, neither idea stands out. Give equal emphasis to both ideas by using two sentences, as follows:

> Thank you, Ms. Long, for your May 12 letter endorsing our newsletter. Beginning with the June issue, your next three copies will arrive at your temporary address.

Placing more than one idea into a sentence may also result in a **run-on sentence**—two or more independent clauses joined without the correct punctuation or conjunctions. A comma is not strong enough to join two independent clauses. If you do not use a conjunction or other connective to join two independent clauses, use a semicolon. For example: *The meeting begins at noon; please arrive at least 10 minutes early.* Notice that a semicolon is required because each clause forms an independent clause. The following run-on sentence contains three ideas:

> **RUN-ON:** Please be prepared to discuss your ideas at the meeting, they don't require typing, if possible, though, you should write them in outline form.

Notice how much clearer the message becomes when split into three sentences:

> **CLEAR:** Please be prepared to discuss your ideas at the meeting. You do not need to type them. If possible, though, write your ideas in outline form.

Give more emphasis to an important idea by dividing it into parts and expressing each part in a separate sentence. Even though the following weak example is not a run-on sentence, the message becomes much stronger as two sentences:

> **WEAK:** We promise you excellent service in the future, and please let us know of any way we can make your next flight more enjoyable.

> **STRONG:** We promise you excellent service in the future. Please let us know of any way we can make your next flight more enjoyable.

3. Vary the Sentence Lengths

For quick, clear, easy reading, write short and simple sentences, right? Wrong! Sentences should *average* about 17 words in length for fast reading. You may use sentences longer than 20 words or as short as 4 or 5 words for variety and emphasis. Imagine the monotony of a message in which each sentence is exactly 17 words long.

Key Point ▶ **Enliven your writing by varying sentence length.**

Varying sentence length vitalizes your writing. A very short sentence placed between two long sentences emphasizes the thought of the short sentence. A few very short sentences help give the message "punch." But too many short sentences one after the other make the message seem fractured or "choppy."

> **FRACTURED:** We received your shipment of February 18. It contained four boxes of designer swimwear, Stock No. 1187. There was one box each in Misses sizes 8, 10, 12, and 14. But we ordered four each in Junior sizes 5, 7, 9, and 11. You can see this on the copy of the order, which is enclosed.

> **STRONG:** Your February 18 shipment of four boxes of designer swimwear, Stock No. 1187—one each in Misses sizes 8, 10, 12, and 14—arrived today. However, the enclosed copy of our order shows four each in Junior sizes 5, 7, 9, and 11.

On the other hand, extra-long, rambling sentences hinder readability. In the following example, the writer has jumbled the ideas to the point at which the reader must reread—perhaps several times—to make any sense.

> **RAMBLING:** In response to your inquiry about our agreement, we desire to enter it upon the record that, out of our six (6) percent commission to be paid to us by the Albrights for making sale of this property for them, we agree to pay you a commission of three (3) percent of the sale price, amounting to $3000, as a service to you and as compensation for the work and expense of closing the sale, and we further agree that no portion of this charge shall be assessed against or paid by the purchaser.

Isn't this rewrite much easier to read?

> **STRONG:** The following states the terms of our agreement: The Albrights will pay our commission for selling this property. We agree to pay you a commission of three (3) percent of the sale price, amounting to $3000, at the closing. We further agree that no portion of this charge will accrue to the purchaser.

Too-long sentences often result from overuse of *and* or *and so* and from too many dependent clauses. A discussion of these two careless writing habits follows.

The "And" or "And So" Habit

In the following sentence, notice how the overuse of *and* weakens the message.

> **WEAK:** We presently employ 93,466 people at 11 sites in the greater Denver area, and so this makes us the third-largest private employer in the area, and we hope you will see fit to include these figures in your brochure, and we thank you for your cooperation.

You can usually correct this kind of error by making several sentences from the long sentences. When you do this, vary the sentence arrangements. In the following rewrite, a prepositional phrase introduces the first sentence.

> **STRONG:** With 93,466 employees at 11 sites in the greater Denver area, Mason Manufacturing ranks as the third-largest private employer in this area. We would appreciate your including these figures in your brochure.

Instead of the expression *and so*, use transitional words such as *therefore*, *consequently*, and *accordingly* to connect clauses.

> **WEAK:** Our supplier does stock PetLove pet doors, and so we can order a replacement flap if you will send us the size.

> **STRONG:** Our supplier does stock PetLove pet doors; therefore, we can order a replacement flap if you will send us the size.

The "Dependent-Clause Chain" Habit

Chains of dependent clauses produce confusing sentences. A series of overlapping clauses introduces new ideas and expands previous ideas so fast that the reader can barely grasp one idea before the next one arrives. Notice all the clauses introduced by *which* in this long sentence:

> **WEAK:** Ms. Jamie Boggan will take Air Pacific Flight 190 at 4:15 p.m., which should arrive in Seattle at 6:10 p.m., which means that you should plan to meet her and accompany her to the tennis awards banquet, which begins at 7:30 p.m.

See how you might correct this problem by making two sentences:

> **STRONG:** Ms. Jamie Boggan will arrive in Seattle at 6:10 p.m. on Air Pacific Flight 190. Please plan to meet her and accompany her to the tennis awards banquet, which begins at 7:30 p.m.

4. Write Concisely

Whether your sentence is long or short, make it concise. **Concise** is the *opposite of wordy;* it is not the opposite of *long*. If your sentences are concise, they contain no wasted words.

You have already studied the wisdom of avoiding needless repetition and of using concise words and phrases. You learned to avoid using three or four words to say something you can say just as well or better in one or two words. Apply that rule to sentences as well.

 **Use only as many words as you need for your message.**

Useless Words

Eliminate words that do not help make your meaning clear or your tone courteous. As an example, the beginnings *It is, There are,* and *There were* generally add nothing to sentences. They also tend to lead you into stiff, formal writing and passive constructions. When you see that you have used one of these beginnings, try rearranging the sentence to eliminate the phrase and to achieve conciseness.

WORDY: There are two choices open to you.

CONCISE: You have two choices.

Look at the next example. Although the sentence is grammatically correct, it can be improved by eliminating the useless words.

WORDY : The reason I cannot attend is that I will be out of town.

CONCISE: I cannot attend because I will be out of town.

Repetitiveness

In the following request message, the writer begins with a vague introductory sentence. The rest of the message is repetitive and rambling and wastes the reader's time.

WEAK: I would like to ask a question about your summer school course offerings in the computer science curriculum. The offerings at the Knoxville campus seem to be geared to upper-level students, and I am having difficulty finding introductory-level courses to take. It would help if you could send me schedules from your Chattanooga, Martin, and Nashville campuses, so that I can decide what I want to take this summer and reserve a dorm room early. When these schedules are available, will you please send them to me at the address below.

The writer's real purpose—to request schedules—is buried in a clutter of unnecessary information. He or she can solve the other problems after receiving the schedules. Isn't this a more forceful request?

STRONG: Please send summer school schedules for the computer science curriculum at your Chattanooga, Martin, and Nashville campuses. My address follows.

The only reason for restating a question or an idea, once it has been asked or said clearly and forcefully, is to gain emphasis. Repeating a question or an idea because you failed to state it clearly the first time is poor writing. In the following example, do you think that it is necessary to thank the reader twice?

Dear Advisory Committee Member:

Thank you so much for attending our advisory committee meeting last week. Your ideas will help us improve our curriculum and give our students the training they need to meet the needs of the community.

Thanks again for your time. We hope to see you again next year.

Sincerely,

The second *thank-you* sentence seems to be a filler because the writer couldn't think of anything else to say. Omitting the repetition makes the letter stronger.

Obvious Statements

If you agree that concise writing helps your message accomplish its purpose, then you will also agree that it is wise to omit facts the reader already knows. When you state the obvious, you waste words and risk offending the reader by implying that he or she is ignorant or forgetful. You also appear to be forgetful or thoughtless—you should realize the reader already knows the information.

Beginning a Message

Obvious statements in business messages usually appear at the beginning. Writers who use obvious statements instead of direct beginnings admit that they don't know how to begin.

If you begin your message by telling the reader that you received his or her letter, which you are answering, or by restating what the reader said in the letter, you are losing the advantage of the letter's most effective position—the opening sentence.

Your answer is evidence that you received the reader's correspondence. Why waste the important beginning of your message telling the reader, "In reply to your letter of March 23, . . ."or "In your letter of May 7 you stated that . . ."? If the reader doesn't remember all the details, a quick glance at the file copy will provide those details. Your job is to give the reader an *answer*, not to echo the reader's words.

Thus, the best way to begin a reply to a business message is usually to answer the reader's question. In Chapter 5 you will read about a few situations when you should *not* begin the message with the main point. The following examples begin with obvious statements:

> **WEAK:** I am in receipt of your letter which is dated September 19. You wanted to know the current prices of our Amadeus microcassette recorders; so I am enclosing our latest price list, which will cover all this information.

> **WEAK:** I am replying to your letter of October 9. With this letter you enclosed a check for $101.25, the total amount due since August.

Notice how the rewritten messages state the same information concisely.

> **STRONG:** The enclosed list shows current prices for our Amadeus microcassette recorders.

> **STRONG:** Thank you for your check for $101.23, which clears your account.

Ending a Message

As with beginnings, writers often have trouble ending messages. After answering the reader's questions and giving explanations, a writer may then resort to trite phrases.

TRITE: Thank you again for your interest in our product. If you need further information with regard to this matter, or if we may assist you in any way, please don't hesitate to contact us.

As we have already seen, once is enough to give thanks; say it twice and you may appear to be overeager. To offer further information or assistance may seem courteous, but it really means that you aren't sure that your answer was complete. Assume that if the reader needs more information or help, you will hear from him or her.

Deleting trite endings, like avoiding obvious beginnings, improves the message. Take this business letter as an example:

Dear Mrs. Rutherford:

SUBJECT: AQUATICS SCUBA GEAR

Thank you for your recent request for more information on the Aquatics scuba gear advertised in the June issue of *Underwater Fantasy*.

We appreciate your interest in Aquatics products. The enclosed literature gives complete descriptive data and specifications—and we are asking our dealer in your area to contact you. The dealer's address follows:

Mr. Doug McNeese
The Dive Shop
7850 Poplar Avenue
Germantown, TN 38138
Phone: (901) 755-3442

Mr. McNeese will give you excellent service and can answer questions about Aquatics scuba gear and demonstrate the ways in which it can make your next dive safer and more enjoyable.

Meanwhile, if we can be of further help to you, just call on us. We'll be glad to assist you in any way.

Sincerely,

Would the letter be weakened if you removed the first and last paragraphs? No. Actually, omitting these two paragraphs makes the message concise and clear.

Go to Student CD-ROM Activity 3-1.

5. Use the Active Voice

Active verbs—verbs used in the active voice—create strong sentences. In the active voice, the subject of the sentence performs the action. On the other hand, in the passive voice, the subject receives the action. Compare these examples:

> **ACTIVE:** Janet gave the report.

> **PASSIVE:** The report was given by Janet.

In the active example, the subject of the sentence—Janet—performs the action. The reader "sees" Janet presenting the report. In the passive example, the subject—report—is not performing the action; rather, the subject is receiving the action. The reader now "sees" the report instead of the presentation of the report. This shifts the emphasis from the action and removes the interest and clarity. This construction not only weakens the sentence but also uses more words than necessary.

The two major disadvantages to using passive constructions are these:

1. Passive constructions require more words.
2. Passive constructions weaken the impact by taking away emphasis from the action and the person performing the action.

 Key Point The *active voice* makes your writing forceful. The *passive voice* weakens and dulls your writing.

Although the passive voice has its place, such as softening a negative statement, you should use it sparingly. For example, if you do not want to place blame for an error, you might use a passive construction in some cases. *An error was found on your report* (passive voice) doesn't accuse the way *You made an error on your report* (active voice) does. Even in a situation like this, you may be able to word the sentence in active voice without accusing. *Please recheck the calculation, for it appears to have a discrepancy* does not accuse, yet it calls attention to the error.

Make people the subjects of your sentences whenever possible, and write in the active voice to give the reader a picture of the subject performing the action. Stress the "people" element in your writing to keep it flowing and lively.

The grammar checker of your word processing software can help you revise your writing by counting and marking passive constructions. Be sure that the suggested revisions correctly express your intended meaning.

6. Vary Sentence Structure

We have seen that a long string of very short sentences can make your writing seem broken or choppy, that a sequence of long sentences makes reading difficult, and that sentences that are all the same length make a message uninteresting. Another fault—constructing all sentences the same way—affects the reader's reaction. A series of sentences with the same construction becomes monotonous and may even seem to insult the reader's intelligence.

Isn't the following paragraph monotonous?

> **MONOTONOUS IDENTICALLY CONSTRUCTED SENTENCES:** The Peanut Festival committee met to plan the events. The parade will proceed from Main

3-1—Individual Responsibility. *What is wrong with the wording in the following sentences?* You did not follow my instructions. You used the wrong figures in that report.

Go to Student CD-ROM Activity 3-2.

Street to the park. The peanut judging competition will then take place. The food booths will then open. The rides will also be open.

Besides varying the length of your sentences, you should also vary **structure** and **pattern**. One way to achieve variety in your writing is with different sentence beginnings. Since the way you begin a sentence almost always determines the pattern for the sentence as a whole, concentrating on beginnings is the logical way to control patterns. See how our monotonous paragraph becomes lively with varied length, structure, and pattern:

> **VARIED STRUCTURE:** The Peanut Festival committee met to plan the festival events. Starting on Main Street, the parade will proceed to the park where the peanut judging competition will begin. Immediately after the competition, the food booths and rides will open.

Another way to vary the structure of your sentences is to use simple, compound, complex, and compound-complex formations.

A **simple sentence** contains *one independent clause:*

> Mr. Barrow borrowed the reading file.

A **compound sentence** contains *two or more independent clauses:*

> Mr. Barrow borrowed the reading file, and he lent it to Ms. Connors.

A **complex sentence** contains *one independent and one or more dependent clauses:*

> After Mr. Barrow borrowed the reading file, he lent it to Ms. Connors, who took it to the Dallas meeting.

A **compound-complex sentence** contains *two or more independent clauses and one or more dependent clauses:*

> After Mr. Barrow borrowed the reading file, he lent it to Ms. Connors; and she took it to the meeting in Dallas.

better not to use

7. Link Sentences Naturally

Just as you arrange words in a sentence for smooth reading, also arrange the sentences in the message. Each sentence should flow naturally from the one that preceded it. That is, one thought should lead to the next.

 Check each sentence in a paragraph to make sure that it connects to the preceding sentence.

In writing sentences that fit together smoothly, you will find it often helps to follow these two tips:

- Refer in some way to the preceding sentence.
- Use connectives (transitional words and phrases).

Some examples of such bridging expressions follow:

Connectives

also	for instance	otherwise
as a result	however	previously
consequently	in addition	similarly
for example	in this way	therefore

In the following example, the sentences seem clear but do not connect smoothly to one another:

> Your proposal has a great deal of merit. A number of questions still require answers. A comprehensive market research program should result in an appropriate solution.

Adding a connective ties the thoughts together:

> Your proposal has a great deal of merit. Although many questions still require answers, we should be able to find an appropriate solution through a comprehensive market research program.

Without connectives, you risk leaving the reader guessing about the relationship between the statements in your message.

> **POORLY CONNECTED SENTENCES:** We agree with many of the suggestions in your report. We plan to implement some of them immediately. We will delay action on the remainder and get reports from other sales representatives.

> **IMPROVED CONNECTED SENTENCES:** We agree with many of the suggestions in your report and therefore plan to implement them immediately. After we have studied reports from other sales representatives, we will consider your other suggestions.

8. Punctuate Sentences Correctly

Writers generally have more trouble with commas than with any other punctuation mark. Omitted commas, unnecessary commas, or misplaced commas frequently distort the meaning of a sentence and may force the reader to reread a sentence several times to understand the intended meaning.

 Correct punctuation helps your reader understand your message.

Omitted Commas

One mistake occurs when the writer omits one of a pair of commas:

> **INCORRECT:** Ronald James, their vice president called while you were away.

> **CORRECT:** Ronald James, their vice president, called while you were away.

Another mistake that can confuse your reader is omitting a comma needed to make your meaning clear, such as *In business clothes make a difference.* The reader may be thinking about *business clothes,* when in fact, you meant to say *In business, clothes make a difference.*

Unnecessary Commas

A writer may incorrectly insert a comma between a subject and its verb, as follows:

INCORRECT: Analyzing the data and presenting recommendations by the end of the month, will be difficult. (The subject is *analyzing and presenting.)*

CORRECT: Analyzing the data and presenting recommendations by the end of the month will be difficult.

Misplaced Commas

Misplaced commas may interrupt the thought of a sentence. In the following incorrect example, the comma placement distorts the meaning.

INCORRECT: The most exclusive, as well as the nearest restaurant, offers banquet rooms for special occasions.

CORRECT: The most exclusive, as well as the nearest, restaurant offers banquet rooms for special occasions.

Let good usage and common sense guide your punctuation. If you do not follow accepted rules in punctuating, will your reader know what your messages mean? Maybe not. Review the punctuation rules in the Reference section.

9. Use Correct Grammar

Basic errors in English may make your reader think that you are ignorant or careless—or both. What is good English, and what are the rules of good English? The "rules" are general agreements among the users of English on how to use the language to achieve certain goals under various circumstances.

 Following the punctuation and grammar rules adhered to by the majority of skilled writers and speakers in the business world will give you credibility.

Subject and Verb Agreement

Business writers sometimes make this glaring error: they fail to make the verb agree with its subject. A verb should always agree with its subject in person and in number.

NONAGREEMENT: Neither the students nor the teachers was at the meeting.

AGREEMENT: Neither the students nor the teachers were at the meeting. (The plural form *were* agrees with the plural *teachers.)*

Review Appendix C on Agreement of Verb With Subject. Remember to check your writing closely for subject and verb agreement.

Parallel Construction

Using parallel construction improves sentence clarity. **Parallel construction** simply means using similar grammatical structures in phrases, clauses, and listings to express similar ideas.

> **NONPARALLEL:** My hobbies include water skiing, knitting, and to go to dances.

> **PARALLEL:** My hobbies include water skiing, knitting, and dancing.

Notice in the parallel version that each hobby ends with an "ing" noun, making the construction parallel.

You can read more about parallel construction in Appendix C.

Carelessness

Carelessness contributes to grammatical errors. Although sloppy writing seems much easier than careful writing, you can develop the habit of editing each sentence until it is mechanically correct.

How do you know what is correct, or standard, English usage? Reading, listening, writing, speaking, studying, and practicing the rules of grammar can help you develop an instinct for correct English usage.

The ability to recite the rules of grammar and punctuation will not necessarily prevent you from making errors. You must develop the ability to recognize your own errors. You can then turn to a reliable reference manual or English handbook for the rules you need to correct your mistakes and to improve your usage habits.

Grammar and Punctuation Rules

Appendix C briefly summarizes grammar, punctuation, and other rules. Review the rules and the examples until you feel confident that you can apply the rules correctly.

You may wish to buy one of the many comprehensive English-usage handbooks. And like every other writer—even the most competent one—you should own and make frequent use of an up-to-date, reliable dictionary.

 Always use a *current* dictionary and reference manual to help you write effective messages.

FORMING AND ARRANGING PARAGRAPHS

After choosing words and combining them to make sentences, you must group the sentences into logical paragraphs. The reader can better understand your intended meaning if your sentences follow a logical order. Take the same care in organizing paragraphs as you do in choosing your words and writing your sentences.

See pg. 101

 Key Point Identify the major subject or purpose of your business message; decide what items make up that purpose; then organize them into paragraphs.

Begin by identifying the major subject or subjects, and identify the items or parts within each subject. Then arrange everything into the order most likely to achieve your purpose. Follow these general guidelines to compose and arrange your paragraphs:

1. In each paragraph, cover one point of the major subject.
2. Vary paragraph length.
3. Keep opening and closing paragraphs shorter than average paragraphs.
4. Fit paragraphs together smoothly.

A discussion of each of these guidelines follows.

1. In Each Paragraph, Cover One Point of the Major Subject

An effective paragraph consists of a group of closely related sentences about one major topic. A paragraph contains a topic sentence, or topic statement, and the sentences that develop the idea.

When you introduce a new topic, start a new paragraph. A new paragraph lets the reader know that a new idea will follow. A paragraph containing unrelated ideas confuses the reader. By starting a new paragraph, you prepare the reader for the shift from one phase of the subject to another.

For example, assume that you work in your company's copy center. You compose a message to inform employees that they may now send their copy orders by e-mail. Each of your paragraphs should contain one part of that main idea. The different paragraphs, therefore, might break down this way:

First paragraph: Inform employees that they may send copy orders by e-mail.
Second paragraph: Give instructions for completing the request form on line.
Third paragraph: Give instructions on procedure for attaching the file to e-mail.

2. Vary Paragraph Length

p. 457 - 459

Most businesspeople are too busy to read a series of long, rambling paragraphs thoroughly; consequently, they may merely skim a line or two in each paragraph. Using one- or two-sentence paragraphs in combination with medium and long paragraphs gives emphasis to your main ideas and keeps the reader's attention.

 **Key Point** Place your main ideas in short paragraphs for emphasis.

You can, as a rule, read short paragraphs faster than long paragraphs. Also, most readers like the breaks that "white space" provides. A paragraph as short as one sentence—or even one typed line—may be effective. But remember that too many short paragraphs, just like too many short sentences, give a broken effect. At first glance, the reader may feel that the page contains too many ideas.

Break a short message into two paragraphs, even when the letter or other type of message contains only two or three sentences. A one-paragraph message rarely looks attractive, and it may give your reader the impression that you didn't care enough to write more than a few lines.

In a long message, vary the length of the paragraphs. For emphasis, use one-sentence and two-sentence paragraphs to call attention to important ideas, especially if longer paragraphs precede and follow. Short paragraphs attract the reader's attention and signal "This is important."

If a paragraph exceeds eight lines, you should consider breaking it into two or three short paragraphs. Think of "reasonably short paragraphs" in a business message as varying from two to eight lines, with an average length of four or five typed lines.

To continue our copy center example, see Figures 3-1 and 3-2. Which of the messages seems easier to read?

FIGURE 3-1 This message is difficult to read with no paragraph breaks.

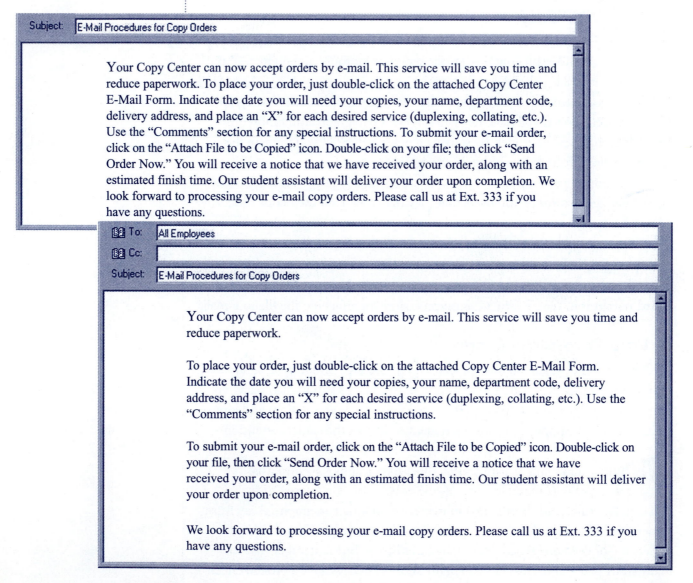

FIGURE 3-2 A message with paragraphing is easier to read.

3. Keep Opening and Closing Paragraphs Shorter Than Average

Brief opening and closing paragraphs give the message a neat, businesslike appearance. Since a reader hesitates when faced with a long mass of words, a short opening paragraph is especially important. A two-, three-, or four-line opening paragraph invites the reader to start reading. In a short closing paragraph, you can often stress the one idea that you want to leave with the reader.

> **OPENING:** Yes, Mrs. Hill, you have earned a five percent discount on your first order.

> **CLOSING:** To get your copy of our free brochure, just fill in the enclosed prepaid card and return it.

 The **most important location** in a message is the *opening*. The **second most important location** is the *closing*.

4. Fit Paragraphs Together Smoothly

You have learned the importance of smooth movement from one sentence to the next. To make a message easy to understand, the paragraphs in the message must also fit together so that the reader will be able to read naturally from the opening paragraph to the closing paragraph without having to reread. Sometimes you can show the relationship of paragraphs more clearly by numbering them or by using connective and transitional words, phrases, or sentences. Look at the following poorly paragraphed business message:

Dear Ms. Johnson:

Thank you for agreeing to speak at the September Educational Office Personnel meeting on March 8 in Tulsa, Oklahoma. The luncheon meeting begins at noon and ends at 2 p.m. We have allowed 45 minutes in the schedule for your presentation.

We confirmed that the banquet room lighting can be adjusted so that the projected images will show clearly on the overhead projector we will provide. I have arranged an e-ticket for your flight, Air East 202, which leaves Baltimore at 7:30 a.m. on the 8th.

I will meet you at Intercontinental Airport and transport you to the Halley Hotel (918-555-8899). We look forward to having you as our special guest.

Sincerely,

Don't you think the following version breaks the paragraphs more logically?

Dear Ms. Johnson:

Thank you for agreeing to speak at the September Educational Office Personnel meeting on March 8 in Tulsa, Oklahoma.

The luncheon meeting begins at noon and ends at 2 p.m. We have allowed 45 minutes in the schedule for your presentation. We confirmed that the banquet room lighting can be adjusted so that the projected images will show clearly on the overhead projector we will provide.

I have arranged an e-ticket for your flight, Air East 202, which leaves Baltimore at 7:30 a.m. on the 8th.

I will meet you at Intercontinental Airport and transport you to the Halley Hotel (918-555-8899).

We look forward to having you as our special guest.

Sincerely,

SUMMARY

You will achieve effective communication through unified structuring of the message at all levels—words, sentences, and paragraphs. A message has unity when all the paragraphs fit together to form an organized, cohesive message.

Check the paragraphs you write to make sure that they relate to each other and to the central theme of the message. Then polish the paragraphs until the message flows smoothly. As you study and practice writing the different types of messages in the later chapters, you will learn to place paragraphs in the best order to accomplish each specific purpose.

Name _____ Date _____

WHAT'S WRONG WITH THESE?

Each of the following items contains one or more of these problems: punctuation errors, fragments, run-on sentences, lack of subject-verb agreement, unparallel construction, wordiness, or passive constructions. On the lines below, write what is wrong in each situation.

1. Reading a good book at the beach, is my idea of a great day.

   _____

2. Looking forward to calling on you sometime soon.

   _____

3. I would like to sell you on one idea the value of my services as a financial counselor can benefit you and your family.

   _____

4. Your videotape will be sent to you next week.

   _____

5. I regret to inform you that the agent from whom you originally purchased your contract is no longer with the company and I am his replacement.

   _____

6. Qualities or skills you should develop include integrity, solving problems, and communication.

   _____

7. There were 20 visitors at our conference.

   _____

8. The awards for Most Valuable Offensive Player and Most Valuable Defensive Player goes to two outstanding athletes each year.

   _____

9. Abby Garner will teach the class, Steve Brown will be the substitute teacher.

   _____

10. In the event your choice is unavailable. We will refund your payment.

    _____

Chapter 3 Worksheet

Name _____ Date _____

USING GOOD SENTENCE STRUCTURE

On the rule next to each of the following sentences, indicate whether the sentence is:

simple (S)	*complex (CX)*	*fragment (F)*
compound (C)	*compound-complex (C-CX)*	*run-on (RO)*

_____ 11. Be sure to ask for permission from each of your references before you send your résumé.

_____ 12. Send copies of the budget to all department chairs, send minutes of the meeting to the associate deans.

_____ 13. When the holiday schedule arrives, we will circulate it, since we must follow the same schedule.

_____ 14. As predicted, interest rates continue to rise, and the economy continues to suffer during this period.

_____ 15. The marketing director suggested a new advertising campaign and asked the staff for creative ideas by next Wednesday.

_____ 16. If you take swimming lessons here, you will also learn CPR; then you can apply for our CPR certification.

_____ 17. Wishing you the best of everything for the new year.

_____ 18. Please visit the artifact exhibit at the museum, we need your support.

_____ 19. The Illinois chapter will meet in Room 208; the Texas chapter, in Room 215.

_____ 20. Updates for computer operators provided by software companies to subscribers on a regular basis.

USING THE ACTIVE VOICE

On the lines below each sentence, indicate whether the sentence is active voice (AV) or passive voice (PV). Then rewrite the passive voice sentences in the active voice.

21. The bank deposit was made by Sue Kruse.

_____

_____

_____

Name _____ Date _____

USING THE ACTIVE VOICE *(continued)*

22. The laser printer makes the best-quality copies.

_____

_____

23. The passive voice sentences were written by Jim.

_____

_____

24. After you prepare the payroll, the tax report needs to be done.

_____

_____

25. A Request for Vacation form should be submitted to the department supervisor from each employee.

_____

_____

IMPROVING WEAK SENTENCES

These examples include sentence fragments and weak sentences. Rewrite them on the lines, adding appropriate punctuation.

26. The order was processed by Larry. (*Note*: Eliminate passive construction.)

_____

_____

27. No matter how well known or how prosperous your business may be. New customers must constantly be added to your clientele. (*Note*: Eliminate fragment and passive construction.)

_____

_____

_____

28. Although your Christmas shopping may be almost done. We would like to suggest a gift that we believe is perfect for a member of your family. (*Note*: Eliminate weak opening and fragment.)

_____

_____

_____

Name _____ Date _____

29. Thank you, Mr. Tenley for the information you sent me on environmental studies, in Minneapolis. (*Note*: Correct punctuation.)

_____

_____

_____

30. In the event your choice has been sold out. Your check or money order will be cheerfully refunded. (*Note*: Eliminate wordiness, passive voice, and sentence fragment.)

_____

_____

_____

31. Please ask Sue to make the changes as quickly as possible and the report should be ready by next Tuesday. (*Note*: Correct switch from active to passive voice, and correct run-on sentence.)

_____

_____

_____

32. Social Security and Medicare benefits have been increased and so we can now offer you better service. (*Note*: Eliminate *and so* and passive voice.)

_____

_____

_____

33. Should you want your check, in the amount of $78.29, returned to you, please say so by indicating on and returning the enclosed self-addressed and stamped postcard. (*Note*: Simplify into shorter, clear sentence.)

_____

_____

_____

34. Refreshments were enjoyed by all of the participants. (*Note*: Eliminate passive construction.)

_____

_____

_____

Name _____ Date _____

IMPROVING WEAK SENTENCES *(continued)*

35. While waiting for the meeting to begin. We heard the good news. (*Note*: Eliminate fragment.)

_____

_____

_____

COLLABORATIVE EXERCISES

36. Work with one or two other students to write one concise sentence from the following repetitious sentences:

Repetitious: Many people find it extremely difficult to save money. They fail to plan appropriately for the future by disciplining themselves to set aside funds for a rainy day. They should recognize the need to save money during their peak earning years.

_____

_____

_____

_____

_____

37. Work with one or two other students to improve the beginning of the following memo:

Weak Beginning: As we come to the end of another record-breaking year at Edwards Manufacturing, I want to take this opportunity to congratulate you on your outstanding sales performance as a manufacturer's representative during your first full year with the company.

_____

_____

_____

_____

_____

PARAGRAPHING A LETTER

Read the following letters and decide where paragraph breaks would be most effective. Indicate appropriate paragraph breaks on the lines following each letter.

Name _____ Date _____

38. Dear Ms. Lindsey:

We have moved! Come see our new veterinary offices at 305 Sweetgum Street, where we now offer state-of-the-art laboratory and grooming facilities adjoining a luxury pet hotel. Your pet, Bootsey, will have the advantage of the latest technology available to veterinarians. And if you need a place for Bootsey to stay, our pet hotel is tops! In addition, our staff visits, grooms, and exercises your pet several times a day. We invite you to stop by between 7 a.m. and 7 p.m., Monday through Friday, for a tour. We think you will find our new "digs" to be a great place for Bootsey.

Sincerely,

_____

_____

39. Dear Mr. Whitley:

Because the law stipulates that the owner of a sole proprietorship and his or her business are one, the owner is personally responsible for the obligations of the business. If you as a sole proprietor incur a debt, it makes no difference whether it is a business debt or a personal debt; you are fully liable in either case. The nature of your business creates several problems that are best solved through insurance. I would like the opportunity to provide you with the type of security benefits that you would have as an employee. I will call you next week to discuss the many benefits available to you.

Sincerely,

_____

_____

Name _____ Date _____

PARAGRAPHING A LETTER *(continued)*

40.   Dear Mrs. Bellows:

Most security-minded homeowners rely primarily on a burglar alarm to protect their residences against burglaries. It takes a burglar only about seven minutes to break into a home equipped with an alarm system, get most of the valuables, and vanish! The police arrive on the scene about 15 minutes after the burglar leaves. Often, the most sophisticated alarm system does not prevent a theft, even though it performed as designed. Now you can protect your valuables conveniently at home or in the office, protected from theft and totally hidden from view. We custom-build hidden safes and walk-in vaults to fit the space available. Call us today at 555-3200 to find out more about the creative ways that Custom Security can install a hidden vault or safe in your home or business.

Sincerely,

_____

_____

_____

Go to an on-line bookstore to find two recently published college dictionaries and two recently published English-usage reference manuals. Look for general dictionaries—not specialty dictionaries such as a dictionary of slang. Be prepared to give your instructor the names of the dictionaries and reference manuals, the copyright dates, the publishing companies, and the prices.

Building Goodwill in Your Messages

In the foregoing chapters you have practiced choosing the right words to compose sentences and paragraphs.
    Effective communications must also establish and maintain goodwill. Chapter 4 will present the foundation you will need to be sure that your messages build goodwill.

Objectives

After completing this chapter, you should be able to:

- Define *goodwill*.
- Use positive language to build goodwill.
- Project a "you" attitude.
- Promote goodwill through a service attitude.

BUILD GOODWILL IN YOUR MESSAGE

Every business is concerned with selling products or services and with selling itself. A business achieves these goals by building and maintaining **goodwill**. Goodwill is an **intangible asset**—a quality that is difficult to describe and measure.

One definition of *goodwill* is the **favorable image** people have of a business. Other terms for *goodwill* are:

- Public relations
- Customer service
- Customer relations
- Business promotion

How can you as an employee help to build and maintain goodwill for your organization? You can project genuine interest in the customer, as well as fairness, courtesy, and friendliness in any contact with customers including your business correspondence. Always keep this goal in mind:

 Every message you write should accomplish its specific purpose and, at the same time, increase the reader's positive feeling toward your organization.

Your messages should create in the reader an impression of a friendly organization that is interested in the people it serves.

A business's correspondence influences what people think about the organization. In addition, what people think often determines where they buy. Consider each letter you write as an **ambassador of goodwill**—an opportunity to influence a person's attitude toward you, and your organization, and possibly even an opportunity to make a sale. Although you do not try to sell goods or services in every message, you do try to sell the organization you represent.

Many message writers inadvertently offend former or potential new customers by conveying an attitude of indifference or by failing to make a conscious effort to build and maintain customer goodwill. The words you choose and the way you put them together play a large part in the impact your message has on your reader.

PROJECT A POSITIVE TONE

 You can build goodwill into your message with the tone you use—tone is the attitude or feeling of the message. The words, sentences, and paragraphs, and the meaning behind them convey tone. Together, these elements form the impression that the message makes on the reader—what the reader "reads between the lines" of the message.

The tone in which you write must be *sincere*, because most people quickly detect words that lack sincerity. The tone should also be *warm* and *friendly*.

Writing with this kind of warm and friendly, sincere meaning is writing with a "you" attitude. The "you" attitude gives a business document a desirable tone and shows sincere interest in the reader.

PROJECT A "YOU" ATTITUDE

Everyday situations—personal or business—may affect both your personal attitude and the attitude you show in your work. How you feel can actually determine *what* you write and *how* you write. If you feel worried, frustrated, or angry, that attitude may show in your letters.

Put distractions aside. Concentrate on representing the organization you work for and satisfying your reader. The attitude projected in the tone of your letter should show the reader that you care, that you are looking at the situation fairly, and that you are genuinely interested in communicating.

Avoid writing from a self-seeking point of view. If the tone of your letter shows an "I" or "me" attitude—that is, if the letter is slanted toward you or your organization—the reader will receive a one-sided message. Instead, put the emphasis on the reader. Make a "you" attitude evident throughout the message.

Three ways to show the "you" attitude and build goodwill in your writing are:

1. Use the words *you* and *your*.
2. Focus on the reader.
3. Put the reader into the picture.

As mentioned, one way to show the "you" attitude is to use the words *you* and *your* often in your writing. But remember that the words *you* and *your* alone do not create a "you" attitude; the content of the sentence must put the reader in a positive light. Look at the following pair of sentences:

> **"YOU" WORDS:** Your error caused the delay, and you alone will be responsible for the extra charges on your bill.

> **"YOU" ATTITUDE:** We are sorry about the delay and will have our shipping department check the shipment; we will, of course, accept responsibility if we are at fault in any way.

Which sentence gives the reader the better feeling? Although the words *you* and *your* do not appear in the second sentence, that sentence conveys a "you" attitude because it views the reader in a positive attitude. The first sentence, on the other hand, uses "you" words but lacks the essence of the "you" attitude. The first sentence places all blame for problems on the reader. Look at another example with "you" words:

> *You* should know that Invoice 1045 will be due on January 27 and that *you* will be charged interest if *you* pay it after *your* due date.

Now see the sentence written with the "you" attitude:

> Your payment for our Invoice 1045 must be received by January 27 to avoid interest charges.

OR: Please send your payment for the invoice by January 27 to avoid interest charges.

OR: To avoid interest charges, send your payment for Invoice 1045 by January 27.

Now read the following excerpt:

"WE" ATTITUDE: *We* have been pleased to sell fine accessories for the home for more than two decades. *We* supply the finest exotic interior items to customers from all over the United States. *We* are proud to be the only dealer in this area to specialize in heirloom tapestries. *Our* record shows at least a 15 percent increase in sales every year since Classic Interiors opened for business in 1975.

The ideas are good, but they give a boastful impression. The paragraph does not focus on the reader at all. As you can see, the words *we* and *our* leave the reader with a negative feeling.

Notice the greatly improved tone when the same ideas are expressed in "you" words and convey a "you" attitude:

"YOU" ATTITUDE: At Classic Interiors it is our privilege to serve as your exclusive heirloom tapestries dealer. Our showroom presents an array of beautiful and desirable interior items that will satisfy your discriminating taste. You will find the exotic home accessories you have always dreamed about—the kind that have kept loyal customers coming back to Classic Interiors since 1975. You can depend on our reputation and experience to provide the selection and service you deserve.

By putting the reader into the picture, the writer creates a reader-centered letter, citing benefits that the customers of Classic Interiors should enjoy. The revised letter has a "you" attitude and maintains goodwill toward the customer. Look at another excerpt:

"WE" ATTITUDE: We are pleased to have you as a new student at Stafford Business College. We offer many advantages to our students. We have the latest equipment in our classrooms, and our faculty and staff are among the most dedicated in the country. We are very proud of our 98 percent placement rate for our graduates.

Now look at the excerpt written with a "you" attitude:

We are pleased to welcome you as a new student at Stafford Business College. You will have many advantages during your student experiences. You will work on the latest equipment in your classrooms, and your faculty and staff represent the most dedicated in the country. You will be pleased to know that 98 percent of our students are placed in good jobs after they graduate.

OR: Welcome to Stafford Business College; we welcome you as a new student. You will have many advantages during your student experience. You will work on the latest equipment in your classrooms and work with a faculty and staff dedicated to preparing you for an office career and placing you when you graduate.

As you work to keep the "you" attitude in your letter writing, keep this in mind:

 Every message you write represents an opportunity to build the goodwill of your reader.

SHOW SINCERE INTEREST IN THE READER

Show a genuine interest in your reader. Write with respect for that person's intelligence, judgment, opinions, and preferences. Remember that if you make statements that are distasteful to the reader, your letter will have the opposite effect from the one you intended.

Avoid a Formal Tone

An informal, conversational style can help your letters show warmth and friendliness. Remember that formal English seems stiff and unnatural to the reader. A simple, personal style is much more appealing.

Compare the following pair of letters. The first uses a stiff, formal style; the second, a more natural, conversational style. Read these two letters as if you were the customer.

FORMAL TONE

Dear Mrs. Whitherspoon:

In accordance with your request of recent date, in which you expressed concern about the damaged merchandise you received on July 9, I have reviewed your case and have reached the decision that full restitution should be made to you.

In view of the circumstances, I am sending to you today the replacement shipment of merchandise. If you will please send the damaged merchandise back to us at your earliest convenience, we will expedite your claim.

Please accept our most sincere apologies for delivering damaged merchandise to you, and we deeply regret the delay and inconvenience that you have suffered.

Sincerely,

Dear Mrs. Whitherspoon:

The new shipment of computer desks should reach you within five days, Mrs. Whitherspoon. So that you will be able to display the desks in your store as soon as possible, our driver will deliver them and pick up the damaged ones.

We are sorry for the slight delay, but we will do our best to see that the latest computer workstations are ready for your customers by the end of the week.

Sincerely,

Which letter would you rather receive? The letters may have similar meanings, but they leave the reader with very different feelings. The second letter sounds natural—it could be a written conversation. Can you imagine being part of a conversation that sounds like the first letter?

Avoid a Condescending Tone

A person new to message writing may "talk down," or lecture, to the reader. A **condescending tone** communicates lack of respect and will surely arouse resentment. Sharing ideas or making suggestions will create a more receptive attitude in your reader than trying to force acceptance of your views. Like most of us, your reader would appreciate being *asked* rather than *told*.

Look at this letter. Would it attract you to Hamilton's back-to-school sale?

CONDESCENDING TONE

Dear Customer:

Now is the time when all smart shoppers are taking advantage of the special money-saving buys at Hamilton's, while our Back-to-School Sale is in progress. School will be starting soon, and crowds of shoppers are trying to buy their children's clothes. You should come in now while we offer the lowest prices of the year and a pleasant shopping atmosphere.

Sincerely,

The message that everyone else is doing something implies that the reader is out of step if he or she is not doing it too. According to this letter, "all smart shoppers" are coming to Hamilton's. Does this mean that the reader is unintelligent if he or she does not shop at Hamilton's? Even without the letter, the reader already knows that "school will be starting soon." Writing that "crowds of shoppers" are in the store may make the reader want to go elsewhere!

A better approach is to stimulate the reader's interest by giving examples of specific sale items and then letting him or her decide that "now is the time" to shop at Hamilton's. The following revision eliminates the condescending tone and helps the reader feel that he or she would be wise to shop at Hamilton's.

CONGENIAL TONE

Dear Customer:

Come in today and take advantage of the special money-saving buys at Hamilton's Back-to-School Sale. Our entire stock of jeans is on sale for 60 percent off the regular price; at these fantastic savings, you will want to stock up.

You will get the best selection of the latest styles at the lowest prices of the year and avoid the crowds by shopping early.

As always, you will get friendly, courteous service from our sales staff.

Sincerely,

Keep in mind that the reader, like everyone else, prefers to think and act independently. He or she is more likely to respond favorably if you make your appeal through sound reasoning.

 Put yourself in the reader's place—after you have written a letter, read it as if you were the receiver and imagine your response.

Do Not Exaggerate

A message sounds insincere when it contains:

- Bragging
- Excessive language
- Flattery
- Overhumility
- Unlikely promises

Look at each of these examples of exaggeration.

Bragging

When describing your products and services, be prepared to prove everything you say. Overstatements and superlatives such as *the best, outstandingly superior,* and *incomparable* seldom sound convincing to the reader unless you give specific evidence to support your claims.

The unreasonable claims made in this boastful message make it sound absurdly insincere:

BRAGGING TONE

Dear Customer:

In your wildest dreams you have never pictured bargains in furniture like those in our showroom today. They are truly the ideal buys of the century! Competitors envy—but never approach—the magnificent choices and prices and the unbelievable service we offer. They are aghast at the fabulous deals we make to move our furniture.

Visit us today during our Labor Day Sale to select your living room, dining room, or bedroom suite of matchless beauty fit for a king at a price a peasant could afford!

Sincerely,

Make your letter believable by telling the reader specifically what your product or service can do for him or her.

This revised letter eliminates the bragging:

BELIEVABLE TONE

Dear Customer:

Now is the time to buy that new furniture you have been wanting; you can choose from a wide selection of styles. All furniture has been marked down from 30 to 70 percent off, and we will match the price of any competitor.

Visit us today during our Labor Day Sale to select your living room, dining room, or bedroom suite at a price you cannot miss.

Sincerely,

Excessive Language

Excessive language in business messages tells the reader that the writer is insecure about the product or service. Flowery words and too many strong adjectives and adverbs may be a way of compensating for a writer's uncertainty about the message.

Extreme politeness makes the following message sound insincere and inappropriate. The lengthy paragraph and the repetition of the reader's name appear unprofessional. Using the reader's name once in the body of the letter personalizes the letter; using the reader's name repeatedly sounds artificial.

EXCESSIVE TONE

Dear Mrs. Nelson:

Yes, indeed, Mrs. Nelson, we shall be more than happy to reserve a cabin for two for a cruise to Bermuda the first week in June. We certainly remember you from last summer. How could we forget such extremely vivacious, glamorous—and altogether charming—guests! It will be marvelous to have you with us again, Mrs. Nelson. We appreciate to the utmost your desire to return for another cruise and are even now waiting—eager to welcome you aboard on June 1, Mrs. Nelson.

Sincerely,

If you eliminate the extravagant language that makes this letter sound insincere, you can create a simple, but personalized confirmation:

SINCERE TONE

Dear Mrs. Nelson:

We appreciate your desire to cruise with us again to Bermuda and are happy to confirm your reservation for June 1–7.

For your enjoyment, we have added a kickboxing class to the recreation schedule. Also, we have just completed construction of a recreational facility, which includes a sauna and a whirlpool.

A brochure of activities for the month of June is enclosed. Your cabin will be ready for you on June 1, Mrs. Nelson.

Sincerely,

4-1:
REPETITION MAY INDICATE AN ERROR.
A sales letter that repeatedly used the reader's name had an error in the database. Every place the reader's name was to appear, the letter had the name of the city and state. Dear Potomac, Kansas, Great news, Potomac, Kansas, you can save...

4-2—Your Opinion, Please. *What impression would you have if you received a letter similar to the one in OOPS?*

Flattery

Flattery can be more damaging than excessive language. Giving a compliment that has been earned is fine, but avoid embarrassing the reader with outright flattery. Does this opening paragraph of a request for information sound sincere?

> **FLATTERY:** Since you are an authority on life insurance, I am sure you can help me. Twenty years' experience as a successful insurance agent should qualify you to answer all my questions.

The writer first flatters the reader and then implies that the reader may not deserve the compliments if he or she cannot answer all the writer's questions! Now look at the revised version:

> **SINCERE TONE:** May I have your advice on these questions, since you are an experienced life insurance agent? **OR** Would you draw from your twenty years' experience in the life insurance business to answer these questions for me?

Does this rewritten opening paragraph eliminate the flattery and sound more sincere?

Overhumility

Overhumility merely shows the reader what little self-respect the writer has. If, as a writer, you apologize to the point of degrading yourself and your organization, you are destroying the reader's faith. Look at the following message. What effect would this message have on a reader?

> **OVERHUMILITY:** Please accept our deepest apologies for the thought-less error we made in sending you a second bill for your December 8 order when you had sent us your check two weeks earlier.
>
> Our accounting department is extremely embarrassed and sorry. We need your business, and we hope you will forgive us.

Saying that you are sorry is appropriate, but a *simple* apology is all that is necessary if you have taken steps to remedy the problem.

This revised message eliminates the excessive humility from the previous example:

> **POSITIVE TONE:** You are right! We did receive your $85 check in full payment of your December 8 order. Please accept our apologies for accidentally sending you a second bill.

Unlikely Promises

If you make promises such as "We will take care of each order the minute it comes into our office" or "Just a telephone call and our technician will be right there," your reader may be skeptical of *everything* you say. Guard against making rash promises for which you may be liable.

A promise likely to be fulfilled is one backed by reliable information. For example, by using a computer database, a businessperson can tell a customer that certain stock is available and can promise shipping dates and methods.

Do not make promises that do not sound believable, as the writer of the following letter did:

Dear Friend:

Whether your unpaid bills are many or not so many, First Financial Company will SOLVE ALL YOUR MONEY PROBLEMS in the bat of an eye! A moment's chat in one of our friendly offices . . . a First Financial check . . . and you can jauntily bid all your financial worries good-bye!

Sincerely,

Readers know that no legitimate lending company can promise instant solutions to everyone's money problems. This revision sounds more believable:

BELIEVABLE TONE

Dear Friend:

Whether you have a few bills or several bills, First Financial Services can help you consolidate them into one easy payment per month. Call one of our financial advisors at 555-8734 for an appointment, or drop by our office between 8 a.m. and 5 p.m., Monday through Friday.

You can have a First Financial check and a convenient, confidential personal payment plan in two days. Some restrictions apply.

Sincerely,

Avoid Doubt, Irritation, or Indifference

Negativism, doubt, irritation, and indifference destroy the sincerity and goodwill in your messages.

Doubt

Be careful not to imply doubt about your reader. Referring to "your claim" or saying "we are surprised" about something the reader said or did implies that you do not believe the reader. Do you detect the tone of disbelief in the following example?

> **DISBELIEVING TONE:** We have not forgotten the $35 payment on your account that is two months past due. We received your explanation of your failure to pay on time a month ago, and we are still waiting for you to pay.

Here is a straightforward revision:

> **STRAIGHTFORWARD TONE:** Your $35 payment is now two months past due. Take a minute right now to write us a check, slip it in the enclosed envelope, and drop it in the mail. Sending your payment today will protect your good credit rating.

Irritation

Revealing that you are irritated does not help you accomplish your purpose. Doing so merely arouses the reader's resentment at your lack of respect. Notice how this message irritates and belittles the reader:

> **IRRITATED TONE:** We have investigated your complaint about your McKenna leaf blower and found that you neglected to charge the battery. We charged it for you and trust that in the future you will take care to check the battery before making unfounded claims about defective merchandise.

A message written in this tone would surely make the reader vow never to buy from this company again. Does this message do a better job of explaining the problem, outlining the action taken, and describing how the customer can prevent recurrences?

> **STRAIGHTFORWARD TONE:** We examined your McKenna leaf blower and found that the battery was dead. We charged the battery for you, and the leaf blower is working fine now. The battery should be charged after every three or four hours of use.

Indifference

One reason retail stores lose customers is **indifference**—an apparent lack of interest or enthusiasm. Whether a store's employees actually display an attitude of indifference does not matter. If the customer perceives indifference—even if it is imagined—the customer is likely to take his or her business elsewhere. A major concern of retailers is to convince customers that they really care about them.

Read the following form letter, which was sent to a customer who complained about a blazer she bought at Jensen, Hart & Co.

> **COLD, INDIFFERENT TONE:** Although Jensen, Hart & Co. attempts to ensure that every customer will get the highest-quality merchandise available, our enormous volume makes it impossible for us to achieve this goal 100 percent of the time.
>
> If you will bring your garment in, we will have someone look at it to ascertain whether we are responsible. Should Jensen, Hart & Co. accept responsibility, satisfactory arrangements will be made.

How can Jensen, Hart & Co. improve customer relations by revising this form letter? The errors in the tone of this letter include the poor excuse that the store's "enormous volume" makes the reader—the customer—unimportant, and the ending, which leaves the reader asking, "satisfactory to whom?" Is this revision better?

PERSONAL TONE: Please bring your wool blazer in, and we will be happy to exchange it. Customer satisfaction is our top priority at Jensen, Hart & Co.

Avoid the Temptation to Criticize, Argue, or Be Sarcastic

When you talk with someone face-to-face, you usually do your best to keep the conversation pleasant. You try to put the other person at ease, and you avoid sounding critical or saying anything he or she might resent. When you write a letter, however, the reader is not present. As the writer, you may find that you are tempted to ignore the reader and to think only of your own feelings.

Criticizing, arguing, or making a sarcastic remark will only reflect poorly upon you and your organization. Remember that in a written message you can't soften the tone by smiling or listening to the reader's side, as you can face-to-face. The reader can only read the words you have written, harsh as they may be. The reader cannot respond or look for other clues to your intended meaning.

Also, *showing anger* in a letter provokes the reader's hostility and makes transacting business difficult or impossible. An effective letter will get the message across while avoiding criticism, arguments, and sarcasm and will project a tone that will enhance human relations.

Go to Student CD-ROM Activity 4-1.

BUILD GOODWILL WITH POSITIVE IDEAS

The reader is more interested in what you *can* do than in what you *cannot* do. You cannot always answer yes to a request, but you can say no with a friendly tone if you **stress the positive** and **play down the negative**. Try to make your messages sound as friendly and helpful as possible, and try to encourage the reader.

Compare the following positive and negative sentences.

> **NEGATIVE:** We are sorry that we cannot deliver your TECH computer hardware by December 1.

> **POSITIVE:** We will deliver your TECH computer hardware just as soon as it arrives from our Chicago warehouse. We expect it to arrive during the week of December 7.

The tone of a message should be positive from start to finish. However, because the mood is set at the *beginning* of a letter, it is especially important that the beginning contain something positive for and pleasant to the reader—even if the message delivers bad news.

How many positive ideas can you find in the following letter?

> **NEGATIVE TONE:** It is my unpleasant duty to inform you that your application for a research grant was not approved. Only five grants were awarded. Unfortunately, the selection committee placed your application sixth on the list, which means it is not eligible for reconsideration until next semester's grants are awarded.

What a depressing letter! But what if it were rewritten to stress the good news that is almost hidden among the many negatives?

4-2:

PROOFREAD YOUR MESSAGES CAREFULLY.
A little negative goes a long way: A department store included a note in its sales brochure announcing its new service: We can **now** *take your orders by phone. Unfortunately, the note was typed and mailed this way: We can* **not** *take your orders by phone.*

POSITIVE TONE: Your application for a research grant placed sixth on a list of 200. Since only five grants were available this time, Miss Jung, the Selection Committee invites you to resubmit your application next semester.

The difference in these two letters is a matter of **attitude** and **tone**. Each tells the reader that the committee did not award her the grant. The second letter, however, softens the blow by telling her that her application was close to the top and may be resubmitted for consideration next semester.

Even a letter with few negative words may sound unpleasant if the tone is not one of pleasant conversation. But, when a letter has many negative words, the overall effect on the reader is most unpleasant.

Compare the letters in Figures 4-1 and 4-2. These letters contain the same facts—but do you sense the difference in tone?

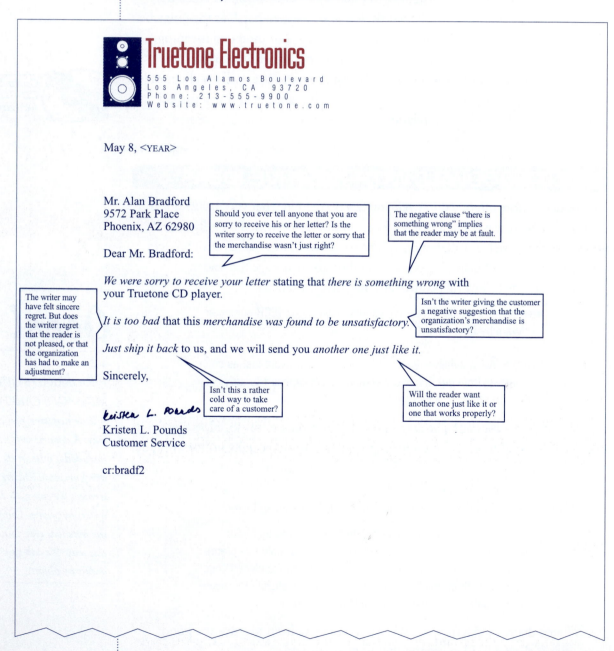

FIGURE 4-1 Although this letter has few negative words, its overall effect is negative.

Truetone Electronics
555 Los Alamos Boulevard
Los Angeles, CA 93720
Phone: 213-555-9900
Website: www.truetone.com

May 8, <YEAR>

Mr. Alan Bradford
9572 Park Place
Phoenix, AZ 62980

Dear Mr. Bradford:

Thank you for writing us about the Truetone CD player we sent you recently. We are sorry that it is not working properly.

We have instructed our carrier to deliver a new system to you next week and to pick up the system you have now.

I am sure your new Truetone system will give you many hours of listening pleasure.

Sincerely,

Kristen L. Pounds

Kristen L. Pounds
Customer Service

cr:bradf2

FIGURE 4-2 Compare this letter to the one in Figure 4-1. Doesn't its tone seem more positive?

PROMOTE GOODWILL THROUGH A SERVICE ATTITUDE

In trying to build goodwill, you can find many ways to project a service attitude in your business correspondence.

 A service attitude includes both a sincere interest in the customer's or client's welfare and the willingness to do a little more, to give a little extra. A well-expressed service attitude will pay dividends (often monetary) for both your organization and you.

In addition to the rewards of a well-expressed service attitude, you will have the personal satisfaction of doing a job well. Your messages should show the reader your genuine desire to serve rather than simply to make a profit and satisfy selfish interests. Some ways to express a service attitude are:

- Anticipate a customer's questions and offer the information.
- Include information you know will be of particular interest, such as an article or a brochure.
- Make it easy for the reader to do what your letter asks by enclosing an addressed, postpaid reply card or envelope.

Gestures like these build and keep goodwill. People will notice and appreciate your thoughtfulness.

Go to Student CD-ROM Activity 4-2.

In messages that contain good news, building goodwill is fairly easy. But when organizational policy or other circumstances do not allow the replies the customers or clients would like to have, building goodwill is not easy. For instance, you may need to:

- Answer no to a customer's or client's request.
- State that the customer or client has made an error.
- State that the customer's or client's criticism of the organization's products or service is unjustified.

Such "problem" letters call for skill and tact—and imagination.

Skillful writers have several ways to build goodwill even in these problem letters. Three often-used techniques to promote goodwill in problem letters are (1) beginning with a "goodwill idea," (2) considering the customer's or client's point of view, and (3) selling your organization's viewpoint.

Begin With a "Goodwill Idea"

Open the letter with something the reader will be pleased to hear, whether the message of the letter is good news or bad news.

Starting a Bad-News Message

In a bad-news message, rather than starting with an unpleasant idea and setting up a barrier between you and the reader, start with an idea the reader likes and agrees with. This way you have a chance to gain the reader's attention while you gradually introduce your point of view.

Starting a Good-News Message

When you write a message containing good news, use an opening that gets immediately to the heart of the subject. Beginning with a goodwill idea does not mean making needless introductory remarks such as:

- May I take this opportunity to . . .
- I am writing to tell you that . . .
- This letter is to tell you that. . .

In Chapter 5 you will learn how to begin your letters.

Consider the Customer's or Client's Point of View

You can build and maintain goodwill by keeping the customer's or client's point of view clearly in mind at all times. Try to discover and point out the benefits to the customer or client when few or no benefits may be apparent. Your message should make it easy for the customer to agree with you. Above all, try to express the organization's point of view in such a way that the customer or client accepts it and is still friendly toward your firm.

 You can build goodwill in all situations if you take time to find out the customer's or client's position. Try to assume the other person's perspective and to look at things the way he or she looks at them.

Sell Your Organization's Viewpoint

In writing business letters for dealing with problem situations, remember that you cannot build goodwill by losing your temper or showing annoyance. Look at the following excerpt:

> You certainly are not entitled to the 2 percent discount you took, as you could clearly have seen if you had read the terms of our invoice.

This writer missed an opportunity to promote goodwill. To sell the organization's viewpoint in this situation:

1. Explain the reasons behind the policy.
2. Point out that the policy is fair because it applies to all customers, including the reader.
3. If possible, show the customer how the policy may benefit him or her in the end.

By using these three steps, the writer of the letter above could have replied diplomatically, as follows:

Dear Mr. Sandusky:

Thank you for your check for $1372.84 in payment of our invoice 8970K for $1400.86.

We notice that you have deducted from the invoice the 2 percent discount offered on payments made within ten days of the date of purchase. The date of your check is September 15, however, and the date of our invoice is August 20. We assume that this was an oversight—that you intended to send your check within ten days.

Naturally, we wish we could allow a discount on payments made within thirty days. Payments made within ten days represent a saving to us, and we are glad to pass these savings on to our customers in the form of lower prices. But, as you can understand, payments made at a later date do not give us these savings to share with our customers. May we have your check for $28.02?

Sincerely yours,

Notice that the writer doesn't *demand* payment but instead gets the reader's interest at the start by drawing attention to the difference in the payment amount and the invoice amount. Then the writer leads the customer gently to the organization's point of view. When the reader gets to the last paragraph of the message, he or she should be ready to answer yes to the question.

The following excerpt destroys goodwill by projecting a "Your business isn't significant to us" attitude toward the customer.

Dear Mrs. Figueiredo:

You are mistaken in thinking that we would consider stocking petite sizes in our Misses Department simply because it would be convenient for you.

Sincerely yours,

Now read a letter that explains the organization's viewpoint but also maintains goodwill.

Dear Mrs. Figueiredo:

Your suggestion that we stock petite sizes in our Misses Department is welcome—particularly since it comes from one of our good customers.

You may be interested to know that our branch store in Raleigh recently featured a selection of petite styles. But these did not sell as well as had been expected, and we discontinued the line. As a result, The Toggery is somewhat reluctant to stock petite sizes here in Somerville just now. We will keep your suggestion in mind, however.

We understand that Michelle's, in the Beale Street Mall, carries a selection of petite styles. You may be able to find what you need there. In the meantime, Mrs. Figueiredo, we look forward to continuing to help your family with other clothing needs.

Sincerely yours,

Shortsighted businesspeople often act as if there were no competition—an unrealistic attitude, to say the least.

Recommending another organization as a source of supply for something you don't carry shows a service attitude. Not only is it helpful, but it makes you look good in the customer's eyes—it's that little extra you didn't really have to give.

Occasionally recommending a competitor won't cost you sales, as some businesspeople fear. Remember that you are the "favored vendor." The customer came to you *first* and wanted to buy from you. You will still have that in your favor after sending the customer elsewhere for something you don't have. If you are afraid that the customer will prefer your competitor's products or service, maybe you should look for ways to improve yours! And if you can't make improvements, at least you can build goodwill by recommending a competitor.

These are only two examples of so-called problem letters that must be written every day in business. Each letter presents an opportunity to build goodwill or to tear it down. Before you begin to write such a letter, think through the situation carefully to decide exactly how you can best do the job and still keep the reader as a customer.

USE LETTERS AS GOODWILL MESSENGERS

If you *care* how your letters sound, you can use them to help build goodwill. Try to visualize each letter as your organization's ambassador, as a salesperson meeting a customer. Keep in mind that a salesperson may be both personable and courteous but still not be successful. Evaluate the effectiveness of your "letter salesperson" in the same way you would evaluate a real salesperson.

 Is Your Letter Salesperson Doing a Good Job?

1. Does the salesperson choose correct, concise words and speak clearly? (Review Chapters 1, 2, and 3 to be sure that your letter salesperson speaks well during the visit with the customer.)
2. Is the salesperson's tone friendly, courteous, and conversational, and yet persuasive?
3. Does the salesperson give the customer satisfaction? (Even if you cannot give the customer exactly what he or she asks for, the good salesperson tries to keep the customer's friendship.)
4. Does the salesperson answer all of the customer's questions completely and promptly, giving all the facts needed to act or to make a decision?
5. Does the salesperson show interest in the customer's point of view as well as a genuine desire to be helpful?

You can supply yes answers to the last three questions about your "letter salesperson" if you follow the suggestions in this chapter.

Answer All the Customer's Questions

An incomplete letter leaves the customer dissatisfied and weakens the organization's chances of building goodwill. It may even lose a customer. The friendliest and most tactful letter you can write does not build goodwill if it fails to provide the needed information.

When you do not know all the answers, you should supply the answers you know and tell the reader how and when you will complete your response. Always *compare your reply with the inquiry* to be sure that you have not overlooked any of the customer's questions—actual or implied.

Suppose someone writes to you about the used cameras you advertised for sale in a national camera magazine. Here is the letter:

Ladies and Gentlemen:

Would you please send me the following information about the used 35-mm camera you advertised in the Winter issue of *Camera Cappers:*

1.   What are the make and model?
2.   What is the cost?
3.   What does the guarantee cover?
4.   What type, size, and speed are the lenses?

Here is your reply:

Dear Mr. Gonzalez:

Our used cameras are Cannon FX 900s with a one-year guarantee on all parts and labor. They sell for the low price of $259.95. All the cameras have been completely reconditioned and tested.

We have only six of these cameras left in stock, so send your order promptly to avoid being disappointed.

Your letter is friendly, courteous, and convincing. But it is not complete. You did not answer the question about lenses. Naturally, the customer is annoyed. He hesitates to order a camera without knowing what lenses are available. The customer wants the camera in time for his son's birthday, which is only two weeks away. He may write again for the information—or he may order from another supplier.

Consequences of Unanswered Questions

Failure to answer a customer's questions makes the customer suspicious. Why didn't you answer the question? What are you trying to hide? Is there some drawback to your product or service you don't want the customer to find out about? If so, what other dishonest thing may you try to do?

The customer assumes that you want to do your best for yourself and your organization. Suspicion leads directly to distrust—perhaps not logically, but that's human nature. And distrust is unlikely to lead to sales.

When You Don't Know the Answer

Admitting you don't have an answer to a customer's question is not wrong. If this is the case, promise to get the answer and then follow through. If there is no answer, say so and explain why. Either course is preferable to ignoring a question.

Remember, a *prompt response* is an excellent beginning to building and maintaining goodwill.

Don't Make the Reader Guess

Often a reply to an inquiry—such as the letter about the camera—is incomplete because the writer has overlooked a customer's question. However, you can answer all the questions and still not say everything the customer needs to know. You may leave out an important detail that you assume the customer knows. The customer then has to guess because you have assumed too much.

For example, a writer may fail to answer a question because the question should be directed to another department. Perhaps after answering the letter, the writer will turn the letter over to the appropriate person, who will then supply the missing answer. But does the reader know this? Even though the writer cannot handle part of the letter, for the customer's sake he or she should not ignore that part of the letter. The writer could avoid making the reader guess simply by adding a short paragraph, such as this:

> I am referring your question about subscribing to *The Executive's Guide* to Mr. Donald Valdez, Circulation Manager. You should hear from him in a few days.

RESELL THE PRODUCT OR SERVICE AND YOUR ORGANIZATION

The built-in purposes of each letter you write should be to:

- Promote goodwill.
- Resell the product and the business.

Reselling means "repeating the selling job that led to the purchase."

Resell Your Product or Service

The purpose of reselling is to assure the customer that he or she made a wise choice in buying the product (even though it may not yet have been delivered) and to keep the customer from complaining or returning the goods. When you resell, you reaffirm the reader's faith in your products, services, and organization.

Resell Your Organization

Reselling your organization involves pointing out the services, guarantees, policies, and procedures that will benefit your reader. Reselling is appropriate in a letter to a new customer, but you should also resell whenever you can tell a customer about a new service or benefit that your company provides.

When Jan O'Neill received the following letter, she probably felt that she had made a wise choice in subscribing to *The Executive's Guide,* a monthly magazine of tips and case studies.

Dear Ms. O'Neill:

Your first issue of *The Executive's Guide* will arrive in a few days. The feature article should be particularly interesting to you, Ms. O'Neill, because it discusses ways you can increase productivity and profits by improving interpersonal skills among your employees.

In the coming months, such noted communications experts as Anne Constantino and Paul Anderson will cover methods you can use to your advantage when communicating with either superiors or subordinates. For example, you will learn ingenious techniques that help get proposals approved and unique approaches that are usually successful in persuading others to go along with your ideas.

We know that you will enjoy reading every issue of *The Executive's Guide* and that it will be as helpful to you as it has been to other executives in the past ten years.

Sincerely,

As you can see, the purpose of this letter is to promote goodwill and resell the product. Chapter 14 will give you more goodwill ideas as you study special goodwill letters.

Each message you write presents an opportunity to build goodwill or to tear it down. Before you begin to write a message, think through the situation carefully to decide exactly how you can best do the job and still keep the reader as a customer.

Use the Goodwill Attitude Checklist to be sure each message you write builds and maintains goodwill.

Goodwill Attitude Checklist

Your message will project a goodwill attitude to your reader when you can answer yes to each of these statements:

	Yes	No
1. Did you focus on your reader with a positive "you" approach?	☐	☐
2. Did you avoid a formal tone?	☐	☐
3. Did you avoid lecturing your reader?	☐	☐
4. Did you avoid exaggerating?	☐	☐
5. Did you avoid showing doubt, irritation, or indifference?	☐	☐
6. Did you avoid criticizing, arguing, and being sarcastic?	☐	☐
7. Did you avoid showing anger?	☐	☐
8. Did you focus on what you *can* do instead of what you *can't* do?	☐	☐
9. Did you consider the customer's or client's point of view?	☐	☐
10. Did you sell the organization's viewpoint?	☐	☐
11. Did you answer all of the customer's or client's questions?	☐	☐
12. Did you open with something the reader will be pleased to hear?	☐	☐
13. Did you avoid making the reader guess?	☐	☐
14. Did you resell your product or service and your organization?	☐	☐

Name _____ Date _____

WHAT'S WRONG WITH THESE?

Indicate on the lines provided what is wrong with each of the following message excerpts.

1. We know from experience that we sell the best-quality air conditioners in the nation.

   _____

2. We are so very sorry that our accounting department made such a terrible mistake.

   _____

3. You are the most wonderful, fantastic client we have ever had the opportunity to serve!

   _____

4. There is something wrong with the weed cutter you returned.

   _____

5. May I take this opportunity to send you our new fall catalog?

   _____

WRITING SENTENCES TO IMPROVE TONE AND BUILD GOODWILL

Revise the following sentence so that it will project a "you" attitude.

6. We must receive all conference reservations immediately, so that we can make the room assignments.

   _____

   _____

   _____

Revise the following sentence to eliminate the negative tone.

7. You failed to give us the shipping number so that we could send your order.

   _____

   _____

   _____

Revise the following sentence to eliminate exaggeration.

8. We here at Stollberg's have the best cheesecake you have ever tasted.

   _____

   _____

   _____

Chapter 4 Worksheet

Name _____ Date _____

WRITING PARAGRAPHS TO IMPROVE TONE AND GOODWILL

9. Revise the following paragraph to eliminate the "we" attitude and use the friendlier "you " attitude.

We are glad to have your business, but we want you to keep in mind our hours. We are open Monday through Saturday from 9 a.m. until 6 p.m. We have many bargains from which to choose. We also have many special sales. We would like to see you soon.

_____

_____

_____

_____

_____

_____

_____

10. Rewrite the following paragraph using positive language and a service attitude.

We were very sorry to hear that one of the pieces of your new luggage set was missing. We were certain that all the pieces were there, but we guess mistakes do happen. Anyway, we are sending you today the 20-inch tote bag that you say is missing. Please let us know if there is anything else that we can do for you.

_____

_____

_____

_____

_____

_____

11. Rewrite the following paragraph to eliminate the "we" attitude and use the more friendly "you" attitude.

We want you to know that we appreciate having you as one of our catalog shoppers. We have decided that we can make catalog shopping easier and more convenient by issuing our new credit card. We are happy to now take your orders by phone as well as by mail.

_____

_____

_____

_____

_____

Name _____ Date _____

COLLABORATIVE ACTIVITY

Work with another person on the following problem situations. Study the partial analyses of each problem, and then describe your objective and write an effective opening paragraph for each problem.

12. In January Mrs. Terri Schultz returned several large cartons of Christmas decorations to Cloud Nine, where you work as a customer service representative. You must reply to her angry letter, in which she insists that the cartons arrived on the day before Christmas, too late for use in her home. You have obtained from your shipping department a delivery slip that Mrs. Schultz signed on December 16, the delivery date agreed upon at the time of purchase.

The customer's request: Mrs. Schultz demands that the store accept the decorations, with a full refund to her.

The organization's policy: The full refund cannot be approved on this seasonal merchandise because the Christmas buying season is over. The store will, however, charge Mrs. Schultz the January sale price, one-half off the regular price, and return the decorations to her.

   a. **Your objective when you write to Mrs. Schultz:**

   _____

   _____

   _____

   _____

   _____

   b. **Goodwill opening paragraph:**

   _____

   _____

   _____

   _____

   _____

   _____

   _____

13. You work for the Portland (Oregon) Realty Company. The manager agreed to delay rental of a commercial studio for one week to give a prospective client, Hugh Steele, time to make his decision. When the manager didn't hear from Mr. Steele within ten days, he leased the studio to another client. Soon afterward, your company received a letter from Mr. Steele stating that he had had a telephone conversation with "a woman" in your office; he claims that he told this woman that he had decided to lease the studio.

Name _____ Date _____

COLLABORATIVE ACTIVITY *(continued)*

The manager never received the telephone message. The letter, correctly addressed and postmarked within the one-week period, had been mistakenly delivered to Portland, Maine.

The client's request: Mr. Steele has asserted his right to lease the studio.

The organization's policy: The company's position is that the company and the other client entered a lease in good faith and that lease is legally binding.

   a. Your objective when you write to Mr. Steele:

_____

_____

_____

_____

_____

_____

   b. Opening paragraph:

_____

_____

_____

_____

_____

_____

_____

_____

_____

Building Goodwill

Search the Internet for at least one Website that has information on building or maintaining goodwill in messages. Compare what you find with the material in this chapter. Provide a short report of your findings.

_____

_____

_____

_____

Planning and Preparing Messages

In the preceding chapters you studied some of the aspects of preparing business messages. You are now ready to take the next important step—planning the message—and then the most important step—actually writing it.

Objectives

After completing this chapter, you should be able to:

- Choose among the direct, indirect, or persuasive approaches for message writing.
- Develop a plan for your message.
- Write a rough draft of your letter or memo.

PLANNING THE MESSAGE

Before you write, you should plan what to include. You do this for the same reason you make a list before you go to the supermarket or prepare an agenda for a meeting—so that you won't forget anything. A good shopping list can eliminate a second trip to the store, and an agenda can prevent extra meetings. A good plan should make it unnecessary to send a second message to complete the job.

As you plan your correspondence, you should start by considering:

- Your own organization.
- The recipient.
- The background and purpose of the message.

Then decide upon the best approach and what you will say.

Consider Your Own Organization

As you begin any new job, you should learn all you can about the organization you will represent. In all your communications you must act on behalf of the organization and treat your personal views as secondary.

Your messages should sincerely reflect the attitudes and policies of the organization. Occasionally, a policy may seem unfair; you may even suggest revisions to that policy. But until a change occurs, you must follow the policy.

Never let a customer or client know that you disagree with your organization's policy. Be sure that your message does not seem to blame another person or department for an error or an unpopular decision.

 In business correspondence, you speak for the organization as a whole—not for yourself or for your department.

The organization or group speaks through you—the writer. Your job is to relay the decisions of the organization in terms that your reader can accept, to bring both sides to agreement. The good message writer represents the organization's point of view while showing the reader that the position is a fair one.

Consider the Recipient

The most important factor to consider when you plan a business message is the person who will read it.

 A business message succeeds only if the reader
- **Reads it.**
- **Understands it.**
- **Reacts favorably to it.**

The more you know about how your reader thinks and feels, the better chance you have of getting the message across. **Adapting to the reader** means *writing with the reader in mind.*

If you know something about the reader's education, for example, you can adapt your vocabulary accordingly. If you know something about the reader's position and ambitions, you can choose a suitably challenging appeal.

To interest and influence the reader, you must be able to look at both your side and the reader's side of a situation. By doing so, you can learn what kind of help the reader expects to find in your message. With practice, you can see things from the reader's perspective as well as from your own, and then you can become successful at persuasion. Remember, one of your goals is to sell the reader on your organization's position.

When answering a letter or other business message, use background information contained in the communication itself. Always read carefully to be sure that you have learned all you can about the situation. If you need additional facts or if you have no letter to answer, scan the files for previous correspondence, call reports from sales representatives, and other pertinent records. And of course, use common sense, as well as your general business knowledge and any specialized knowledge of your organization, to decide what background facts are important and how you can best use them to make your message successful.

Consciously practice adapting to the reader as you write all your messages, and you'll soon master the technique. Just remember to:

- Think through the situation.
- Imagine your reader as best you can.
- Write directly to your reader.

Consider the Background and Purpose of the Message

A business message grows out of a need to communicate.

 To plan your message efficiently, you must understand:
Why you need to send the message.
The response it should bring.

As you think through your message and the background facts, the **purpose** becomes clear. For example, the purpose of a credit manager's writing a collection letter might be "to collect $125 from Travis Yates without losing him as a customer." And the purpose of Travis Yates' reply might be "to pay $50 on my account and promise the store the $75 balance in 30 days."

Choose the Best Approach

As you plan the best way to accomplish your purpose, you will need to decide upon the best approach—the most effective order in which to present the ideas in your message.

 Business messages fit into one of these three categories:
- **Routine or informational and "yes" messages.**
- **"No" messages.**
- **Persuasive and sales messages.**

Routine or Informational and "Yes" Messages

Routine messages that *request or transmit information* represent the largest part of business correspondence. When you want to ask for or give routine information, write simple messages or use standardized wording.

Keep routine and "yes" messages straightforward, since they *tell the reader what he or she wants to hear.* This type of message can get directly to the point; therefore, the term **direct approach** describes the arrangement of the parts.

"No" Messages

Messages that *give the reader bad news* or refuse the reader's request can cause problems. You must carefully prepare these "no" messages to avoid causing anger or loss of goodwill. These problem situations call for an **indirect approach.**

Persuasive and Sales Messages

The third group of business messages includes those in which the writer must *persuade* or "sell" the reader on an idea. Such messages may be:

- Sales letters that attempt to obtain an order for a product or a service.
- Sales promotions that try to set up a future sale without pressing directly for an order.

Messages of this type use the **persuasive approach.**

Let's examine how these three approaches—*direct, indirect,* and *persuasive*—work so that you can learn to choose the right one for each situation. As we discuss common business situations in later chapters and apply these three approaches, you will see how you can vary them to fit a wide range of writing situations.

ORGANIZING YOUR MESSAGE

Now that you have a general idea about each of the three approaches—direct, indirect, and persuasive—we will take three situations and follow the steps in choosing the best approach.

The Direct Approach

 In the direct approach, *start with the good news.*

When you can tell your reader yes or transmit good news, you have the easiest and most pleasant writing task. Good news will put the reader in a friendly, receptive frame of mind for anything else you say.

Follow the good-news opening with the next most pleasant point for the reader, then the third most pleasant, and so on. The last paragraph of the message should build goodwill and leave the reader in a cordial mood.

Examples of the routine types of correspondence that use this approach, the *direct approach,* are the following:

- Requests for appointments or reservations.
- Requests for information about products and services.

5-1—Storing Messages. *If you routinely type letters with the same wording, how could you most efficiently store those paragraphs with your computer software?*

- "Yes" answers to inquiries and requests.
- Favorable settlements of adjustments and credits.
- Goodwill messages.   *Kiss up*

In summary, then, whenever you can say yes or otherwise tell your reader something he or she wants to hear or will be pleased to hear, use the direct approach. Start your message with that information. Analyze the following example, a situation that requires the direct approach:

THE SITUATION: Ms. Karen Brown, owner of Classic Eyewear, has asked for credit by filling out Beaumont Designer Eyewear's credit form and supplying references. The credit manager for Beaumont, a wholesale dispensary for frames and sunglasses, has checked the references and will extend credit to Classic. Beaumont's manager needs to inform Ms. Brown of the good news.

THE ORGANIZATION'S POLICY: Beaumont has set Classic's credit limit at $5000. Beaumont will bill Classic for purchases through the 15th of each month. Payment is due by the 28th.

THE LETTER'S JOB: The writer should welcome the customer, explain the credit terms, talk about Beaumont's service, and look forward to the customer's orders.

THE APPROACH: Because Beaumont has good news for Ms. Brown, the writer should select the direct approach. See the letter to Ms. Brown in Figure 5-1.

Beaumont Designer Eyewear

9947 East Parkway, Norfolk, Nebraska 68701-8360
Send Correspondence to: P.O. Box 8360 • Phone: 402-555-9378 • Website: www.beaumonteye.com

April 9, <YEAR>

Ms. Karen Brown
Classic Eyewear
3357 Tower Road
Norfolk, NE 68701-6631

Dear Ms. Brown:

Beaumont welcomes you as a credit customer. You may begin using your charge account immediately. Just provide your account number, 409-1440-7, for each in-store or telephone order. For telephone orders, choose either overnight or two-day delivery service.

You may charge purchases up to $5000 a month. Your monthly statement will provide a detailed listing of purchases through the 15th of each month. Payment will be due on or before the 28th of each month.

Come in soon to see our newest frames and sunglasses, or browse through the enclosed catalog. We look forward to serving you.

Sincerely,

Jordan Anderson

Jordan Anderson
Credit Manager

js
Enclosure

FIGURE 5-1 This letter starts with the good news—the direct approach.

The Indirect Approach

Having to give the reader bad news or to say no poses a problem in business writing. If you blurt out the bad news in the first sentences of your message, the reader will quickly become disappointed, angry, or both. Such feelings will color the reader's interpretation of everything else you say. If you start with the refusal, the reader isn't likely to accept your explanation, if he or she reads it at all! If the information brings bad news to the reader or if it reflects negatively on another organization or person, use the **indirect approach.**

 Follow this rule for the indirect approach: *Place the bad news in the middle.*

Place a "buffer"—a cushion—between the reader and the bad news by beginning and ending with a positive message. Using a buffer paragraph follows common sense. People would rather hear good news than bad news. You can help break the bad news gently by organizing your message as follows:

1. Buffer Paragraph

Begin with something in the situation that you and the reader can agree on. It may be only that the reader was right to come to you with the problem. If there are no points of agreement, pay the reader a compliment (but don't flatter), or say something friendly. However, you must not appear to be saying yes. The reader will not forgive you for misleading him or her if later on in the message you say no. And your buffer paragraph must relate to the subject of the message; it should not be a time waster.

2. Reasons and Refusal

After the buffer paragraph, give the reasons for refusing or for giving the bad news. Begin with your best reason for refusal, go on to the next best, and so on. After giving the explanation, use another paragraph for the actual refusal. Be sure that the reader will understand the message, even though the bad news may be subtly implied. But also be sure you leave the reader feeling receptive, even though he or she may not be getting the desired answer.

3. Ending

By the end of the message, you are past the rough parts. You can then offer a counterproposal to what the reader asked or resell your point of view. Even a bad-news message should end on a hopeful note.

The following types of correspondence use the *indirect approach:*

- Appointment or reservation refusals.
- "No" answers to inquiries and requests.
- Invitation rejections.
- Order refusals.
- Adjustment and credit refusals.
- Job applicant rejections.

Because you must give reasons for saying no when you use the indirect approach, these messages are almost always longer than direct approach messages. The following situation uses the indirect approach:

THE SITUATION: Each year Formal World Inc., a manufacturing company, purchases classified telephone directory advertisements in cities where it has franchises. Mr. David Harbor, an independent dealer with an exclusive franchise to rent and sell Formal World products in his area, wants the manager to also purchase advertisements in two nearby suburbs. The marketing manager for Formal World Inc., Leslie Peterson, must answer a letter from Mr. Harbor.

THE ORGANIZATION'S POLICY: Formal World purchases advertising only in classified telephone directories serving areas where it has stores. Since this dealer is not located in the suburbs but inside the city limits, the company will place advertising only in the city directory.

THE LETTER'S JOB: Refuse Mr. Harbor's request for company-paid advertising in the two suburban directories. Explain the policy behind the refusal: The company has more than 800 stores; if it buys something for one, it must do the same for all; the costs would be excessive; requests would come in for the company to purchase advertising in directories in neighboring counties and towns.

THE APPROACH: Since the manager will have to say no, the letter should begin with a buffer paragraph and use the indirect approach. Notice that the letter in Figure 5-2 requires more careful wording than the direct approach letter in Figure 5-1.

FORMAL WORLD INC.

82 Broadway, Dryden, NY 13053-9100
Phone: 518-555-9788 • E-Mail: formal_world@def.com • Website:www.formalwear.com

March 2, <YEAR>

Mr. David Harbor, Manager
Formal World
P. O. Box 5488
Ellisville, MS 39437-5488

Dear David:

We agree that advertising in the Yellow Pages is important for getting the word out about our products. We also agree that the more of it we can do, the better.

Last year we considered the possibility of altering our policy on telephone directory advertising. We calculated the cost of placing advertising for each of our 806 stores in all the telephone directories within 125 miles of the store's location. It came to a staggering $965,000 a year! Even for only those directories in areas our stores actually serve, the cost was more than $650,000.

Since we would, of course, have to apply the same policy to each store, we regret to say that we cannot increase our telephone directory advertising.

Any increase in one area of our advertising budget would affect other areas, and we know the importance you and our other franchisees place on our magazine and Internet advertising, as well as our sponsorship of the Wedding Fair. Such activities, as part of Formal World's master marketing plan, have proved to be very effective.

In spite of increased competition, Formal World Inc. has increased its share of the market, thanks to energetic dealers like you. We intend to continue to provide you with the best products on the market and to aggressively support you in your successful sales and rental efforts.

Sincerely,

Leslie Peterson

Leslie Peterson
Marketing Manager

ah

FIGURE 5-2 Because this letter refuses the reader's request, the writer used the indirect approach.

5-1:
ERRORS IN MEANING WILL CONFUSE A READER. *This sentence appeared in a refusal* letter, *but the typist typed a* w *instead of a* t *in one word.* We will *now* be able to meet your due date. *Naturally, the reader was confused.*

The Persuasive Approach

As discussed earlier, persuasive messages make special requests or try to sell the reader a product, a service, or an idea. Getting the reader to do what you want, to accept what you say, or to agree with you calls for the **persuasive approach.**

If you want to write effective sales messages, take this advice from an advertising copywriter: "Don't use formulas. Rely on your knowledge of why people buy things." Successful copywriters can make readers imagine themselves using the product or service or benefiting from the idea. When you can accomplish this goal, you can close the sale.

 Remember this rule for the persuasive approach: *Place the "call for action" at the end of your message.*

A good sales message will be structured something like this:

1. Attention

In the opening paragraph, you should *promise or imply some benefit or reward for the reader.* This captures the reader's attention, sets the tone of the message, and prepares the reader for what follows.

2. Interest

Second, you will arouse the reader's interest if you *describe how the product or service would benefit the reader.* Write with a "you" attitude to help the reader imagine himself or herself using the product or service.

3. Desire

Next, *give physical details of the product or service,* such as dimensions, materials, and specifics about the guarantee and service. These details will help clinch the sale by whetting the reader's desire for the product or service.

4. Action

Finally, *ask for the reader's response*—or for the order, if appropriate. The request for action should make the reader's response as easy as possible.

These four steps represent as much of a formula for a sales message as you will need. No two products or services are alike, nor are any two groups of prospects. Each must be treated individually if you are to get the response you want.

Examine the following example of the persuasive approach:

> **THE SITUATION:** The Life Insurance Division of Floridian Insurance Company has started a new campaign to sell additional insurance to current policyholders.

> **THE LETTER'S JOB:** Persuade current policyholders to purchase additional insurance with their accumulated dividends and arrange for future dividends to purchase more insurance. A form included with the letter and authorizing these changes will provide a convenient way for the customer to enroll.

THE APPROACH: Get the reader's attention in the opening sentence by making a statement that makes the reader stop and think, and then continue reading. To see the persuasive approach in action, read the letter shown in Figure 5-3.

FLORIDIAN *Insurance Company*

LIFE INSURANCE DIVISION
One Allen Center • Orlando, FL 32610 • Phone: 317-555-2929

May 18, <YEAR>

Mr. Dean Talbert
33890 Maple Corner Drive
Sanborn, NY 14132

Dear Mr. Talbert:

Did you realize that your life insurance policy has accumulated dividends of $1431? As you know, the interest earned on the dividends must be reported as income each year.

Instead of paying taxes on the interest, why not put that money to work? You can buy $2366 in additional paid-up insurance with your accumulated dividends. And you can apply future dividends to keep your investment working for you.

Look at the advantages of using your dividends in this way:

1. You will no longer have interest to report as income.
2. The paid-up insurance will increase the death benefit to your beneficiary.
3. The cash value of the additional paid-up insurance is guaranteed never to be less than the dividends declared.
4. The purchase is made at net cost—there is no charge to purchase this additional paid-up insurance. As you can see, at present each $1 in dividends will buy about $1.65 of additional paid-up insurance.

If you would like to take advantage of this opportunity, please sign the enclosed form and return it to me in the enclosed envelope.

Cordially,

Joseph Grove

Joseph Grove

cw
Enclosures

FIGURE 5-3 This letter uses the persuasive approach.

Go to Student CD-ROM Activity 5-1.

You will study more techniques for writing sales messages in Chapter 12.

You can choose the best approach for each message by anticipating the reader's reaction and by considering the type of message you are creating, as illustrated in Figure 5-4.

CHOOSING THE BEST APPROACH

Anticipated Reader Reaction	Type of Message	Message Approach*
Reader will be **pleased.**	Good news	Direct
Reader will be **displeased.**	Bad news	Indirect
Reader will be **neutral** (neither pleased nor displeased) or will have at least **some degree of interest.**	Neutral or informational	Direct
Reader will have **little or no initial interest.**	Persuasive	Persuasive

*Refer to Figure 5-6.

FIGURE 5-4 Choosing the best approach.

DEVELOPING A PLAN

After you choose the best approach, you should begin planning the content and organization of your message. You can make your ideas concrete by writing them down.

Writing a Plan

Besides clarifying your thoughts, a written plan ensures that you won't forget any important details and makes the actual writing of the message faster and easier. A written plan helps especially when you begin to learn to write business messages. After you have had more practice, you may find that you need to write plans for only the most complicated and most important messages you prepare.

Keep your written plan *brief and simple*. Jot down or type a few words for each point you want to make. Or, you might make notations in the margins of the letter or memo you plan to answer.

Planning Procedures

Many beginning business writers have found the procedures outlined in Figure 5-5 helpful as they developed planning skills. Try to follow these steps exactly in planning your first messages. Later, as you gain experience, you may eliminate some of the steps and adapt the procedures to your own work habits.

STEPS FOR PLANNING YOUR MESSAGES

Procedure	Example

Step 1
Write down the main purpose and all secondary purposes of the message concisely.
	Primary Purpose:
	    To provide cost estimates for printing.
	Secondary Purpose(s):
	    To convince the reader that we are dependable.
	    To confirm exact printing specifications.

Step 2
Jot down all points to be covered in the message to accomplish primary and secondary purposes.
 	
Include every detail you think of (whether important or not) as you think of it.
 	
This process (called **brainstorming**) will stimulate both good and bad ideas that can be sorted out later.
	Brainstorming List:
	Itemize paper, printing, collating, and shipping costs for 750, 1000, and 1250 copies.
	    Customer to supply binders.
	    Delivery within ten days.
	    Thank her for estimate request.
	    Confirm specifications in her letter.
	    Speedy delivery.

Step 3 Strike out any items from the list made in Step 2 that can be omitted without sacrificing friendliness or completeness. Watch for repetitious ideas that brainstorming often produces.	Edit Brainstorming List: Draw a line through "Speedy delivery." (You already listed "Delivery within ten days.")
Step 4 Choose the best approach. Determine reader reaction and appropriate approach (direct, indirect, or persuasive).	Determine Reader Reaction and Approach: Reader will be pleased; use direct approach.
Step 5 Based on the approach you chose, number the items in the edited brainstorming list in the order in which you will cover them in your message.* The result will be a plan from which you can quickly compose a draft of your message.	Arrange Items in Proper Sequence: 1. Thank her for the estimate request. 2. Confirm specifications in her letter. 3. Customer to supply binders. 4. Itemize paper, printing, collating, and shipping costs for 750, 1000, and 1250 copies. 5. Delivery within ten days. 6. Call me with questions.

*Refer to Figure 5-6.

FIGURE 5-5 Steps for planning your message.

Organizing the Message Plan

Figure 5-6 summarizes the direct, indirect, and persuasive approaches to message writing. You can use this chart in combination with Figure 5-5, which is more general, or alone as you further develop your skills at planning the various kinds of messages.

PSYCHOLOGICAL ORGANIZATION FOR BUSINESS MESSAGES

The Direct Approach   **Direct Plan**
(For Inquiries, Requests, Good News, "Yes" Messages)

Opening	State the specific information needed. **OR** Make your request. **OR** Start with what the reader wants to hear (good news).	Main Idea or Good News
Middle	Specific questions to help reader give answer. Details. Explanation of good news.	Details or Explanation
Closing	Specific request for action tied with appreciation. Goodwill. Resale of organization and/or product or service.	Goodwill or Resale

The Indirect Approach   **Indirect Plan**
(For Negative News)

Opening	Pleasant, neutral—but relevant—statement (never start with bad news).	Buffer
Middle	Reasons, explanations, or facts about the negative news—tell reader *why*. Make explanation reader-oriented and positive—*tell what you can do instead of what you can't do.*	Reasons and Explanations
	Give bad news *after* the reasons.	No—stated or implied
Closing	Pleasant, relevant comment to end on a positive note.	Buffer

(continued)

FIGURE 5-6 The direct, indirect, and persuasive plans for writing a business message. The bold rules in each plan indicate where the main point of each message goes.

The Persuasive Approach (For Sales Letters and Special Requests)			Persuasive Plan
Opening	Relevant idea that gets the reader's attention.	_____ _____	Attention
Middle	Explanation and description that expand on opening idea and get the reader interested.	_____ _____ _____	Interest
	Reader benefits that will convince reader to take the action you request. (Mention warranties, guarantees, and enclosures. Play down cost and other possible negatives.)	_____ _____ _____ _____ _____ _____	Desire or Conviction
Closing	Request for action that is courteous and specific, and makes it easy for the reader to say yes.	_____ _____ _____ _____	Action

FIGURE 5-6 *(continued).*

WRITING A ROUGH DRAFT

You have studied all the facts related to your message, made notes on what you should say, selected the best approach, and decided on the best order for saying it. Now, you must turn your plan into a letter or memo. Keep in mind two factors that have influenced your planning: (1) your reader and (2) your reason for writing.

 To accomplish its purpose, a message should meet these requirements:

- Its content must be correct and appropriate.
- Its style must be clear and natural.
- Its tone must build goodwill.

Remember also to build goodwill with every message you write by:

1. Emphasizing the things the reader wants to hear.
2. Avoiding negatives and other statements unpleasant to the reader.
3. Using friendly words and reflecting a sincere desire to serve.

Because you must keep in mind so many things while writing your message, you will probably do a better job if you prepare a rough draft. In composing the first draft, *concentrate only on content.* Keep these tips in mind while writing:

- Develop your rough draft directly from your plan or outline.
- Prepare the draft with double spacing to allow space for marking revisions.
- Write on paper, type directly into the computer, or dictate to a machine as quickly as you can.
- Don't take time to check spelling, grammar, style, tone, or references to your text—yet. (While looking up a point, you might forget an important idea.)
- Write the message in your own words. Write naturally—as if you are speaking.

In actual business practice, most writers do not use a detailed outline. But for long, complex messages and for problem messages, most writers do jot down an informal outline and make a rough draft.

In Figure 5-5 you saw an example of the procedure to follow in getting your ideas down. Now see how those ideas look as a rough draft as shown in Figure 5-7.

ROUGH DRAFT

We want to thank you for asking us to estimate the cost of printing your new company manual, "Quality Control Procedures." We are delighted to be of service.

Your letter specified that the new manual will be 207 pages long. It will be printed on 8 ½ x 11," 20 lb. white paper and all pages will be 3 hole punched, collated, inserted into loose leaf binders which Victory Industries will be providing. As you requested and based on these specs we have itemized the costs of paper, printing, collating, and shipping for quantities of 750, 1000, and 1250 copies.

	750 Copies	1000 Copies	1250 Copies
Paper	$336.75	$449.00	$561.25
Printing	123.75	151.00	176.25
Collating	29.25	39.00	48.75
Shipping	23.25	31.00	38.75
	$513.00	$670.00	$825.00

If you wish to discuss these estimates, please call me. As soon as you select the quantity and deliver you typed pages and loose leaf binders. We will process your order and deliver the manuals to your office within ten days.

FIGURE 5-7 This first draft was written rapidly. It contains abbreviations, shortcuts, and errors, which will be edited.

After you write the rough draft, you will edit and correct the draft, prepare the message in its final form, and then proofread.

Go to Student CD-ROM Activity 5-2.

SUMMARY

Planning will help you write effective messages. Start your plan by considering your own organization, the message recipient, and the purpose of your message. Then decide which approach—direct, indirect, or persuasive—best fits your situation.

In addition, use the Planning and Preparing Messages Checklist to help you plan your messages carefully and choose the right approach for each writing situation.

Planning and Preparing Messages Checklist

You will successfully plan and prepare your messages if you can answer yes to each of these questions:

	Yes	No
1. Did you consider your own organization's attitudes and policies?	☐	☐
2. Did you consider your reader's point of view as you planned your message?	☐	☐
3. Did you analyze the reason for sending your message and consider the response it should bring?	☐	☐
4. Did you choose the right approach for the situation?	☐	☐
5. For the direct approach, did you start with the good news?	☐	☐
6. For the indirect approach, did you place the bad news in the middle of the message?	☐	☐
7. For the persuasive approach, did you place your "call for action" at the end of your message?	☐	☐
8. Did you write down your main purpose and all important points and make a draft?	☐	☐

Name _____   Date _____

WHAT'S WRONG WITH THESE?

The following are poor examples of business messages. On the lines below, write what is wrong.

1. Dear Mr. Jones:

    We regret to inform you that we cannot accept your application to Midland State College. We have certain minimum standards for entrance, and you do not meet those standards.

    You must have a 2.5 grade point average to transfer into our program, and your transcript shows a 2.43 grade point average.

    If you bring your average up to our standards, we will process your application.

    Very truly yours,

_____

_____

_____

2. We received your e-mail offering to supply us with almonds for resale. As our store name says, we are the Peanut Hut. We've always sold peanuts and nothing but peanuts. Adding almonds to our stock would not fit our tradition or our name.

    We are willing to try some new products to add a little variety to our business. We would like to order 50 pounds of almonds for immediate delivery.

_____

_____

_____

Chapter 5 Worksheet

Name _____ Date _____

CHOOSING THE BEST APPROACH

Each of the following problems states a purpose for writing a message. Read each purpose; then write (1) what the reader's reaction will be (pleased, displeased, neutral, little interest) and (2) which approach you as the writer would take (direct, indirect, or persuasive).

3. To confirm a reservation.

   Reaction: _____   Approach: _____

4. To refuse a request for credit.

   Reaction: _____   Approach: _____

5. To send a brochure that a client requested.

   Reaction: _____ or _____   Approach: _____

6. To ask for an opportunity to demonstrate your new energy-saving device.

   Reaction: _____   Approach: _____

7. To decline a speaking invitation.

   Reaction: _____   Approach: _____

8. To thank a customer for placing a large order.

   Reaction: _____   Approach: _____

9. To interest a potential customer in advertising in your magazine.

   Reaction: _____   Approach: _____

10. To grant a request to replace a defective product.

    Reaction: _____   Approach: _____

11. To reject a job applicant.

    Reaction: _____   Approach: _____

12. To ask for more information about a product advertised on television.

    Reaction: _____   Approach: _____

13. To compromise on an adjustment.

    Reaction: _____ Approach: _____

14. To collect an overdue account.

    Reaction: _____ Approach: _____

15. To congratulate a former classmate on a promotion.

    Reaction: _____ Approach: _____

16. To notify club members of an upcoming meeting.

    Reaction: _____ Approach: _____

17. To turn down an invitation to a business dinner.

    Reaction: _____ Approach: _____

18. To order a free booklet.

    Reaction: _____ Approach: _____

19. To ask for donations to the United Way campaign.

    Reaction: _____ Approach: _____

20. To thank a personnel manager for a job interview.

    Reaction: _____ Approach: _____

BRAINSTORMING AND WRITING LETTER PLANS

Brainstorm and jot down all the items that you might include to write the letters described below. Then select the items you need and arrange them in the correct order according to the approach you choose.

21. Situation: Santa Maria College, a satellite campus of a community college, will begin offering evening classes next year. The college has planned an open house for prospective students next month. Plan a letter to employees of local manufacturing businesses to invite potential students to the open house.

    Primary purpose of letter: _____

    Secondary purpose of letter: _____

Name _____ Date _____

BRAINSTORMING AND WRITING LETTER PLANS *(continued)*

Reader's reaction: _____

Approach: _____

Brainstorming list:

_____   _____

_____   _____

_____   _____

_____   _____

_____   _____

22. Situation: You are an assistant to Janis Temples, president of The Watchdog Corporation. She has decided that Watchdog's conference room should be modernized. Plan a letter to Bob Pishkur, an interior designer with Designs With Style Ltd., to ask for an appointment to discuss and get a bid on redecorating the conference room.

Primary purpose of letter: _____

Secondary purpose of letter: _____

Reader's reaction: _____

Approach: _____

Brainstorming list:

_____   _____

_____   _____

_____   _____

_____   _____

_____   _____

_____   _____

23. Situation: Reply to a letter from a Girl Scout troop (20 members) requesting a tour of your manufacturing plant (your company makes breakfast cereal). Because of health and sanitation regulations, you discontinued tours five years ago. You can send product samples for each scout and lend the troop a color film or videotape showing the manufacturing process.

Primary purpose of letter: _____

Secondary purpose of letter: _____

Reader's reaction: _____

Approach: _____

Brainstorming list:

_____   _____

_____   _____

_____   _____

_____   _____

24. Situation: You are the personnel manager of Winnetka Company. Plan a letter, to be mailed to the employees' homes, telling employees about the company picnic. This will be the company's first picnic, and your goal is to get all employees and their families to attend. Make up the specific information. Your message should be so clear that no employee will call you with questions.

Primary purpose of letter: _____

Secondary purpose of letter: _____

Reader's reaction: _____

Approach: _____

Brainstorming list:

_____   _____

_____   _____

_____   _____

_____   _____

_____   _____

_____   _____

OUTLINING AND PREPARING A ROUGH DRAFT

You are the assistant sales manager for Brasel Professionals, a placement service for office temporaries. You must answer a request for "more information about Brasel's services" from Mr. Jason Byrd, Office Manager of Independent Researchers Inc., 121 Ashlea Drive, Fort Worth, TX 76129.

Name _____ Date _____

OUTLINING AND PREPARING A ROUGH DRAFT *(continued)*

Your letter should have two purposes: (1) to impress upon Mr. Byrd that he should think of Brasel whenever he needs temporary office help and (2) to smooth the way for a representative to call on him.

The outline and letter plan notes you have made follow:

Monica Randolph (our sales representative) will call

Established 1966

Professional help when you need it

{ Clients include Fortune 500 (give example)

Clients include small firms (give example)

{ Well-trained administrative assistants

Clerical help (filing clerks)

Others (typists, receptionists)

Accounts receivable help

Telephone survey specialists

Page 4 of brochure (research services)

{ Wide range—help for one day or one year

Sales rep—appointment

{ Staff is experienced

In business for many years

Research specialists (brochure, p. 4)

Thank you

25. What will be the reader's reaction to your letter? What approach will you use?

Reaction: _____

Approach: _____

26. Revise the outline notes given, crossing out unnecessary or repetitious items and joining related items. Number the items in the order in which you would present them in the letter. Then, in the space provided, rewrite your notes in the revised sequence.

_____

_____

_____

_____

_____

_____

_____

_____

_____

_____

_____

27. Based on your outline, prepare a draft (preferably by composing on the computer) of the letter to Mr. Byrd.

_____

_____

COLLABORATIVE EXERCISE

With your team members, prepare a rough draft for the situation in question 24 (Winnetka Company).

_____

_____

Searching for Advertising Practices
When you write persuasive messages, you must not promise anything you cannot deliver. Search the Internet for information on deceptive advertising. Go to the U.S. Federal Trade Commission Website <www.ftc.gov> and find information about consumer protection. Choose a special area of advertising (for example, advertising dietary supplements, food, furniture) that interests you and print out guidelines for advertising those products.

NOTES

Chapter 6

Composing, Editing, and Proofreading

Communicating well through writing means producing error-free communications that meet the highest professional standards. Business professionals and support personnel all must develop the skills to produce such communications.

Composing, editing, and proofreading skills have always been important, but advances in office technology have made these skills essential to many jobs. Word processing software and computers have accelerated the production process and have changed the nature of many jobs. But technology will never replace the tasks of composing, editing, and proofreading. These skills are essential—and sharpening them can give your career a boost.

Objectives

After completing this chapter, you should be able to:

- Describe the advantages of different methods of composing messages.
- Plan dictation.
- Explain methods for improving your editing skills.
- Explain methods for improving your proofreading skills.

COMPOSING THE MESSAGE

Transferring the thoughts from your mind to written words can happen in several different ways. Let's look at each one briefly.

Composing at the Keyboard

With computers on most employees' desks in today's workplace, more and more executives are typing their own correspondence. In addition, laptop computers allow composing at the keyboard anytime and anyplace.

The advantage of composing at the keyboard is that you can see your words on the screen and quickly review what you've written. Skill in typing is an asset for anyone; obviously, the faster you can type, the more productive you will be.

 A minimum typing speed of 25 to 30 words a minute should be considered an essential communication skill in today's technological world.

Writing in Longhand

Writing by hand, although very time-consuming and costly, is still a common way of originating business correspondence. Typical writing rates of about 10 to 15 words a minute are very slow compared to other methods of originating correspondence, such as typing or dictation.

Dictation

Dictating correspondence using current technology is a productive way of generating letters, memos, and reports. In addition to saving time, dictation frequently results in a more conversational style, avoiding the formality that often creeps into business writing. Although dictating to a secretary has decreased as businesses have embraced technology, many executives still use dictation machines. In addition, voice-recognition software is becoming a popular way to dictate correspondence directly into the computer. But for dictation to be efficient, whether by voice recognition or by dictating machine, it is necessary to plan before dictating.

The guidelines in Figure 6-1 will help you form good dictation habits.

FIGURE 6-1 Preparing to dictate.

1. Know how to compose good business messages—with appropriate style, tone, psychological organization, and degree of persuasion.

2. Plan your dictation time by selecting a quiet location and avoiding interruptions. Twenty minutes of concentrated dictation is likely to be more productive than an hour of interrupted dictation.

3. Gather all the data you will need, the correspondence to be answered (underline the points to be covered), and the enclosures. If you are writing a reply, reread the communication you are answering.

4. Clearly define the purpose of the communication to be dictated. Determine precisely the reaction you want from the reader, and keep that desired reaction uppermost in your mind.

5. Visualize your reader. A communication is always more effective if it is written with its specific audience in mind.

6. Prepare an outline, decide on the plan, and determine the order in which your facts and ideas should be presented.

7. Be sure that you know how to operate your equipment before you begin your dictation, whether you are using a dictation machine or voice recognition software.

Using a Dictation Machine

Using a dictation machine is fast and convenient. You can dictate at any time, and you can dictate as fast as you can talk. Portable dictation machines allow dictation 24 hours a day, seven days a week, from anywhere in the world. Dictating allows business executives, attorneys, or doctors to hand over a very time-consuming part of communication, the mechanical act of producing correspondence, to someone else—the administrative assistant or transcriber. Executives can dictate in automobiles, trains, hotel rooms, and airports, as well as in their own homes.

A disadvantage is that you must have the appropriate equipment and dictation skills. Dictation may look easy—but it's not. To compose a concise, unified message orally requires a good deal of practice and a working knowledge of the principles of effective communication. Follow the guidelines in Figure 6-2 to improve your dictation skills.

1. Relax and speak clearly and distinctly. Speak in your natural voice at a fairly constant speed, a little more slowly than your normal rate.

2. Use voice inflection, and vary the tone of your voice. You will then avoid a monotone and help the transcriber recognize where punctuation goes, as well as where the instructions leave off and the message itself begins.

3. Start by giving any information the transcriber will need, such as your name and department. If the material is confidential, say so at the beginning. State what format the item should take (letter, memo, etc.), whether you want a rough draft or final copy, and when you will need it.

4. Indicate how long the document should be stored.

5. Indicate the type of stationery, letter style, and preferred punctuation style. List any enclosures and give the names and addresses of copy recipients.

6. Spell names, addresses, technical terms, and any other unfamiliar words. If the transcriber has access to correspondence files, you may omit this step.

7. Dictate complete phrases or thoughts, and pause at natural points.

8. Indicate punctuation marks, paragraph breaks, and the placement of tables or lists.

9. Clarify long figures. For example, say, "Gross revenue totaled two hundred million, three hundred ninety-four thousand, eight hundred sixty-seven. That's two-zero-zero comma three-nine-four comma eight-six-seven."

FIGURE 6-2 Dictating to a dictation machine.

6-1:

USE CORRECT SPELLING.
An administrative assistant transcribed an executive's dictation, "I have reserved two isle seats at the stadium."

(continued)

FIGURE 6-2 *continued*

10. Give corrections clearly and as soon as you are aware of the error. You will make errors or change your mind as you are dictating. Say, for example, "Correction. Substitute this sentence . . . . Or, "Correction. Change that to forty-eight dollars and fifty cents."

6-1—Pronunciation. *With a partner, practice enunciating this sentence. Be sure to pronounce every (ev-er-e) syllable.* Everybody traveling the Intercontinental Highway should enunciate every word, every syllable, and every sound, and move his or her lips distinctly and noticeably.

Dictating With Voice-Recognition Software

Although voice-recognition systems have been used for years in customer service activities, creating documents by voice input is relatively new. In the early voice-recognition systems, a user would speak each word separately, pausing between words. The newest systems recognize continuous speech—natural language processing with no pausing between words. Current voice-recognition systems, available for use with word processing software, store vocabularies of thousands of words that are ready for use. They are capable of storing many more thousands of words. As you dictate a message, your words appear on the computer screen. Some executives use this dictation method to create a rough draft; they then give the draft to an assistant to proof and finalize.

This technology is a productive way to create printed documents with accurate spelling. However, you must have the proper training in order to achieve high accuracy. Each user must "train" the system to make it fit the individual and follow specific procedures for instructing the software to format a message, handle punctuation and paragraphing, and make corrections. The benefits of voice-recognition technology include reduced costs and hands-free dictation.

Dictation skills are becoming extremely important as voice-recognition technology becomes more common. Good enunciation skills are essential. And you still need good language and proofreading skills to find errors, such as sound-alike homophones, like *capital* and *capitol* and *their* and *there*.

Figure 6-3 lists a few tips for using voice-recognition technology.

FIGURE 6-3 Tips for using voice-recognition software.

1. Be sure that your computer has enough memory for the software program.

2. Follow the software instructions exactly.

3. Train and dictate in a quiet place.

4. Speak normally without pauses.

5. Enunciate your words.

6. Make corrections according to the system's instructions.

Collaborative Writing

As the availability of information has increased, and access to that information has become easier, collaborative writing has become a popular way of composing reports and other business correspondence. In collaborative writing, teams composed of two or more people work together on complex memos, letters, or reports.

6-2—Spelling Accuracy. *What other ways might a voice-recognition system spell they're?*

 Writing in teams of two or more members is called **collaborative writing.**

Collaborative writing is particularly useful when a project requires input from different skill areas. For example, one team member might provide the artistic aspects of a project and another member could calculate the cost of each part of the project.

Internet Activity

**6-1
Finding Information on Groupware**

Access the Internet and use the key word *groupware* to find information about collaborative computer software. Prepare a short report on your findings.

TAKING RESPONSIBILITY FOR ERRORS

If you do your own composing, editing, and proofreading, obviously *you* are responsible for any errors you make. But who is responsible for errors when a support person transcribes your dictated communication or types your correspondence?

Although it is the support person's job to transcribe dictated communications into final form, the writer is ultimately responsible for the final draft. The impression the communication makes will be attributed to the *signer*. However, if the originator made a mistake, that does not excuse the support person for not catching and correcting the error. You should work as a team with the mutual goal of producing error-free correspondence.

Learning how to edit and proofread will help you check communications closely.

 Editing means *revising* a communication that often is still in rough draft form. **Proofreading** means checking the *final* copy to make sure it is free from errors.

EDITING THE MESSAGE

Editing not only involves correcting spelling, grammar, punctuation, and similar errors but also encompasses much more. Editing requires looking at a written communication critically to see whether revising the content will improve it.

Written messages containing incorrect facts, figures, dates, and even more serious errors are made every day. Avoiding these and other errors in written communications is a matter of knowing the rules of language usage and of developing editing and proofreading skills.

Edit carefully before preparing final copy. Editing requires at least two readings.

First Reading—for Meaning

Pay attention to details. If you do not concentrate and pay attention to meaning, you may overlook problems and errors. Many errors go undetected because the document originator or the typist, or both, have merely "eyeballed" the message for typing accuracy but have not *read it for meaning and sense.* Consult your notes, dictionary, thesaurus, or usage handbook if any word, phrase, or sentence doesn't look or sound quite right.

You want your business messages to reflect an image of you as an intelligent, professional writer.

Try to look at the rough draft through the eyes of the reader. The reader will notice a polished message but will pay even more attention—negative attention—to one that contains errors.

Because of a slip in dictating or a careless typing error, the letter may say something you did not intend to say—even something that may irritate or offend the reader.

 Most people *do* notice flaws in business communications they receive and react with either irritation or amusement.

Mistakes in meaning often occur because the typist misreads notes, misunderstands dictation, is distracted by interruptions, or is thinking about something else. Concentrate on ideas instead of meaningless words. Be sure that each sentence makes sense; then check the overall message for *content, tone, and style.*

✔ Checklist for Content, Tone, and Style

	Yes	No
1. Is the meaning so clear throughout that the reader cannot misread or misunderstand?	❏	❏
2. Does the message use the best approach—the one most likely to achieve your purpose?	❏	❏
3. Does it reflect the "you" attitude?	❏	❏
4. Does it sound positive, natural, and sincere?	❏	❏
5. Will it keep the reader's friendship and interest?	❏	❏
6. Are the paragraphs "choppy," too long, or poorly organized and connected?	❏	❏
7. Do these paragraphs contain sentences that are incomplete, "choppy," too long, wordy, or awkward?	❏	❏
8. Does the message contain words that are used incorrectly, words that are too general, or words that can be eliminated?	❏	❏

The answers to these questions will tell you whether you need to rewrite one or two paragraphs or the whole message.

Second Reading—for Mechanical Accuracy

Check the message word by word to be sure that it is appropriate and correct in every detail.

Checklist for Mechanical Accuracy

	Yes	No
1. Are capitalization, number usage, and the use of abbreviations, apostrophes, hyphens, and so on, appropriate?	☐	☐
2. Are any words misspelled? Review the list of Words Frequently Misspelled in Business Communications in Appendix C.	☐	☐
3. Should any punctuation marks be changed, inserted, or omitted to make the message clear and easy to read?	☐	☐

The *spell checker* and *grammar checker* of your word processing software can help you ensure mechanical accuracy. The checkers have built-in lists of grammar and style errors and highlight potential errors or weaknesses, such as passive voice, subject-verb agreement, mixed verb tenses, and missing words. The writer still needs a solid background in grammar and punctuation to know whether to correct the highlighted material.

 Word processing software spell and grammar checkers can alert you to potential errors; however, you cannot rely on the checkers to find all errors or to provide the correct revisions.

Editing a Hard-Copy Draft

If you are revising a printed copy of a document, use **proofreaders' marks,** or **revision symbols,** to mark changes or corrections in a standard way, so that all typists and business writers can understand them. Some common proofreaders' marks are shown in Figure 6-4. A more comprehensive list appears on the inside front cover page.

 Always use standard proofreaders' marks in a contrasting color when revising a printed copy.

6-2:

USING A GRAMMAR CHECKER.
A grammar checker marked this sentence as passive construction: A letter will be sent to you by my assistant requesting your choice of seats. *The executive composing the letter accepted the checker's suggested revision:* My assistant requesting your choice of seats will send a letter to you.

∧	= insert
≡	= change to capital letter
ℓ	= delete
⊙	= insert a period
⌣	= close up
#	= insert space

FIGURE 6-4 Proofreaders' marks.

Proofreading symbols provide an easy system for marking corrections. When editing, use a *contrasting color* so that the marks will be readily noticed. If more than one person is editing a paper copy, each person should use a different color.

Look at the edited rough draft shown in Figure 6-5, which illustrates the use of proofreaders' marks. The editor marked changes and corrections on the printed copy, and then the typist made the changes and corrections on the computer to produce the final version shown in Figure 6-6.

We want to thank you for asking us to estimate the cost of printing of your new company manual, "Quality Control Procedures." We are delighted to be of service. In your letter it specified that the new manual will be 207 pages long. It will be printed on 8 ½ x 11" 20 lb white paper and all pages will be 3 hole punched, collated, inserted into lose leaf binders which Victory Industries will be providing. As you requested and based on these specs we have itemized the costs of paper, printing, collating, and shipping for quantities of 750, 1000, and 1250 copies.

	750 Copies	1000 Copies	1250 Copies
Paper	$336.75	$449.00	$561.25
Printing	123.75	151.00	176.25
Collating	29.25	39.00	48.75
Shipping	23.25	31.00	38.75
TOTAL	$513.00	$670.00	$825.00

If you wish to discuss these estimates, please call me. As soon as you select the quantity and deliver you typed pages and loose leaf binders. We will process your order and deliver the manuals to your office within ten days.

FIGURE 6-5 An edited rough draft.

PRESTO PRINT

560 Peachtree Boulevard • Atlanta, GA 30312 • Phone: 404-555-2000 • E-Mail: aster@aol.com

August 1,<YEAR>

Mr. Watson M. Villines
Manager, Purchasing Department
Victory Industries
6900 Carlisle Avenue, S.E.
Atlanta, GA 30303

Dear Mr. Villines:

Thank you for asking us to estimate the cost of printing your new company manual, *Quality Control Procedures.* We are delighted to be of service.

Your letter specified that the new manual will be 207 pages long and will be printed on 8 ½- by 11-inch, 20-pound white paper. All pages will be three-hole punched, collated, and inserted into your loose-leaf binders, which Victory Industries will provide.

As you requested, based on these specifications we have itemized the cost of paper, printing, collating, and shipping for quantities of 750, 1000, and 1250 copies.

	750 Copies	1000 Copies	1250 Copies
Paper	$336.75	$449.00	$561.25
Printing	123.75	151.00	176.25
Collating	29.25	39.00	48.75
Shipping	23.25	31.00	38.75
TOTAL	$513.00	$670.00	$825.00

If you wish to discuss these estimates, please call me. As soon as you select the quantity and deliver your typed pages and loose-leaf binders, we will process your order and deliver the manuals to your office within ten days.

Sincerely yours,

Amanda Starling

Amanda Starling
Manager

kdv

FIGURE 6-6 Proofread the final draft carefully.

Editing a Soft-Copy Draft

In collaborative projects, team members may want to show their suggested revisions to other members directly on the computer. The team members may have special software, or they may use the formatting features of their word processing software to show their suggested revisions. The highlighting or shading feature of the software accentuates changes; the strike-through feature shows proposed deletions.

Go to Student CD-ROM Activity 6-1.

PROOFREADING THE MESSAGE

Proofreading the final copy is the last step in the process of preparing a business message. *Proofreading is not the same as reading.* It takes time to proofread because you must pay attention to small details. Figure 6-7 lists the characteristics of good proofreaders, and Figure 6-8 explains the steps to follow in proofreading.

FIGURE 6-7 Characteristics of good proofreaders.

1. Are good spellers.
2. Know punctuation and grammar rules.
3. Are detail-oriented.
4. Know what types of errors are frequently missed.
5. Take ample time to proofread.

After you have corrected and printed a message, proofread it against the original edited version to be sure that you *made all revisions and added no new errors.* You have now progressed to the final step in the letter writing process: determining whether the finished product is mailable.

FIGURE 6-8 Proofread in four steps.

1. Word processing programs now check spelling and grammar automatically as you type unless the computer settings have been changed. Some misspelled words are corrected automatically; for example, *teh* is changed to *the.* Words not recognized by the program's dictionary and double words *(in in)* appear underlined in a color or otherwise flagged. If you are composing your first draft, you want to type as fast as the ideas come and not stop to make corrections. After you finish your draft, you can then activate the spell checker and grammar checker and make all corrections.
2. Proofread the document on screen starting at the very beginning.
3. View the entire document on screen to check placement of elements on the page. ("View" is a word processing feature that allows you to see the document on the screen as it will appear when printed.)
4. Print the document and proofread the hard copy. (Some people find errors more easily on the hard copy than on the screen.)

Oops!

6-3:

PROOFREAD CAREFULLY.

This sentence appeared in an applicant's résumé: I am an excellent poofreader.

The right way to proofread is to scrutinize every detail of every part of the letter, starting with the date. Many business letters are sent without dates and signatures because of carelessness. Be sure to check for errors in numbers; an error in typing the street address or ZIP Code may delay a letter several days. The frequent errors listed in Figure 6-9 need special attention when you proofread a letter.

FIGURE 6-9 Proofread for these frequent errors.

1. Confusion of similar words—*to, too, two; quite, quiet; its, it's; your, you're; led, lead; hear, here; by, buy; there, their.*
2. Transposition of letters within a word—*from* for *form; cats* for *cast.*

3. Transposition and repetition of words—*it if is* for *if it is; will let let you know* for *will let you know.*

4. Omission of one or more letters of a word, especially in words with double or recurring letters—*adress* for *address; excelent* for *excellent; Febuary* for *February; determing* for *determining.* The *spell-as-you-go* software feature usually corrects or marks this type of omission for you.

5. Omission of words, of phrases, of spaces between words, and of one of a pair of commas, dashes, quotation marks, or parentheses.

Go to Student CD-ROM Activity 6-2.

Read the letter Will McGoof of Bronco Airlines wrote (see Figure 6-10). What do you think Ms. Bishop's reaction is likely to be?

711 Gamblers Boulevard
Denver, CO 41215
Phone: 1-800-Cockpit
E-Mail: wmcg@yahoo.com
Website: www.bronco.com

February 10, <YEAR>

Ms. Vonnie Bishop
3315 Keats Road
Spokane, WA 98406-3452

Dear Ms. Bishop:

Good News! Bronco Airlines will begin service to and from Spokan on March 1. Sign up today for Bronco's Frequent Flyer Program, your passport to a world of fee or discounted travel.

You'll like Bronco Airlines because of our low fairs, convient air schedules, and excellent personnel service. When your seated in our Business Section. Your copy of "The Wall Street Journal" will be waiting for you.

Take our Early Bird fright to Seattle for only $49 or to to Portland for only $69. Save money-save the day-that's the Bronco spirit!

See the enclosed bronco world route map and the brocure describing our fully automated Frequent Flyer Program. Then call you Bonco agent to make your first reservation and accumulate your first bonus pints!

Sincerly,

Will McGoof

err

Enclosures

FIGURE 6-10 This letter made a very poor impression on the reader because the originator and the transcriber who produced it failed to proofread. How many careless errors can you find in the letter?

Keep in mind, too, that a poorly formatted letter will not make the best possible impression on the reader. As you proofread, skim the letter for errors in format and style. Attractive arrangement and balanced placement are also important to the appearance of the letter. Make sure that the appearance of your letter does not detract from the message. Appendix A, Formatting, will give you more information about specific letter parts, their placement, arrangement styles, formats, and envelopes.

The steps the typist followed in preparing the final Presto Print letter (shown in Figure 6-6) are listed in Figure 6-11; these steps will also help you type the letters you write in good form before you mail them or submit them to your instructor.

FIGURE 6-11 Steps for preparing a final document.

1. Select the appropriate stationery, letter style, and format for the letter. (Appendix A will help you with these details.)

2. Type the heading or date line, inside address, salutation, body (the message), complimentary closing, signature, and any special notations.

3. Proofread and correct the letter word by word, sentence by sentence, and as a whole *before you print the final copy.* Always spell-check and/or look for errors marked by the software. Then give spelling, punctuation, and grammar a final check even though you have typed carefully and consulted your dictionary or reference manual as you edited the copy.

Figure 6-12 is designed to build your awareness of the types of errors observed most frequently in written business messages. Which items on the list do you have difficulty with? Turn to the Reference section to review those trouble spots and to learn how to correct errors as you edit and proofread written communications.

Before you give final approval to any written message, ask yourself the following questions:

1. Is it courteous?
2. Is it clear?
3. Is it complete?
4. Is it concise?
5. Is it correct?
6. Is it consistent?

If you identify weaknesses in these areas and correct them, you'll be making the finishing touches that ensure that your written communications will be as close to perfect as possible.

FIGURE 6-12 The most common errors in written business communications.

1. Comma usage

2. Sentence structure (run-ons and fragments)

3. Subject-verb agreement

4. Spelling

5. Typographical errors—omissions, transpositions, repetitions

6. Verb tense

7. Word usage—homonyms, pseudohomonyms, synonyms

8. Style and format

9. Paragraphing

10. Redundancies

11. Parallel structure

12. Active and passive voice (shifting voice and overuse of passive)

13. Placement of modifiers (misplaced and dangling modifiers)

14. Plurals and possessives

15. Capitalization

16. Contractions

17. Double negatives

18. Pronoun usage

19. Adverbs, adjectives, and articles

20. Prepositions and conjunctions

21. Compound words (one word, two words, or hyphenated)

22. Number usage

23. Word division

24. Abbreviations

25. Quotation marks with other punctuation

SUMMARY

Composing, editing, and proofreading skills are essential in today's business world. Well-written, error-free communications make a positive, lasting impression on your readers. On the other hand, sloppy, error-ridden messages reflect badly on you and your company. Editing and proofreading thoroughly ensure that your messages will be effective.

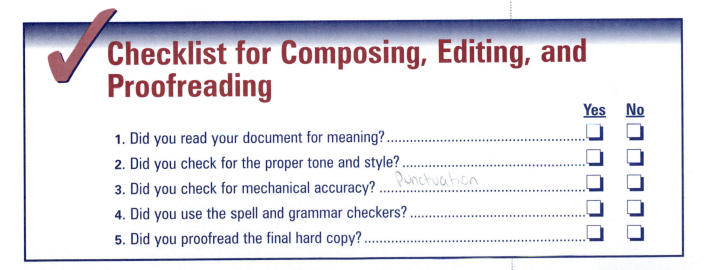

✔ Checklist for Composing, Editing, and Proofreading

	Yes	No
1. Did you read your document for meaning?	☐	☐
2. Did you check for the proper tone and style?	☐	☐
3. Did you check for mechanical accuracy? *Punctuation*	☐	☐
4. Did you use the spell and grammar checkers?	☐	☐
5. Did you proofread the final hard copy?	☐	☐

Name _____   Date _____

WHAT'S WRONG WITH THESE?

Locate any spelling, typing, and mechanical errors in the following sentences. Use proofreaders' marks to indicate changes on the sentences, and then write the errors on the lines provided.

1. The computer specialist will install the new printer in in the student learning center next week.

    _____

    _____

2. Renew you subscription to our best-selling magazine "Professional Writing" by completing and returning the enclosed card today.

    _____

    _____

3. The restaurant will close at ten p.m. on New Years eve.

    _____

    _____

4. We hope you will be among the crows visiting our store during our Jaunary White Sale.

    _____

    _____

5. I received a memo form the accounting dept. outlining our firms' travel and entertainment policies.

    _____

    _____

6. Spread sheet software save a great deal of time in recordkeeping for our department.

    _____

    _____

7. Both managers' were transferred to another state.

    _____

    _____

8. The sale ended last week therefore the memory telephone is now available at the regular price of $59.95.

    _____

    _____

Name _____ Date _____

DICTATION PRACTICE

9. Practice dictating the following letter on a dictating machine, if available, or to a classmate. Pause at the end of each line.

Operator, this is [your name] of the Athletic Department.
My telephone extension is 2030.
I have one letter. I need a rough draft, double-spaced on plain paper.
The final letter will be run on Athletic Department letterhead and merged with the alumni and fans
mailing list.
Use today's date.
Leave room for the inside address.
Dear [Name]:
The Ramada Inn, 160 Union Avenue
parenthesis across from the Peabody Hotel
close parenthesis
is the official Alumni-Razorback Fans Headquarters
in Memphis for the Liberty Bowl Game. paragraph
Come by our information booth
in the lobby of the hotel starting at 1 p.m.
Wednesday, December 26. paragraph
So that all alumni and fans can gather and
vent their enthusiasm before the game,
the Alumni Association will sponsor a reception
in the East Conference Room
on the second floor
from 3 p.m. until 5 p.m.
on Thursday, December 27.
The Association has planned a pep rally for 4:30 p.m.
Paragraph
Since the game has been sold out,
we look forward to a tremendous turnout
from Arkansas alumni and fans.
Make your reservations now at the Ramada
to ensure your spot at Razorback Headquarters.
Call us at 901-555-5261.
Sincerely,

10. From the outline on the next page, dictate a letter giving the same message as in the letter in Problem 9.
Then compare your dictation with the script in Problem 9.

Name _____ Date _____

Paragraph 1:	Liberty Bowl headquarters: Ramada Inn, 160 Union
Paragraph 2:	info booth Wed 26th at 1 in lobby
Paragraph 3:	Alumni Assn. reception Thurs. 27th 3–5; East Conf. Rm. 2nd Fl.; Pep rally at 4:30
Paragraph 4:	reservations—Ramada ph no. 901-555-5261; expect great Arkansas turnout

11. If you have voice-recognition software that is "trained" for your voice, dictate from the finished letter.

EDITING AND PROOFREADING PRACTICE

12. Figure 6-13 is an edited draft; Figure 6-14 shows the corrections in place. Compare the two copies to be sure that the typist made all the corrections and did not introduce any new errors. Use proofreaders' marks to correct errors.

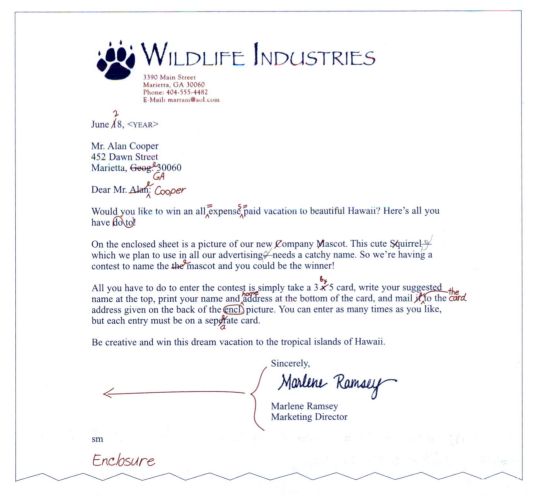

FIGURE 6-13 An edited draft.

Name _____ Date _____

EDITING AND PROOFREADING PRACTICE *(continued)*

WILDLIFE INDUSTRIES

3390 Main Street
Marietta, GA 30060
Phone: 404-555-4482
E-Mail: marram@aol.com

June 28, <YEAR>

Mr. Alan Cooper
452 Dawn Street
Marietta, GA 30060

Dear Mr. Alan:

Would you like to win an all-expenses-paid vacation to beautiful Hawaii? Here's all you
have to do!

On the enclosed sheet is a picture of our new company mascot. This cute squirrel—
which we plan to use in all our advertising—needs a catchy name. So we're having a
contest to name the mascot and you could be the big winner!

All you have to do to enter the contest is simply take a 3 by 5 card, write your suggested
name at the top, print your name and home address at the bottom of the card, and mail
the card to the address given on the back of the enclosed picture. You can enter as many
times as you like, but each entry must be on a separate card.

Be creative and win this dream vacation to the tropical islands of Hawaii.

Sincerely,

Marlene Ramsey

Marlene Ramsey
Marketing Director

sm

FIGURE 6-14 The final version of Figure 6-13.

13. Edit the following message using proofreaders' marks.

Inclosed for your review are three plans for remodeling your office
on Main St. I have tried to include everything on your spec sheet in
in each of these planes.

Two of the palns require taking out an interior wall but
I think the increased utilization of space and the overall
appeareance will be worth the expense of removing the wall.
I am still waiting on bids form schick office supply company
and arnold's office supplies for the office chairs and desks.

Name _____ Date _____

COLLABORATIVE ACTIVITY: PROOFREADING A LETTER

Remember the error-laden Bronco Airlines letter? (See Figure 6-15.) Work with a partner to find 18 careless spelling, typing, and mechanical errors; use revision symbols to mark the errors. Then type the letter and proofread it carefully before printing the final letter.

BRONCO AIRLINES
711 Gamblers Boulevard
Denver, CO 41215
Phone: 1-800-Cockpit
E-Mail: wmcg@yahoo.com
Website: www.bronco.com

February 10, <YEAR>

Ms. Vonnie Bishop
3315 Keats Road
Spokane, WA 98406-3452

Dear Ms. Bishop:

Good News! Bronco Airlines will begin service to and from Spokan on March 1. Sign up today for Bronco's Frequent Flyer Program, your passport to a world of fee or discounted travel.

You'll like Bronco Airlines because of our low fairs, convient air schedules, and excellent personnel service. When your seated in our Business Section, Your copy of "The Wall Street Journal" will be waiting for you.

Take our Early Bird fright to Seattle for only $49 or to to Portland for only $69. Save money-save the day-that's the Bronco spirit!

See the enclosed bronco world route map and the brocure describing our fully automated Frequent Flyer Program. Then call you Bonco agent to make your first reservation and accumulate your first bonus pints!

Sincerly,

Will McGoof

err

Enclosures

FIGURE 6-15 Follow the instructions above.

Voice Recognition and You
Go to two or three Websites of companies that offer voice-recognition software. Compare features, system requirements, and prices.

PART 2

Writing Effective Messages

The professional business world is becoming increasingly sophisticated and complex. In today's businesses the flow of accurate, reliable information and ideas through effective communications is essential to efficient operations.

In Chapters 7 to 9 we will look at various types of memos, letters, or e-mail messages—from the routine to the specific—that ask for information, make requests, or answer inquiries. Chapter 10 provides guidelines for writing and acknowledging orders.

In Chapter 11 you will learn how to write letters asking for credit and how to create collection letters when payment is overdue.

Chapter 12 shows you how to "resell," the way to persuade your reader, and how to create effective sales flyers. Then, in Chapter 13, you will learn the proper way to write a message when something is wrong, the proper way to reply to a claim letter, and how to protect one's rights.

To help you learn how to write business messages with the primary purpose of generating goodwill, Chapter 14 discusses writing thank-you, congratulation, condolence, and other friendly messages.

Here are the chapters in Part 2 that enhance what you have already learned in Part 1 and continue your letter-writing steps to proficiency:

professional business writing

Chapter 7

Writing Memos, E-Mail, and Other Routine Communications

Whether you write only for yourself or write communications for your employer, you will need to be able to write different kinds of routine messages.

Examples of routine messages are requests for information, answers to routine inquiries, acknowledgments, referrals, transmittals, invitations and replies to invitations, follow-up letters, and meeting notices. These messages take different forms—memos, e-mails, letters—and will usually follow the basic outline for good-news and neutral-news letters (direct approach). But whether you are writing for your supervisor or for yourself, remember to *keep your routine messages brief*.

Objectives

After completing this chapter, you should be able to:

- Identify routine forms of communication.
- Write routine memos, e-mail, and routine letters.
- Compose various routine messages, including:
  - Acknowledgments
  - Referrals
  - Transmittals
  - Invitations and replies
  - Follow-up correspondence
  - Meeting notices

ROUTINE COMMUNICATION RESPONSIBILITIES

You have five responsibilities in handling routine communications:

1. **Check incoming communications for factual discrepancies.** Errors in dates and figures are especially common. Suppose you receive a letter that mentions the date of a monthly meeting as Tuesday, May 6. Automatically consult the calendar to verify that Tuesday is the 6th. If Tuesday is the 7th, you must check further and get a clarification. In your response, you might tactfully ask, "Am I correct in marking the calendar for Monday, May 6, for the monthly meeting?"

2. **Record all promises you make of further correspondence.** For example, when you mention that you or your employer will write again in a few weeks to arrange a meeting, immediately enter a reminder on your calendar or your tickler file. (A **tickler file** is a filing system arranged by due date to keep track of deadlines.) At the appropriate time, follow up with the promised correspondence.

3. **Confirm in writing all appointments and invitations arranged verbally.** Embarrassing and costly mix-ups often occur when someone does not confirm in writing the time, place, and other details arranged in telephone and in-person conversations.

4. **Recognize the importance of sending goodwill messages promptly.** Regularly check newspapers, trade journals, or Internet sites for news items that suggest occasions for sending letters of appreciation, congratulations, and other goodwill messages to clients or other business contacts.

5. **Proofread all correspondence you write.** Errors in typing, spelling, and word usage reflect unfavorably on you, your employer, and the organization you represent.

In the first part of this chapter, we will study the different forms of routine correspondence. Then you will learn how to write routine messages for the different situations you will find in most businesses.

 Your ability to write routine communications is an important asset. Many people in management positions have found that the ability to organize, set priorities, and write effectively contributed to their career advancement.

FORMS OF ROUTINE WRITTEN COMMUNICATIONS

Routine written communications can take many different forms—memos, e-mail, letters, faxes, and more. The form you choose for your routine written correspondence depends on several factors:

- Whether your communication is internal or external.
- How formal or informal your message is.
- How quickly your message should be delivered.

Memorandums (Memos)

Internal memorandums, or **memos,** are written communications that are distributed *within a business organization.* In many organizations, particularly large ones, memos exchanged internally far outnumber external communications in the form of letters. In all organizations, in-house memos are vital to efficient operations. And every memo has a job to do, whether it's a simple reminder, a persuasive request, or an informational message.

The memo format is valuable for internal communications because a memo:

- Carries a special informality and gets a friendly reception (because both writer and reader are part of the same organization).
- Provides a written record, whereas a phone call does not.
- Can be delivered instantly by e-mail or fax (discussed later in this chapter).

The main reason for using memos as interoffice correspondence is to *save time.* Memos are not typed on letterhead stationery, nor do they require the formality of an inside address, salutation, or complimentary closing. The simple format of interoffice memos permits the writer to concentrate on the content.

Routine memos serve the same purpose *within* an organization that letters serve *outside* it. Memos are used to:

1. Transmit
2. Instruct
3. Announce
4. Congratulate
5. Express appreciation
6. Inform
7. Direct
8. Request
9. Reply
10. Confirm
11. Recommend
12. Persuade

Many organizations tell their employees to *put in writing all important information that crosses their desks,* in order to:

- Clarify who has responsibility for the information.
- Be sure that the appropriate people see the information.
- Keep written records.

Even a file copy of a simple transmittal memo is valuable in case the original memo is lost, because it lists the documents that were attached and tells when they were sent.

The following guidelines for writing routine memos will help you learn to communicate effectively within your organization.

Tone

The tone of a memo may differ from that of a letter or a report written to someone outside the organization, because the writer is often more interested in *presenting facts* than in persuasion. The writer is willing to let the reader form his or her own opinions. Although the memo writer does not forget about tact, courtesy, and friendliness, he or she assumes that the reader—a coworker—will work with the writer to serve the needs of the organization.

In most organizations today, the trend is toward *informality* in tone of memos. Generally, memos addressed to people above the writer's rank are more formal than memos addressed to people at the same level or below the rank of the writer.

 The tone of a memo depends on the rank of the writer in relation to the rank of the reader.

Other factors that influence the formality of a memo include:

- The personalities of the reader and the writer.
- The reader's background knowledge of the subject.
- The subject matter itself.

For instance, a memo announcing the recreation schedule for the annual picnic would obviously differ in tone from a memo justifying costs that have run over budget.

The effective memo writer will weigh all these factors before writing a memo and will give the message a final reading from the reader's viewpoint.

Organization

Good organization of a message appeals to a reader because a *logical order* allows the reader to review material quickly and easily. A poorly organized memo will confuse the reader and may require a second or even a third reading.

Organize your memo by following one of the three approaches for writing effective business messages. (For a detailed review of the approaches, see Chapter 5.)

Direct Approach

Most memos follow the *direct approach*.

1. Present the main idea in the opening statement.
2. Give supporting details or facts.
3. Conclude with a statement of future action or a request for further guidance.

Indirect Approach

Occasionally you may decide that the *indirect approach* (used primarily for bad news) is a better plan. For instance, if you are presenting conclusions and recommendations that you know the reader will be opposed to, you may be wise to first give the details and facts leading up to the conclusions and recommendations. Don't waste words, but do lead the reader to come to your conclusion by first explaining and building a strong case. The indirect approach follows this plan:

1. Give background details, facts, or explanations.
2. Present conclusions and/or recommendations.

Persuasive Approach
A memo requesting a special favor or approval of an idea should follow the *persuasive approach*.

1. Get the reader's attention.
2. Create interest by showing a benefit to the reader, if possible.
3. Encourage the reader to say yes by presenting your logic.
4. Make the request.

Sequence of Message
The most important rule for writing effective memos is to write from your reader's point of view. Too often, writers allow a dictatorial tone to creep into their memos. *Will you please . . .* is a better beginning than *You will . . .* Just as in writing letters, the memo writer should use the "you" attitude and should note benefits to the reader.

In a routine memo using the direct approach, follow these steps:

1. State the purpose first.
2. Give the message.
3. End with conclusions, suggestions, or a goodwill thought.

Let's look at each of the parts of a memo.

The Opening: The Purpose
The first sentence determines whether your reader will continue to read or toss your memo into the wastebasket. The opening paragraph should:

- Be reader-oriented ("you" attitude).
- Get the reader's attention.
- Use a convincing, positive tone.
- Contain the main point (unless you have negative news).

If you have negative news, lead up to the main point by first giving some facts, reasons, or explanations.

In a direct approach memo, make the purpose of your memo clear in the opening. You may refer to a:

- Previous memo, fax, or e-mail message.
- Meeting or teleconference.
- Phone conversation or voice mail message.
- Topic of mutual interest.

Here are examples of how to state the purpose of a memo:

> The information you requested explaining the nature of the entertainment expense I submitted on my September 27 Travel and Entertainment Expense Report follows.
>
> **OR**
>
> At the June meeting of our Credit Union Board, I was asked to recommend a method for collecting delinquent loans. I submit the following ideas for your consideration prior to our next meeting on Tuesday, August 4.

OR

> During my recent visit to the Philadelphia office, I observed several ticket-processing procedures that I believe would result in greater efficiency in our office. I would like to share these ideas with you.

The information that follows the opening will be valid and pertinent if you *identify your reason for writing* first.

The Middle Paragraph(s): The Message

In the middle paragraph(s), *cover all points,* such as:

- Give the *causes* if you bring up a problem and the *reasons* for your suggested solution.
- Tell *why* as well as *how* when writing a directive.
- Provide enough information so that the reader can *understand* new procedures and *follow directions.*
- Give realistic and logical explanations.
- Give the reader the benefits of your plan if you are using a persuasive strategy.

The first of the sample openings given in the preceding section would be followed by a middle paragraph such as this:

> The entertainment expense was for taking Don and Martha Story to a dinner theater. Don Story is vice president of Saulter Company, the largest client in my division.

If the middle section of your memo contains several related items, consider numbering them or starting each one on a separate line preceded by a dash or a bullet to make reading easier. Again, the key to writing this section is to cover all points. Memos that offer insufficient information not only cause confusion but also cast doubt on the abilities of the writer.

The Ending: Conclusions or Suggestions

The ending should be a separate paragraph expressing *a goodwill thought* or giving *conclusions or suggestions for future action.* Tie your conclusions or suggestions to the statement of purpose or the recommendation made in the opening and support your conclusions by the facts presented in the middle of the memo. The ending might, for example:

- Summarize the important points you have listed.
- Interpret a table or graph.
- Suggest future action.

Here are some examples of memo conclusions:

> Although this expense exceeded our company guidelines for an evening meal, Bruce Weinard, my division sales manager, asked me to make a special effort for such a good customer. Therefore, I feel that this expenditure is justified.
>
> **OR**
>
> The statistics presented above demonstrate the need for us to upgrade our telephone system. I suggest that we authorize Pete Symanski to ask for proposals and bids for a new phone system.

Most routine memos will be effective if you:

1. Orient your writing to your reader and follow the suggestions in this chapter.
2. Edit each memo for clarity, logic, and psychological effect.
3. Proofread very carefully.

 Composing and transmitting an informative, useful message should be the primary goal of every memo writer.

Memo format may vary. For general guidelines on formatting memos, see the Formatting appendix. Also see Figure 7-1 for an example of a memo that was created with a word processing template. You will learn how to use the memo format to create informal reports in Chapter 17.

interoffice memorandum

to:	Ms. Georgia Pullen
from:	Randall Burrell *RB*
subject:	Customer Service Improvement Suggestions
date:	11/21/<YEAR>
cc:	Helen Caplen

At the October meeting of our Customer Service Improvement Circle, you asked me to survey the floor sales staff for their suggestions on improving service.

The floor staff had a number of good suggestions, which I have listed below:

- Acknowledge every customer with a greeting and a smile.

- Do not follow a customer around, but be available as soon as the customer is ready.

- Send thank-you notes to first-time purchasers.

- Provide free coffee for shoppers.

- Offer assistance in carrying purchases to the customer's automobile.

- Give discount coupons for next purchase.

- Provide customers with a "How Are We Doing?" card to give us more ideas for improving service.

These suggestions show that our sales staff is truly interested in improving customer service. I would like to discuss how we might implement some of these suggestions at your convenience.

lk

FIGURE 7-1 A memo created from a word processing template.

E-Mail

With today's technology and need for instant information, **e-mail (electronic mail)** has become a major way for organizations to communicate internally and externally. Delivery of a memo by hand may take a day or more to get from one floor or building to another; delivery of a letter externally can take even longer. E-mail is sent via computer and appears on the receiver's monitor on command. An e-mail message uses an informal memo format. E-mail can be easily answered by clicking on "Reply" and typing a brief response.

Memos and letters can be easily transmitted by e-mail by inserting or attaching computer files to e-mail messages.

 Be as careful in writing your e-mail as you are with other correspondence, and do not put any confidential information in e-mail.

Keep these points in mind when using your business e-mail:

1. Keep your e-mail messages short. If you have a lengthy message, it is usually better to write a memo or letter using your word processing software; and then send the memo as an **attachment** to your e-mail.

2. So that you will not forget to insert your attachment, make it a practice to insert the attachment *first*—before writing the message in which you say you are attaching a document.

3. Always provide a descriptive subject in the heading. The e-mail recipient can then quickly know that your message is business—not junk mail.

4. Follow grammar, spelling, punctuation, and capitalization rules. Sloppy e-mail reflects badly on the writer.

5. Never write anything confidential in e-mail messages—e-mail is not confidential. And even though you may delete a message, it remains on the company's e-mail server. Retrieved e-mail messages have been used in court as evidence of wrongdoing by employees.

6. Send messages only to those people who need the information. Be careful in your use of "global" e-mail lists—such as lists of "All Employees," or "All Managers."

7. Do not use your company's e-mail for personal business. Many companies have policies that can include dismissal of the employee for abusing the e-mail system.

8. Even if your company does not have a policy banning personal use, do not use company time to send and receive your personal e-mail. In addition, act professionally and resist the temptation to pass on cute graphics and "thoughts for the day" type of messages that are so rampant on e-mail. These useless messages take up space on the company's e-mail server. Also, many people resent receiving "junk mail" on their computers, just as they resent having to go through and discard paper "junk mail."

9. Although **emoticons** (<u>emo</u>tional <u>icons</u>—symbols used to suggest facial expressions) may appear in informal e-mail to express feelings, avoid using them in your business e-mail messages. A few examples of these symbols, which are also called *smileys* and are constructed sideways, follow:

:-) smiling face

:-] sarcastic smirk

8-) wide-eyed look

10. Do not use all-capital letters for your messages. Type the usual upper-case and lowercase letters. Using all-capital letters means that you are shouting, according to e-mail "etiquette."

11. Always use a spell checker and proofread your e-mail carefully before sending it. Because e-mail is so handy and quick, many writers tend to forget that the recipient may find errors and think of you as a careless writer. An example of an e-mail message is given in Figure 7-2.

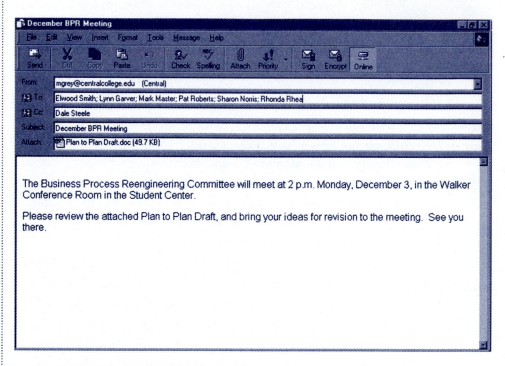

FIGURE 7-2 An e-mail. Be sure to include any attachments.

Routine Letters

Most business organizations use a letter format for external communications. The letter format is more formal than the format used for memos or e-mail. But both letters and memos have a job to do, whether it's a confirmation, a thank-you message, or a persuasive request.

The letter format is valuable for routine external communications because it:

- Presents a formal appearance.
- Provides a written record.
- Provides the complete company name, address, telephone number(s), and in many cases, the e-mail address of the writer and the Internet address of the company.

Routine letters, like routine memos, serve to:

1. Transmit
2. Instruct

3. Announce
4. Congratulate
5. Express appreciation
6. Inform
7. Direct
8. Request
9. Reply
10. Confirm
11. Recommend
12. Persuade

Follow the guidelines you learned in Chapter 5 to plan and prepare your letters.

Most *routine* letters will follow the direct approach. However, you may need to use the indirect and persuasive approaches in some situations. (For a detailed review of the approaches, see Chapter 5.)

Remember to write even routine letters from your reader's point of view. For example, begin with *Will you please . . .* rather than *You will . . . .* In addition, always edit letters for clarity, logic, and psychological effect. For guidelines on formatting letters, see the Appendix A, Formatting.

 Just as in writing memos, use the "you" attitude and note the benefits of your suggestions to your reader when writing routine letters.

Fax Messages

Letters or memos that need to be immediately transmitted from one office to another are often sent via facsimile (fax) machines. A **facsimile machine** is a scanner that is connected to telephone lines and can transmit a document in a matter of minutes from one office to another. A fax resembles a photocopy of a document.

A few points to remember about sending faxes:

1. Be careful when you send or receive confidential faxes. A fax that arrives while the intended recipient is away from the machine could be examined by any passerby.
2. Be sure to include the *recipient's* name and phone number on the cover page so that the fax will be delivered to the intended recipient.
3. Be sure to include the *sender's* name and phone number on the cover page so that the recipient can call if there is a problem.
4. Check to see whether all the pages are transmitted. If in doubt, call the recipient to confirm that all pages were received.

You may use a full-page cover sheet or a small stick-on label to show information about the fax transmission. Word processing software includes templates or "wizards" that will make cover sheets and send faxes quickly if your system is configured to do so. Examples of a cover page and a transmitted document are given in Figure 7-3.

7-1
Searching the Internet for a Famous Case
In the late1990s the U.S. government subpoenaed the e-mail records of Microsoft Corporation as evidence in its antitrust case against Microsoft. Find the status or outcome of this litigation on the Internet. Has the case taken on greater significance as the years have passed?

FIGURE 7-3 A fax cover page and accompanying document.

02-11-<YEAR>   10:18   913 555 2839   M. L. LaRue, Jr.   p. 01

36896 Lone Oak St.
Lexington, KY 42501
Fax: 913-555-2839
Phone: 913-555-1837
mllarue@cwiz.net

M. L. LaRue, Jr.

Fax

To:	Larry Clooney, Raintree Inc.	From:	M. L. LaRue, Jr. *MLL*
Fax:	213-555-9898	**Date:**	February 7, <YEAR>
Phone:	213-555-3869	**Pages:**	2
Re:	Consulting Invoice	**CC:**	[Click here and type name]

☐ **Urgent**   x **For Review**   ☐ **Please Comment**   x **Please Reply**   ☐ **Please Recycle**

• **Comments:**

Larry — I would appreciate your placing my invoice in line for early payment. Thanks.
ml

02-11-<YEAR>   10:18   913 555 2839   M. L. LaRue, Jr.   p. 02

36896 Lone Oak St.
Lexington, KY 42501
Fax: 913-555-2839
Phone: 913-555-1837
mllarue@cwiz.net

M. L. LaRue, Jr.

November 19, <YEAR>

Mr. Larry Clooney
Raintree Inc.
10300 Cosby Way
Georgetown, TX 73901

Dear Larry:

INVOICE

CONSULTING SERVICES RENDERED OCTOBER 1—31, <YEAR> $7,500.00

EXPENSES TO BE REIMBURSED:

Copying	38.50		
Parking	10.00		48.50
		TOTAL	**$7,548.50**

THANK YOU!

M. L. LaRue, Jr.

M. L. LaRue, Jr.

rt

Self-Stick Notes

Self-stick notes have become very popular for writing reminders or simple instructions. Attaching a self-stick note to a form that needs a signature is much quicker than writing a cover memo.

Preprinted Message Forms

Information that is regularly collected in a routine office task is often recorded on a preprinted message form.

Since every organization conducts at least some of its business over the telephone, most organizations use a preprinted telephone message form. Complete the telephone message form entirely and verify the following information while the caller is still on the line:

- Phone number. Always get a phone number and *repeat it* to the caller.
- Caller's name and company affiliation, if any. Ask the caller to spell his or her name (unless you know the name), and include both first and last names on the form.
- Message. Repeat the message to the caller to be sure that it is accurate.

Many other types of message forms are available: routing forms for publications and long reports, service request forms, and photocopy request forms. An organization can save time by developing a form to communicate information especially when high volume warrants doing this.

The key for successful use of such preprinted business forms is to *complete them accurately.*

Informal Notes

Use small notepads for brief, informal messages that need to be done quickly. The notepads, usually 4 by 6 inches, can be plain paper, but many organizations have notepads printed for their employees with a heading such as:

- From the Desk of John Doe
- A note from John Doe
- John Doe, Graphics Department

You may write or type these messages. *Sign* and *date* informal notes, just the way you do with other business communications.

You may use an informal note for a coworker who is busy or away from the office temporarily. Informal notes can also be used to transmit material or serve as a reminder on a file copy. An example of an informal note is shown in Figure 7-4.

Message-Reply Forms and Memo-Letters

Message-reply forms provide space for both the writer's message and the addressee's reply. These two-way message forms are popular with field representatives who do not always have support personnel available to type their correspondence.

very informal

FIGURE 7-4 An informal note.

From the desk of . . .

Molly Romano
Birds Unlimited, 993 Bay Area, Tampa, FL 32610
912-555-1010   mromano@birds.com

10/22

Sue –

I need to talk with you sometime today about your order.

Molly

The message-reply form is very quick to use and easy to reply to; the snap-out form is a preassembled carbonless pack that provides:

- An original for the recipient.
- A copy to return to the writer.
- A file copy for the writer
- An extra copy for a third person, if needed.

A **memo-letter** uses a preprinted form to send a message, in memo format, to a branch office or to a field representative of the sender's organization. Because the representative may work in a small office or in an office in his or her home, or may be traveling from one field location to the next, faxing the message may be impractical. Often handwritten, a memo-letter provides a copy for the sender.

WRITING ROUTINE COMMUNICATIONS

Acknowledgments

You will want to write messages to acknowledge receipt of (1) letters or messages that cannot be answered immediately, (2) information or material, (3) gifts and favors, (4) remittances, and (5) orders.

Messages That Cannot Be Answered Immediately

When you receive a communication that you must hold for someone else's attention, business courtesy requires that you send a **stopgap communication.** This type of message is a short, direct acknowledgment that explains (1) why an answer will be delayed and (2) when it may be expected.

Be careful not to obligate anyone or give out confidential information about why the person who needs to handle the situation is not able to answer immediately. An acknowledgment message might read like this:

> Dear Mr. Melecosky:
>
> Thank you for your May 14 letter asking Ms. Langas to speak at your meeting on July 10.
>
> Ms. Langas is out of the office this week. As soon as she returns, I will make sure that she sees your letter.
>
> Sincerely,
>
> Jeanene Lowery
> Assistant to Ms. Sharon Langas

 Never give out confidential information or obligate someone when you write stopgap letters.

Another example of a stopgap message is one written to explain that you will need more time to prepare a complete answer. Often a person asking for information does not realize that it might take several days and communication with several departments to get the facts together for a reply. When this is the case, send a short message (it might be an e-mail rather than a letter) to explain the delay. You might say:

> You can expect the information you requested in your March 21 letter in a few days. In order for my report to be helpful to you, I must get data from both the sales and the advertising departments.
>
> I am glad to cooperate with you on this project and expect to send a complete answer by the end of the week.

When a delayed reply is a common occurrence, you may send an e-mail, a form letter, or a postal card. If a letter is best, you can easily make a form letter appear to be an individually written letter using your computer. If you were employed in an office that handled numerous property loss claims, for example, you would build goodwill by acknowledging each claim on the day you received it with a brief message such as:

Dear Ms. Wong:

We have received your recent notice of loss, and it is receiving our prompt attention. You will receive a reply as soon as we complete your property loss evaluation.

Sincerely,

Information or Material

You should write acknowledgments when you receive packages, requested information, and other messages or materials. These acknowledgments should be direct, concise, and courteous. These acknowledgments should also (1) thank the reader and (2) include the details needed to identify the items received, since they become a record for the files. A form message may be useful for many similar acknowledgments. The following example illustrates the principles of good writing for a routine acknowledgment of signed contracts.

Go to Student CD-ROM Activity 7-1.

Dear Ms. Sennhenn:

The signed contracts relating to the Kestell case arrived this morning. Thank you for sending them so promptly.

Sincerely,

Gifts and Favors

Write simple and sincere thank-you acknowledgments for gifts and favors as well as for congratulatory and other goodwill letters you receive from clients and friends.

> Dear Mr. Fabrizio:
>
> You were most generous to send copies of your interesting booklet *Dictation for Productivity* for all the members of our office staff.
>
> Your commonsense approach to dictating—with checklists and clever illustrations—will certainly help the dictators and office support personnel in our company.
>
> Sincerely,

Remittances

You may not need to acknowledge remittances by check because the sender's canceled check serves as notice of payment. However, some managers believe that the goodwill gained by a written acknowledgment outweighs the time and expense of writing the letter. A letter acknowledging a remittance should:

1. Be brief.
2. Express appreciation.
3. Give the amount and form of remittance.
4. Tell what the remittance was for.
5. Build goodwill through a warm, friendly tone.

Two occasions on which you should *always* send a letter acknowledging a remittance are:

1. When a customer pays his or her first invoice.
2. When the remittance is an unusually large one.

> Dear Mr. Lopez:
>
> Your Check 482 for $1500 arrived today, and we have credited your account.
>
> We do appreciate your prompt payment, which reduces your account balance to $1000.
>
> Sincerely,

Orders

See Chapter 10 for a discussion of acknowledgment of orders.

Referrals

At times, someone other than you can better answer a message you received. If the person you refer that message to is not in the same office or, for any other reason cannot reply immediately, you should send a referral message to the writer. Send a copy of this message, along with a request to reply, to the person to whom you are referring the matter. A short, courteous referral message follows:

Dear Mr. Sharmila:

Thank you for inquiring about service on your telephone answering machine. Our distributor would be the best person to answer your questions.

I am therefore referring your question to Mr. Adam Passavage, manager of the Service Department at Columbia Private Telephone Inc., 186 Technology Avenue, Shadtpoint, OK 74956, telephone 209-555-1699, e-mail address adam_passavage@columbiapri.com.

        Sincerely,

        Jessica Johnson

ct
c: Adam Passavage

Transmittal Letters

Transmittal letters are cover letters sent to accompany information or articles. We will discuss cover letters in Chapter 9. The transmittal letters you write may be as simple as this one, which was sent to a dealer:

Dear Mrs. DeBaraba:

Here are the advertising mats you requested.

We appreciate your interest in promoting the Schwinn bicycle in Milwaukee's newspapers.

Sincerely,

Invitations and Replies to Invitations

You may be called upon to write or answer two types of invitations: formal and informal.

Formal Invitations

Figure 7-5 shows a formal printed invitation. Before preparing a formal invitation, refer to an up-to-date book of etiquette (one of the essential reference books in the office) for correct wording and arrangement. Before printing the invitation, be sure to check a proof copy for accuracy of dates, time, place, spelling, and other details.

Invitations that include an **R.S.V.P.** (which means "please reply") *require an answer.* Some invitations include a reply card for you to complete and return; others will have a phone number so that you can reply by phone.

The Board of Directors
of
Bayshore Credit Union

cordially invites you and your guest
to a reception
for our retiring president

George S. Camarro

at seven o'clock on Friday evening
the twenty-eighth of May
nineteen hundred and ninety nine
at the Greensboro Country Club
2 Mason Road

R.S.V.P.   *Black Tie*

FIGURE 7-5 A formal invitation. A reply card would be enclosed with this invitation.

Informal Invitations

A more casual letter format is appropriate for informal invitations. In addition to "inviting," these invitations should provide the following specifics about the event:

- The day, date, and time
- The place
- The type of function
- The reason for the function
- Who is included in the invitation
- The dress requirements (if any)
- A request for a reply

Here is an example of an informal invitation:

Dear Mr. Vann:

Please join me for lunch on Friday, June 8, at the Venice Garden restaurant at 12 noon. I hope that you and all the other members of the Restoration Committee for the Southern Aire Opera House can come.

We will be discussing specific suggestions for the October fund-raiser. Come prepared to share your ideas.

Will you please let me know by Monday, June 4, whether you will be able to attend the luncheon and meeting?

Sincerely,

When accepting an invitation:
- Express pleasure with the invitation.
- Confirm all the details.
- Make it clear exactly who will attend. However, do not ask to bring extra people.

If you must refuse the invitation, *express regret.* An acceptance of an informal invitation might look like this:

Dear Ms. Gilley:

I am delighted to accept your invitation to speak at the annual meeting of the National Association of Physical Therapists in San Diego on Friday, November 9.

As you suggested, I have made a reservation for Friday night at the Comfortlodge on Toronto Road. My flight (Air South Flight 526) should arrive in San Diego at 4:10 p.m., and I will take the Comfortlodge shuttle directly to the hotel and meet you in the lobby at 6 p.m.

I look forward to seeing you on November 9.

Sincerely,

Follow-Up Communications

You may need to follow up, for example, on information or articles that you requested but have not received or enclosures that were omitted from correspondence. Follow-up messages should:

- Use a tone of reminding rather than of criticizing.
- Be brief, but include enough information for the recipient to recall the earlier communication or discussion.
- Identify the promised item(s).
- Tell what you want the recipient to do.

Here are two examples of follow-up correspondence:

We have not received the committee report on proposed changes in insurance coverage, which was promised for last Friday, April 3. Mrs. Johnson needs this information to prepare for a meeting with the insurance company on the 13th. Therefore, please forward the report to Mrs. Johnson so that it arrives by April 10.

Your letter of March 24 indicated that a copy of the Treasurer's Report for the American Chemical Society was enclosed. However, the report was not in the envelope when the letter reached us. Will you please send us another copy today?

Meeting Notices

Meetings result in the exchange of ideas and the making of decisions. Sending notices about meetings is another type of routine correspondence that you may handle. Use your calendar or tickler file to help you remember when to send out meeting notices. An e-mail or written notice is the best way to remind people about meetings because you are repeating the details and sending the identical information to each person. A meeting notice should include the following information:

- Day and date of meeting
- Meeting time
- Meeting place
- Purpose of the meeting
- What to bring, if anything
- Agenda or list of discussion items if several items are to be discussed
- List of invitees

In addition, if refreshments will be provided, include that information on your meeting notice.

An e-mail meeting notice might look like the e-mail you saw earlier in this chapter in Figure 7-2. A written memo notice might look like this:

MEETING NOTICE

WHO: Quality Assurance Team

DATE: Wednesday, August 30, <YEAR>

TIME: 2 p.m.–3:30 p.m.

PLACE: Conference Room D

PURPOSE: Regular Monthly Meeting

AGENDA: Discussion of *Quality Report V*

Recommendations for improving usable product rate—Plastics

New product line preview

Suggestion box proposal

Please bring with you *Quality Report V*, which we distributed at the July meeting. You should also bring your written recommendations for improving the usable product rate in the Plastics Department.

Brad Meachum, Chairperson

You will study reports, such as agendas and minutes, and additional information about meetings and meeting correspondence in Chapter 16.

Go to Student CD-ROM Activity 7-2.

Messages of Appreciation, Congratulations, or Sympathy

On occasion you may need to write a letter to someone who is celebrating an engagement, a wedding, an anniversary, or a similar happy event. You may also need to write a letter to offer sympathy for a death or personal misfortune. Chapter 14 discusses these goodwill messages.

SUMMARY

Routine messages can take the form of memos, e-mail, letters, self-stick notes, and other formats. Whether your communication is internal or external, how formal or informal you want the message to be, and how quickly you need the message delivered determine its format.

Routine messages can be acknowledgments, referrals, transmittals, invitations, replies to invitations, follow-ups, meeting notices, or messages of appreciation, congratulations, or sympathy. The ability to write routine communications is an important asset in the business world.

✓ Writing Routine Correspondence Checklist

Writing Routine Correspondence

	Yes	No
1. Did you check for factual discrepancies?	☐	☐
2. Did you record all promises you made?	☐	☐
3. Did you confirm appointments and invitations in writing?	☐	☐
4. Did you send goodwill messages promptly?	☐	☐
5. Did you choose the appropriate form for your message?	☐	☐
6. Did you use the appropriate tone?	☐	☐
7. Did you choose the right approach?	☐	☐
8. Did you proofread all correspondence?	☐	☐

Name _____ Date _____

WHAT'S WRONG WITH THESE?

On the lines provided, write what is wrong with the following statements.

1. Please R.S.V.P. by Friday, March 25, for the Gala to be held in the Grand Ballroom on Friday, March 13.

   _____

   _____

2. E-mail text: *Carolyn Robertson, manager of purchasing, makes a salary of $63,500.*

   _____

   _____

3. Routine memo text: *I want you to send me copies of every contact you have with Ralley Company employees.*

   _____

4. Stopgap letter text written by administrative assistant: *Ms. Riley is on a cruise in the Caribbean this week; however, I am sure she would love to speak at your meeting next month.*

   _____

5. Informal invitation text: *Please join us for refreshments on Monday, June 3, in the Heritage Room of the Lodge Hotel, to honor Gerald Kidman for his 30 years of service to the company.*

   _____

   _____

CHOOSING THE RIGHT FORM OF ROUTINE CORRESPONDENCE

Background for Problems 6 to 10. You are the assistant to Ralph Waller, vice president of Delectables, Inc., a food processing company. Mr. Waller is also a member of the executive board of the Colorado Historical Society. He left this morning on a two-week vacation, and you must handle his correspondence while he is away. On the lines provided, write which type of routine correspondence you will use for each situation (for example, acknowledgment via memo or e-mail).

6. You have received a letter from John Kinsey, public relations director of Kinsey Productions, Inc., asking the dates of the Old West Festival that Delectables cosponsors each year. You have this information on the festival:

   Begins at 10 a.m. on June 2 with a parade down Main Street.
   Festival ends on June 5 after fireworks display that begins at 10 p.m.
   Delectables, Inc., has cosponsored the event since 1966.
   Profits go to local food banks for the needy.
   Activities include food booths and demonstrations about pioneer days.

   Type of routine communication needed: _____ Memo _____

Name _____ Date _____

7. Your electronic calendar indicates that you need to send notices today for a meeting of the New Products Committee (which Mr. Waller chairs). The regular monthly meeting will be Tuesday, February 23, at 10 a.m. in the 6th floor conference room. The meeting usually lasts about two hours. Committee members should bring their new *Policies and Procedures Handbooks* with them.

Type of routine communication needed: _e mail_____

8. You have received a letter from Constance Riker, manager of Riker's Whole Foods, Inc., asking for information about stocking Delectables' products in her store. Tom LaPorta, marketing manager of Delectables, handles all such requests.

Type of routine communication needed: _letter_____

9. Today 100 copies of the pamphlet *Packaging for Promotion* arrived. Mr. Waller had requested them from a friend, Linda Suggs, who owns Creative Packaging. Mr. Waller wants to give them to the sales managers as inspiration.

Type of routine communication needed: _memo_____

10. You have received a letter from Kathrine Burney, director of student services at Mainland College, asking Mr. Waller, an honor graduate of Mainland, to present the commencement address at this year's graduation ceremony on Friday, June 15, at 2 p.m.

Type of routine communication needed: _letter_____

WRITING ROUTINE MESSAGES

Plan and prepare clear, concise memos, e-mails, or letters for the following problems. Organize the information, plus any other information you wish to assume, into effective interoffice memos. Type your messages on a computer, if one is available.

11. Write an e-mail to your supervisor, Lilly Fisher, requesting the first week of the month after next month (use current dates) as vacation time. You want to attend your sister's wedding, which will be held at an out-of-state location.

_____

_____

_____

_____

_____

Name _____ Date _____

WRITING ROUTINE MESSAGES (continued)

12. Prepare a memo using today's date to Bart Andrews, safety director, asking the dates and times of the next CPR training course to be offered by the company. Tell him that you want to take the course because no one in your division of the company is certified since Frances Sanders retired last month.

_____

_____

_____

_____

_____

13. On a recent flight to Boston, you read a magazine called *The Executive's Guide to Communication and Motivation,* which you found very interesting. You think the magazine would be helpful to other people in your office. Prepare a memo to your office administrator, Clarice Schroeder, asking her to subscribe to the monthly magazine in your organization's name. The yearly subscription rate is $24. Attach the magazine subscription card to your memo.

_____

_____

_____

_____

_____

_____

14. As human relations director, write a memo to tell all full-time employees of changes in medical insurance premiums. The insurance carrier has just notified you that, effective the first of next month, the medical insurance premium will go up by $15 a month for each employee. The current rate is $160 a month. The coverage for dependents will remain at $190 a month. The additional $15 will be automatically deducted from their paychecks starting the first of next month.

_____

_____

_____

_____

_____

Name _____ Date _____

15. Prepare a congratulatory e-mail that your regional manager, Howard Schwartz, can send to all sales personnel. Mr. Schwartz received an e-mail today from the New York office announcing that the Southern Region exceeded its goals for the fiscal year—gross sales were 148 percent of last year's sales. Your message, though short, should project jubilance.

_____

_____

_____

_____

For Problems 16 to19, assume this working situation: You are an assistant to Ms. Freida Ireland, Marketing Director, Lakeview Medical Center, 500 Logan Avenue, Berea, OH 44017. In addition to her responsibilities at the Medical Center, Ms. Ireland has had a leadership role in the Berea United Way for several years and last year served as general chairman of the fund drive.

16. Write a letter for your own signature to the administrator of Children's Research Hospital, 800 Harmon Street, St. Petersburg, FL 33733, to transmit a copy of last year's *Lakeview Medical Center Annual Report.* Ms. Ireland met the administrator, F. M. Hoskins, on a recent business trip and promised to send him an annual report.

_____

_____

_____

_____

17. Write a letter for Ms. Ireland's signature to welcome Ronald L. Hurst, a new member of the board of Lakeview Medical Center. Mr. Hurst is president of Natural Foods, Ltd., 98967 Merchant Boulevard, Berea, OH 44017. Invite Mr. Hurst to lunch at noon next Wednesday at the River Oaks Country Club. Ms. Ireland wants to discuss matters concerning the Medical Center. Ask Mr. Hurst to respond by telephone or e-mail to let you know whether he can accept the invitation.

_____

_____

_____

_____

_____

_____

_____

Name _____ Date _____

18. Prepare the copy for the printer to invite the Foundation Members to the annual black-tie Recognition Program on Friday, May 28, at 7 p.m. at River Oaks Country Club, 333 River Oaks Drive. Ask for a reply.

_____

_____

_____

_____

_____

_____

_____

_____

_____

_____

_____

19. Your follow-up file indicates that you should have received facilities utilization statistics (occupancy rate of hospital beds) for the past six months from the Accounting Department yesterday. Ms. Ireland needs the statistics for a marketing report she is preparing. Prepare an e-mail from you to Rita Calvert in Accounting. Ms. Ireland's report is due one week from today.

_____

_____

_____

_____

_____

COLLABORATIVE WRITING: WRITING AN EFFECTIVE MESSAGE

With another classmate, choose one of the situations in Problems 6 to 10 above and write an effective message. Provide addresses and other facts as needed. Type your message if possible.

_____

_____

_____

_____

_____

_____

Name _____ Date _____

PROOFREADING ACTIVITY

Proofread the following memo, and mark the errors using proofreaders' marks.

MEMO TO: Michael Seinfeld

  FROM: William T. Lawless

DATE: February 2, <YEAR>

SUBJECT: Location for JUNE Staff Meeting

   I recommend that we have our June staff meeting at the diamondhead executive conference center on Paradise Aisle.

Paradise Isle is located in the rolling hills of of Arkansas, overlooking a crystal-clear 30,0000-acre lake. The recreational attractions includes a championship 18-hole golf coarse, clay tennis courts, sailing, and guided fishing and float trips.

To conclude the meeting and reward they staff for an excellent first half, we could have the banquet on the 4-star resort, Paradise Isle Inn.

Please look over the enclosed brochure and let me no your thoughts.

vb
Enclosure

Search the Internet for Netiquette

Find several sites that provide e-mail etiquette (or "netiquette"). List at least ten rules for proper etiquette. Also cite your sources. You may use this format to cite your Internet sources: Jones, P., May 5, 2000. History of the comb. Retrieved June 21, 2000, from <http://www.combhistory.org/index.html>.

_____

_____

_____

_____

Chapter 8

Writing Inquiries and Requests

The most common types of documents written are inquiries and requests. People write **inquiry messages**—messages that ask for information—when they want to know more about a product or service. People write **request messages** when they want a specific action taken. Inquiry and request letters and memos can be grouped into four types:

1. Appointment and reservation requests (direct approach)
2. Buying inquiries (direct approach)
3. General requests (direct approach)
4. Persuasive requests (persuasive approach)

Objectives

After completing this chapter, you should be able to:

- Write appointment requests.
- Write reservation requests.
- Write buying inquiries.
- Write general requests.
- Write persuasive requests.

As indicated, the first three types use the direct approach, and the fourth uses the persuasive approach. Let's look at each of these four types of inquiries and requests. Notice the difference in approach between the letters and memos that will benefit the reader and the ones that will benefit the writer.

APPOINTMENT AND RESERVATION REQUESTS

 A writer sends an *appointment request* to set up a meeting and a *reservation request* to reserve a facility or to make overnight accommodations.

Because a business person's schedule is busy and often changing, these messages must include exact dates and all other necessary details to prevent misunderstandings.

Use the direct plan (see pages 89 and 90), and follow these four suggestions for appointment and reservation requests:

1. Make Sure That the Facts Are Accurate

Think of the problems one error in the date could cause for the reader and for you. You can prevent such errors by always giving the day of the week with the date. Develop the habit of checking the day and date with your calendar every time—don't trust your memory!

2. Give All Necessary Details

Remember, simple requests should be concise and specific. (See the paragraphs that follow and the letters illustrating them.)

3. Keep the Tone Courteous and Friendly

Write with the attitude of "please" rather than in a demanding tone.

4. Keep the Closing Simple

Expressing appreciation, indicating future action, or remarking that you look forward to your future meeting or trip are appropriate ways to end an appointment or reservation request.

Requests for Appointments

You will have occasion to make, change, and cancel appointments. The same information is needed whether you make these requests in writing or by phone.

Scheduling Appointments

Details to include when you are requesting appointments are:
- Day of week and date
- Time
- Place
- Purpose of the appointment or meeting

Notice that the following letter gives these details and then asks for confirmation:

> Dear Mr. Willis:
>
> On Tuesday, May 22, at 3 p.m., I would like to demonstrate for you our brand-new Equity Model XL color scanner in our office showroom at 8208 Technology Drive. Yes, professional-quality color scanning at reasonable prices can be yours today.
>
> On Tuesday you can see for yourself the increased capabilities of the Model XL as described on the enclosed color brochure.
>
> I'll call you next week to make sure that this date and time fit your schedule.
>
> Sincerely,

When scheduling appointments, you may save some time and correspondence if you offer alternate dates and times.

Rescheduling Appointments

If you must change the time or date of an appointment, do it as soon as you know that this will be necessary and give a satisfactory reason. The other person deserves better than a last-minute excuse.

The following sample letter:

- Asks for a change in the date of an appointment.
- States the reason for the change.
- Gives the reader the opportunity to set the date for the next appointment.

> Dear Mr. Willis:
>
> Will it be convenient for me to demonstrate our new Equity Model XL color scanner to you next Thursday instead of next Tuesday? Can we reschedule our meeting for May 24 at 3 p.m.?
>
> We are exhibiting at a business and office products show in Milwaukee on May 22 and 23, and I have been assigned to work at that exhibit.
>
> If Thursday, May 24, is not convenient for you, would you suggest a later date? I'm looking forward to meeting with you.
>
> Sincerely,

8-2:

VERIFY DATES FOR EVENTS
The caterer for a lunch meeting of 25 people did not arrive at the expected time. When the administrative assistant called, the caterer responded that he thought the meal was to be served the next day. What would you have done if you'd been the caterer?

Canceling Appointments

If you must cancel an appointment, it is courteous to do so as soon as you know you must cancel. Notify the person by the quickest method possible—usually the telephone and, if appropriate, follow up with a brief note of apology. Being dependable is an important personal trait. Being a no show is not acceptable in the business world.

Be aware that some organizations (resorts, restaurants, airlines, professional people such as doctors and attorneys) may charge a cancellation fee if you do not give adequate notice. When canceling a hotel reservation, be sure to get a cancellation number and keep it with your records.

Requests for Reservations

Although you may make reservations by phone, confirming the reservation in writing is usually a necessity for some types of reservations and events.

Special Events

Reserving a facility such as a meeting room or arranging for a banquet or dinner requires advance planning. Depending on the event, "advance planning" may be several days to several years prior to the event. Put your request in writing so that there is no misunderstanding about what is needed. Many hotels and restaurants have a banquet manager or meeting planner who can help you plan for special events. You should include these details when you make special event reservations:

- Day of week and date
- Time (beginning and ending)
- Place (including name of meeting room)
- Menu or refreshments (if applicable)
- Special equipment needed (VCR, computer, microphone, etc.)
- Room setup (tables in rows, or in a circle, speaker's podium, etc.)
- Purpose of the event
- Cost (if applicable)

Overnight Accommodations

Include the following details when you make reservations for overnight accommodations:

- Number of adults and number of children
- Number of rooms
- Number and size of beds per room
- Number of nights
- Arrival and departure days and dates
- Smoking or nonsmoking
- Name of the convention or group meeting you are attending (if applicable)

 If you will arrive after 6 p.m., you should guarantee a reservation for overnight accommodations by sending a deposit or providing your credit card number and expiration date.

Ask the hotel to send you a *written confirmation* of the reservation details, including the rate and the confirmation number. If the hotel does not provide written confirmation, ask for a confirmation number and write it down. This will enable you to verify the details and to present the confirmation number upon your arrival.

You may wish to request a corporate rate when you make the reservation if your travel is business related.

Here is a sample reservation letter:

8-4—Know the Meaning of Terms
What does a guaranteed reservation *mean?*

Anaheim Marriott Hotel
700 West Convention Way
Anaheim, CA 92802

Attention: Reservations Department

Ladies and Gentlemen:

Please reserve a room with one double bed for one adult for six nights—Sunday, April 24, through Friday, April 29—at the corporate rate. I will be attending the National Information Systems Convention. I would appreciate receiving a written confirmation before April 1.

Sincerely,

BUYING INQUIRIES AND GENERAL REQUESTS

 A buying inquiry asks for information about products or services the writer is interested in purchasing. In a **general request**, the writer seeks information without intention to buy or sell.

Buying inquiries and general requests ask for details and facts the reader can give with a minimum amount of time, effort, and expense. When you write a buying inquiry or a general request, you are asking for information. Use the direct plan (pages 89 and 90), and follow the six suggestions listed in the following sections:

1. Begin With Your Questions
Get to the point immediately and tell the reader exactly what you need to know. In other words, use the direct approach.

2. Word Each Question Carefully
Ask for specific information to avoid ambiguous questions.

Use Questions Rather Than Statements

Notice that the question that follows is shorter than the statement. And the *question mark* immediately tells the reader that *an answer is expected.*

> **POOR:** I would like to know the colors in which Bradley Mills stain-resistant carpet is available.

> **IMPROVED:** What colors are available in Bradley Mills stain-resistant carpet?

Make the Questions Specific, Not General

A general question usually brings a general answer that often repeats what you already know instead of giving you the details you want.

> **VAGUE:** What can you tell me about your computer?

> **SPECIFIC:** How does your computer compare with the Satellite II computer in price, features, memory size, and portability?

Avoid Questions That Can Be Answered Yes or No

Some questions can be specific but still may not elicit an answer that will tell you what you really want to know. A "yes" answer would be satisfactory for a question such as "Do you have it in stock?" But what about a "yes" answer to "Is it available in any other color?"

> **POOR:** Is the guarantee on the Sony MiniDisk player a good one?

> **IMPROVED:** What is the length of the guarantee on the Sony MiniDisk player and what does it cover?

3. Briefly Explain Why You Are Asking

Include all facts—such as the use you plan to make of the information requested—that will help the reader answer you. This is especially important if you are requesting general information with no intention of buying products or services. If you are writing in response to an advertisement, you should mention the:

- Name of the publication
- Date of the publication
- Page number

You may even wish to include a copy of the ad.

4. Omit Details Not Helpful to the Reader

Incidental comments lengthen a letter unnecessarily and make it harder for the reader to determine the exact information you want.

5. Make Each Question Stand Out

A letter that groups several questions in a single paragraph is hard to answer. The reader must make a special effort to identify each question and may easily overlook one.

8-5—Answering Yes or No Questions

Answer this question with "yes" or "no": Have you stopped cheating on tests? What are the implications of a "yes" answer? A "no" answer?

Go to Student CD-ROM Activity 8-1.

When you have more than one question, you can make the questions stand out by numbering them, bulleting them, or putting each question in a separate paragraph.

You may include explanations at the beginning or at the end of a letter, or in the paragraph that contains the question (see question 2 in Figure 8-1), whichever is most appropriate.

1206 NE Douglas • Lee's Summit, MO 64086
(816)525-8182

October 8, <YEAR>

The Swiss Colony
1112 Seventh Avenue
Monroe, WI 53566-1364

Ladies and Gentlemen:

Subject: End-of-year gifts for customers

Please send me answers to the following questions about your products:

1. Can you ship the orders directly to each of our customers with a personalized gift card indicating that the gift is from our company?

2. What gifts or products do you have in the $20 to $25 price range that would be appropriate for all of our customers? We know that some of our best customers have food allergies and diet restrictions, so we're interested in nonfood items for this year's appreciation gift.

3. What kind of quantity discount would be available if we order 75 or more items?

I look forward to hearing from you so we can place our order in time for a December 15 delivery date.

Sincerely,

Charles A. Hicks

Charles A. Hicks
Sales Manager

lg

FIGURE 8-1 A buying inquiry that uses the direct approach and puts the questions in a numbered list. Notice that each question ends with a question mark to indicate to the recipient that an answer is expected. (Letterhead courtesy of Computer Connection.)

6. Stop When You Are Finished

Too many writers tend to repeat in the closing of the letter statements they have already made, just because they do not know how to stop. Examples of a good way to end are:

> I am looking forward to receiving the information.
>
> **OR**
>
> I will certainly appreciate receiving the information.

You will see the importance of following these writing suggestions as you begin to answer inquiries and requests in Chapter 9.

A request for cooperation, time, gifts, or favors, without intention to buy or sell, is a **persuasive request.** These requests should use the persuasive approach.

Such letters attempt to persuade readers to spend time or money or to go to some trouble to help the writer—usually without benefit to the readers.

November 3, <YEAR>

Dear Friend:

The smell of crayons . . . the excitement of receiving a new book . . . the bright colors of a new toy . . . these are gifts you can provide to the children at The Center for Children's Services.

Did you know that CCS provides licensed child care for 90 children? The child care program provides a secure and stimulating environment for children while parents complete their education, embark on job training, or enter the workforce.

This year's Children's Light Festival will ensure that our child care program will have stimulating and safe materials for the children we serve. By sponsoring a light display this holiday season, you can make a difference in the lives of 90 children all year long.

Your contribution will go directly to fund educational and art materials that will enrich the lives of our community's children. We are asking you today to please support early childhood education. A stimulating environment early in life can set the tone for a lifetime of learning.

With your gift, we can make great progress toward a bright future for Danville's children . . . from infancy through the elementary years.

Please . . . fill in the attached sponsorship sheet and mail it today.

Sincerely,

Jillian McKinnon Hurley

Jillian McKinnon Hurley, President
Board of Directors

Enclosures

FIGURE 8-2 An effective persuasive message asking for a contribution in support of a worthwhile program. An *altruistic appeal* is used; it stresses the benefit to others (the children). The closing sentence makes it easy for the reader to respond. (Letter and letterhead courtesy of Center for Children's Services.)

The Center for Children's Services letter in Figure 8-2 shows how a persuasive letter can effectively capture the interest and secure the cooperation of the reader with its approach and its use of the "you" attitude. When you write a persuasive request, use the persuasive plan on pages 93 and 94 and follow the five suggestions listed in the following sentences:

1. Begin With Something That Will Interest the Reader

You already know a great deal about the opening paragraphs of persuasive letters from the discussion in the section "Choose the Best Approach" in Chapter 5.

The approach for persuasive requests is entirely different from the approach for direct inquiries. When you ask someone about a product or service he or she is trying to sell, the reader becomes interested because the inquiry is an opportunity to sell. But when you ask for a gift or favor, you must point out the advantage to, and stimulate the interest of, the reader. If the request is made bluntly or selfishly, the reaction is likely to be "Why bother?"

 Since you want a favorable response, avoid starting with the request. Get the reader interested in your story before asking for an answer.

Successful persuasive approaches often appeal to altruism, reader benefit, individual responsibility, or personal experience.

Altruistic Appeal

The altruistic (or benevolent or philanthropic) appeal puts its emphasis on *benefits to others,* as illustrated in this opening paragraph of a letter from the Organ Transplant Fund:

> Dear Mrs. McQuean:
>
> You can have a powerful impact on another human being. The power to preserve another person's life depends upon your decision. Your generosity and caring can extend life for another . . .

Reader-Benefit Appeal

The reader-benefit appeal is illustrated in the following excerpt from a sales manager's plea to sales associates to improve their personal appearance:

> Dear Miss Ruez:
>
> How often do you take time for a second look at your appearance? Your customers do every day.
>
> Your appearance is a preview of the way you might handle your customers' business. When you take pride in yourself, your customers feel that you also take pride in what you do for them.

Individual-Responsibility Appeal

A lawmaker used the individual-responsibility appeal in this request for information from state agency personnel:

Dear Mr. Aspirian:

You are part of a carefully selected group of finance and administrative industry executives receiving this letter. Over the last five years, your experience and leadership have played a major role in increasing educational funding in the national budget.

Your answers to the enclosed questionnaire are vital to law-makers who are negotiating to preserve educational funding.

Personal-Experience Appeal

Recalling a pleasant childhood memory is an example of a personal-experience appeal. This excerpt, from a letter trying to persuade the reader to donate money to help underprivileged children attend summer camp, illustrates this appeal:

Dear Mr. Lee:

Remember the contrast of the icy cold water to the sweltering outdoor temperature when you dived into the river as a kid at summer camp? Leaving the inner city and the asphalt jungle for a week of camping in the great outdoors is an experience youngsters never forget. The thrill of cabins, sleeping bags, and campfire cooking lives on in their memories, and the experience of closeness and sharing with role models shapes their adult lives. A donation of only $50 will enable us to send a child to Camp Kikima for one week this summer.

2. Follow Through With the Reason for the Request

After you select the strongest theme for your approach, you should follow through with an explanation of your request. Use the "you" attitude in explaining the reasons for your request.

Emphasize an Advantage to Someone Other Than the Writer

Explain the advantage to the reader or the reader's organization—as illustrated in this paragraph from a letter asking wholesale clothing buyers to complete a questionnaire for a fashion merchandising organization.

> Your cooperation in this project will be of definite help to the garment industry, as you can readily see. But it will be of even more benefit to you as buyers, because the results of the survey will be used by our members to develop better merchandising methods and to give better service to individual buyers.

Compliment the Reader

A complimentary reference to the reader is an effective technique in persuasive requests. This sentence, from a letter asking a member of the Sales and

Marketing Executives Club to address the Phi Beta Lambda Chapter, gives a compliment to the reader:

> We know that any pointers you can give us on sales and marketing techniques will be stimulating and helpful to our students.

3. State the Request in Definite and Specific Terms

 Key Point After getting your reader's interest and giving your explanation, make your request. Be sure that the reader knows (1) exactly what you want and (2) how and when he or she is to respond.

Notice how explicitly this writer requests the cooperation of an organization member:

> Specifically, Jennifer, these are the things I am asking you to do:
>
> 1. Attend the monthly meetings.
>
> 2. Chair the Fundraising Committee. You are to form the committee and send a list of the members to the Secretary by March 1. Submit a plan for this year's events to the Secretary by April 15. Your annual committee report will be due on July 30.
>
> 3. Serve as adviser to the Budget Committee. Your experience should be especially valuable to this committee, and I have asked the chairperson, Vikki Edwards, to contact you directly.
>
> 4. Write a cover letter for the attached questionnaire, which will be sent to all members.

The following letter was written by an administrative assistant:

Ladies and Gentlemen:

Please send me some information about the paper you make that is used for letterhead stationery.

I've been asked to do some research and write a proposal to recommend the paper and layout for new letterhead stationery for my organization. Specifically, I'd like to know:

1. What weight of paper do you recommend for letterhead?
2. What percent of cotton fiber content should the paper have?
3. Is it proper to use colored paper for letterhead?
4. What information should be included in the letterhead?

Could you please reply by July 7, since my proposal is due a few days after that?

Sincerely,

The good organization of this letter makes it easy to answer. You will read a clear, concise, and specific response in Chapter 9.

4. Stimulate Action With Closing Remarks

Closing remarks should stimulate action by suggesting that compliance will be easy and satisfying. Doesn't this closing paragraph make viewers feel that supplying the information requested by a television station will be simple yet worthwhile?

> Our questions are easy to answer. We will not use your name—no one will try to sell you anything. We have stamped the ballot—so no postage is necessary. But we *do need* your vote—so please fill in the few blanks on the enclosed ballot, fold it, seal it, and drop it in the mail.

5. Reflect an Optimistic Outlook

Effective persuasive letters show an appreciation of and confidence in the reader's favorable response. Sincere belief in people and an optimistic outlook shine through every paragraph of most successful persuasive letters.

Notice the positive tone in the following excerpt from a persuasive request:

> This will be the most important vote you will cast between now and November 2. And this vote will count more, because you are one of only 1500 AMS members but just one of 50 million voters in the presidential election.

Here is another excerpt using the positive tone:

> For many of us, our Phi Mu Foundation experience has been a spark that has helped light our lives. Your financial support of the Foundation today can create a living endowment to light many more lives yet to come.

More complex persuasive requests will be discussed in Chapter 12.

SUMMARY

Inquiry and request messages are the most common types of written documents. Appointment requests (including making, changing, and canceling appointments), reservation requests, buying inquiries, and general requests all use the direct approach.

Most of these messages contain questions. Follow the guidelines for writing good questions and end the questions with question marks. Giving complete and accurate information in these messages will help ensure that your communication will accomplish its purpose and get the answer or information you need.

Persuasive requests are written when you ask for cooperation, time, gifts, or favors from your reader without any intention to buy or sell. Common approaches in these messages appeal to altruism or benevolence, reader benefit, individual responsibility, and personal experience. Use the persuasive approach to write an effective persuasive request.

Name _____ Date _____

WHAT'S WRONG WITH THESE?

The inquiries in Problems 1 to 5 are poorly worded, incomplete, wordy, or ambiguous. On the lines provided, write what is wrong with each inquiry.

1. What would be the cost of engraving the 14-karat gold bracelet in your catalog?

   _____

   _____

2. Could you give me information about renting a van?

   _____

3. What can you tell me about the cruise you advertised in the paper the other day?

   _____

4. Do you think the scanner will pick up the emergency channels of any other cities?

   _____

5. How much should I expect to pay for a hotel close to Disney World?

   _____

6. What is wrong with this letter? On the lines provided, write the five questions the writer is trying to ask.

Ladies and Gentlemen:

While visiting a friend last week, I saw his cellular phone, which is a Model C400, and I liked it. So I decided I might like to have one of my own. However, since my friend's phone was a gift, he didn't know anything about the cost, and other details. I'm wondering whether you could answer some of the questions that my friend couldn't answer. I would like to know the cost of the phone if I ordered it from you and how much the service connection fee would be. My friend's phone is installed in his car, but I wonder if it also comes in a portable model. Also, I'd like to know whether it comes with a warranty and whether insurance against theft or damage is available. If you will please answer all these questions, then I can decide whether to buy or not to buy a Model C400 cellular phone.

Sincerely,

Name _____ Date _____

_____

_____

_____

_____

_____

_____

PLANNING AND COMPOSING INQUIRIES AND REQUESTS

7. **Improving questions.** On a separate sheet of paper, rewrite the questions in Problems 1 to 5. Follow the guidelines for writing effective questions. Make sure that your revision is concise and that it asks for the exact information needed. Assume any information you need to improve the questions.

8. **Rewriting an inquiry letter to improve it.** On a separate sheet of paper or on the computer, compose an improved version of the letter in Problem 6. Refer to Appendix A and rewrite the letter; address it to Cellular One, 3876 Willett Avenue, Indianapolis, IN 46200, and sign the letter using your own name.

Use separate paper to make a plan for each message in Problems 9 to 13. Follow the suggestions given in the section "Steps for Planning Your Message," in Chapter 5. On separate sheets of paper (or on the computer), compose a rough draft for each plan, edit each rough draft, and then prepare (preferably type) each letter in correct format. Assume any information you need to be specific in each inquiry.

9. **Appointment letter.** On a separate sheet of paper, write or type a letter to Mr. Collins to set up an appointment on the first Wednesday of next month to review the requirements for this year's Interstate Industries annual report. You work for Interstate Industries; Mr. Collins works for Sun Graphics Inc., the graphic arts firm that

Richard Collins
Manager

Sun Graphics Inc.

148 Industrial Parkway
Parsons, Kansas 67357
Phone: (316) 555-6200
E-Mail: rcollins@aol.com

PLANNING AND COMPOSING INQUIRIES AND REQUESTS *(continued)*

handles your company's printing (see business card on this page). On the lines below, write your letter plan.

Letter plan:

_____

_____

_____

_____

_____

10. **Reservation letter.** Make reservations for you and three other executives at the Embassy Suites, 51 South Gilbert Street, Albuquerque, NM 87120. You want separate rooms for the nights of April 7 and 8. You will be arriving around 10 p.m.; you need to know the checkout time as well as the room rate. Mention that a list giving the names and addresses of the other three executives is enclosed (you do not need to prepare the list).

Write your plan on the lines below.

_____

_____

_____

_____

_____

_____

_____

11. **General request letter.** On separate paper, write or type a letter to Pitney Bowes Inc., One Elmcroft Road, Stamford, CT 06926, asking for ten copies of the free booklet *Download Postage from the Internet and Print It From Your PC,* which was advertised in this month's issue of *Office PRO.* You plan to distribute the copies to the administrative assistants in your organization. Also, ask for some literature about a postage meter suitable for an office mailing fewer than 200 pieces a day. Write your letter plan below on the lines provided.

Letter plan:

_____

_____

_____

Name _____ Date _____

_____

_____

12. **Persuasive request letter.** As president of the student advisory council of your school, write a persuasive request to Don Newcombe, a noted lecturer, whose office address is 104 Harvey, Philippi, WV 26416. Ask Mr. Newcombe to address an assembly on the topic "Drugs and Alcohol." The assembly will be held on the first Friday of next month at 2 p.m. in the conference center. You can pay travel, meals, and hotel expenses but no fee. Write your letter plan on the lines provided below.

Letter plan:

_____

_____

_____

_____

_____

13. **Persuasive request letter.** As November approaches, the general manager of FM radio station Rock 103—The Eagle, asks you to assist in preparing for the Christmas "Come In and Warm Up" charity project. Following the general manager's instructions (see note on this page), write a persuasive request in the form of a script to be read on the air. Write your letter plan on the lines provided below.

Letter plan:

_____

_____

_____

_____

_____

_____

_____

_____

_____

_____

_____

_____

FROM THE DESK OF

ELAINE AESCHELIMAN

Claudia,

Please write the script for our public service announcement for the annual "Come In and Warm Up" Christmas project. Ask our listeners to donate their used coats to be cleaned compliments of Tigers Cleaners at 1400 Poplar Avenue, sorted by size, and given to the homeless.

Be sure to mention the convenient drop box on our parking lot at Fourth and Vine and that we need the coats by November 15 to allow time for cleaning.

ROCK 103 – THE EAGLE

COLLABORATIVE WRITING

Composing an Inquiry Letter *You and your teammate(s) are employed by Mrs. Betsy Porter-Peck, a partner at Porter and Peck law firm, 85 Walden Street, Concord, MA 01742. As president of her high school graduating class, she is responsible for planning the upcoming ten-year class reunion of Messick High. Compose an inquiry letter for Mrs. Porter-Peck to Ms. Trudy Noyes, banquet and convention manager of the Four Seasons Hotel, 1919 Union Avenue, Omaha, NE 68056, asking her to quote rates including:*

- A banquet room to seat 125 to 150 people for the last Saturday night in May (assume that the calendar shown here is for the current year).

MAY

SUN	MON	TUE	WED	THU	FRI	SAT
○ FM 5	◑ LQ 12	1	2	3	4	5
6	7	8	9	10	11	12
13	14	15	16	17	18	19
20	21	22	23	24	25	26
27	28	29	30	31	● NM 19	◐ FQ 27

- A dance floor and stage for a six-piece band to provide after-dinner dancing.

- A dinner menu of shrimp cocktail, grilled chicken breast, baked potato, mixed vegetables, apple or cherry pie à la mode, and iced tea and coffee.

- A two-night room package (ask for a discounted rate) for the last Friday and Saturday nights in May for class members who want to spend the weekend.

Ask the hotel to confirm all details by January 15 so that you can finalize the plans and arrangements and send the invitation letters out. You will also need a podium and microphone for the welcoming remarks at 6:30 p.m.; dinner should be served at 7 p.m.; dancing will begin at 8:30 p.m.; and the banquet room should be reserved until 12 midnight. You prefer round tables seating eight to ten people each. Twelve people will be seated at the head table. Your decorating committee will handle table decorations and a floral centerpiece for the head table. Prepare a rough sketch of the room setup (arrangement of tables and chairs) to include with the letter. Brainstorm with your teammate(s) about the items to be included in the letter and prepare a letter plan. Compose the letter and make a sketch of the room setup (arrangement of tables and chairs) as an enclosure. Write your letter plan below.

Letter plan:

_____

_____

Name _____ Date _____

_____

_____

_____

_____

_____

Search the Internet for Hotels in Your Town or City

You've received a letter from an out-of-town relative who is coming for the weekend and wants to know what hotels are in your town or city. Connect to the Internet and type in the following URL: <http://www.athand.com/>. Look for a list of hotels and motels in your town or city that you can mail or fax to the relative. Complete the Internet form with the following information:

Category: hotels and motels _____

City: your city or town _____

State: your state _____

Click on "Find It" _____

On next Web page:

Scroll down page and fill in categories as follows:

Category: hotels and motels _____

City: your city or town _____

State: your state _____

Scroll up and choose Hotels and Motels again.

Click on "Find It." _____

If your instructor asks you to, print a list of the hotels and motels in your city or town. Pick one of the hotels and look at the map on the Website. Is it accurate?

Chapter 9

Writing Replies to Inquiries and Requests

Answering inquiries and requests effectively gives you the opportunity to gain both business and goodwill.

After completing this chapter, you should be able to:

- Answer yes to inquiries and requests.
- Answer yes to persuasive requests.
- Answer no to inquiries and requests.
- Write form replies to inquiries.
- Write cover letters.

 Answer an inquiry the same day you receive it, if possible, while the sender's interest is highest. A *prompt answer* improves the chance of turning an inquirer into a customer or client.

If you cannot answer an inquiry immediately, write to explain the reason for the delay and to give a time when you can send an answer. Many organizations spend thousands of dollars on advertising to attract inquiries and then throw away the results of that advertising by the haphazard way they handle the inquiries. It takes no more time to answer a letter today than to answer it next week, and the results will be better.

ANSWERING YES TO INQUIRIES AND REQUESTS

Use the direct approach (see page 89) when you say yes to an inquiry or request, and be sure to follow the suggestions listed below in your reply.

1. Give the Exact Information Requested
Say in the first sentence that you are granting the request or answering the inquiry.

 A common error in answering inquiries is failure to answer some of the questions asked. Prevent this common error by *marking on the letter of inquiry the points or questions to be addressed.* Before you send your reply, double-check the original letter to confirm that you have adequately covered each point or question.

When answering yes to a request for an appointment or reservation, repeat in your letter all the details such as day, date, time, and place. The following letter illustrates an answer to a request for a reservation:

Dear Mr. Gustavson:

We were happy to receive your registration form and deposit for the 21st Century Marketing Conference to be held from Monday, April 3, through Friday, April 7, in Washington, D.C.

The Washington Hilton has set aside a block of rooms at a special discounted rate for conference attendees. The rate is $92 for a single, $112 for a double. To make reservations, call 800-555-2000 before February 1.

Transcontinental Airlines is offering conference attendees up to 40 percent off the regular fares. To make flight reservations, call 800-555-4000, and refer to identification number J0969.

When you arrive at the conference, be sure to register before noon on Monday, April 3, so that you can attend the 1 p.m. special roundtable discussion by market analysts.

Sincerely,

2. Express Appreciation for the Inquiry

Tell the customer, either directly or by implication, that you are glad that he or she has written to you about one of your organization's products or services. Write in the spirit of service and goodwill. The tone of your reply should express your appreciation.

3. Sell Your Organization or Product

Put "sell" into every letter you write. An inquiry tells you that the customer was interested when he or she wrote, but what guarantee do you have that the interest is still "hot"? Stress the benefit of converting interest into action.

4. End With a Positive Closing

If appropriate, offer to give further assistance and end with a goodwill closing.

When inquiries are clear, concise, and specific, they are easy to answer. Take a moment to review the good example of an inquiry letter in Chapter 8 on page 164. The following reply was written. Because all of the customer's questions could be answered positively, the writer used the direct approach.

9-1—Timely Responses *What exactly is the time limit for a prompt response?*

Dear Mr. Crump:

Enclosed are samples of the paper we recommend for letterhead stationery. We are happy to answer the questions in your June 15 letter because the content and design of your organization's letterhead create a first and lasting impression of your organization.

1. Letterhead is printed on 16-, 20-, or 24-pound paper. The weight is figured as the weight of four reams of 8 1/2- by 11-inch paper.
2. Paper for letterheads should have a minimum of 25 percent cotton fiber content. Paper to be used for documents that need to be kept for more than 10 years should contain 100 percent cotton fiber content. The heavier the weight and the higher the cotton fiber content, the higher the quality (and the price) of the paper.
3. Although white is the most commonly used color of paper for letterheads, colors like beige, ivory, pale blue, pale mauve, and pale green are gaining in popularity.
4. A good letterhead should answer the questions "Who?" (name of your organization), "What?" (the nature of your business), and "Where?" (mailing address, phone number, and fax number). Many organizations also include e-mail and Website addresses as well as a logo or trademark.

Enclosed is a booklet called *The Letterhead Analyzer,* which gives an analysis of the psychological effect of different colors used for letterheads. The booklet also contains several sample letterheads that won awards for outstanding design and layout last year.

I suggest that you hire a professional graphic artist to help you with the design of your letterhead. If you have additional questions, please write again or call me at (109) 555-3312.

Sincerely,

Go to Student
CD-ROM
Activity 9-1.

 When you reply to a letter containing several questions, be sure to *answer every question completely,* using one of these formats:

1. **Put each answer in a separate paragraph.**
2. **Number each answer, as the writer of the preceding letter did.**

If you have a positive answer for every question, numbering the answers is easy to do. If you do not have a positive answer for every question, *start with your most positive answer* and work your way down to your least positive answer. This sequence will prevent you from starting your letter with a negative answer. Reread the inquiry letter shown in Figure 8-1 on page 160; then read the reply in Figure 9-1.

1112 7th AVENUE, MONROE WI 53566-1364

October 11, <YEAR>

Mr. Charles A. Hicks
Sales Manager
Computer Connection
1206 NE Douglas
Lee's Summit, MO 64086

Dear Mr. Hicks:

We appreciate your interest in our products and are happy to answer all of the questions in your October 8 letter.

1. We will ship orders directly to your customers with a personalized gift card containing your message.
2. I have enclosed a catalog showing a wide variety of nonfood items in the $20 to $25 price range.
3. You will receive a 10 percent discount on an order of 75 items or more.

For your convenience, a preaddressed postage-paid order form is enclosed with the catalog. After you've looked through the catalog, please give me a call at 1-800-555-6389 if you have additional questions or if you need more information about any of the items in the catalog. You can also place your order by calling us toll free at 1-800-555-9678 from 8 a.m. until 9 p.m. Monday through Friday.

Sincerely,

Sheri O'Neal

Sheri O'Neal
Sales Manager

Enclosures

FIGURE 9-1 This letter gives a yes answer to an inquiry and uses the direct approach. The writer numbered the answers because several questions were being answered. Notice that the letter has been answered promptly and that the writer builds goodwill by offering further help. (Letterhead courtesy of Swiss Colony.)

ANSWERING YES TO PERSUASIVE REQUESTS

It's easy to answer a persuasive request when you can say yes. A smiling "Here it is" or "I'll be glad to" just about sums up the reply. Follow the direct approach, and use the suggestions listed here:

1. Start With a Cheerful Yes

Open your letter with the good news that will make your reader happy.

> I'll be at the seminar to help in any way I can. The solution to the customer service problems is important to me, too, and I'm glad you planned the seminar.

If you grant the request grudgingly or with reservations, you will probably lose the goodwill you could expect to gain by saying yes.

2. Confirm Details of the Request and Acceptance

You can confirm the details in the first paragraph, along with your yes response, as in this opening sentence:

> We are pleased to enclose the entrance requirements to our graduate business program.

Otherwise, use the next paragraph for the confirmation, and *repeat the details of the request* to be sure that you and the reader agree. For example, a letter accepting an invitation to give a presentation at a meeting should confirm the day and date, time, place, subject, and length of the talk. Or, if a contribution is enclosed, the letter should state the amount and purpose.

3. Ask for Additional Information

Even though you are making a positive response, you may need additional information to follow through on the request.

For instance, a speaker accepting an invitation to conduct a seminar wrote:

> Can you provide a screen so I can show a PowerPoint presentation during my talk?

A volunteer agreeing to act as coordinator of the annual LeBonheur Children's Hospital Benefit Auction wrote:

> Will you help me by sending a copy of last year's budget, timetable, and invitation list?

4. Give "Something Extra" When the Gesture Seems Appropriate

If you give more than is expected, the reader will feel good about coming to you. You will have increased the goodwill that is the ultimate goal of every letter you write.

Offer to Do More Than Requested

The "something extra" may be an offer to do more than requested. For example, a professor is invited to speak at the Louisiana Business Education Association (LBEA) convention in Alexandria, with expenses paid but no fee.

The professor not only accepts but also offers to come at no expense to the nonprofit organization:

> Since I will be in Alexandria that week on other business, I shall be happy to speak to the LBEA convention on Monday, May 1, or Tuesday, May 2, at no expense to your organization.

A college graduate sends a contribution to the alumni fund and writes:

> I'll be glad to call the members of my class and add a little personal persuasion to the fine letter you sent them.

Express Interest and Offer Further Help

The "something extra" may be an expression of interest and willingness to help further if asked.

A travel agent sends the brochures requested by a student and closes the letter with:

> Just write me if I can give you any more help. I certainly want that geography report to earn an A.

A business executive sends an author the sample letter requested, with permission to reproduce it, and closes the letter with:

> Please let me know when I can help you again. When will your book be published? I'm interested in purchasing copies for my office staff.

A cooperative attitude is evident in the following reply a benefits coordinator wrote to a mortgage company's request for written confirmation of relocation benefits for an employee:

Dear Mrs. Donovan:

As I confirmed to you by telephone, Nova Industries has agreed to extend the one-year clause in the "Policy and Procedure for Relocation of New Employees" for Robert O'Keefe to August 31, <YEAR>.

Section 3.3, page 4, "Expenses Associated With the Purchase of a New Home," is enclosed for your reference.

If you need additional information about the relocation expenses for which Mr. O'Keefe will be reimbursed, please call me at 601-555-4000.

Sincerely,

ANSWERING NO TO INQUIRIES AND REQUESTS

When you must say no, use the indirect plan and deliver the bad news gently and tactfully. Strive to let courtesy and thoughtfulness shine through your letter.

A gracious refusal is much like a persuasive request—you are asking your reader to accept your decision as the only fair answer under the circumstances.

You have already seen these principles applied to writing letters in which it was not possible to say yes. Do you remember how tactfully a store said "not now" to the customer who asked it to stock petite sizes (Chapter 4, page 80)? How a firm said no to a request from one of its retailers to purchase advertisements in two suburban telephone directories (Chapter 5, page 97)? Take a few moments now to review those letters.

 Remember that a no letter has two purposes:
1. **To say no.**
2. **To keep the goodwill of the reader.**

To accomplish both purposes, consider the following suggestions:

1. Approach the Message as an Opportunity to "Talk It Over"

Give your reader whatever encouragement you can—not just a plain no. If you think, "I must decline this invitation or this order or refuse this request," you will probably write negatively. But you will probably write constructively if you think, "What can I do to encourage this person even though I have to say no?"

2. Start With a Friendly Buffer Paragraph

When you receive a letter that begins, "It is my unpleasant duty to inform you that . . . ," or "I'm sorry to tell you that we cannot grant your request . . . ," don't you immediately close your mind to whatever else the writer may say? You think that the writer is not interested in helping you, in building goodwill, or in keeping your friendship. The writer seems concerned only with saying no and getting an unpleasant task completed. But suppose the letter begins this way:

> Your proposal for a joint meeting of Phi Beta Lambda (PBL) and Future Business Leaders of America (FBLA) is exciting, Maria.

Aren't you more likely to read the rest of the message with an open mind?

3. Tell the Reader *Why* You Cannot Say Yes

In your explanation, imply that you would rather say yes than no. And try to compliment the reader in some way. Although her request to book a video was denied, the PBL president who received the following explanation felt that she had chosen a worthwhile video:

> Many PBL groups throughout the nation have enjoyed *Preparing for Your First Job Interview.* In fact, Lisa, it is our most popular video. Last March we had three additional copies made so that it would be available to more clubs, but even these are booked well in advance.

4. Avoid a Negative Refusal

 Explain *before* you refuse. A blunt no should be avoided.

If your letter does a good job of explaining, the reader will realize that you cannot do what he or she has asked—the no is inferred. If you must state your refusal (to be sure your reader knows that you are not granting the request), avoid emphasizing it or putting it in negative terms. Sometimes limiting expressions, such as *only* or *exclusively*, may substitute for negatives such as *regret*, *apologies*, and *cannot*. Notice how this business letter dwells on the negative and almost obscures the positive points:

Dear Sir:

We are very sorry that your portrait has been damaged. This rarely happens to Dixie photos.

I regret to advise that we cannot hold negatives for a long period of time, because we lack sufficient storage space; therefore, we will not be able to reprint your portrait. I am, however, processing a refund in the amount of $15.95, which you should receive within the next two weeks. I am also returning the damaged 5 by 7 portrait to you with a free coupon.

Please accept our apologies for this problem, as we greatly value your patronage.

With kindest personal regards,

The following letter shows interest in the reader and tries to keep his business while refusing the request.

Dear Mr. Brooks:

We were happy to hear that your family was so pleased with your portraits. And we are sorry that one was damaged. Because our storage space is limited, however, all negatives are destroyed ten days after an order has been filled.

Your 5 by 7 portrait is being returned, along with a refund of $15.95. You should receive both in about two weeks.

Please use the enclosed coupon for a complimentary 5 by 7 color portrait when Dixie Photos returns to Dayton on December 1.

Sincerely,

5. Give Encouragement and, When You Can, Give Help

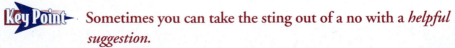 **Sometimes you can take the sting out of a no with a *helpful suggestion.***

For example, a department store representative, in declining an order for an article not carried by the store, may tell the customer where he or she can make the purchase. The reservations manager of a New Orleans hotel, not able to make the requested reservations, suggested:

> If you can conveniently defer your arrival in New Orleans until May 15, we shall be glad to reserve a double room for you and your wife. If you must be here on May 10, you might write for help to the Greater New Orleans Hotel Association at 105 Poydras Street, New Orleans, LA 70112, or call them at 1-800-555-2323.

The public relations manager at Lakeside Hospital responded to a graduate student's request for help with a research study by making the student aware of another possible avenue:

> Although Lakeside has no funds available to help with your worthwhile project, state funds have been appropriated to support research projects that will benefit the inner-city areas. I suggest that you present your proposal to the State Health Agency at 1800 Peachtree Boulevard, Atlanta, GA 30303.

6. Close Pleasantly With a Look Toward the Future

In your last paragraph, *don't stress or repeat the negatives.* For example, closing with "We hope that our inability to grant your request does not inconvenience you too much" would leave the reader thinking how dissatisfied he or she is about your refusal.

Also, *do not include an apology in your last paragraph.* Saying "We are sorry that we couldn't send the information you requested" accents what you *can't* do. Instead, emphasize what you *can* do. Some possibilities include:

- A substitute suggestion.
- An expression of your desire to cooperate further.
- A wish for the reader's success.
- A pleasant off-the-subject remark.

Would you agree that the following letter says no graciously to a job applicant?

Dear Miss Wisner:

It was certainly a pleasure to meet you this week and have the opportunity to discuss career opportunities at World Wide Travel Inc.

Because of its position as a leader in the travel industry, World Wide Travel Inc. offers unique public relations challenges and opportunities. I think that you would find the travel industry an exciting one to work in.

Although we currently have no openings in public relations, I will keep your résumé in our active file for 90 days, and I will call you if we have a job opening that fits your skills and abilities.

We sincerely appreciate your interest in World Wide Travel Inc.

Cordially,

9-1— Saying No to a Request With an Alternative *Why is it a good idea to offer your reader an alternative suggestion when you have to say no to a request?*

Go to Student CD-ROM Activity 9-2.

To save time and money, form messages and cards, merged letters, and guide letters are often used to reply to inquiries.

Form messages can be printed in advance or on an as-needed basis. They may be prepared in connection with advertising campaigns to take care of the flood of inquiries expected. The form letter in Figure 9-2 was prepared to answer inquiries about lodging and tours at Mammoth Cave National Park. In this case, a form letter is also a cover letter (as described in the next section).

Mammoth Cave National Park

Mammoth Cave, Kentucky 42259
Phone: 502-555-2225
Website: www.mammothcave.com

Dear Prospective Visitor:

We are pleased to answer your request for information about Mammoth Cave National Park. The enclosed material should answer many of your questions about the area.

We appreciate your interest in Mammoth Cave and look forward to having you visit the park soon.

Sincerely yours,

Ron Hartley

Ron Hartley, Superintendent

Enclosures 2

FIGURE 9-2 A form letter, prepared in advance, can be especially useful if you have a flood of inquiries.

Oops!

9-2:

ANSWERING INQUIRIES ACCURATELY

Bill sent a letter to the motor vehicle department asking how to renew his driver's license early because he would be out of the country on a six-month assignment when his license was due to expire. He received a form letter telling him how to get a license to drive a semitrailer. What lesson can be learned from this?

Merged letters are form letters that appear to be written specifically for the recipient. A merged letter is always more impressive than a photocopied or printed form letter. Merged letters are prepared on a computer by merging a database of names and addresses with a form letter that contains codes indicating where the variable information is to be inserted. It is also possible to include variable data such as a delivery date or an order number in the message. This is the method Tryon Clinic uses to prepare personalized letters to new patients, as illustrated in Figure 9-3.

Another type of form message is a **guide letter.** With this type of letter, individual paragraphs are stored and printed. The writer chooses which paragraphs to include in the letter. The writer must use caution when selecting paragraphs to be sure that the message conveys the intended meaning.

THE TRYON CLINIC
Health Care for Women

1114 Kennedy Boulevard / Tranquility, NJ 07860 / Phone: 973-555-1130 / E-Mail: tryon1114@compuserve.com

June 28, <YEAR>

Mrs. Debbie Brown
9345 Morning Grove Cove
Cordova, TN 38018

Dear Ms. Brown:

Welcome to our office.

We look forward to meeting you and getting acquainted. To help you feel more comfortable with our specialty and office procedures, we have enclosed a patient information booklet. Please feel free to ask any of our staff members about the subjects in your booklet.

To save you time during your visit, please complete the enclosed patient medical history and bring it with you. This form will become part of your medical record and will familiarize us with your medical background.

If we can be of further assistance before your visit, please call us at 973-555-1130.

Sincerely,

THE TRYON CLINIC

Roseanne Peters
Office Manager

RP:nf
Enclosures 2

FIGURE 9-3 Note the warm, friendly tone of the form letter Tryon Clinic uses to prepare patients for their first visit.

WRITING COVER LETTERS

 The purpose of a **cover letter** is to accompany other items such as advertising brochures, flyers, price lists, catalogs, coupons, tickets, checks, reports, and business forms. Sending one of these items to a customer, client, or dealer without comment would be a bit abrupt, like walking in without knocking. Writing a short, friendly cover letter to accompany such items is both courteous and helpful.

Usually a cover letter accompanies the item being sent. If the item is bulky, the cover letter may be attached to the outside of the package or mailed separately, as in the following example:

Dear Customer:

We are pleased to mail in a separate package the carpet samples you requested.

If you need help in making your selection or placing your order, just call 800-555-8000 and ask for one of our decorators. Your order will be filled within two weeks.

Sincerely,

A cover letter *tells the purpose of and points out pertinent details about the item sent.* The sender can describe how the receiver may use the accompanying item and can stimulate interest and prompt action. A cover letter also becomes *a file record of the date and the reason* something is sent or received.

A cover letter that accompanies a shipment of merchandise can establish personal contact with customers and can lay the foundation for future sales. Sending the merchandise would be enough, but the cover letter adds the "something extra" that can strengthen the goodwill between an organization and its customers or clients.

Mail-order houses often receive requests for their catalogs, which are usually offered free in advertisements. When someone asks for a catalog, a sales opportunity is created. A cover letter can focus attention on the catalog. Such letters may be form letters that have been prepared to generate interest in specific products or in categories of products.

Suggestions for writing a cover letter for merchandise or literature follow:

1. Start by Identifying the Item
Introduce the enclosure pleasantly by identifying the item and your reason for sending it (possibly in response to the reader's request).

2. Stress the Reader's Use of the Item
The fact that you are sending something isn't important. The fact that *your reader can use or enjoy it* is important. Avoid these phrases when referring to enclosures:

"I am enclosing . . ." (selfish-sounding)
"You will find enclosed . . ."(should be obvious)
"Enclosed please find . . ." (Must I hunt for it?)
"Enclosed with this letter is (are) . . ." (wordy—*with this letter* is not needed)
Simply use:
"Enclosed is (are) . . ." (concise)

3. Be Specific, but Choose Details Carefully

Arouse interest in the enclosure by referring to specific advantages he or she may gain from it. Mentioning page numbers and marked excerpts in a booklet can stimulate reading and encourage buying. Remember, though, that the letter is only one part of the message and should never overshadow the enclosure.

4. Close With a Forward Look

Write a closing designed to promote *goodwill and future business.* Even when there seems to be no immediate possibility of a sale, try some sales promotion. And be sure to stress the service attitude.

The letter that follows is a form letter as well as a cover letter. It introduces the organization's personnel through a professionally prepared color brochure.

Dear Mr. Faust:

The warm, sincere welcome you received when you placed your business account with First Security Bank shows our commitment to making your association with us as pleasurable as possible. We are happy to have you as our business associate.

Accompanying your new checks is a brochure highlighting our account representatives and customer service personnel, who take great pride in working for our customers. They are dedicated to meeting the needs of you, the customer, because we believe people do business with people they like.

At First Security Bank we are dedicated to making our customers our number one priority. Our greatest compliment is a satisfied customer.

Sincerely,

SUMMARY

Inquiry and request messages can mean potential business for an organization. These messages should be answered promptly—while the interest is at peak level.

When replying to an inquiry or request, you can say yes or you can say no. Use the direct approach when saying yes; use the indirect approach when saying no. If you must say no, remember to say no in a way that will keep the customer's goodwill.

Many organizations use form messages to save time and money when replying to inquiries and requests. Pay close attention to ensure that these messages answer the questions in the inquiry or request.

Cover letters (which can also be form letters) are sent with an enclosure and are a wonderful opportunity to resell your product and your organization.

Name _____   Date _____

WHAT'S WRONG WITH THESE?

1. On the lines provided, indicate what is wrong with the following reply to a prospective customer's inquiry about Bright and White toothpaste:

> Dear Sir or Madam:
>
> We received your May 2 letter. As requested, we are sending a sample of our new toothpaste called Bright and White.
>
> Your sample of Bright and White toothpaste was mailed today. You will like the new fresh taste and extra fluoride protection you will get from Bright and White. Bright and White is being distributed this week to drugstores and discount stores in your area.
>
> Sincerely,

_____

_____

_____

2. The writer of this poor reply probably lost a customer as well as a promotional opportunity. On the lines provided, tell what is wrong with the following reply:

> Dear Customer:
>
> Referring to your letter of November 15, I am sorry to tell you that the video game Super Sleuth Incorporated, about which you inquired, is currently out of stock and will not be available until early January. We deeply regret that you cannot receive this game in time for the holidays, but perhaps you would like to try ordering some of our other games. You will find several in our current catalog.
>
> Sincerely,

_____

_____

_____

Name _____ Date _____

PLANNING AND COMPOSING INQUIRIES AND REQUESTS

For each message in Problems 3 to 9, use the lines provided to make a plan for replying to the inquiries or requests. Follow the suggestions in the section "Steps for Planning Your Message'" in Chapter 5. Then write a rough draft from each plan, edit your rough draft, and prepare (preferably type) each letter in an acceptable format.

3.   **Answering yes to an inquiry letter.** You are an assistant to Mr. Cecil Neff, sales manager. Write a reply to the following letter from Mrs. Myler. Base your reply on the price list shown below.

March 25, <YEAR>

The Picture Place
315 South Steward
Iola, KS 66749

Ladies and Gentlemen:

The manager of our local Camera Club suggested that I write to you about making pictures from slides. I would like to have several prints of a recent slide.

How much would these prints cost?

Respectfully,

Martha Myler

(Mrs.) Martha Myler
519 Sherman Street
Meadville, PA 16335

Your photographs will be the same superior quality that won four National Awards for us!

50 reproductions $49.99
30 reproductions $29.99
12 reproductions $12.00

Finished photographs 2½ by 3½ inches
Kansas residents add 6 percent sales tax
Postage prepaid
Include remittance with order

Letter plan:

_____

_____

_____

_____

_____

_____

_____

_____

_____

_____

_____

_____

Name _____   Date _____

4. **Answering yes to an inquiry letter.** You are the commercial exhibits manager for the Pyramid Convention Center. Write a reply to the letter shown below. Send application forms and an information brochure for prospective exhibitors at the upcoming National Business Education Association meeting. Deadline for reservations is January 1, cost per exhibit booth is $500, and this year's meeting will be from April 2 to April 5 from 9 a.m. to 5 p.m. in the Presley Exhibit Hall on Concourse One. You expect 5000 people to attend.

USA PUBLISHING COMPANY

516 East 42 Street / Las Vegas, NV 89104 / Phone: 702-555-1152 / Website: www.usapublishing.com

December 15, <YEAR>

Commercial Exhibits Manager
Pyramid Convention Center
1001 Egypt Avenue
Louisville, KY 40201

Dear Commercial Exhibits Manager:

USA Publishing Company would like to reserve space in the Pyramid for the National Business Education Association meeting from April 2 to April 5. We will need two booths.

Please send me an application form, a schedule of events, a list of convenient hotels, and any other information I will need.

Sincerely,

Diane Fumich

(Mrs.) Diane Fumich
Marketing Representative

ra
01exhib

Letter plan:

_____
_____
_____
_____
_____
_____

Name _____ Date _____

PLANNING AND COMPOSING INQUIRIES AND REQUESTS *(continued)*

5. **Answering no to an inquiry letter.** Write a reply to the letter in Problem 4 in which you turn down Diane Fumich because you have sold all the exhibit space. Offer to put her on the mailing list to receive an invitation to exhibit at next year's meeting on April 3–6.

Letter plan:

Buffer

No: Explain

Offer put on Mailing List

Buffer

6. **Answering yes to a persuasive request.** Write a reply to the persuasive request in the letter below and send your Check 354 for $20. Also, offer to distribute some of the association's pamphlets to all members (30 people) of your bowling league.

ALA
AMERICAN LUNG ASSOCIATION

1-800-LUNG-USA   http://www.lungsusa.org

Dear Friend:

We are writing to you because the American Lung Association is very much in need of your help.

Your gift of $5 in the last campaign was put to good use in vital health programs fighting emphysema, bronchitis, asthma, tuberculosis, smoking, and air pollution.

Today, the need for your assistance is even greater. Lung disease—especially emphysema—is a serious threat to the health of the people in your area.

We hope you will consider a gift of $5 or more—but any amount will be greatly appreciated. An addressed envelope is enclosed for your convenience.

Sincerely yours,

Lois Morrisey

Lois Morrisey, Volunteer
32 Circle Drive
Rossville, Illinois 60963

js
Enclosure

Name _____ Date _____

Letter plan:

_____

_____

_____

_____

7. **Answering no to a persuasive request.** Write a no answer to the letter in Problem 6. Explain that you cannot contribute this year because you were injured in a car accident a few months ago and have many expenses related to the accident that are not covered by insurance.
Letter plan:

_____

_____

_____

_____

8. **Writing form replies to inquiries.** You work for Terri White, director of marketing, Lincoln Trail College, 880 University Drive, Robinson, IL 62454. She receives many requests each day for such items as class schedules, catalogs, housing literature, campus maps, applications for admission, financial aid, Booster Club event schedules, and University Foundation brochures. Mrs. White asks you to write a form letter that can be used to reply to all these requests for information. The form letter will be stored on the computer and merged with the addresses of the inquirers to send individually addressed replies. Use your form letter to answer a request from Eric Fraley for an application form and a college catalog.
Letter plan:

_____

_____

_____

_____

9. **Writing a cover letter.** Write a cover letter to a prospective customer to be mailed out along with a miniature magnetic menu and a coupon good for a free pizza with the purchase of a pizza (of the same size) from the Best Pizza in Town Restaurant.
Letter plan:

_____

_____

_____

COLLABORATIVE WRITING

Writing Letters as a Team Work with a teammate to plan and rewrite the replies in Problems 1 and 2 so that they follow the principles of an effective reply to an inquiry or request.

PROOFREADING EXERCISE

Using Proofreaders' Marks Use proofreaders' marks to mark the errors in the following letter:

Dear Mr Pate:

Thank you for you interest in touring Crunchy Cereals plant. Because of the health and and sanitation regulations of our state govenment, we had too discontinue tours about a year ago. I am enclosing a video that show the manufacturing process form the time the grain are brought into our plant until the boxes of cereal leaves the plant. I've also enclosed a coupon for a complementary box of our newest cereal, Crunchy Oats.

Sincerely,

Finding Stock Prices on the Web

Your supervisor has asked you to find out the current stock price for AT&T. Go to the Website for AT&T <http://www.att.com> and find the current price of stock. Send an e-mail to your supervisor (or instructor) or write a memo giving this information. Be sure to include in your message the date and time of the stock quote as well as the price.

Chapter 10

Writing and Acknowledging Orders

Chapter 9 presented information to help you become expert in writing replies to inquiries and requests. You will again build upon the concepts you have been perfecting and move ahead in your writing skills in Chapter 10. The following new skills will become yours as you study this chapter:

- Writing orders, not just hints

- Acknowledging orders that demand special attention

- Refusing orders using the appropriate approach

Objectives

After completing this chapter, you should be able to:

- Organize and write order messages.
- Choose the correct forms for order acknowledgments.
- Organize and write routine, special, and refusal acknowledgments.

PLACING ORDERS

To operate its business, every organization must purchase products or services. Telephone and Internet ordering has become popular. Mail-order companies include order forms with their catalogs for customers who prefer to mail or fax their orders.

Most large companies use a purchase order system to order goods. The person who needs an item initiates the process by completing a purchase requisition or other form, either a paper or computerized form. After appropriate approval(s), someone in the purchasing department of the company prepares and mails or faxes the purchase order to the **vendor** (the seller of the goods).

Smaller companies, however, may not use a formal purchase order system. Their employees may order by telephone, Internet, catalog form, or letter. We will discuss two ways to order merchandise or services—order forms and order letters.

Order Forms

Most companies include *order forms* with their catalogs because they:
- Help the buyer give complete information.
- Are faster and easier to read than order letters.
- Are convenient for both the buyer and the seller.

Complete all applicable blanks on order forms, and be sure that you write legibly on forms that must be prepared by hand.

Many companies now encourage ordering over the Internet. A company's Website provides an easy-to-follow format and an order form that gives immediate feedback on product availability. The order will not be accepted by the system unless all necessary information is provided. After sending an Internet order form, a customer usually receives a message of confirmation by e-mail.

Reputable companies try to make sure that their sites are secure so that their customers will feel safe using account and credit card numbers. Be very careful about giving account and credit card numbers over the Internet.

Order Letters

Although you may use the Internet, the telephone, or a form for ordering, there may be times when you need to write a letter to order merchandise or services. If no order form is available or if you need to include explanations that will not fit the form, you will need to write an *order letter* to fax or mail. An order letter should be organized like an order form and should contain the same information.

Order letters are easy to write because (1) getting the attention and interest of your reader is no problem (your letter is bringing business) and (2) no convincing or persuading is necessary. All you have to do is write an order letter that can be read quickly and that makes it easy for the reader to fill the order. If you write clearly enough so that the recipient knows what you want and if you make satisfactory plans to pay for the item, you'll get an answer.

Give every order letter the familiar *who, what, where, when, why,* **and** *how* **test to be certain that it will accomplish your purpose.**

Here are five suggestions for writing effective order letters:

1. Write Orders, Not Just Hints

Legally, an order letter is the "offer" portion of a contract. The "acceptance" portion of the contract is completed when the seller sends the merchandise. Use specific and direct openings such as "Please send me . . ." or "Please ship . . ." rather than vague phrases such as "I'm interested in . . ." or "I'd like to . . . ."

2. Provide a Complete Description of Each Item

Include the following information in your order letter:

- Quantity ordered.
- Catalog (or model or stock) number.
- Name of product.
- Description of product, including as much of the following as is appropriate: (1) color, (2) size, (3) material, (4) grade or quality, (5) pattern, (6) finish, and (7) any other details available.
- Unit price.
- Total price for desired quantity.
- Any other information that you have, including where you saw the product advertised.

3. Organize the Information in a Clear Format

To make your letter easy to read, do one of the following:

- Write a separate, single-spaced paragraph for each item, and use double spacing between paragraphs.
- Arrange your order in a tabular form similar to that used on an order blank.

When you need to give several sets of numbers, items, and prices, tabular form is clearer than writing the information in sentences.

4. State Payment Information

Give the form of payment to be used (personal check, money order, credit card, or credit account number). Be sure to add any shipping charges and sales tax that may be part of the total cost. If you want the item charged to a credit card, give the credit card number and the expiration date. Also, if the printed name on the credit card differs from the signature and typed name on the letter, be sure to give the exact name of the cardholder.

5. Specify Shipping Preferences

Give the shipping address, or say that you want the merchandise to be sent to the address above (your return address) or below (if your address appears below your typed signature).

If you need the merchandise or service by a certain date, be sure to include that date in your order letter. And if you have a preference, include the method

10-1:

FILLING ORDERS CORRECTLY.

A woman ordered reindeer boxer shorts for her husband, to be delivered to their home, and, on the same order form, she ordered a pink gown for her grandmother, to be delivered to her grandmother in another city. Both items were to be gift-wrapped. When the husband opened his gift, he was surprised to find a pink gown. And the grandmother was pretty shocked at seeing the reindeer boxer shorts!

of shipment. Otherwise, the seller will choose the shipping method and may delay sending the merchandise. For example, you may need the merchandise in a hurry and be willing to pay the extra cost of air express.

Merchandise is shipped *FOB destination* (seller pays shipping charges, which are included in the price of the merchandise) or *FOB shipping point* (buyer pays shipping charges over and above the cost of merchandise).

Look at the well-written order letter that follows:

Go to Student CD-ROM Activity 10-1.

October 9, <DATE>

Action Treadmills
183 North Oak St.
Tavares, FL 32778

Ladies and Gentlemen:

Please send the following treadmills, as advertised in your fall catalog on page 15:

Quantity	Item No.	Description	Price	Total
3	A-1000	Programmable Treadmill	$4395	$13,185
		Shipping and handling		220
		TOTAL		**$13,405**

Enclosed is my check 2402 for $13,405. Please ship the treadmills to Sports Clubs of America, 35 Mason Road, Akron, Ohio 44313. We would like to receive them before November 1.

Sincerely,

Randy Robinson

dm
Enclosure

ACKNOWLEDGING ORDERS

With the current intense competition for customers, sellers strive to fill orders promptly and provide quick delivery via overnight or express mail. So, no separate acknowledgment is usually necessary. However, in some cases, such as back orders, customized or personalized orders, discontinued items, gifts, or deliveries to other addresses, acknowledgment is needed. Legally, an acknowledgment message completes the contract of a sale, but its major purpose is to encourage future orders. An acknowledgment message is an opportunity to resell your product and organization. The way the seller handles the order may determine whether the buyer will send future orders. Send acknowledgments promptly.

 Use acknowledgment messages to resell your product and your organization.

Replies to Orders

You may send an acknowledgment reply in the form of (1) a postal card, (2) an acknowledgment form, (3) a duplicate invoice, (4) an e-mail, or (5) an individual letter.

1. Postal Cards

Large businesses such as catalog houses and department stores doing business with customers by mail may use acknowledgment cards. Some firms send printed general acknowledgments, but most firms use printed form cards that show a description of the order and the expected date of shipment (see Figure 10-1). Smaller firms may use preprinted form cards that provide space in which specific order information may be written.

> Thank you for your order for
>
> Item #P3988—Heirloom Entertainment Center
>
> We will ship your order on or before
>
> April 12, <YEAR>
>
> BRADLEY'S FINE FURNITURE

FIGURE 10-1 Mail acknowledgment cards immediately.

2. Acknowledgment Forms

Acknowledgment forms are usually preprinted and have the general appearance of a letter. Several different items are listed, and an open box is in front of each item. The sender puts a check mark, either by hand or by computer, in the boxes that apply to the particular order.

3. Duplicate Invoices

When an order is processed, the seller prepares an invoice and makes a copy for the customer. If the copy goes to the customer separately from the filled order, it may be marked "Acknowledgment—This Is Not an Invoice," or something similar. When the customer receives the acknowledgment, he or she knows that the seller is processing the order. The customer also knows the final cost, payment terms, and estimated shipping date. A duplicate invoice is the least effective method of acknowledgment, however, because the customer may resent receiving a copy of the bill before receiving the merchandise.

4. E-Mail Acknowledgments

If your company receives orders on its Website or provides a space on its order forms on which the customer may write an e-mail address, acknowledgments may be sent by e-mail. You may program your Website ordering system to automatically acknowledge orders, or you may use a standard e-mail form. Again, send these acknowledgments promptly.

5. Individual Letters

The individual letter does the best job of building goodwill. With computers generating most of the paperwork in today's businesses, individual acknowledgment letters are now economically feasible. We will discuss the contents of acknowledgment letters in the next sections of this chapter.

Form acknowledgments are acceptable as long as they reflect the same care in preparation that the organization gives to filling the order. A poorly printed card or letter or error-ridden e-mail message will give the customer the impression that you will also be sloppy in filling the order. A cold, formal acknowledgment can make you seem cold, formal, and uncaring.

When form messages acknowledge orders, revise and update them periodically so that your frequent customers will not receive the same wording several times.

 Build goodwill for your company by acknowledging orders promptly with individualized messages.

Situations Requiring Acknowledgment Messages

In several situations, acknowledgments are critical to your business. These situations are described in the next sections.

1. A Customer's First Order

Never miss the opportunity to make your first impression on a customer a positive one. Welcome the customer, and encourage him or her to buy from you again.

2. An Incomplete or Unclear Order

When details are omitted from an order, it is important to ask for the missing information without placing blame on your customer. Just ask for the information you need to fill the order and encourage a quick response by enclosing a reply envelope.

 Avoid placing blame for missing order information—just ask for what you need.

3. An Unusually Large Order

Let your customer know that you noticed and appreciate the large order. Begin with your thanks and specify what was ordered. Give other pertinent information and conclude with a goodwill statement.

 Your customers will appreciate receiving acknowledgments for large orders or first orders.

4. An Order for a Discontinued Item

Here is a real opportunity to sell something by suggesting another product. When you do not have the exact item a customer has ordered, you may send a form message to the customer and include information about the substitute item. Your acknowledgment message might include wording similar to this:

Go to Student CD-ROM Activity 10-2.

THANK YOU FOR YOUR INQUIRY

The enclosed flyer describes an item similar to the one you requested. We think that you will find this item equal or superior to the discontinued item. Please use the enclosed order form and return envelope to let us know your decision. Our money-back guarantee ensures your satisfaction.

5. An Order Requiring a Delay in Shipment

Occasionally shipment will be delayed because an item is out of stock. You can help keep the customer's goodwill by telling when you will ship the merchandise.

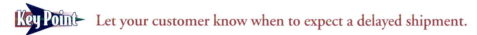 **Let your customer know when to expect a delayed shipment.**

6. An Order for a Product Sold Only Through Dealers

Although it may be your policy to sell your products only through dealers, it is never a good idea to use the phrase "it is our policy"—a customer's reaction may be that you should change your policy. Just explain your policy. If you must get this idea across, say "it is our practice" instead. This phrase isn't quite as strong.

7. An Order From a Customer Who Has Poor Credit

Sometimes an order must be refused because of the unsatisfactory condition of the account of a customer who is buying on credit. In these cases, try to find an alternative payment method that would allow you to complete the order. You might offer to send the merchandise COD or ask the customer to send 50 percent of the payment before you ship the merchandise. Or if you accept bank credit cards, offer that option to the customer.

The first three kinds of orders above require routine acknowledgments, the next two require special acknowledgments, and the last two require acknowledgments refusing the orders. We will discuss three types of acknowledgments next.

 Try to offer an alternative payment method for customers with bad credit.

Routine Acknowledgments

 When you can make complete and accurate shipment, your acknowledgment message should follow the *direct*, or *good-news*, approach.

1. Start With the Good News

Tell when and how you will ship the merchandise. Assure the customer that you are handling the order promptly and efficiently. Be careful not to promise delivery on a specific date. It is safer to state when you *shipped* the merchandise. Remember that *order* is the word for what the buyer sends; the seller sends *merchandise*—not an order.

2. Repeat the Essential Details of the Order

Give the date of the order, order number, product name(s), quantity, size, cost, and any other applicable information. Remember that a listing is easier to read in a tabular form than in a paragraph.

3. Build Goodwill

Thank your customer for the order and emphasize your service attitude by stressing how your product or service can help. Use a sincere and friendly tone. To be sure that your message projects the best image of you and your organization, make the letter look professional.

4. Resell Your Product and Your Organization

Reassure the reader about the quality of the merchandise and the reliability of your organization. Show genuine interest in the customer and a desire to serve. Avoid using self-centered phrases like "Our product . . . ," "We also make . . . ," and "We'd also like to sell you . . . ." Use the "you" attitude, and be specific. Tell the customer that you are looking forward to future orders.

Special Acknowledgments

Sometimes you cannot fill the order as you receive it because information on the form or in the letter is incomplete or you no longer carry the item. Or perhaps shipment will be delayed. An acknowledgment message for bad-news situations like these should use an *indirect plan* or *approach*. Place the emphasis on what you *can* do rather than on what you cannot do. Avoid negative words such as *can't, delay, unable, won't, failed, forgot, error,* and *mistake.* Include the appropriate items for the situation from the list that follows. Your content will depend upon the circumstances.

 Follow the *indirect approach* for bad-news acknowledgment messages.

1. Thank the Customer for the Order

Indicate your appreciation for the order, or say something favorable about the merchandise.

2. Repeat the Order

List the essential details of the item(s) ordered.

3. Address the Problem Appropriately

Specify the information you need to complete the order (avoid emphasizing the customer's error), state the reason for delayed shipment, or suggest an alternative product. If you ask for a response from the customer, include a reply card, a return envelope, a toll-free telephone number, or e-mail address to help you get a prompt, complete answer.

4. Give Shipping Information

State when and how you will ship the merchandise.

5. Resell Your Product and Organization

You can effectively resell in a special acknowledgment by mentioning the quality of your products and the reliability of your organization. By reselling the merchandise, you remind the customer that delivery is worth waiting for.

6. Promote Goodwill in the Closing

A goodwill closing should indicate your desire for the customer to be satisfied with the merchandise and your desire to give good service to your customer.

Figure 10-2 shows a letter acknowledging an incomplete order.

Redi-Check

2100 Minutemaker Boulevard • Waltham, MA 02154
Phone: 201-555-7746 • Fax: 201-555-6635 • E-Mail: redicheck@aol.com

March 15, <YEAR>

Mr. Bob Jones
693 Gilbert Street
Hampton, VA 23366

Dear Mr. Jones:

Thank you for your order for 200 Deluxe Checks, Stock No. 54, which we received today.

Please sign the enclosed order form and return it to me in the enclosed postpaid envelope. Your signature is only a formality but a necessary one. We will mail your Deluxe Checks as soon as I receive this order form.

This new style of check is very popular, and I am sure you will be pleased with your selection.

Sincerely,

Steve Hughes, Manager
Customer Services

jm
Enclosure

FIGURE 10-2 A letter acknowledging an incomplete order.

Acknowledgments Refusing Orders

Sometimes you must refuse an order. Your organization may sell only through dealers, or you may be unable to ship the merchandise on credit because of problems with the customer's account.

Messages refusing orders call for the *indirect plan* or *approach*, or the "sandwich approach"— the bad news is placed in the middle of the letter.

Use the following outline for these messages:

1. Start With a Buffer
Thank the customer for the order, and repeat the details.

2. Give an Explanation
In a positive way, tell *why* you cannot complete the order and stress what you *can* do, along with the advantages to the reader. Offer to help the reader in any way you can—give the name of the nearest dealer, explain credit terms, or offer an alternative solution.

3. Say No
The sentences leading up to the refusal will imply that "No" is coming. Be sure that your refusal is clear.

4. End With a Buffer
Resell your organization and your products.

Notice how the indirect approach is followed in this letter to Mr. O'Reilly:

Dear Mr. O'Reilly:

Thank you for your order for one pair of Bostonian shoes, size 10D.

The Bostonian shoe is well made and has been the best-selling shoe in the United States for many years. People who take pride in their work make this shoe and use only the finest materials.

Because we want you to be perfectly happy with our new Bostonians, we are returning your money order for $120 and requesting that you contact Bob Surdell at Style Step Shoes, 3356 Monroe Street, Spokane, WA 99202.

Bob is one of our leading dealers, and he will make sure that your shoes fit perfectly for your comfort.

We are enclosing a brochure showing our latest styles, along with a coupon worth $5 on your new Bostonians.

Sincerely,

Rich Lanter

mc
Enclosures
c: Mr. Bob Surdell

This letter will make Mr. O'Reilly feel that the refusal is actually advantageous to him. When you present the reasons for saying no, a reasonable customer will understand.

Acknowledgment messages provide an excellent opportunity to build goodwill and encourage future orders.

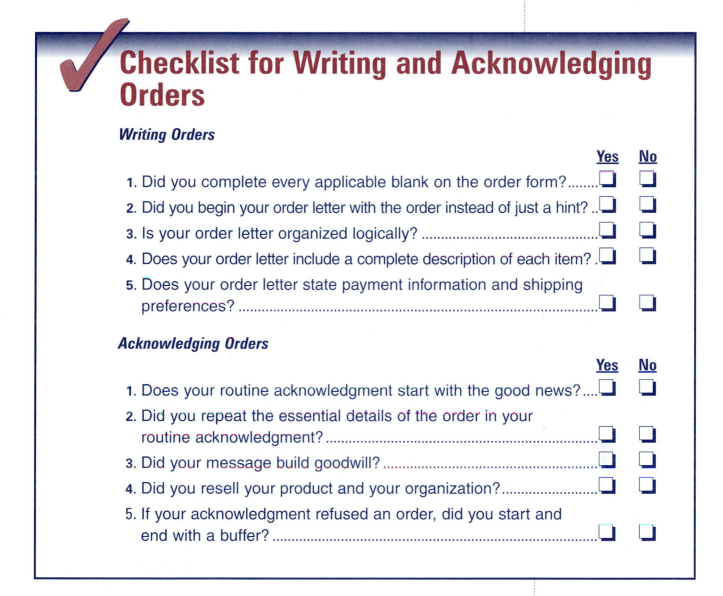

Checklist for Writing and Acknowledging Orders

Writing Orders

	Yes	No
1. Did you complete every applicable blank on the order form?	❑	❑
2. Did you begin your order letter with the order instead of just a hint?	❑	❑
3. Is your order letter organized logically?	❑	❑
4. Does your order letter include a complete description of each item?	❑	❑
5. Does your order letter state payment information and shipping preferences?	❑	❑

Acknowledging Orders

	Yes	No
1. Does your routine acknowledgment start with the good news?	❑	❑
2. Did you repeat the essential details of the order in your routine acknowledgment?	❑	❑
3. Did your message build goodwill?	❑	❑
4. Did you resell your product and your organization?	❑	❑
5. If your acknowledgment refused an order, did you start and end with a buffer?	❑	❑

SUMMARY

Your company depends on timely delivery of goods and services to keep its business going. It is important to place orders correctly and professionally.

Likewise, to stay in business, every organization needs to receive orders for its products and services. The way you fill those orders affects your future business. Acknowledging orders in a timely and professional manner helps ensure that you will have repeat customers and build a good reputation for your company. Your writing skills will help your company accomplish these goals.

Name _____ Date _____

WHAT'S WRONG WITH THESE?

On the lines provided indicate what is wrong with each of the following order acknowledgment excerpts.

1. Dear Ms. Bowman: You failed to include the size of the dress you ordered.

    _____

2. Dear Mr. Tines: The item you ordered (item 2357, sweater) has been discontinued. Sorry. Sincerely,

    _____

3. Dear Mr. Lawson: Your order No. 2393 for three sets of our Deluxe Culinary Knives is back-ordered. Thank you for waiting. Sincerely,

    _____

4. Dear Ms. Taylor: I'm sorry but we regret to inform you that your credit is below par. Therefore, we cannot fill your order.

    _____

5. Dear Ms. Lyles: We cannot fill your order because we are wholesale only. You will have to find a dealer in your area.

    _____

WRITING ORDER LETTERS

Plan and prepare (preferably type) the following order letters.

6. A friend told you about a small family-owned business, Creations Limited, 124 McLean Avenue, Hawley, MS 39205. You have an ad from the May 3 issue of the local newspaper, in which this company advertised 3- by 6-inch leather pocket diaries, Item No. K-553, that would make good holiday gifts. Each diary costs $17.95, including tax, plus $4 for shipping and handling up to five items. Personalization is $3 per diary and is limited to 22 letters and spaces. Order personalized diaries for four of your friends, relatives, or business associates. Enclose a check and have the merchandise delivered to you.

HELP OUT

Volunteers to work in national parks or forests as backcountry guides, campground hosts, wildlife observers, or trail workers. For a 108-page annual directory of jobs, send $5 to: AHS/Helping Out, 1015 31st St., N.W., Washington, DC 20007.

---

7. Write a letter ordering the directory described in the advertisement at left, which is from the November 18 edition of *Today's News*. Have the directory mailed to you, and enclose your check.

Name _____ Date _____

WRITING LETTERS ACKNOWLEDGING ORDERS

Plan and prepare (preferably type) acknowledgments for the following situations.

8. **Acknowledging a large order.** You are the marketing manager for Valley Fruits, Inc. Acknowledge a large order from Mr. T. C. White, P.O. Box 2525, Harlingen, TX 78820. He ordered gifts for 12 addressees, all of them monthly deliveries of fresh fruit, for a total of $2380. Valley Fruit will refund the customer's money if the customer is dissatisfied.

9. **Acknowledging an incomplete order.** You are the sales manager of Video House. You receive the following order letter from George Green. You have two VCRs on sale this month for $400. Model 6450 is a 4-head VHS VCR, and Model 6250 is a 2-head VHS VCR with on-screen programming. Write Mr. Green a tactful letter asking which model he prefers. Make it easy for him to reply, and use this opportunity to build goodwill and resell your product. This month, you are including two free blank videotapes with each VCR.

202 McKinley Street
Concord, NC 28025
October 10, <YEAR>

Video House
5661 Western Avenue
Charleston, SC 29411

Please ship one of the VCRs you have on sale this month for $400.

Ship the VCR to me at my address in the heading. Please charge my bankcard No. 5349-0516-1019-7889, which expires March <YEAR>.

Sincerely,

George Green

Name _____   Date _____

COLLABORATIVE ACTIVITY

Writing a Refusal *Work with another person to write a tactful refusal message acknowledging the letter on the next page. Your organization sells your products exclusively through local dealers. Refer Dr. Thomas to Ms. Gina Goerlich, manager of The Sticker Gallery, 1743 East Main Street, Cleveland, OH 44106. Explain that the Sticker Gallery carries a complete line of your stickers. Include a statement promoting or recommending the store. Send your current catalog, which illustrates more than 700 stickers, along with the letter.*

Jon Thomas, M.D.
1355 Winnette Drive
Cleveland, OH 44102
February 8, <YEAR>

Stuck-on-You Designs, Inc.
3800 Ala Moana Avenue
Honolulu, HI 96822

Please send 5000 assorted smelly stickers to me at the address above. Charge the order to my bankcard No. 1234-567-891-232, or send me an invoice.

Jon Thomas, M.D.

cs

Name _____ Date _____

PROOFREADING EXERCISE

Proofread the following order letter. Mark errors with proofreaders' marks.

October 1, <YEAR>

Mr. David R. Bush
9565 San Felipe Dr.
Tallahasse, FT 32109

Dear Mr. David:

Thank you for you September 20 letter requesting 7 Premium Class Office Chairs. Your order will be shipped today by Truckers, Ltd., and you may expect delivery within three days.

You new chairs carry a ten-year guarantee and meets the most highest ergonomic standards.

We appreciate your business, Ms. David, and look forward to your future orders.

Sincerely yours',

Researching Credit Card Security
Log onto the Internet and find at least three Internet businesses that provide online order forms. Find out how these companies can guarantee that your credit card information will be confidential. Print out their guidelines or policies regarding this issue.

Chapter 11

Writing Credit and Collection Messages

Chapter 10 presented the basic information for you to learn to write order letters, use order forms, and organize and write routine, special, and refusal acknowledgments. Chapter 11 will build on the knowledge and skills that you have perfected and will give you additional skills so that you can:

- Write letters requesting, investigating, extending, or refusing credit, and

- Write appropriate letters for customers who have not paid their bills in a timely manner.

Objectives

After completing this chapter, you should be able to:
- Organize and write credit messages.
- Organize and write collection messages.

For convenience and security reasons, customers purchase products and services on credit. By extending credit, the seller simplifies the purchasing process and attracts customers who do not wish to pay with cash. Credit purchases allow the customer to get the product or service. The seller gets a *promise* that the customer will pay later. If the customer delays or refuses payment, the seller usually begins the collection process.

WRITING CREDIT MESSAGES

Communications concerning credit fall into four basic categories:

- Requesting credit.
- Investigating credit.
- Extending credit.
- Refusing credit.

Because credit is such a large part of the operation of most organizations today, form letters are often used for communications regarding credit. With technology, businesses can generate form letters to look like individually prepared documents.

Requesting Credit

Customers wishing to establish credit will write or telephone the organization's credit department for a credit application form. The form usually requests both personal and business information such as:

- Name, address, Social Security number, telephone number, and date of birth.
- Name and address of current employer, position, length of employment, and monthly compensation.
- Bank and other credit references.
- Rental or mortgage payment, auto payment, and other installment loans and revolving account information.

Customers want to establish credit mainly for *convenience*. Consumers can:

- Buy now and pay later.
- Avoid carrying cash or writing checks.
- Receive advance notice about sales, promotions, and other special events.

Investigating Credit

Because you are trusted with the applicant's information, you must handle carefully all facts related to the credit rating of that organization or individual. Your employer will advise you of procedures and laws governing what you can and cannot do or say during the credit investigation. Upon receiving a credit application, the credit department will verify the information on the application by sending a form letter, such as the following, to the banks and credit references listed by the applicant:

Ladies and Gentlemen:

SUBJECT: Credit Inquiry

The following applicant has given your name as a credit reference:

Ms. Jane R. Smithson
Suite 111
Turret Towers
4432 Lamar Lane
Houston, TX 77077

We would appreciate your providing us the information listed below:

- Date the account was opened
- Terms of the account
- Credit limit
- Current balance
- Past due amount
- Date of last activity
- Payment history
- Remarks

Please use the postpaid return envelope provided. Your reply will remain confidential.

Sincerely,

To save time, many businesses order credit reports from credit bureaus or services. These reports provide the following information:

- Open accounts
- Paid accounts and date of payoff
- Payment histories
- Slow payment records (30, 60, 90 days)
- Charged-off accounts (uncollected accounts)
- Bankruptcies
- Credit inquiries (who has made inquiries about this account)

Most credit services also provide rating scores to help businesses make credit risk decisions.

Evaluating the Credit Information

The credit department decides whether to extend or refuse credit based on the applicant's *credit standing* or *credit rating*.

- **Credit standing** means the reputation of an individual for financial responsibility.
- **Credit rating** means a credit agency's appraisal—based on reports from creditors—of a credit standing at any one time.

Traditionally, the following **four Cs of credit** form the basis for extending credit privileges:

1. **Character** refers to a sense of honesty and ethical dealings with others. It means meeting obligations and is demonstrated by *willingness to pay.*
2. **Capacity** is the *ability to pay.* It is evidenced by income or potential income.
3. **Capital** refers to tangible assets in relation to debts. Capital also determines the *ability to pay* if the debtor does not pay willingly.
4. **Conditions** refers to the general business trends, the local business environment, or current consumer demand.

Extending Credit

Few letters are more welcome than one extending credit. Writing such a letter is a pleasant task. You are telling someone who has applied for credit—who has completed an application form, and whose credit standing you have investigated—that he or she rates high enough to be given credit privileges. That is good news to anyone!

When writing a message extending credit, use the *direct approach* and the following outline as a guide:

1. Welcome the new charge customer, and express the wish for a pleasant association.
2. Outline special privileges that are available.
3. Explain the terms of payment.
4. Encourage the customer to use the new charge account, and enclose promotional material.
5. Build goodwill by indicating your eagerness to serve the new customer well.

The letter in Figure 11-1 uses the good-news approach and covers each of these five points. The writer begins with a welcome and the good news that the customer's credit account is ready for use. The second paragraph calls attention to the significance of the enclosed credit card. The writer might have noted other privileges that charge customers receive, such as advance notice of sales. Details about terms and payment, essential for new customers, appear in the middle of the letter after the good news and before the sales promotion appeal and pleasant ending.

Many retail stores notify credit applicants of acceptance by a form message that welcomes the new credit customer and explains the credit process. However, a personalized credit acceptance letter goes much further in strengthening a credit relationship, building goodwill, minimizing collection problems, and increasing sales.

The major reason organizations sell on credit is *to increase profits.* Sales figures increase because credit customers buy more merchandise on a regular basis.

Orchids and More Outlet

883 Floral Way / Philadelphia, PA 19100 / Phone: 888-555-2900 / Fax: 888-555-2905 / Website: orchidoutlet.com

March 10 <YEAR>

Mrs. Constance Cordello
444 East City Road
Dayton, PA 19150

Dear Mrs. Cordello:

Welcome to Orchids and More Outlet's family of happy customers who use the convenience of credit. You will be pleased that your account is ready for use when you visit our store. Our staff will do everything possible to make your shopping experience a pleasant one.

The enclosed credit card offers you access to our wide selection of plants and accessories for you and your home—at reasonable prices. You will receive a monthly statement of your purchases shortly after our closing date, the 25th of each month. You will have until the 15th of the next month to pay your bill.

Mrs. Cordello, we invite you to enjoy the convenience of your charge account by taking advantage of this month's special—Lady Slipper Delight. You may also use our convenient telephone or online shopping. We also deliver!

Bring this letter and receive a 10 percent discount on your total purchase when you use your credit card for the first time. See you soon.

Sincerely,

John Bridgeton

John Bridgeton
Accounts Manager

pm
Enclosure

FIGURE 11-1 Note how this letter uses the direct approach and covers all five points in the outline.

Refusing Credit *Indirect*

Your organization cannot afford to extend credit to every customer who asks for it. After evaluating the credit information you have gathered, you must decide whether the account would be more likely to (1) increase sales and profits or (2) become an uncollectible account.

If the information gathered indicates that an applicant for credit is a poor credit risk, a *credit-refusal* letter is necessary. The credit-refusal letter is a difficult letter to write, because you are telling the applicant that credit cannot be approved. Use the *indirect approach* when writing this letter.

Go to Student
CD-ROM
Activity 11-1.

 Key Point Every credit-refusal letter has two objectives:
1. To say no tactfully.
2. To keep the goodwill of the customer.

Your goal is not to discourage credit buying but to convince the applicant that buying on a cash basis now will be advantageous. The main reasons for refusing credit are:

1. Lack of established credit.
2. Overextension of credit, which may result in an inability to pay on time.
3. Unwillingness to pay that which is owed according to credit reporting agencies.

Regardless of the reason(s) for refusing credit, the letter that refuses must be clear about why credit is not extended. A harsh credit refusal can cause the loss of the customer's current cash business. It can also discourage the customer from reapplying for credit later.

Consider this credit refusal written to a college student who applied for credit from an oil company:

Dear Ms. Michaels:

Regretfully, we do not issue credit to unemployed college students.

Please reapply after you are employed full-time. Until then, we want to encourage you to remain a cash customer. We will do all we possibly can to make your purchases of our gasoline and related products worthwhile.

Sincerely,

How would you react to this curt refusal? In this example, the harsh, direct approach does not demonstrate goodwill toward the credit applicant. How could you rewrite this credit refusal, de-emphasizing as much as possible the reason for the refusal? A better approach appears below:

Dear Ms. Michaels:

Your credit application is a clear indication that you are satisfied with our efforts to serve your automobile needs. Thank you for sending it to us.

Because college students have a difficult time building a credit rating while they are committed to getting an education, we would like to make a suggestion to you.

Once you are employed full-time, please send us another credit application. We will be happy at that time to welcome you as a new addition to our growing family of charge customers.

In the meantime, Ms. Michaels, let us continue to serve you on a cash basis. We are eager to attend to your future automotive needs.

Sincerely,

The opening statement serves as a buffer because it is positive in tone. The reason for refusal is indicated clearly enough, although not stated outright. The key to this refusal is the interest shown in reevaluating the applicant's credit status later. Also, a closing message inviting her *cash* business helps to establish goodwill, despite the refusal.

WRITING COLLECTION LETTERS

An important part of being competitive in business is the ability of an organization to effectively deal with customers who do not pay their bills. It is certainly not a pleasant task to remind or urge customers to pay, but it is a critical function of business not to ignore this inevitable problem. When customers do not send payments on time, businesses send reminders to the customers stating that payment is past due. Messages that attempt to collect are referred to as **collection letters;** they are written because of the need to persuade customers to pay.

 The purpose of collection letters is:
1. **To get the money owed.**
2. **To keep the customer's goodwill and future business.**

Collection Letter Series

Most organizations use a series of collection letters that they send at predetermined intervals, beginning with a statement of account and ending with a last demand for payment.

Statement of Account

Most organizations send statements each month to their credit customers. These statements provide the customers with a record of charges and the total amount due.

When customers do not pay on time, the business may send a duplicate copy of the statement. A friendly reminder such as "If you haven't sent us your payment, please do so today!" may be added to this statement.

Impersonal Reminder

If the customer still does not pay, the organization may send a printed letter that is not personalized. At this early stage, a company takes the position that the customer is trustworthy and intends to pay. The tone of the reminder message is friendly, as illustrated in Figure 11-2.

Go to Student CD-ROM Activity 11-2.

FIGURE 11-2 A gentle reminder such as this one may be all that is needed to secure payment.

Secure Life Insurance Company
945 Security Boulevard/Bay City, TX 77501/Phone: 281-555-5800/Fax: 281-555-5801

Please . . .
. . . Have you forgotten your payment that is now due?

As you know, your Secure insurance policy is designed to protect your family from financial difficulty when you are gone. Because missing a payment can cancel this protection, we urge you to send us the amount due as soon as possible.

Please don't delay! Keep you and your loved ones *secure* by sending us your payment now.

Another impersonal reminder might be a form letter in which you fill in the date, inside address, and account information to give it a more personal touch, as illustrated in Figure 11-3.

883 Floral Way / Philadelphia, PA19100 / Phone: 888-555-2900 / Fax: 888-555-2905 / Website: orchidoutlet.com

January 27, <YEAR>

Mr. David Nguyen
13911 Jackson Freeway
St. Louis, MO63144

Dear Mr. Nguyen:

We value having you as one of our charge customers.It is important, though, that you make your payments promptly each month.You may have forgotten last month's minimum payment of $35 on your Account No. 7-21338-446.

To protect your credit, please send your payment in the enclosed envelope. If you have sent your payment, please accept our thanks. If a problem exists with your account, please contact us as soon as possible.

If you need any additional information, please call.We are here to help.

Sincerely,

Anna Kempler

Anna Kempler
Collections

zp
Enclosure

FIGURE 11-3 You can merge individual information into a computer-generated form letter to make the reminder more personal.

Personal Reminder

As an alternative to using a computerized form letter, you may wish to send a personal message—usually no more than a couple of paragraphs. Take care to ensure that the customer will consider it a reminder—not a *demand* for payment. It attempts to persuade the person to pay and does not intimidate. The following message illustrates the tone used in such a reminder:

Dear Mr. Cheng:

Enclosed is a duplicate of your credit charges from December 20,<YEAR>. It is a friendly reminder that the balance on your account with us is past due. Please take a few minutes today to send us your check for $105.77.

Use the postpaid addressed envelope provided for your use. Thank you for your business.

Sincerely,

Request for an Explanation

When a credit customer does not respond to personal reminder messages, you can assume that something is preventing the customer from paying. The customer may be unhappy with the purchased merchandise or may be facing financial difficulty. Whatever the reason for holding up payment, you want the customer to (1) explain why the payment has not been made or (2) settle the account.

The following letter illustrates the approach generally used in requesting an explanation:

Dear Mrs. Perez:

We are concerned about your overdue account. We have sent several reminder notices, and we expected to receive your check for $264.32 in the mail. So far, we have not.

Circumstances may be preventing you from paying your account. If so, please write or call me. I am certain we can work out a payment arrangement after we know what your situation is.

Just think how good you will feel, Mrs. Perez, when you pay your account.

Sincerely,

Note that the writer of this message did not threaten. The tone reflects the assumption that the customer is basically honest. The object of the message is to get the money owed and to keep the customer's future business.

If the customer writes or calls you to explain why he or she has not paid, it is important to maintain a service attitude. Is the customer lacking cash? Ask for a smaller or minimum payment. Is the customer dissatisfied with the product or service in some way? Come up with a mutually agreeable resolution to the problem. Your service attitude will help you keep the customer's goodwill.

Appeal(s) for Payment

The next collection message is an appeal to the credit customer to pay. This is a stern letter, but calmly written. *Typical appeals are to the customer's pride or sense of fairness.*

Your appeal for payment should not threaten to take the debtor to court unless you actually plan to. Give the person another chance to save a good credit standing by sending payment before the deadline—usually 10 to 12 days from the date of the letter. The following letter is an example of a courteous request for payment that appeals to the customer's pride and sense of fairness:

11-2:

CHECK BILLING DATES
A doctor's billing service sent computerized form letters to a husband and wife asking for past-due payments. Knowing that their insurance should have paid, the wife closely examined the notices and was surprised to see a billing date of one year and four months earlier. The bills were indeed paid, but the computer was just a bit late sending notices.

Dear Ms. Broomfield:

Your good credit reputation enabled you to make a purchase from us more than three months ago. We were glad to place your name on our credit list at that time, and we made it clear that accounts are due on the fifteenth of the month after the purchase was made. When you made your purchases, Ms. Broomfield, you accepted those terms.

Your credit reputation is a valuable asset. We want you to keep it that way because of the advantages it gives you. You have enjoyed a liberal extension of time; but to be fair to our other customers, you must pay the amount that is past due by March 2. Will you please send us your check for $150.88 today?

Sincerely,

Last Call for Payment

The final message is an appeal to customers to pay so that the delinquent account does not have to be given to a collection agency or an attorney. In this letter a customer is given one last chance to save a good credit standing by sending payment before the deadline—usually five to ten days from the date of the letter. *Never threaten the customer; state the consequences simply and regretfully.* Notice that the following letter tries to keep the friendship of the customer by stressing interest in fairness:

Dear Ms. Murphey:

Your credit reputation is important to you, Ms. Murphey.

For some time now, we have been writing to you in an effort to clear your balance of $303, explained in the attached statement. So far, you have not sent us a check or an explanation, although six messages have called the debt to your attention.

Can we still settle this account in a favorable way? If you send your check for $303 now, you can continue to buy luggage and accessories on our regular credit terms. The agreement with our collection agency, however, does not allow further delay. We must assign your account to the Meritt Collection Agency unless it is resolved within ten days.

The choice is yours. If your check reaches us by November 16, your credit standing with us will still be good and our friendly business relations will continue.

Please mail your check for $303 today. Protect your credit reputation.

Sincerely,

If you discover that the customer does not intend to pay, you will need to consult a collection agency or lawyer about possible legal strategies.

Payment Acknowledgment

When a customer writes you about a past-due account, answer with a personal letter. Do not send the remaining letters from the collection series. When the customer responds to a collection letter with his or her payment, send a special thank-you message.

Dear Mr. Langston:

Thank you for your check for $327.93. Your account has been marked "paid."

Your cooperation in this matter enables us to continue to serve you in every way we can.

Sincerely,

SUMMARY

Customers purchase products and services on credit for reasons of convenience and security. Businesses extend credit to attract customers and to simplify the purchasing process.

To minimize losses, companies offering credit must carefully verify and evaluate the information on all credit applications. If the applicant meets the "four Cs of credit," the company sends a direct approach letter extending credit. On the other hand, if the information gathered indicates that the applicant is a poor credit risk, an indirect approach credit-refusal letter is necessary.

Organizations must take steps to collect debt from customers who do not pay their bills. A collection letter series is an effective way to deal with this unpleasant situation.

Name _____ Date _____

WHAT'S WRONG WITH THESE?

Indicate on the lines provided what is wrong with each of the following credit or collection message excerpts:

1. Credit inquiry: Send all the credit information for Ms. Julia Kerr as soon as possible.

   _____

   _____

2. First sentence in extending credit letter: Here's your new credit card.

   _____

   _____

3. Credit refusal: You do not qualify for credit with our company.

   _____

   _____

4. First notice for a late payment: If you do not pay now, we will take you to court.

   _____

   _____

5. Last call for payment: Obviously, Mr. Smith, you do not care about your account.

   _____

   _____

WRITING CREDIT MESSAGES

Prepare (preferably type) the following credit messages.

6. **Extending Credit.** Ms. Joyce Stannington, 87 North Street, Texas City, TX 77590, applied for a charge account at Melissa's Fine Clothing, 120 The Strand, Galveston, TX 77500. After checking her credit rating and finding it satisfactory, the store opened an account for her. Write the credit approval letter to welcome Ms. Stannington as a new credit customer. Remind the customer of the credit terms (15 percent discount on all purchases made on the first day the credit card is used, payments due on the fifteenth of each month), and enclose an information sheet listing specific credit terms. Follow the outline provided in this chapter for writing messages to extend credit.

7. **Refusing Credit.** Mr. James Sessleton applied for a credit card with your company, Pentium Plus Processors. You checked Mr. Sessleton's credit history and found that he has nine charge accounts with

Name _____ Date _____

WRITING CREDIT MESSAGES *(continued)*

unpaid balances. His history also indicates numerous past-due accounts. Write a message that is tactful but reflects an understanding of the customer's problems. Be fair and helpful while trying to acquire his cash business. Mr. Sessleton's address is 1899 Strawberry, Splendora, TX 77008.

WRITING COLLECTION MESSAGES

Prepare (preferably type) the collection messages in Problems 8 to 10.

You work in the Credit Department at Maybree's. Mr. Thomas J. Wellingstone opened an account four months ago. You have billed each month, but Mr. Wellingstone has not paid. You have sent a duplicate statement and a personal reminder, but he has not responded. Mr. Wellingstone's address is 998 Southmore Boulevard, Pleasanton, TN 78055; he owes $235.87. In your letters, supply dates for sending payment as appropriate.

8. It is April 1. Prepare a message requesting an explanation.

9. It is April 15. Mr. Wellingstone has not responded. Prepare a message using an appeal approach.

10. It is May 1. Mr. Wellingstone has still not responded. Prepare a message for the last call for payment.

COLLABORATIVE ACTIVITY

Beginning a Collection Series Work with another person to write an impersonal reminder that would be included with a duplicate statement as the first step in a collection series. Supply a business name and the type of business you represent.

PROOFREADING EXERCISE

Proofread the credit message on the next page. Mark errors with proofreaders' marks.

Search the Internet for Credit Card Opportunities
Search the Internet for types of credit cards that you can apply for online. Write a short report of your findings. Discuss how you feel about the security of obtaining credit online.

Name _____ Date _____

November 23, <YEAR>

Dear Ms. Smith;

Enclosed is a duplicate statement and terms agreement.We are sorry that you did not
recieve your copy.Us here at Thompson's strive for quality work and we apologize for
any inconvenience caused by our' error.

You are important to us; we do appreciate you're business.Please except the enclosed
coupon worth $10 toward your next purchase.We cannot do to much to win your trust.

Sincerly,

Laura Whitmore

pm
Enclosure

NOTES

Chapter 12

Writing Persuasive Messages

Chapter 11 presented the basics of credit and collection letters and gave you practice composing letters based on these situations. Chapter 12 will continue to build your skills and knowledge, concentrating on persuasive messages to customers and dealers.

Objectives

After completing this chapter, you should be able to:

- Plan persuasive messages.
- Write persuasive messages to customers.
- Write persuasive messages to dealers.

WRITING PERSUASIVE MESSAGES

To some extent, every message is a persuasive message. You are promoting your organization's image and goodwill. In this chapter, we will talk about the messages that have as their main purpose to sell products or services.

Direct mail promotions, especially the kind sent to consumers, often use some device to get the customer—the "prospect"—to open the envelope and read the message. "Free Gift Inside!" or "Urgent—Open Immediately!" or a similar message may be printed on the envelope. Inside, the consumer may find a letter, a brochure, and a coupon, plus other items that make up an impressive package. Yes, much of it is "junk mail," but people have become so accustomed to having it appear in their mailboxes that even organizations that have products or services of real value sometimes feel that they have to "shout" for attention.

Persuasive messages to business people may use all the devices of direct mail but usually get to the point without resorting to gimmicks. We will focus on persuasive messages as businesses use them.

Persuasive messages are an effective selling tool for several good reasons:

- **Cost.** The cost of producing and mailing a large quantity of sales letters is less than the cost of reaching the same number of prospects by producing and buying time for a radio or television commercial or producing and buying space for a newspaper or magazine ad.
- **Selectivity.** The seller may select a mailing list according to profession, geographic area, income, interests, and so on. By selecting the mailing lists carefully, the seller is virtually assured of reaching a certain number of "qualified" prospects.
- **Personalization.** Computer software enables the sender to address a specific customer as if he or she were the only person receiving the offer, when, in fact, these sales messages are produced quickly and inexpensively in large quantities.
- **Adaptability.** Basic sales information can be adjusted quickly for specific prospects.

Direct mail persuasive messages do, however, have certain drawbacks. Because many people look upon all direct mail as junk mail, a sales message may be discarded before it is read, even though it is well written and makes a spectacular offer. In addition, even a "successful" persuasive message will usually draw a positive response from no more than 5 percent of the total number of people receiving the mailing.

Letters written specifically for direct mail selling are not the only persuasive messages. The writer who acknowledges receipt of a large order will write a thank-you letter that will also *resell* the customer. The writer who introduces a new sales representative to a customer is paving the way for that representative to call for an order. And the writer who tries to persuade a superior to approve a project or an expense must sell that person on the reasons the project or expense should be approved. Therefore, every business writer must keep in mind the principles of writing persuasive messages. These principles are described on the next page.

12-1—Check for Redundancy. Is the word free *necessary in* free gift?

1. Know Your Products and Services

Be aware of the advantages and disadvantages of your products and services, why they appeal or should appeal to people—in fact, know as much as you can about them.

2. Know Your Potential Customers

Learn everything you can about your customers: *who* they are, *where* they are, *what* their needs are, and *how* to get through to them.

3. Know How Sales Are Made

Concentrate on what motivates people to buy, what appeals are likely to prove successful, and how to get people to act.

4. Remember the Basics of Effective Writing

Apply the writing principles you have learned, especially those that pertain to persuasive messages, and practice the techniques of clear communication.

PLANNING SALES LETTERS

Before you can begin actually drafting a sales letter, take five important planning steps, as described in the next section. Until you complete this planning, it is virtually impossible to write an effective persuasive message.

1. Analyze the Prospects in Terms of the Product

First, identify the characteristics that describe the most likely prospects for your products or services. From research or experience, build a "composite" prospect. The age, gender, occupation, geographic location, financial status, and other characteristics of the "average" prospect determine what appeals will be used in the letter. Defining your targeted customers' characteristics helps you discover the needs and desires of these prospective buyers.

For example, you would not try to sell a "Sixty-Five Plus" insurance plan to college students. Nor would you try to sell homeowners' insurance to apartment dwellers.

2. Prepare a List of Prospects

Next, you need a good mailing list. The obvious place to start is your organization's own list of customers. You can also buy lists from organizations that specialize in compiling and selling mailing lists. To be a good sales tool, a mailing list must contain the correct names and addresses of people or organizations that have in common the characteristics that make them likely prospects for your products or services.

3. Analyze the Product in Terms of the Prospects

What specific feature of the product or service makes it attractive or useful or appealing? What features should you emphasize? What features should you deemphasize? (You will have done part of this analysis already.) Letters that present a product in terms of what prospective buyers think of it and how they can use it do more than make sales—they win satisfied customers.

4. Decide on the Central Selling Point (CSP)

The **central selling point (CSP)** should be the item of information most likely to persuade the prospect to buy a product or service. After analyzing the prospects and the product, build your letter around this central selling point. The CSP might be appearance, durability, comfort, convenience, price, or any other positive feature that is likely to have the greatest influence on your reader's purchasing decision.

5. Make a Plan for the Letter

One formula for a sales presentation is **AIDA**—attention, interest, desire, action. First, get the prospect's attention—get him or her to read the letter—by promising a benefit. Then, arouse interest by helping the prospect to imagine using the product or service. Next, try to convince your reader of the desirability of buying the product or service. Finally, attempt to get your prospect to act—to send in an order or to subscribe to your service.

Many good sales letters will not fit such a set pattern. Rather than let a formula dictate the letter, the effective persuasive writer will link the product or service with the prospect's desires and needs by giving sufficient factual information to be convincing.

WRITING PERSUASIVE MESSAGES TO CUSTOMERS

The purpose of your persuasive message is to arouse in the reader the impulse to buy and use your product or service. After you have planned your message, follow these suggestions when you write a sales letter:

1. Capture Reader Attention and Interest in the Opening

The opening sentences of a sales message are critical. If the prospect does not read the letter, no sale will result, no matter how good the offer is. To get the message off to a fast start and to get the prospect reading, the CSP and the promise of a benefit to the buyer should be woven together at the beginning.

The opportunities for different forms, styles, attention-getting ideas, gadgets, devices, and so on, are limited only by your active imagination. Often you can capture the reader's attention in one of the following ways:

- Arrange the first sentence as a headline—perhaps in all-capital letters or in color—or as an address block, as illustrated in Figure 12-1.
- Use a humorous cartoon or a striking color display.
- Attach a simple gadget such as a coin, stamp, piece of string, or button.

FUN STOP

1200 West Colorado • Phoenix, AZ 85073
Phone: 602-555-2100 • Fax: 602-555-2200 • Website: www.party/havaaparty.com

June 7, <YEAR>

Make the Fun Stop
Your First Stop . . .

. . . Whenever you need party supplies or equipment.

Whether you want a highly sophisticated glamorous event or a great birthday party,

The Fun Stop
is for you!

Whatever you need to make your party special is waiting for you. From tablecloths to balloons to party favors—you can find it at the FUN STOP.

To help you plan your event, use the enclosed party-planning guide. Come in to see our selection—bring this letter with you and you will receive $10 off any purchase of $50 or more.

Sincerely,

James Kirkwood

James Kirkwood
Manager

Enclosure

FIGURE 12-1 This effective persuasive letter from The Fun Stop offers the reader a special discount just for bringing the letter to the store.

If you use an attention-getting device, be sure that it leads right into the heart of the message. For instance, the cartoon may be a pictorial presentation of the CSP of the letter and an attached stamp may be described as "the postage needed to send for a Passport to Adventure."

Key Point Remember that any unusual opening should point toward the reader benefits you stress in the letter.

The following are some popular persuasive openings with sufficient "you" appeal to capture the reader's *interest*—not just momentary attention.

An Answer to a Problem, Need, or Desire of the Reader

Almost all successful persuasive openings provide answers to problems or needs, or fulfill desires. This basic kind of opening is usually a winner, because we are all interested in finding answers to our problems. It is also a natural opening, because the answer is always the use of the product or service advertised.

A sales message introducing a water purifier began:

> You can have clean, crystal-clear water *free* for 30 days with America's most advanced water purification system! We'll include a year's supply of filters *plus a valuable mystery gift!*
>
> Would you like to maintain your health with pure drinking water? It's easy—with the amazing new . . .

An Unusual Headline, News Item, or Statement of Fact

An obvious statement like "Spring is just around the corner" or "School will be starting again in a few weeks" lacks imagination and attracts no attention or interest. But an unusual headline, news item, or statement of fact usually leads the prospect to read further.

The following three openings are excerpts from successful sales messages:

> Every issue in government and politics has three sides—the *pro* side, the *con* side, and the *inside*. GOVERNMENT REVIEW gives you <u>all</u> sides.
>
> ATTENTION: PEOPLE WHO HAVE SUBSTANTIAL MONIES IN SAVINGS ACCOUNTS, CERTIFICATES OF DEPOSIT, ETC.
>
> U R G E N T   R E M I N D E R:
>
> The deadline is 12:01 a.m.

A Thought-Provoking Question

A question with an obvious yes or no answer—such as "Could you use more income?" or "Do you appreciate quality?"—is usually boring. But a question that challenges the reader to do some thinking is an excellent way to arouse interest in a message. Often, a question is better than a statement because it gives the reader a share in the idea. While thinking of an answer to your question, the reader may sell himself or herself on your idea. Naturally, the idea—the answer to the question—involves the use of the product or service you are selling. Look at the following example:

> NOT ENOUGH TIME AND MONEY?
>
> WHAT CAN *YOU* DO ABOUT IT?

Notice the opening question of the Sterling Insurance letter in Figure 12-2. This message is general enough so that it could be customized for your entire mailing list of customers.

Secure Life Insurance Company

945 Security Boulevard / Bay City, TX 77501 / Phone: 281-555-5800 / Fax: 281-555-5801

October 1, <YEAR>

Mr. David S. Evann
5429 Dewberry Lane
Decatur, AL 35602

Dear Mr. Evann:

Have you thought about how your family will make your house payments if you are too ill to work?

Most insurance policies don't pay the mortgage if you are unable to work. Sterling Insurance has a solution—a new policy that will pay the mortgage in cases of prolonged illness or disability.

Mr. Evann, you can now have "peace of mind" knowing that your home is protected against loss of income.

Take a moment now to complete and return the enclosed postpaid card. Take steps today to ensure protection for your home.

Sincerely,

Lynn J. Walters

Lynn J. Walters
Insurance Specialist

jt
Enclosure

PS: Do both you and your spouse work? If so, you may prefer to have insurance that covers both of you.

FIGURE 12-2 This persuasive letter is effective because it arouses the reader's interest, encourages the reader to see how he or she could benefit from the offer, and makes it easy to respond.

A Witty Comment or an Adaptation of a Familiar Saying

A clever phrase, a play on words, or a quotation of a familiar saying usually gets attention. But such openings must be closely related to the central selling point. This is a line from a Hart Drug Corporation letter about cold medicines:

A HART TO HEART TALK ABOUT A COLD PROPOSITION

Another witty example is a letterhead in which the organization name—Statewide Message Service—appears as skywriting:

Skywriting soon disappears . . . but Statewide Message Service makes sure that your messages don't.

Oops!

12-1:

WATCH USING A PLAY-ON-WORDS APPROACH.

Using a "play-on-words" approach requires careful proofreading. A hotel, Towne Suites, advertising suites at a sweet deal had to reprint its ad: . . . Treat Yourself to a Sweet Deal. Rest and Relaxation at Towne Sweets.

An Anecdote, a Fable, or a Parable

A story opening—if the story is a good one—usually arouses interest. It is effective as a sales letter opening if it relates to the CSP of the letter and does not overshadow the message itself. Read the following opening from a writer whose organization has placed a bid to win a project:

> As a child, did you ever look into the night sky and wish upon a star?

> We are wishing to hear from you about the September price quotation.

Go to Student CD-ROM Activity 12-1.

2. Keep the Message Interesting and Informative

Skillfully build the interest aroused by your opening sentences. A sales letter with even one slow, undeveloped paragraph usually means one more letter in a wastebasket. Your letter about a product or service succeeds when it leads the reader to say, "I didn't know that this product (or service) would do that for me. I want (or need) it."

3. Build the Message Around the Reader

The benefits the reader *thinks* a product or service offers will influence his or her decision about buying. Often a prospective customer knows little or nothing about your product or service you offer and has no interest in learning about your product or service when starting to read your letter. Bring your reader into the picture by showing how he or she can enjoy your product or service in a special way or how it can save time, energy, or money.

Your sales message will hold the reader's interest when it gives information on how to live more comfortably or how to do a better job. Specifically, your message may appeal to one or more of the *basic wants* of people everywhere:

- The desire to be comfortable, healthy, and attractive to others.
- The desire to have attention, praise, material possessions, relaxation, and enjoyment.
- The desire to avoid pain, trouble, and criticism.
- The desire to protect personal reputations and families.

Your message may stress an appeal to reason—*the rational appeal*—or an appeal to desire—*the emotional appeal.*

 Most successful sales messages combine **rational appeals** (appeals to reason) and **emotional appeals** (appeals to desire).

People seldom buy something just because they have a logical reason for buying it or just because they desire it. Usually, their buying depends upon both reason and desire. A rational reason to buy a car is that you *need* it for transportation. But you make decisions about style, color, and other features based on what you *like*.

One benefit of your product or service usually appeals most forcefully to a targeted group of readers. Make this benefit the CSP of a letter to that group. As you develop this leading appeal, back it up with a discussion of other benefits that may also appeal to the prospect.

Suppose you are selling shoes. Although your CSP may be durability, you would certainly mention such features as good fit and comfort. In another letter, your CSP may be style. While stressing that the shoes are stylish, you may also mention that they fit well, are comfortable, and keep their fine appearance with continued wear.

In every letter, develop the appeal from the reader's viewpoint.

4. Use Accurate Information and Show Sincere Interest in the Reader

Concentrate on facts, not on opinions or exaggeration. Misinformation in a sales letter is unethical and can endanger the success of the message. Your reader may be fooled by misrepresentation and may believe you once, but not twice. Remember that most organizations depend on repeat sales for their profits.

Sincerity in selling means that the service you offer will be useful, practical, and economical for the buyer. Your sales message will not reflect sincere interest in the reader unless you believe that, when you make a sale, you make a friend. Remember that *making friends—developing trust—is the key to making repeat sales.*

5. Convince Your Reader That the Time to Respond Is Now

Imagine yourself talking with, instead of writing to, the prospective buyer. Think of the reasons the person might give for not buying or for waiting until later to decide. Then answer those objections in your letter *before* the reader has a chance to think of them.

At times, the reader may object or hesitate because he or she cannot accept everything you say the product will do. So you must present *evidence* to back up your statements. Three kinds of evidence often used to effectively support sales claims follow:

A Vivid Description of How the Product or Service Can Be Used

Why does the reader *need* your product or service? To answer this question, take a problem-solving approach. First, you must identify a problem that the reader has. Then, in your message, present your product or service as a solution to that problem.

A Sample, a Trial Use, or a Money-Back Guarantee

Sometimes you can provide tangible evidence—a free sample or a trial use of the product or service—so that your reader can personally test the claims. Another way to convince the reader that all you say is true is to give a money-back guarantee. Or you may suggest that no payment is necessary unless the customer is satisfied that the purchase lives up to the sales promises. Notice how well the writer of the following excerpt from a sales letter understands the importance of evidence:

12-1—Check for Reasoning *Critique this: Many companies that sell magazine subscriptions use sweepstakes or contests as a way to get their readers' attention. In fact, many begin with the statement "You have just won $10 million!" Describe the effectiveness of this type of persuasive message.*

Perhaps you are skeptical. It's natural for you to want proof about a sales claim. I want to prove mine by having you try the SENTRY SAFETY system in your own home for 30 days. You be the judge. Either the SENTRY SAFETY system is good—and will work well—or I get it back.

You don't need to make up your mind now. Just mail the enclosed postpaid card. In a few days the SENTRY SAFETY system will be there for you to try.

Performance Facts and Endorsements by Users

Facts based on actual experiences with a product or service or testimonials from current customers provide strong sales support. Both performance facts and testimonials are sometimes included in sales letters. More often, though, the surveys and tests, as well as authentic endorsements, are included in brochures or other literature enclosed with the letter.

If your reader delays a decision to buy, his or her enthusiasm for the product may decline. To encourage an early decision, sales offers may include incentives such as a reduced price or added features. Suppose you are trying to persuade a reader to buy an air conditioner in January. The prospective customer may ask, "Why should I buy now—why not wait until summer when I'm ready to use it?" or "I don't think I can afford that right now." A sales letter would not mention these objections, of course, but may anticipate them. Sales incentives may include:

- *The reduced January sale price:* Regular prices return in February.
- *The storage plan:* Seller holds the air conditioner until the customer requests delivery and installation.
- *Extended credit arrangements:* The first payment is delayed until April 1.

 A good persuasive writer anticipates and overcomes customers' objections.

6. Avoid High-Pressure Selling

Never try to force the reader to buy. Do not mention that the reader needs what you are selling. Most people resent being told what they need. Sales letters usually get better results by telling what the product or service can do and then leaving the decision to buy to the reader. Avoid exaggerated comparisons between your product or service and that of your competition.

7. Introduce the Reader to the Enclosure

If you send a brochure or other enclosure—and you usually do—you can make it an integral part of your sales message if you keep two ideas in mind:

First, refer to any enclosures only after you have provided enough information to interest the reader. Make the reader want to finish reading your letter before making a decision about buying.

Second, refer to your enclosure by suggesting that the reader observe something interesting about it. Offer a specific course of action. The sentence "I have attached a reply card" sparks no interest and prompts no action. In contrast, the reader is drawn to action by these directions: "All you have to do is check your choices on the enclosed postpaid reservation certificate, fold it, seal it, and drop it in the mail."

8. Talk About Price at the Best Psychological Moment

Naturally, somewhere in your letter you must talk about the cost of the item you are selling. Few people decide to buy before they know the cost. If you think the reader will consider the article a bargain at your price, stress the price—as good news—by mentioning it near the beginning of the letter. Price may even be the CSP headlined in the opening sentences. But if you think the price may seem high to the reader, present it toward the end of the letter. Make the reader *want* the product before he or she knows the cost. And make the cost seem less by telling how much the reader is getting for the money. Notice how cost is linked to benefits in this excerpt from the next-to-last paragraph of a letter:

Teachers and parents have discovered the tremendous value of *Science and Nature Magazine* in educating youngsters through the mystery and fun found only in this fantastic nature and science-oriented magazine. It's filled with great pictures and true stories about children around the world, science and adventure, games and puzzles—everything a child loves. A gift subscription for a full year (12 issues) of *Science and Nature Magazine* is only $20.

Another excerpt showing the same technique follows:

Try our new magazine, *Gardens Beautiful,* free for one month. You are under no obligation. If you are not absolutely delighted, write CANCEL on the invoice and owe nothing. But if you love gardening and *Gardens Beautiful* as much as I think you will, you pay only $15.95 for the next 12 issues.

9. Close With a Request for Action

The closing paragraph of your letter often is the key to getting the reader to act. Without specific, easy-to-follow directions, the reader may only *think* about buying the product or service. *Your closing paragraph should tell exactly what to do.* Be positive—assume that the reader wants to do as you ask. Be specific also; for instance:

- Tell the reader to complete and send in the enclosed order form.
- Ask the reader to come into the store for a demonstration session—tell *where* and *when* the session will take place and *what* it will include.
- Tell the reader to invite a representative to call, and give the representative's name, phone number, and office hours. Whenever you can, mention a reason for acting at once.

Remember that the longer the reader waits before acting on your suggestion, the less likely he or she will act at all. Even when the reader is interested in the product and wants to buy, a little push for action is usually needed. Your closing paragraph can provide that push with this *three-way call for action.* In closing, tell the reader all of the following:

- What to do.
- How to do it (make it easy).
- Why it should be done promptly.

Notice how the words in italics in these closing paragraphs from an effective sales promotion letter use the three-way call for action.

> Take just a moment to *jot your name on the enclosed postpaid order card, drop it into a convenient mailbox,* and we'll see that your Whirlwind Vacuum Cleaner is on the way in less than a week.
>
> If you send a check or money order, we will pay all express charges. Or, if you prefer, we'll send the Whirlwind Vacuum Cleaner COD. Just check the appropriate box on the order card.
>
> *With a Whirlwind Vacuum Cleaner, your next cleaning job will be the easiest ever!*

Short closing paragraphs often combine the three persuasive elements in one or two sentences:

> There's no need to bother with a check at this time—we will be glad to bill you later—but do *avoid missing a single exciting issue* of *WORLD-WIDE TRAVEL TODAY* by *returning the postpaid card today.*

You cannot prepare an effective sales letter if you think of the recipients merely as names on a mailing list. Instead, write to a group of people who are alike in at least one aspect—their need for your product or service. The more attributes the members of the group have in common, the easier it is to relate your sales information to the individual reader's interests.

Notice that the sales letter in Figure 12-3 is not a high-pressure sales approach but does ask for action.

April 28, <YEAR>

Ms. Glenda Bonnette
Bonnette's Supply
P.O. Box 49067
Houston, TX 77730

Dear Ms. Bonnette:

Your business demands a great deal of you. Your time is limited. Your decisions are often critical. When you need answers, you need them NOW.

COMMUNICATIONS CENTRAL can help put the resources you need to make those decisions—*where* you need them, *when* you need them, and *how* you need them. You can maintain constant contact with your office and clients, all with your own custom-designed communication system. Whether you need local, national, or international service, we can design a system for you.

Give me a call today at (281) 555-5535, or complete the enclosed reply card. I will be happy to answer any questions you may have and to provide you with a personal demonstration of a communication system designed to meet your specific needs.

Call today and stay in touch tomorrow.

Sincerely,

COMMUNICATIONS CENTRAL

Emily De La Rosa

Emily De La Rosa
Communications Representative

lp
Enclosure

FIGURE 12-3 Note how this effective sales letter asks for action. Merging the letter with a mailing list of prospective customers can easily individualize it.

WRITING SALES LETTERS TO DEALERS

Before you prepare a sales promotion letter for a prospective customer, ask yourself, "How will this customer benefit from the product or service I'm selling?" Then plan your letter around the answer: Your product will help your reader to have more fun, to do a better job and do it more quickly and easily, or to save money.

When the prospective customer is a dealer, you should ask the same question. However, the answers—the benefits to the reader—will be different. Dealers are interested in products and services that will help them do their jobs better, increase profits, and decrease expenses. Therefore, you should use a somewhat different sales approach in letters to dealers.

You can stress two important benefits in sales letters to dealers, turnover and markup, as discussed in the following sections.

1. Emphasize Quick Turnover

Naturally, a retailer is more interested in how much product can be sold in a short time than in any other fact about the product. No matter how much potential profit you can make on an item, if it sits on the shelf, it earns no profit for the dealer. Letters to dealers should stress how fast the product will sell—how fast it will "turn over"—and give facts to prove its popularity with the dealer's customers.

2. Stress a Profitable Dealer Markup

After salability, the dealer's next interest is markup, the difference between the price the dealer pays for the product and the price at which it is sold. (This difference is not the profit; other selling expenses must be deducted before the dealer makes a profit. But turnover and markup are important factors in determining the profit.) Your sales letter should convince the dealer that the difference between the buying price and the selling price is large enough to ensure a satisfactory profit.

The opening paragraph in letters to dealers usually gets attention and arouses interest if it tells what the product or service can do for the reader. A successful opening may be a direct comment about the salability of and markup on the product, like the following:

A quick sale and a 60 percent markup are yours

When a customer spots

REAL SOUND STEREO SYSTEMS

On your showroom floor!

Direct the whole letter to the dealer. Talk about customers' use of the product and the features they will like. Talk about prices and about the advantages of buying in quantity. Stress the ways in which you (the manufacturer and/or distributor) can help the dealer increase the sale of your products. Some dealer aids you may suggest are:

- Your national advertising, which will bring customers into the store asking for the advertised product or service.
- Scannable or camera-ready copy for the dealer's newspaper advertising.
- Display materials and suggestions.
- Envelope stuffers, posters, catalogs, and other publicity items.

A variation of the dealer sales letter, about a promotional package offered by Promotions Unlimited, follows:

Dear Mr. Simpson:

How do your customers react to the words "FREE" and "WIN"? The TREASURE CHEST (shown in detail in the enclosed brochure) will appeal to passersby because you offer them the opportunity to WIN it! All the prospective customer has to do is complete an entry blank with name and address and drop the form into a box!

In one package, you get everything you need for a successful promotion: the TREASURE CHEST containing prizes for the whole family, a giant, colorful window poster, 1000 entry blanks, and an entry box.

The cost? Only $59.95 each! The result? The TREASURE CHEST will bring shoppers inside your doors!

Take a moment to complete the postpaid order card and drop it into the mail. Your TREASURE CHEST will be shipped the day after we receive your order. If you are not completely satisfied, just return the package within 10 days, and you will owe nothing.

If you enclose your check with your order, we will prepay all freight charges.

Sincerely,

WRITING REPLIES TO INQUIRIES AS PERSUASIVE MESSAGES

Every inquiry about your products or services is important, because it opens a door for your sales message. Sales promotion letters written to answer requests for information are often called **invited** or **solicited sales letters.**

The big difference between invited sales letters and other sales promotion letters is that you start invited sales letters with a direct answer to a question asked in the inquiry. You do not need an attention-getting opener. The reader is interested in the answers to his or her questions. You can best hold that interest by answering all questions—direct and implied—completely and promptly.

In invited sales letters you should, of course, stress the advantages to the reader of using the product or service. And you should close with the three-way call for action.

WRITING A SALES LETTER SERIES

A series of sales promotion letters may be sent to prospective buyers when the seller believes that one letter will not accomplish the job of selling the product or service. The two most common kinds of sales letter series are the wear-out series and the campaign series.

Wear-Out Series

You would prepare a number of letters for this series. *Each letter is complete in itself and independent of any other letters* or advertising plans. Send the first letter to a selected list of prospects. Then, send the other letters at intervals to each prospect who has not ordered. The series continues for as long as the seller believes that the prospect may still be in the market. Every letter in the series tries to get an order. You would use this type of message mainly for selling *inexpensive merchandise.*

Campaign Series

This series requires a number of letters, *each one building on the preceding letter.* As you plan these letters, decide on the number of letters to be sent and the intervals—often 10 to 15 days—at which they will be sent. Plan to send a complete series of letters to each prospect; ordinarily, you would not expect an order from your prospect until all the letters had been received. Frequently, this direct mail advertising is coordinated with newspaper, magazine, radio, and TV publicity. Use this type of letter series primarily for selling *expensive merchandise.*

Go to Student CD-ROM Activity 12-2.

SUMMARY

Every message you write is in some way a persuasive message. Your messages are an extension of you and of your organization. Persuasive techniques include:

- Capturing the reader's attention
- Keeping the message interesting
- Building the message around the reader
- Using accurate information and showing interest in the reader
- Convincing your reader that the time to respond is now
- Avoiding high-pressure selling
- Introducing the reader to the enclosure
- Talking about price at the best psychological moment
- Closing with a request for action

When your customer has purchased your product or service, you have maintained goodwill with reselling.

Name _____ Date

WHAT'S WRONG WITH THESE?

Indicate on the lines provided what is wrong with each of the following message excerpts.

1. First sentence used as attention-getting device: Come one, come all.

    _____

2. Last sentence of a persuasive message: We hope to hear from you soon.

    _____

3. Third letter in a campaign series: Please call us today for information on how you can receive our new vegetable slicer for only $5.95.

    _____

4. Letter to a dealer: Even though this merchandise is not a "quick seller," you can still make a profit.

    _____

5. Letter to a customer who has already purchased the product: We appreciate your purchase; unfortunately, this product proved to be unsatisfactory. We will no longer be able to offer this item.

    _____

ANALYZING SALES LETTERS

6. Collect three pieces of direct mail advertising, and mark the AIDA (attention, interest, desire, action) parts of each letter. Keep the letters for Problem 7.

7. On a separate sheet of paper, list the appeals (both emotional and rational) used in each of the letters in Problem 6.

WRITING PERSUASIVE MESSAGES

Prepare (preferably type) the following persuasive messages.

8. Write a letter to persuade your readers to purchase a subscription to *Movie Moments* magazine. The price is $13.95 for 12 issues.

9. Write a promotional message to prospective book buyers. As a representative of a major book retailer, you are responsible for writing a sales letter to announce your new book club. New members can get three free books of their choice if they agree to purchase six additional books within the next 12 months. Supply a customer name and address and the name of your company.

Name _____ Date _____

COLLABORATIVE ACTIVITY

Writing to a Dealer *Plan and write a letter to sell planning calendars in leather binders to retailers.*
These are nice calendar systems that will appeal to the dealer's customers. The dealer will like the markup. Be
sure to describe the calendars' features and the uses to which the customer might put them. You are enclosing
an order form. The suggested retail price is $35; the dealer's cost is $22 each for a minimum order of 25.

PROOFREADING EXERCISE

Proofread the following persuasive message. Mark errors with proofreaders' marks.

Dear Freind:

Are you always looking for knew ways to beautify your home. Do you have your dream
home pictured in your mind? We can help you make those design decisions.

Whether you tastes run from country to formal, you can choose form thousands of
beautiful accessorys for your home and garden. We have a wide range of decorative
items including the new garden ornaments.

Check the box on the enclosed reply card to recieve your free catalog. If you mail your
card today you will never regret it. Beautiful inexpensive objects are waiting for you and
you will be able to decorate your home exquisitely.

Sincerely,

Identifying Commercial Websites
Many Internet sites are commercial sites trying to sell merchandise or services. Search the
Internet for at least two sites that you find appealing. Print the first page of each site. Prepare a
short report identifying the attention-getting devices used and any appeals that you can identify.

Chapter 13

Writing Claim and Adjustment Messages

In Chapter 12 you studied persuasive letters of various types. You then practiced your new skills and knowledge as you composed various persuasive messages. In Chapter 13 you will continue to build on the following skills:

- Requesting and granting an adjustment

- Writing a denial for an adjustment

- Writing a compromise to an adjustment

You will find these types of messages to be especially important in offices that work with adjustments or claims. In your personal life, you may have need of an adjustment on a product that you purchased. Knowing how to secure an adjustment will be very important.

Objectives

After completing this chapter, you should be able to:

- Compose an effective message requesting an adjustment.
- Respond to a claim by granting an adjustment.
- Write a professional claim response that denies adjustment.
- Respond to a claim by compromising on an adjustment.

Ideally, everything runs smoothly in the operation of an organization—no mistakes, no problems, no defects, and no misunderstandings. However, even in the best-managed organizations, dissatisfactions are sure to occur. In recent years consumer movements and federal legislation have made both buyers and sellers more aware of problems caused by business errors. When products or services do not meet customers' expectations, the customers are disappointed and usually complain.

Customer complaints should not be called *complaints*, because *complaint* suggests irritation, unpleasantness, negativism, and even anger. Using a word with such negative connotations could lead to a bad attitude toward customers. Letters or other messages about such complaints should be called **claim letters** or **claim messages.**

Consider these questions: Would you rather have satisfied customers spreading good reports about your organization or unhappy customers complaining about your products or services?

Can you satisfy unhappy customers if you don't know why they are dissatisfied? Unless someone tells an organization that something is wrong, the organization may never know and may repeat the error.

 Before the Internet became popular, marketing researchers estimated that every time a customer felt offended or wronged, 125 people would hear about it—either directly or indirectly. The ability to communicate via the Internet now makes it possible for an unhappy customer to tell millions of people about such a problem. With this potential for negative publicity, reputable organizations are eager to discover, analyze, and correct defects in their products and services as well as problems with how customers are treated.

An organization's primary source of information about such defects is from customers' requests for adjustment.

Many organizations actively seek information about potential problems by providing checklist-type questionnaires for customers to complete. Some businesses mail follow-up questionnaires to customers along with postpaid, preaddressed envelopes. See the "How Are We Doing?" questionnaire in Figure 13-1.

WRITING CLAIM MESSAGES

When you need to make a claim, you may be able to handle it easily over the telephone or by e-mail; but in some situations, you may need to write a claim letter. Some companies take letters more seriously than telephone calls. A claim letter provides a written record that helps protect your rights. In fact, some

13-1—How Can You Complain About a Company? *To whom can you complain if a company will not try to resolve your problem?*

Tabor Automobiles, Inc.
963 Pine Street, Pasadena, CA 99670;
Telephone 904-555-1817; Website taborautos.com

HOW ARE WE DOING?

Dear Customer:

Thank you for bringing your automobile to Tabor for service. Please tell us how we are doing by answering the following questions. Then, drop the postpaid card into a mailbox. We appreciate your response.

	Yes	No	Not Applicable
Was your service representative courteous and helpful?	❏	❏	❏
Was your car repaired to your satisfaction?	❏	❏	❏
Was your car ready at the agreed-upon time?	❏	❏	❏
If applicable, did the service manager return any replaced parts to you?	❏	❏	❏
Did you feel the charges were reasonable?	❏	❏	❏
If you waited, was the waiting room clean and comfortable?	❏	❏	❏
If you used our courtesy car, was the driver prompt and polite?	❏	❏	❏

If you have other comments or suggestions for ways we can improve our service, please write them below:

_____

_____

_____

_____

_____

FIGURE 13-1 One automobile dealer asks its customers to complete this questionnaire.

companies will not even consider a claim unless it is written. Others recommend that you write your claim. For example, on the reverse side of some credit card statements you might find a billing rights section such as this:

> If you think that your bill is wrong, write us on a separate sheet within 60 days. Although you may telephone us, doing so will not preserve your rights.

Although some claims may be handled by telephone, protect your rights by making claims in writing.

Reputable organizations want to keep your goodwill and will do the fair thing; therefore, you should assume that the problem was unintentional. When you write a claim message:

Don't show anger or disgust.

Don't argue or threaten.

Don't try to persuade.

Just tell your story calmly and clearly, with confidence that you will be treated fairly.

 When writing claim letters, just state the facts in a professional manner.

> **WRITING CLAIM MESSAGES**
>
> - **Give identifying information.**
> - **Explain what is wrong.**
> - **Ask for a specific adjustment.**

A letter making a claim and requesting an adjustment will be easy to write if you think of it as a three-step process, as follows:

Step 1: Give Identifying Information

Describe the original transaction with all pertinent facts, including these:

- The date and place of purchase.
- Terms of payment.
- A copy of the sales slip or receipt.
- An account number.
- An invoice number.
- Salesperson's code number or name, if available.

Step 2: Explain What Is Wrong

Present all the facts and details clearly to give your reader a complete and unbiased picture on which to base the adjustment decision. Give a clear, concise explanation of the problem. To determine whether your explanation is clear, reread it as though you were unfamiliar with the situation or ask a coworker to read it.

Step 3: Ask for a Specific Adjustment

Tell the reader what you think should be done. If you are not sure what the adjustment should be, ask the reader to study the circumstances and determine the fair solution.

A clear, complete, concise, and courteous request for an adjustment follows:

Dear Customer Service Manager:

On May 15 I ordered a framed original Salvador Dali lithograph, Catalog No. 49367. I sent Purchase Order 3861 with Check 8639 for $775, which included shipping and handling.

When the lithograph arrived on June 1, the glass was broken and one corner of the lithograph was torn.

I am returning the damaged lithograph to you today via United Parcel Service. Please send a replacement or a refund.

Another well-written message requesting an adjustment follows. Notice that this writer reverses the order of the three steps, but the letter gets the job done just as well.

Ladies and Gentlemen:

Please repair or replace my calculator watch, Model C863, and return it to me at the address above.

After six months of use, the musical alarm has stopped working.

Enclosed is my watch, a copy of the sales receipt showing the date of purchase, and a copy of your warranty, which guarantees material and workmanship for one year.

RESPONDING TO CLAIM REQUESTS

An **adjustment letter** or **message** is a response to a claim. When a business determines that a claim is justified, some adjustment is made. A business may also decide to make an adjustment to maintain or to build goodwill even if the claim is questionable.

Customer satisfaction and goodwill are such important assets that progressive organizations have established customer services, consumer affairs, or customer relations departments to respond to customer claims promptly and graciously. Adjustment personnel should strive to resolve customer claims fairly, quickly, and tactfully, because business success depends on customer satisfaction. Whether a claim is granted or refused, the adjustment letter should strive to build and keep customer goodwill.

 To succeed in business, always try to respond to customer claims fairly and quickly.

13-1:

BEING COURTEOUS.

James wrote a scathing letter to the telephone company complaining that his telephone bill had nine calls on it last month from his house to a city he never calls. He dropped the letter in the mailbox. Then he picked up his own mail, which included a letter from his mother. In her letter, she asked him to send a copy of his long-distance bill so that she could reimburse him for the calls she had made from his phone during her visit last month. James had completely forgotten that she had made the phone calls.

Go to Student CD-ROM Activity 13-1.

Form letters are commonly used in adjustment correspondence; but even a form letter, carefully written without trite phrases, can stress personalized service and genuine concern for the reader.

Read the following two form letters—routine adjustment letters used for problems with magazine subscriptions. Which letter would you prefer to receive?

Dear Sir or Madam:

This letter is to acknowledge receipt of your recent communication relative to your subscription.

It is necessary that you complete the enclosed form and return it immediately.

We will get back to you when we have located and corrected the problem with your subscription.

Dear Ms. Monfredini:

Thank you for letting us know that you have not been receiving your copies of *Stars and Stripes*.

We are checking with our Circulation Department to see what happened. Unless we need additional information from you, you can expect to start receiving your copies of *Stars and Stripes* within ten days.

We appreciate your interest in our weekly news publication.

The second letter is more personalized than the first and is not so brusque, even though it, too, is a form letter.

Writing Responses Granting Adjustments

RESPONSES GRANTING ADJUSTMENTS

- Give the good news.
- Explain and say thank-you.
- Resell your product or service.
- Resell your organization.

Key Point **Start with the good news when you are granting an adjustment.**

When granting a request for an adjustment, follow these general steps:

Step 1: Give the Good News First
Tell the reader that you are gladly granting a full adjustment. Don't let the reader feel you are doing him or her a favor, even if you believe that you are making a

special concession. Instead, convince the reader that goodwill and friendship are more important to you than the money involved and that your organization always wants to take good care of its customers.

Step 2: Give an Explanation and a Thank-You

Express sincere appreciation for the adjustment request. Acknowledge your reader's inconvenience in writing the letter or message and waiting for the adjustment. Emphasize that you welcome this opportunity to set things right. Let the customer know how he or she has helped the organization improve its products or service.

Stress your organization's effort to prevent further customer dissatisfaction. Accept the blame and apologize if your organization is at fault. If appropriate, explain what caused the problem, but don't blame the computer. Most people know that computers don't make errors—only the operators do. Don't make the mistake of saying to your reader, "This will *never* happen again." No one can promise that. If appropriate, explain what your organization is doing to prevent a repetition of the problem.

Step 3: Resell the Product or the Service, and Resell Your Organization

End the message positively. Don't end with a negative phrase, such as "We hope you do not have any more trouble with your Valic Vaporizer." The best ending for a letter granting an adjustment makes no reference to the original problem. End on a note that implies future dealings, and don't overlook the possibility of doing some effective sales promotion for related products or at least some reselling of your organization. If possible, offer the customer a discount on the next order, especially if your company was at fault.

See how these steps are used effectively in the following letter:

Dear Mr. Dailey:

Your new Sun-Safe door awning is on its way to your home. It should arrive in a few days.

Thank you for returning the original awning, which was torn near one of the grommets. Rather than repair the awning, we are happy to send you a new one in the same pattern. Your new awning is made of an improved, highly durable material and comes with a one-year warranty.

When you need exterior accessories, you will find that we carry a wide variety—from outdoor benches to fountains and statuary. You can rely on our guarantee of high quality and "satisfaction or your money back."

Sincerely,

Go to Student
CD-ROM
Activity 13-2.

Note how the letter to Mr. Dailey is organized. First comes the news he wants to hear most—a new awning is on its way. The writer's thanks and explanation are next. Finally, the appeal for another sale is made. This is appropriate because the company has granted an adjustment and satisfied the reader.

Notice the difference in the tone of the following two messages from an Internet mail-order company (see Figures 13-2 and 13-3). Which message would you rather receive?

FIGURE 13-2 An e-mail to Kimberly Morris.

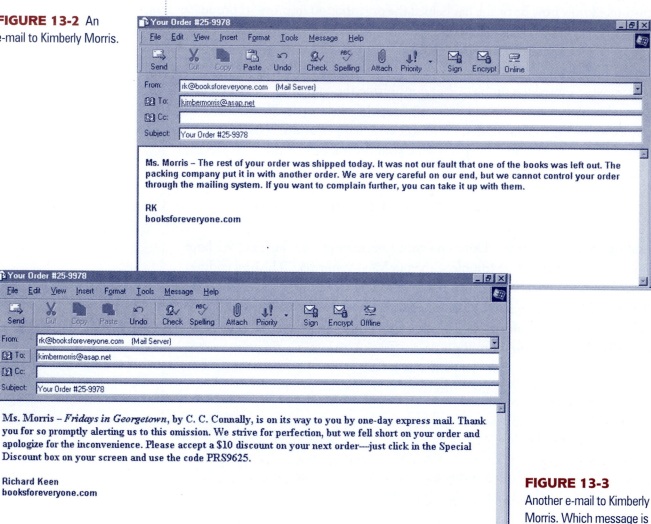

FIGURE 13-3
Another e-mail to Kimberly Morris. Which message is more effective?

Writing Responses Denying Adjustments

An adjustment is not always the appropriate response to a claim. After considering the customer's claim, you may determine that you cannot grant an adjustment. Organizations least like to send—and customers least like to receive—messages that deny adjustments.

 Messages denying adjustments have two purposes:
1. To say no.
2. To rebuild customer goodwill—a difficult task.

Use the effective buffer-paragraph technique when writing messages denying adjustments. Be courteous even when you are answering an angry or distorted claim. If you answer sarcastically, you may lose both your self-respect and your customer. Completely ignore any insults in the message you have received; concentrate on writing an answer that is friendly, rational, and professional. The cost to keep the customer you have is usually less than the cost to find a new customer.

 Denying an adjustment does not mean that you will lose your customer; be fair and refrain from sarcasm.

RESPONSES DENYING ADJUSTMENT

- Start with a buffer.
- Explain.
- Say no.
- End with a buffer.

Follow these four steps when denying a claim:

Step 1: Start With a Buffer

Support the reader's point of view in your buffer paragraph. Since the customer probably thinks that he or she is right, try to coax—not force—him or her to accept the logical solution. Assure the customer that you appreciate the problem and have given individual consideration to the request. Because the requested adjustment is important to the reader, your letter should show that the reader's point of view is also important to your organization.

Step 2: Explain

Present your explanation before the decision. Stress what *can* be done and emphasize your goal—to be fair to all customers. Don't blame and don't argue. Avoid unfriendly, negative expressions such as *your complaint, your error, you misinterpreted, you neglected, you claim, you are mistaken, our records show,* and *your ignorance.* With a truthful and tactful presentation, lead the customer to accept your solution as the only reasonable one.

Step 3: Say No

State or imply that you cannot grant the adjustment.

Step 4: End With a Buffer

Try to leave the reader in a pleasant frame of mind. A friendly but concise closing is even more important when the adjustment is not granted.

Review the indirect approach in Chapter 5 and the Chapter 9 section "Answering No to Inquiries and Requests" for other techniques to help you write effective bad-news messages.

The writer of the following letter realizes the importance of convincing a customer of the organization's position and keeping her as a customer. Read the denial response to Ms. George's request for repair or replacement of her printer.

Dear Ms. George:

You are right to expect high-quality merchandise from Dexter Computers, Ms. George. We stand behind our products when they fail as a result of defects in material and workmanship, as our warranty states.

We appreciate your sending your Model XC printer to us for analysis. We found a sticky residue on the memory board indicating that something had been spilled on it. This residue has caused the electronic components to malfunction. Our service technician estimates that cleaning and repairing your printer would cost $125.

Although we would be glad to repair your printer at a cost of $125, you might consider replacing the printer with our newest Model XXC, currently on sale for $145 with a manufacturer's rebate of $40, which would bring your final cost to $105. The enclosed brochure describes the features of Model XXC.

Please let us know whether you want us to repair or replace your printer. You may call us toll-free at 1-800-555-9911.

Sincerely,

Writing Responses Offering Compromise

You may decide to compromise on an adjustment. In some situations, both the seller and the buyer share responsibility for the problem. In other situations, it is not clear who is responsible. Remember that businesses want to correct problems so that they will keep the customer's goodwill.

 Always try to offer a compromise—your customer will appreciate an option rather than a "no."

> **RESPONSES OFFERING COMPROMISE**
>
> - Start with a buffer.
> - Explain.
> - Say no.
> - Offer compromise.
> - End with buffer.

Follow these steps when writing a message that offers a compromise on an adjustment:

Step 1: Start With a Buffer

Reflect pleasant cooperation in the buffer opening. But don't imply that you are granting the request. If the customer thinks that you are granting the request in the first sentence, he or she may not read the rest of the letter.

Step 2: Explain

State the facts and reasons thoroughly and courteously—but keep the explanation concise. By giving a logical explanation first, you may be able to prevent a negative reaction from the customer.

Step 3: Say No

State or imply the refusal. Make the refusal clear, but de-emphasize it.

Step 4: Offer a Counterproposal or Compromise

Give this offer willingly and graciously or not at all. Remember to let the service attitude show.

Step 5: Use a Buffer Closing

Suggest what action the customer should take, but leave the decision to him or her.

In the following letter, the writer tries to retain the customer's goodwill by repairing the product with no labor charge, even though the warranty has expired:

Dear Mr. Johnson:

As a Sun Lover Pool Company customer, you should expect satisfaction because our pledge is based upon the terms of our sales agreements, including warranties.

Replacement of the two gaskets in your swimming pool pump should resolve your problem. Because the two-year warranty on your pump is no longer in effect, we will not be able to credit your account. However, we will gladly replace the gaskets for you at the cost of the parts, $48.50, with no charge for labor. Our top-quality replacement gaskets are more resistant to chlorine and other swimming pool chemicals than the original gaskets.

If you will please complete and return the enclosed authorization-for-repair form, we will repair your pool pump and ship it back to you within ten days.

Sincerely,

SUMMARY

If you are the consumer and are disappointed in a product or service, the best way to receive a favorable response from a business is to state the facts of the situation clearly and unemotionally and request whatever adjustment seems fair. You will help protect your rights by making your claim in writing.

On the other side, progressive companies must respond to claim messages. The manner in which the response is written determines whether the customer will remain a customer or take his or her business elsewhere.

Writing Claim and Adjustment Messages Checklist

Writing Claim Messages

	Yes	No
1. Did you give all necessary information in your claim letter?	☐	☐
2. Did you explain the problem?	☐	☐
3. Did you ask for a specific adjustment?	☐	☐

Writing Responses Granting Adjustments

	Yes	No
1. Did you give the good news first?	☐	☐
2. Did you give an explanation and thank the writer?	☐	☐
3. Did you resell your product or service and resell your organization?	☐	☐

Writing Responses Denying Adjustments

	Yes	No
1. Did you start with a buffer?	☐	☐
2. Did you give an explanation before saying no?	☐	☐
3. Did you end with a buffer?	☐	☐

Writing Responses Offering Compromise

	Yes	No
1. Did you start with a buffer?	☐	☐
2. Did you give an explanation before saying no?	☐	☐
3. Did you offer a counterproposal or compromise?	☐	☐
4. Did you end with a buffer?	☐	☐

Name _____ Date _____

WHAT'S WRONG WITH THESE?

In the space provided, write what is wrong in each of the following situations:

1. Claim letter text: Dear Customer Service Manager: I will never again order another thing from you. Refund my money immediately to the above address for the enclosed necklace. Your ex-customer, Mary Bell.

   _____

   _____

2. Compromise adjustment letter text: Dear Mr. Lewis: I cannot give you your money back on the above-referenced order. You can, however, come to the store and exchange the item. Sincerely,

   _____

   _____

3. E-mail message denying adjustment: You are right to expect only premium-quality merchandise from us, Ms. Hoventown. However, we are sorry to say that we cannot refund your money. We hope you will enjoy future purchases from us. Sincerely,

   _____

   _____

4. Letter granting adjustment: Dear Mr. Bradley: Thank you for returning the microphone. You must have pulled it out of its connector slot too hard to have broken it in that manner. Your new TRS-10 microphone is on its way to you today. It should arrive within the week. We are sending it free of charge as it should have withstood your pulling on it. Sincerely,

   _____

   _____

WRITING ASSIGNMENTS

On September 20 Lila Peters ordered a solar yard light from a newspaper ad (shown here). The light was supposed to be a gift for a coworker on October 15. Lila specified that her friend's house number be engraved on the inset plate. The light, along with a credit card ticket (shown at left on the next page), arrived on October 30. Lila wrote the letter shown on the next page.

SOLAR YARD LIGHT

Brighten Your Yard With Outdoor Lighting That Needs No Wiring!

Light glows an average of 6 to 8 hours at night

Free engraving on inset plate (maximum of 10 characters). Please specify engraving desired and allow 3 to 4 weeks extra.

Item No. S239C, $58. Shipping and handling included.

**Sunspot Solar Products
989 Monroe Blvd.
El Paso, TX 72991**

Name _____   Date _____

SUNSPOT SOLAR PRODUCTS
989 Monroe Blvd.
El Paso, TX 72991

DATE: 10/26/<YEAR>
MERCHANT#:   111222333
TRAN #:   0008

ITEM#:   S239C
PURCHASE: Solar Yard Light
AMOUNT: $85.00

ACCT: 4144000888999 EXP:0803
AUTH CODE: 009977
NAME: LILA PETERS

X _____
- -
I AGREE TO PAY ABOVE TOTAL AMOUNT
ACCORDING TO CARD ISSUER AGREEMENT
THANK YOU

TOP COPY—MERCHANT
BOTTOM COPY—CUSTOMER

Dear Stupid Solar Light Company:

You idiets sure took you sweet time to send my order and you also goofed it up royally!!!

First-I don't appreciate being charged $85 for a solar light advertised for $58. Did you think you could make a few extra bucks that way and I'd never notice? Well, I'm not that stupid. I happen to read credit card tickets.

You also greatly inconvenenced me. I wanted this for my friend's birthday but it is passed now and I had to by something else. Your ad promised quick delivery and I ordered this over a month ago.

You better credit my credit card account immediately; in fact, you should give me a big discount (half-price would be good) to make up for your error. If you don't, I want to return the light for a complete refund.

Ms. Lila Peters
2986 Saturn Way
Boise, Idaho

---

5. Rewrite Lila's claim letter.

6. As customer relations manager at Sunspot Solar Products, answer Lila's angry letter and grant the half-price adjustment she requested.

7. As customer relations manager at Sunspot Solar Products, answer Lila's angry letter but refuse the adjustment. You can't resell the light because of the engraving. The ad said that engraving would take three to four weeks extra. Correct the credit card charge. Suggest that Lila give the light for another occasion.

8. You own Uptown Construction Company and receive the claim letter on page 265. Compose a compromise adjustment letter. Explain that your cabinetmaker was unable to provide cherry wood because of a nationwide shortage and that it was necessary to use oak to complete the remodeling job on schedule. You will invoice the customer for the cabinets as agreed, but you will pay for and install mulch in the flowerbeds.

Name _____   Date _____

WRITING ASSIGNMENTS *(continued)*

J&J Consultants
2739 Star Drive
Memphis, TN 38114
901-555-3388

September 25, <YEAR>-

Mr. William Anderson
Uptown Construction Company
7396 Fannin Street
Nashville, TN 39025

Dear Mr. Anderson:

Your contract for remodeling our office building provides for installation of cabinets in our employee break room. Although the cabinets have been carefully crafted and installed as expected, they are not made of cherry, as specified in the contract.

We do not feel that the inconvenience and interruptions warrant replacing the cabinets, but we do feel that we should not be charged for them. I am requesting that the cost of the cabinets be deducted from your final bill.

Also, we were disappointed to learn that the flowerbeds were not mulched after the landscaping was completed. Although mulching was not specified in our contract, we feel that mulch should be included in the cost of the landscaping.

Otherwise, we are very satisfied with our remodeled building and are especially pleased that you finished a week ahead of schedule. We will be happy to recommend Uptown Construction in the future.

Sincerely,

Lawrence W. Harkins

Lawrence W. Harkins, Manager

bc

COLLABORATIVE ACTIVITY

Developing Form Messages *You and a partner recently started an Internet gift shop called <giftshop.com>. Your business is growing so fast that you do not have time to compose individual e-mail messages to respond to customer claims. Your system can be programmed to send automatic responses, with a description of the specific item involved inserted into the e-mail message that goes to the customer. Work with one or two other students to compose the wording for two form messages. Indicate where individual insertions will go. You need messages for the two kinds of returns described on the next page.*

Name _____ Date _____

1. **Grant adjustment on returns. You accept returns on items that are not personalized as long as the product has not been damaged. Compose a form message crediting the customer's account.**

2. **Compromise. Your Website clearly states that no credit will be given for personalized items. Therefore, you need a message denying credit if the product was personalized. However, you will grant a $10 credit on the next order over $50.**

PROOFREADING ACTIVITY

Use proofreaders' marks to show all errors in the following claim letter. You should find about ten problems with this letter.

Dear Sir:

On November 31 I ordered one pare of binoculars, Item No. BNN773, for 55.95.

The binoculars arrived on November 12. After trying them for two days, I decide they

weren't no good for watching sports events and so I decided to return them. I want you

to credit my bank card No.5580-566-823-009 and send a copy of the credit to myself.

Sincerely,

Search the Internet for Claim Examples
Go online to the Better Business Bureau. Find out how to file a complaint about a charity, an automobile dealer, or another type of business.

_____

_____

_____

Writing Goodwill Messages

Chapter 13 gave you experiences working with claim messages: writing messages to request, grant, and deny adjustments. You learned how to use a buffer to begin and end a message in certain types of situations. In Chapter 14 you will develop your expertise in writing messages that are sometimes more social than those you have written in other chapters.

Objectives

After completing this chapter, you should be able to:

- Know the appropriate situations for sending goodwill messages.

- Apply the principles for goodwill messages.

- Write messages to thank, announce, express get-well wishes and sympathy, congratulate, invite and welcome, and maintain or reactivate business.

Most business messages have two purposes:

1. To do a specific job, such as ask for or give information, transmit literature, make a sale, or collect an account.
2. To build goodwill.

Every message should try to build and maintain goodwill even if it has another job to do. Sometimes, however, communications have the sole purpose of building goodwill.

 Goodwill messages have only one purpose—to create or maintain good business relations.

Messages written only to build or maintain goodwill are unique because they are messages that *do not have to be written*. If such messages were not sent, no material change in the situation would result. But when someone takes the time to send a goodwill letter, the recipient appreciates and remembers that letter. Often, valuable improvements in human relations are the result of such letters. For maximum effectiveness, send a goodwill message within two or three days of the event that prompted you to write.

What is *goodwill*?

 Goodwill is the favorable attitude and feeling that people have toward an organization or business. Goodwill is an intangible commodity that will ultimately result in increased business for you and your organization.

When an organization shows interest in and respect for a person, that organization has the goodwill of that person.

The personal touch of a goodwill message builds good human relations both inside and outside the organization.

 Internal Goodwill Letters

Goodwill letters to employees and other associates make the organization's work go more smoothly.

 External Goodwill Letters

Goodwill letters to customers show interest—and that is the best way to keep customers. (About two-thirds of the customers who stop buying at a store drift away because of the store's indifference.)

Recipients of goodwill letters especially appreciate them because they are unexpected. Businesspeople seldom take the time to write letters they don't have to write. Therefore, when some businesspeople make this effort, they and their organizations are remembered for their interest in people. This kind of reputation pays off in more satisfaction among customers and employees and in more sales and profits. In addition, goodwill messages almost always reflect well on the sender.

Typical goodwill messages include:

- Messages of thanks
- Congratulatory messages
- Announcements, invitations, or welcome messages
- Messages that express get-well wishes or sympathy
- Messages that maintain or reactivate business

All these messages share one purpose: *to gain the reader's goodwill by showing sincere interest in the reader.*

Whatever their specific purpose, goodwill messages share these characteristics:

- Reader approval
- Friendliness
- Naturalness
- Enthusiasm
- Sincerity

Sincerity is probably the most important characteristic, because a goodwill message that does not sound sincere defeats its purpose. You may recall that these characteristics apply to other successful business messages as well.

 Write goodwill messages sincerely, and keep the spotlight on the reader.

Any goodwill message you write will probably be successful when you can answer yes to the following questions:

1. If you were the reader, would you honestly like to receive this letter or memo?
   A goodwill message does its job only when it makes the reader feel good.
2. Will the reader feel that you enjoyed writing the message and that you mean everything you wrote?
   If the reader detects a bored, indifferent, or overeager tone, he or she may doubt your sincerity and interest.
3. Did you keep the spotlight on the reader?
   To make the reader feel important, put your organization and yourself in the background and convince the reader you wrote the letter *just for him or her.*
4. Did you omit specific sales material?
   The reader will feel let down if your personal good wishes are only a prelude to a sales pitch.

Look at the goodwill letter in Figure 14-1. This letter, from a restaurant supply company, salutes one of the restaurants it supplies for its contribution to the community's homeless people.

Baker's
Restaurant Supply Inc.

294 GRAYSON ROAD   ATLANTA, GA 39721   PHONE: 309-555-2928

January 15, <YEAR>

Mr. Herbert Whitcher, Owner
Café Longoria
5629 Blueberry Drive
Atlanta, GA 39726

Dear Herbert:

It is such a pleasure to be associated with a civic-minded and generous business owner
like you, Herbert. I saw the article in *Atlanta Today* commending you and your employees for donating your surplus goods to the homeless shelter.

Although we all bear the responsibility for helping our homeless, not many of us put the
time and effort into trying to solve this problem.

I salute you for your community service.

Sincerely,

Dogan Baker

Dogan Baker

ap

FIGURE 14-1 This goodwill letter salutes another business for its community service.

THANK-YOU MESSAGES

Just as you can find many occasions for writing personal thank-you messages,
you will also find many opportunities for writing thank-you messages to build
goodwill in your organization.

 You will find many opportunities to say thank-you or well
done. Build goodwill for your organization by taking advantage
of those opportunities.

Routine Thank-Yous

You can send messages of appreciation to:

- A new customer for a first order.
- An established customer for:
    A particularly large order.
    The payment of an overdue bill.
    The last installment of a special-account purchase.

- An individual or an organization that responds to a special appeal or completes a spectacular job.
- Someone in your own organization who makes a suggestion that proves worthwhile or who does something extra.

You may also want to send such messages to:

- Customers who order regularly and pay their bills on time.
- Employees who continually do their work well but unspectacularly.
- Individuals and organizations who cooperate on everyday jobs but get little attention.

Other opportunities for sending thank-you messages are special occasions, special services, and extra responsibilities.

Special Occasions

Businesspeople who want to enhance customer relations frequently send goodwill messages marking major events, such as anniversaries and holidays.

The letter from Honolulu Party Supplies to a caterer in Figure 14-2 projects a warm tone. Who would guess it's a form letter? Word processing software makes it simple to personalize.

HONOLULU **Party Supplies**

'eiki Avenue / Honolulu, HI 93720 / Phone: 214-555-3322

January 3, <YEAR>

Ms. Gabrielle Kent
Kent Catering
1389 Oahu Road
Honolulu, HI 93732

Dear Ms. Kent:

As the new year begins, Honolulu Party Supplies thanks you for your friendship and for the business you have given us during the past year.

In just a few weeks, we will open our second store at 3737 Wapiti. The building contains 22,000 square feet filled with everything imaginable to meet all your party needs.

We hope to continue serving you in the coming year. Together, we can make all your catering events successful.

Sincerely,

HONOLULU PARTY SUPPLIES

Jennifer S. Taylor

Jennifer S. Taylor

st

FIGURE 14-2 This thank-you letter is a personalized form letter.

Special Services

Another opportunity for a goodwill message is acknowledgment of a special service. Your organization could take the service for granted, but you build goodwill by writing a thank-you letter that the recipient does not expect. See the friendly message from Georgia Lambert to Mr. Bailey in Figure 14-3.

PHI CHI BETA *OUR CHILDREN FIRST*

793 Laundry Drive • Redlands, CA 93720 • Phone: 904-555-1122

August 15, <YEAR>

Mr. Phil Bailey, Owner
Bailey's Department Store
293 Main Street
Redlands, CA 93721

Dear Mr. Bailey:

On behalf of the members of Phi Chi Beta and the children in the "Our Children First" program, I want to thank you for opening your store especially for us yesterday.

As you know, burglars entered our storage area Tuesday night and took the clothes and supplies we had collected for the children. Our members had worked hard for two months collecting those items for the children and were determined that the children would have those items before school starts.

You were so gracious to keep your store open on the holiday so that we could replace the items before school starts Monday.

Sincerely,

Georgia Lambert

Georgia Lambert

cn

FIGURE 14-3 A thank-you letter the recipient would not have expected.

Go to Student CD-ROM Activity 14-1.

Extra Responsibilities

Sometimes a message of appreciation is the only "pay" a person gets for accepting an extra responsibility. In these situations, a thank-you letter is necessary. The president of a college sent the following letter to a professor, with a copy to the dean who is the professor's immediate supervisor.

Dear Professor James:

Thank you for giving your time to help our recruitment efforts at last week's College Day. The students seemed to thoroughly enjoy your presentation, and several students commented that they hope to have you as an instructor.

I appreciate your willingness to represent the University. Your professionalism is a great asset to the community.

Sincerely,

J. W. Carlton

J. W. Carlton, President

c: Dean Samuel Starr

14-2—Sending a Copy of Thank-You Message
Why is it a good idea to send a copy of the thank-you message to an employee's supervisor when the employee has given extraordinary customer service?

CONGRATULATORY MESSAGES

A message of congratulations (see the congratulatory letter in Figure 14-4) or commendation is much like a message of appreciation.

- Both recognize and express interest in a worthwhile achievement.
- A message of appreciation says thank-you and implies well done.
- A message of congratulations says well done and implies thank-you.

Yeager
Transportation Company

3391 Glendale Valley Road / Dalton, AL 32921 / Phone: 314-555-5888

July 18, <YEAR>

Ms. Loretta Bradford
City of Dalton
P.O. Box 283
Dalton, AL 32910

Dear Ms. Bradford:

Congratulations on your election to City Council. We need more people like you in our city government, and I am proud to be one of your constituents.

If anyone at our company can help you or the other members of the council, let me know. We will be delighted to be of service.

Sincerely,

Randall S. Yeager

Randall S. Yeager
Vice President

rk

FIGURE 14-4 A congratulatory letter.

When your friends celebrate special events or receive honors, you want to congratulate them. In the same way, businesspeople use congratulatory messages on such occasions as:

- Anniversaries
- Graduations
- Births
- Marriages
- New businesses or homes
- Promotions
- Elections
- Retirements
- Various awards and rewards

These pleasant messages foster a favorable image of you and your organization in the recipient's mind. For instance, this brief congratulatory note went to an executive who had recently become president of the company.

14-3—Why is a written thank-you or congratulations better than merely saying thank-you or congratulations?

Dear Ms. Simmons:

Congratulations on your recent promotion to president of Amstat, Ltd. It is well deserved.

I am sure that the business will grow and prosper under your capable leadership.

Sincerely,

Notice the encouragement in the following letter to a new travel agent who has just landed her first corporate account.

Dear Cynthia:

Landing that first account is an important milestone. Congratulations! We in the travel industry appreciate the time and effort that goes into persuading a potential client to choose a new travel agent.

You're off to a good start, and you'll see your account list grow quickly now.

I hope to see you in Chicago next month for the Advanced Sales Training School. Until then, keep up the good work!

Sincerely,

It is important to distinguish goodwill messages from sales messages. A goodwill message may be an attention-getting device for sales promotion. Compare these two messages:

GOODWILL MESSAGE: Congratulations to the proud parents from Cradle Club Child Care. (A beautiful baby diary accompanies the message.)

SALES MESSAGE: Our sincerest congratulations on the new arrival in your home. We can help you with all of your baby clothes and supplies.

In the first example, the emphasis is on goodwill when a leading child care service sends a beautiful gift to new parents with the congratulatory message. In contrast, emphasis is on sales promotion when a retail store that specializes in infant products sends the parents a message that includes an obvious sales pitch.

Certainly the contractor who received the following sales message was not fooled into thinking that it was a sincere, personal message simply because it began with a congratulatory statement.

> Dear Mr. Knight:
>
> Congratulations on your selection as contractor for the new River Oaks Shopping Mall in Macon!
>
> You, as the contractor, will be interested in selecting quality building materials and supplies. We assure you that our pipe and plumbing supplies can meet your needs . . .

A letter like this one is pure sales promotion with a gimmick opening—it's not likely to build goodwill. A goodwill message should focus attention on the occasion that inspires it. If the writer seems more interested in his or her own organization than in the important events in the reader's life, the reader naturally feels tricked.

Remember that when you write a letter on your organization's letterhead, you speak for your organization as well as for yourself. Your organization is talking *through* you. Thus, when you write a congratulatory message on letterhead stationery, whatever good feeling you arouse in the reader will be for your organization as well as for you personally. Your reader will remember your organization (because you used its letterhead); don't spoil the good impression with an unnecessary sales pitch.

 Build goodwill by focusing attention on the occasion that inspires the goodwill message—don't sabotage your message with a sales pitch.

Oops!

14-1:
ALWAYS CHECK SPELLING
Happy Lines ad in newspaper: "Congradulations on your anniversary!"

ANNOUNCEMENTS, INVITATIONS, OR WELCOME MESSAGES

Businesses have numerous occasions to build goodwill by sending announcements, invitations, and welcome messages to employees, customers, and clients.

Announcements and Invitations

Examples of goodwill announcements and invitations are:

- Announcements of a new business, a new location, or an expansion or reorganization of facilities. These usually include an invitation to visit.
- Announcements of the appointment of a new official or a new representative of the organization.
- Announcements of a new service or policy, often inviting the reader to use it—for instance, when a store announces extended store hours.

A bank announces a new Internet banking service in this example:

Dear Customer:

For your convenience, you may now access your account and do almost all of your banking online. Apply for loans, pay your bills, and check your account balance with a few clicks of your mouse!

Just go to <www.yourbank.com> to try it out. We think you'll like what you see.

Sincerely,

In some companies, formal announcements and invitations are printed in a formal style. Consult a reference manual or an up-to-date etiquette book for the proper wording.

14-1—Learn the Meaning *What does R.S.V.P. mean?*

Welcome Messages

A welcome message is a morale builder that usually has a sales flavor. You may want to write a letter to welcome:

- A new employee
- A new resident of the community
- A new member of a club
- A new customer or subscriber
- A new dealer

While avoiding a specific sales promotion, welcome messages invite readers to call or visit and may include information about the company's services or products.

For example, messages welcoming new residents of a community can benefit both the receiver and the sender. Many retail stores and service firms use these letters regularly to build goodwill and gain new customers.

A typical welcome message is organized as follows. It:

1. Begins with a statement of welcome.
2. Comments favorably on the newcomer's choice of a place to live.
3. Mentions what the firm has to offer.
4. Perhaps even includes a special discount to encourage the customer to come into the store.

Key Point Welcome messages can invite readers to call or visit but should always avoid specific sales promotions.

Notice the friendly tone and service attitude of this letter from a bank president to new customers:

Dear Mr. and Mrs. Littleton:

I was pleased to learn today that you have opened an account at National Bank of Greenville.

In extending to you a warm personal welcome, I want to assure you that our personnel stand ready to assist you with all your banking needs.

We sincerely appreciate your confidence in us, and we will do our best to make your association with us both pleasant and profitable.

Sincerely,

GET-WELL WISHES AND SYMPATHY MESSAGES

When a personal friend or a business acquaintance is ill, you may want to write a note or letter. If the illness is not serious, you can send a humorous get-well card or a cheerful note or letter. If the illness is serious or the person is recovering from a major operation, send a more subdued note or letter. It is appropriate to send a more serious message in this type of situation—not a humorous card that might offend.

Be optimistic when you write to someone who is ill. Mention once at the beginning of the message how sorry you are about the illness. Then talk about a return to normal life, as the writer of the following letter did:

Dear Joseph:

I am sorry to hear that you're in the hospital and hope that, with rest and care, you'll be up and about again soon.

Meanwhile, if I can do anything for you, just give me a call. I wish you a speedy recovery and a quick return to the office.

Sincerely,

Messages expressing sympathy or condolence are often the hardest to write, and many people tend to delay writing such messages until it is too late to send them.

 **Go to Student CD-ROM Activity 14-2.**

The usual occasions for sympathy messages are serious illness and death.

 Sympathy messages are usually short. Be careful not to seem curt, which might make you seem to be unfeeling; however, you should be concise.

As a rule, limit your messages of sympathy to two paragraphs:
- The first paragraph expresses sympathy.
- The second paragraph is a calm and optimistic look toward the future.

Read the following example of a sympathy letter:

Dear Mr. Taylor:

We were all saddened to learn of the death of your company president, Ms. June Dodge. For many years my staff and I enjoyed a close and pleasant business relationship with her. Few banking executives deserve greater respect and admiration.

We know that the memory of June will be with you through this difficult period of adjustment and continue to inspire you in the years ahead.

With sympathy,

14-2:

CHECK THE SPELLING AND USAGE OF PERSONAL NAMES

A manager wrote a welcome letter to Mr. and Mrs. John Appleby, 538 South Drive, Seattle, WA 93726. In the last paragraph, to put a personal touch on the letter, he said, "Mr. and Mrs. Appleton, we look forward to serving you."

Notice that the above letter uses the word *death*—not *passed away, expired,* or other euphemisms.

If you knew the person well, you can add a personal touch to your message by sharing a special remembrance. For example:

> I worked with Sally on the banquet committee; her positive attitude and her enthusiasm kept the rest of us going and made the banquet a great success.
>
> **OR**
>
> I'll never forget how nervous I was my first day on the job. But the first person to welcome me with a big smile was Ken. He made me know that I was going to like working there.

 Add a *personal touch* to a condolence message by citing some small thing the person said or did that showed him or her to be a kind, considerate, and thoughtful person.

This intimate touch, something personal that you alone are able to share about the deceased, will be appreciated and will be comforting to family members or friends.

MESSAGES THAT MAINTAIN OR REACTIVATE BUSINESS

Many organizations use routine customer cooperation as an occasion to send a goodwill letter, as illustrated in the following letter to a new customer who has just made the final payment on a special 90-day account. The acknowledgment—although not necessary—showed that the writer was interested in the customer, and thus it built goodwill.

Dear Ms. Barnes:

Your special account is now marked "Paid in Full"! We appreciate your check for $348 and thank you for your prompt payment.

Customers like you have made possible our growth and success during the past 37 years and will determine our future progress.

Of course, you are welcome to call on our Credit Department as well as any of our other departments whenever we can help. Won't you do this—at any time and often, Ms. Barnes?

Cordially,

It is also a good business practice to send messages to customers whose accounts have been inactive for a long time. This is a way of discovering why former customers are no longer using their charge cards—whether some failure on the organization's part is responsible for lost business. Or the letter may try to persuade customers to start using their charge cards again.

Letters that follow up after a customer has purchased a product or service build goodwill because they show the organization's interest in customers' reactions and its desire to improve its products and services. Read what a full-service hair salon wrote to a new customer:

Dear Jan:

We really appreciate your recent visit to Hilda's Salon for your hair care and manicure needs.

We hope you found our salon to be a pleasant environment with friendly, helpful people to take good care of you. Most important, we hope that you are happy with your hairstyle and manicure.

The enclosed $5 coupon can be used any time within the next six months. Come in soon—let us keep your nails polished and your hair styled to your satisfaction.

Sincerely,

PRINCIPLES FOR GOODWILL MESSAGES

The following checklist summarizes the principles you should emphasize in writing a goodwill message:

1. Write sincerely and with feeling.
2. Make the reader feel important.
3. Keep your message as natural and friendly as a person-to-person chat.
4. Send the message promptly.
5. Avoid the use of humor in goodwill messages—a very fine line exists between humor and sarcasm. Don't take any chances that may lead the reader to misinterpret your goodwill message. You're safer to write a straightforward, sincere message.

Writing Goodwill Messages Checklist

Use the following checklist when writing goodwill messages:

	Yes	No
1. If you were the reader, would you honestly like to receive this letter or memo?	☐	☐
2. Will the reader feel that you enjoyed writing the message?	☐	☐
3. Were you sincere?	☐	☐
4. Did you write naturally?	☐	☐
5. Did you keep your message friendly?	☐	☐
6. Did you keep the spotlight on the reader?	☐	☐
7. Did you omit specific sales material?	☐	☐
8. Did you avoid the use of humor?	☐	☐

SUMMARY

The purpose of a goodwill message is to create or maintain good business relations. Messages that thank, congratulate, announce, invite, welcome, or express sympathy or get-well wishes will ultimately result in increased business for you and your organization.

Successful goodwill messages have in common with other successful business messages the characteristics of reader approval, friendliness, naturalness, enthusiasm, and most important, sincerity.

Name _____ Date _____

WHAT'S WRONG WITH THESE?

Write what is wrong with each of these messages, which were intended as goodwill messages.

1. We at Jacksonville Sales, Inc., wish you a speedy recovery. We have a great sale going and hope that you can stop by before the sale ends.

   _____

   _____

   _____

2. Congratulations on your promotion. Now that you are manager, you can be the one to decide which contractor to hire. And we know that you will find us to be the best in the field.

   _____

   _____

   _____

3. We at United Janitorial Service—the Cleanest Cleaners in Cleveland—welcome you and your business to the community. We are the top janitorial service in town, and we want your business.

   _____

   _____

   _____

4. I am sorry to hear that you're in the hospital with a hernia. I had a hernia about two years ago, and it was really rough. It took a very long time to get back to normal.

   _____

   _____

   _____

WRITING

For each of the following problems, prepare a message that will build goodwill. Make a plan, write a rough draft, edit the rough draft, and prepare (preferably type) each letter on a separate sheet. Supply details to make your messages cordial and interesting.

5. Write one of the following appreciation messages, substituting a more original approach for the usual "thank-you for" opening:

   a. As general manager of WKLL, the public broadcasting television station in your area, you need to thank the viewer who has donated an oriental rug for the semiannual fund-raising auction.

Name _____ Date _____

WRITING *(continued)*

b. You are president of your college's student advisory council. Write a letter to a nationally known tennis personality to express appreciation for the inspiring statements the speaker made at your college graduation. The speaker talked about drugs and alcohol.

6. Write one of these two letters of congratulations:

   a. Write to one of your former high school teachers who has received the Citizen of the Year award in your hometown. He or she has long been active in community affairs.

   b. As president of your town's Economic Development Corporation, write to Mary Meeks, owner of Meeks Industries, to congratulate her on the recently completed addition to the plant and the new production line, which will provide 125 new jobs.

7. Plan and type an acknowledgment and thank-you message. As president of Phi Beta Lambda, your college's business club, you asked the manager of a local supermarket to donate food items. The manager has agreed to donate $200 worth of food. Your club will use those items at the campus Spring Festival, in a food booth, with sales proceeds going to help pay for the group's trip to the state convention.

COLLABORATIVE ACTIVITY

Writing Congratulatory Messages *One team member is to write a message commending your employee for his or her extra work on a project. You are also sending a large fruit basket. The other team member should respond to your nice words and gift with an appropriate thank-you message. Assume any other facts needed.*

PROOFREADING ACTIVITY

Using proofreaders' marks, indicate all errors in the following letter of commendation:

> Deer Stacy:
>
> On behalf of Lyon Communications, thank-you for you suggestion to eliminate Form A22 for reporting equipment problem. By using a on-line system to report these problem, the company will safe at least $4,000 each yr. in paper costs and employee time.
>
> We appreciate your bringing these extra cost to our attention, we will certainly consider any future suggestions. Keep up the good work!
>
> Sincerely,

Name _____ Date _____

Search the Internet for Online Greetings

Go to <www.Hallmark.com> or <www.bluemountain.com>. Look through the various kinds of online greeting cards available. Find several examples of appropriate wording for condolence or get-well messages.

_____

_____

_____

_____

_____

PART 3

Writing Other Effective Communications

As you know, writing effective communications is an important task that requires planning and revising to make the message clear and understandable. Remember that your goal is not only to make all your documents so clear that they can be understood but also to make them so clear that they can't be misunderstood.

In Part 1 you studied the principles of good writing, including:

- Choosing the right words, writing sentences and paragraphs, and building goodwill.
- Composing, editing, and proofreading.

In Part 2 you studied how to write effective documents, such as:

- E-mail
- Orders, acknowledgments, credit and collection messages, persuasive messages, claim and adjustment messages, and goodwill messages.

In Part 3, the chapters listed below present the concepts that you will need to continue your study of other effective messages:

In Chapter 15 you will study special types of communications written to public officials and the media. These communications will go to editors, lawmakers, and those in the media services.

Chapters 16 and 17 will concentrate on reports: notices, agendas, minutes, and collaborative reports. You will also compose memo reports as well as learn how to make an oral presentation based on a report.

Chapter 18 emphasizes writing directions, instructions, and abstracts. You will also practice writing a summary or synopsis of a document.

Here are the chapters in Part 3 that enhance what you have already learned in Parts 1 and 2 and continue to build your business writing skills:

professional business writing

Chapter 15

Writing Public Officials and the Media

You learned how to write order letters, acknowledgments, and similar types of communication documents in the previous chapters as you perfected some of your grammar and proofreading skills. In Chapter 15 you will continue to perfect your skills as you discover how to write messages to:

- Lawmakers

- Editors

- Media

Objectives

After completing this chapter, you should be able to:
- Write a legislative letter to a lawmaker.
- Write a service letter to a lawmaker.
- Write a letter to the editor.
- Write a news release.
- Prepare a newsletter.

WRITING LETTERS TO LAWMAKERS

Writing letters to lawmakers is one of the most meaningful ways you can participate in our democratic system and be sure your voice is heard. Good citizens and progressive organizations take an interest in the world around us because laws affect all aspects of our lives and the organizations in which we work.

 Key Point Lawmakers represent the citizens who live in their district. These citizens are called the **constituents** of the lawmaker.

Lawmakers are very interested in how their constituents feel about issues being considered by legislative bodies. Many lawmakers seek opinions on current issues through questionnaires mailed periodically to constituents along with regular newsletters.

 Key Point The best and most convincing way to express your opinion to a lawmaker is through an individually written letter.

You may wonder, "Will my letter really make a difference?" With rare exceptions, lawmakers not only read their mail but are very interested in the contents. Letters that aren't read by the lawmaker are handled by key staff personnel who relay the contents to the lawmaker.

Your letter, just like your vote, does count. Although your letter alone may not change or add a law, your opinion combined with the opinions of many other constituents, can result in change. In a number of cases over the years, Congress has repealed a law because of the avalanche of mail opposing it.

Many lawmakers receive more than 6000 pieces of mail each week, and they are unanimous in their view that letters are an important aspect of learning the feelings of their constituents. It would be difficult for any lawmaker to vote against an issue that is backed by numerous letters of support from constituents.

Which lawmaker do you write to? *There are federal, state, county, and local lawmakers.* Determine which level of government has jurisdiction over the subject you are concerned about and write to that lawmaker. For example:

Public aid questions	Write to someone at the state level
Social Security or federal taxes	Write to someone at the federal level
Rezoning property to open a business	Write to a local lawmaker

Characteristics of a Good Letter to a Lawmaker

The following sections provide guidelines to use when writing to a lawmaker.

1. Give Complete Information About How You Can Be Reached

Be sure to include your address and a phone number where you can be reached during normal business hours. Use your organization stationery *only* if you are representing the views of your organization. Otherwise, use your personal stationery or plain paper with a complete heading, including your phone number.

Oops!

15-1:
WRITING LETTERS TO PUBLIC OFFICIALS
Jessica wrote to her senator in Washington, D.C., asking to have the graduation requirements changed in her high school. Did she write to the right person?

2. Address Your Lawmaker Properly

Consult a good reference manual for correct titles and salutations. It is appropriate to address most lawmakers as "The Honorable . . . ." Many newspapers publish a list of names and addresses of area lawmakers at least once a week. The library and the Internet are also good sources for this information.

3. Use a Subject Line

Identify the topic you're writing about. If the topic is a bill, include the bill name and number, if known, or the popular title. Remember, more than 20,000 bills are introduced each year, so this identification is important.

4. Be Concise

Discuss only one issue in each letter, and do it concisely. Organize the letter using the direct approach, and present your points in a clear, logical order.

5. Use Your Own Words

Form letters and postcards with identical wording have less impact than a carefully thought-out individual letter. Petitions with dozens of signatures carry little or no weight, because lawmakers know that many of these signatures are from disinterested people who have signed a petition because they were asked, not because they feel strongly about the issue.

6. Tell Why and How

When expressing your opinion about a bill under consideration, tell *why* you feel the legislation is good or bad and *how* the legislation affects you and other citizens in your district or state. Give factual personal examples and observations to strengthen your case. Do not exaggerate. Use facts and figures, and include copies of pertinent articles and editorials from newspapers and magazines. You could also prepare a brief, easy-to-follow fact sheet to enclose with your letter. A fact sheet might look like this:

Fact Sheet

Keep the three-way stop at the intersection of Logan and Woodlawn Avenues

- Almost 20 years ago a three-way stop was installed at this intersection because a grade school student was struck and killed by a speeding car as she walked home from school.
- Traffic is twice as heavy today as it was 20 years ago.
- Many children (20 to 25 children of elementary school age) still live in this area and must cross the street daily.
- Schoolchildren board and disembark from a school bus at this intersection.
- The city bus (which was not in operation when the stop signs were put up) would be more exposed to accidents, since it turns south on Logan from Roselawn. When the bus turns south, there is limited visibility to the north because the street curves at this point.
- Without the stop sign at this intersection, Logan would be the longest stretch of residential street in this city without a stop sign or signal to slow the traffic.

Remember: *why* you believe that the legislation is good or bad and *how* the legislation affects you, your coworkers, your profession, your community, or other people in your district or state are the most important parts of your letter to a lawmaker.

7. Be Courteous and Rational

Avoid starting your letter with the cliché "As a citizen and a taxpayer . . . ." Your lawmaker will likely view this kind of opening in a negative way. Don't be rude to your lawmaker or threaten him or her with a statement such as "If you don't vote for this bill, I won't vote for you in the next election!" This makes you appear emotional, unstable, and irrational. If you are perceived this way, what you have to say will have little or no credibility. Logical reasons work much better than threats. The wording of your letter should be courteous and professional.

Be sure to sign your letter. Anonymous letters are disposed of, unread.

8. Watch Your Timing

Express your views as early as possible, before decisions have been made. Write early in the legislative session before a bill comes to a vote of the full legislative body. After a bill has been introduced, write to the committee members when the hearings begin and to your lawmakers before the bill comes to the floor for debate and vote. Your lawmakers are glad to hear from you any time, but obviously your letter is more effective if it arrives while your lawmakers are still deciding how to vote. The Congress and many state legislatures have telephone hotlines or Internet sites so that interested citizens can find out the current status of bills.

Almost all lawmakers answer their mail. If the reply you receive is just a brief acknowledgment, write again to ask for more specific information from your lawmaker, for instance:

- How do you stand on the issue?
- Do you support or oppose the bill?

A follow-up letter will show that you're really interested.

Don't send a photocopy of your letter to other lawmakers who represent you. Courtesy dictates that you write each one individually—an easy task with word processing.

Constructing a Letter to a Lawmaker

Type your letter if at all possible, because a typed letter looks more businesslike and more professional (and is usually easier to read) than a handwritten letter. If you must write in longhand, be sure that your writing is legible and that your name, address, and phone number are included. You must include your address to receive a reply.

 Letters written to lawmakers fall into two general categories: (1) legislative letters and (2) service letters.

Legislative Letters

Legislative letters deal with legislation, or laws, that affect everyone. For example, raising the speed limit on interstate highways or requiring seatbelt use by all passengers in a vehicle would require a legislative letter. Use the direct approach in these letters. A typical outline for a legislative letter is given in Figure 15-1.

(use plain paper unless you are writing on behalf of your organization)

Current Date

The Honorable _____ _____
House of Representatives
Room Number and Building Name
City, State ZIP Code

Dear Representative _____:

Subject: (Give the bill number or identify the issue)

Paragraph 1
- State your support of (or opposition to) the issue you're writing about.
- Include the bill number, if known, and popular title.

Paragraph 2
- Tell *why* you support (or oppose) the issue, giving local and/or personal examples, experiences, and observations.
- Quote statistics (and their sources), if available, to back up your view.
- Enclose copies of published articles supporting your view.
- Explain *how* this issue affects you, your family, your colleagues, your community, and/or your state.

Paragraph 3
- Ask the lawmaker to sponsor or support (or oppose) the legislation discussed in the preceding paragraph(s).

Paragraph 4
- Express appreciation for the lawmaker's having considered your views.
- Ask for a reply.

Sincerely,

Your name

Street address
City, State ZIP Code
Phone number

Enclosure (if appropriate)

FIGURE 15-1 This plan for a letter to a lawmaker is used for a *legislative letter* (one that deals with laws that affect everyone). Legislative letters should be mailed to the lawmaker's state or federal office.

Legislative letters should be mailed to the lawmaker's state or federal office address because your lawmaker must work with other lawmakers and committees to get legislation passed.

Service Letters

Service letters involve requests to help individuals cut through the red tape (procedures and paperwork) of government programs. For example, an individual may inquire about Social Security or veterans' benefits, immigration and passports, or other programs operated by state or federal governmental agencies. These letters also use the direct approach. A typical outline for a service letter is shown in Figure 15-2.

(use plain paper for this letter)

Current Date

The Honorable _____ _____
United States Senate
Room Number and Building Name
City, State ZIP Code

Dear Senator _____:

Subject: (Name the agency and give your identification number)

Paragraph 1
- Concisely state the background of the problem.
- Be sure to give information in chronological order.

Paragraph 2
- Explain your problem.
- Tell what you've done to attempt to solve your problem.
- Enclose copies of any pertinent documents.

Paragraph 3
- Give written permission for your lawmaker to examine your records or files.

Paragraph 4
- Ask for what you need to solve the problem.
- Ask for a reply.

Sincerely,

Your name

Street address
City, State ZIP Code
Phone number

Enclosure (if appropriate)

FIGURE 15-2 This plan for a letter to a lawmaker is used for a *service letter.* Service letters should be mailed to the lawmaker's local office.

Service letters should be sent to the lawmaker's local or district office because these offices handle most service work. Because of the Privacy Act of 1974, you may need to provide a signed privacy release authorizing your lawmaker to contact the federal or state agency on your behalf.

Internet sites for additional information about the Privacy Act of 1974 and the Freedom of Information Act are:

<http://www.tncrimlaw.com/foia_indx.html>

<http://www.usdoj.gov/04foia/index.html>

<http://www.ins.usdoj.gov/graphics/aboutins/foia/index.htm>

<http:/usgovinfo.about.com/newsissues/usgovinfo/Library/foia/ blprivacyact.htm>

Sending Your Message

Technology now makes it possible to send messages by a variety of methods. Today, many lawmakers have a Website with a direct link to e-mail. A survey of members of Congress conducted by OMB Watch (a nonprofit interest group in Washington) has shown which forms of communication congressional offices take most seriously. In order of importance, they are:

1. Personal letters
2. Personal visits
3. Telephone calls
4. Faxes
5. E-mail
6. Petitions
7. Preprinted postcards
8. E-mail form letters

At the time of publication of this book, the results of the study "Congressional Use of the Internet" could be found at <http://www.american.edu /academic.depts/spa/ccps/research1.htm>. The article "Speaking Up in the Internet Age: Congress and Internet Communication: Use and Value of Constituent E-mail and Congressional Web Sites" was at Website <http://www.ombwatch.org/ombw/>.

Follow-Up Letters

Even though your lawmakers are paid to represent you and to help you, courtesy requires a thank-you letter when they have voted the way you want them to vote on legislation and/or helped you as a result of a service letter. Review the section "Thank-You Messages" in Chapter 14.

WRITING LETTERS TO EDITORS

A letter to the editor is an excellent way to reach a large audience. The "Letters to the Editor" section of newspapers is often one of the most widely read sections. Community leaders and lawmakers learn the public's feelings about current issues from these letters. Nearly all groups in the media encourage their readers, listeners, or viewers to send written responses to their publications, programs, and editorial comments. People who write these letters of response are eager to share their convictions, knowledge, and concerns with others.

Concerned citizens and conscientious organizations write letters to editors to:

- Share a view.
- Express a concern.
- Correct an error or misleading information.
- Suggest an improvement.
- Give information.

 People tend to accept as fact anything that is printed or broadcast. Therefore, a person should feel an *obligation* to write a letter to the appropriate news media when a report is erroneous or misleading.

Characteristics of an Effective Letter to the Editor

The following suggestions will help you write an effective letter to the editor. Although the focus here is on letters to be printed in newspapers or magazines, the same suggestions apply to preparing an editorial message for a radio or television broadcast.

1. Get Right to the Point

Say outright why you're writing the letter. Give enough details so that your letter is meaningful to all readers, even those who know nothing about the topic. Answer the obvious questions that will be in readers' minds.

2. Be Brief—Discuss Only One Topic

Short words and sentences make your letter more readable. Keep your letter short, but do include all the important points. Remember to limit your letter to one topic.

3. Be Rational

Even though you may be responding to something that really angers you, resist the temptation to write a sarcastic rebuttal. Emotionally charged letters help increase readership at your expense. You'll be embarrassed when you see your angry letter in print. Your letter should be polite and professional.

4. Use Good Taste

Avoid insulting a race, religious group, political faction, ethnic group, or minority. Letters that are libelous or contain personal attacks are not published by reputable editors.

15-1—Check the Meaning of Words
What *does* libel *mean*?
What *does* slander *mean*?

5. Be Fair and Accurate

Every story has two sides. Your argument isn't weakened by showing an awareness of another approach. Be certain that all your data and facts are accurate. The best approach is: If you can't prove it, don't use it.

Constructing a Letter to the Editor

Here are some guidelines for formatting and delivering your letter.

1. Follow the Rules

Most publications have an *editorial page* where letters to the editor are printed. Usually the publication provides some guidelines for how these letters should be prepared. Most newspapers and magazines accept e-mail or faxed letters to the editor. Space is limited, so pay particular attention to length specifications. If no length guidelines are given, limit your letter to 200 to 300 words. (Messages to be broadcast are often even shorter. Contact the radio or TV station for guidelines.) Representatives of the publication may edit letters for length, accuracy, and good taste.

2. Type Your Letter

Ideally, your letter should be typed double-spaced with indented paragraphs and wide margins.

3. Meet the Deadline

If your letter is triggered by a recent news story or editorial, write your letter the same day, while the topic is still news. If you are responding to a recent article or letter to the editor, be sure to mention that fact in your letter and give the title of the letter and date of publication. If you wait too long, your letter may not be considered for publication.

4. Identify Yourself

 Always sign your letter to the editor with your full name, title (if pertinent to the topic), and address. And include a telephone number where you can be reached during the daytime. Before publishing your letter, most editors will call to verify that you actually wrote it.

Your name and address (city and, if relevant, state) will probably be published with your letter. A few newspapers will withhold signatures if the editor feels that the circumstances warrant it, but most will not. Magazine editors are more likely to withhold from print a name or location if the writer requests this and the topic is sensitive, but a letter still must be signed. Anonymous letters lack credibility and are seldom published.

The outline in Figure 15-3 can be adapted to most letters to the editor.

15-2—Length of Letters for Publication *Why is it important to limit your letter to the word count given by the publication?*

15-3—Letter Formatting *Why is it a good idea to double-space your letter and use wide margins?*

Current Date

Letters to the Editor
Name of newspaper or magazine
Street address or P.O. Box
City, State ZIP Code

Dear Editor:

Paragraph 1

- Tell what topic your letter is covering.

- Tell what your stand or position is on the topic.

Paragraph 2

- Give your explanation, facts, and reasons.

- Give specific examples, if appropriate.

Paragraph 3

- Give your summary or conclusion.

Your full name
Title (if pertinent to the topic)
Organization name (if pertinent to the topic)
Street address or P.O. Box
City, State ZIP Code

Phone number (where you can be reached during the day)

FIGURE 15-3 This plan is used for an effective letter to the editor. Note that the body is double-spaced because the letter is to be published.

WRITING NEWS RELEASES

The news release, like a letter, is used to build goodwill and promote your organization.

Go to Student CD-ROM Activity 15-1.

 A **news release,** also called a **press release,** announces something that has happened or will happen. It is prepared for the media by someone representing an organization or business. The purpose of a news release is to inform the public and create a favorable image of the company or organization.

An article about your organization or business that appears in the news and business section of a newspaper or magazine is more believable and gets more attention than the same information given in an advertisement.

Larger organizations may have a public relations department to handle this aspect of promoting the organization, but all employees have a responsibility to contribute to good public relations and to their organization's positive public image. You may be responsible for writing the final copy of a news release or for preparing a draft to be edited and polished by the public relations department. Or you may write a news release for a service or professional organization to which you belong.

News releases may announce:

- A new or improved product or service.
- The appointment or promotion of a top executive.
- New or expanded facilities.
- Awards earned or community services donated by employees or the organization.
- Financial activities.
- Any news that shows a positive, progressive organization.

Subjects or events that promote an organization's positive image are appropriate topics of news releases.

Characteristics of a Good News Release

 Since a news release is really a news story, write it in a *journalistic style* with the *most important information first.* Give the relevant *who, what, why, where, when,* and *how* information in the first paragraph of a news release.

Give the information in descending order, with the most newsworthy information first and the least important details last. If the release must be cut, the editor can easily remove the least important information from the end of the release.

Constructing a News Release

Avoid starting your news release with the name of your organization or its chief executive officer. You don't want the editor to view your news release as an advertisement in disguise.

Although portions of certain types of news releases (promotion and new product announcements, for example) are edited and routinely published in trade journals and the business section of many newspapers, others will be printed or broadcast only if the editor considers the information to be newsworthy. In these cases, the information in the opening paragraph must grab the reader's attention.

The media will be more likely to use your news release if you start with a local-news, human-interest, or public-service "angle," or perspective.

Here are some examples of how a news release might emphasize these angles:

LOCAL NEWS: *Centralia native* Alice M. Jacobs yesterday was named president of . . .

HUMAN INTEREST: Mike Kennedy, the volunteer firefighter who last week *rescued an 8-year-old girl* from the icy Middlefork River, will be honored this evening at 7 p.m. at the City Council Meeting. Kennedy, a travel agent at Williams Travel Firm, . . .

PUBLIC SERVICE: Ballet Central is on its toes again, thanks to *a donation of 100 pointe shoes* from Braun Shoe Company . . .

Editors welcome brief, concise news releases, but they would rather have too much information than too little. "Too much" can be edited; "too little" may cause time-consuming telephone calls and could result in the release being tossed into the wastebasket.

Follow these suggestions when preparing a news release:

15-2:
ALWAYS CHECK FACTS AND FIGURES
A news release said: "Lisa Smith, third grade teacher at Maple School, was honored for her many years of service to the school. She is retiring after 3 years of service."

Observe how these suggestions were followed in the routine news release in Figure 15-4.

Many word processing programs today have *news release templates,* which are formatted with the information needed in news releases. These templates may be arranged differently from the guidelines given here, but the basic information is included. Using a news release template saves time.

From: Pat Foster
Good Sports International
3378 Logan Street
Colby, KS 67701
301-555-7000

March 14, <YEAR>

FOR IMMEDIATE RELEASE

VICE PRESIDENT NAMED AT GOOD SPORTS

Stephanie Morris has been named vice president of operations at Good Sports International in Colby, Kansas. The announcement was made by Angela Trower, company president.

Ms. Morris will be responsible for all aspects of the marketing operations. Her professional affiliations include serving two terms as president of the American Marketing Association in Kansas. Currently, she is president of the Colby Chamber of Commerce and a member of the Colby Public Library Board.

Ms. Morris, a native of Topeka, Kansas, is a graduate of the University of Illinois at Urbana, Illinois. Her career interest began when she was a summer intern at the Nikki plant in Somerville, Kansas.

END

FIGURE 15-4 This news release gives all the information needed and is typed correctly.

NEWSLETTERS

Go to Student CD-ROM Activity 5-2.

Communication is a major ingredient in the smooth operation of any organization. A newsletter should educate and inform an audience whose members have similar interests. To get the same information to each employee, customer, or member, many groups publish periodic newsletters. A newsletter may be:

- Printed and distributed.
- Attached to an e-mail message so that it can be opened and printed.
- An e-mail message.
- On a Web page on the Internet.

Types of Newsletters

15-4—Look Up Word Meanings *What does* periodic *mean?*

 Newsletters are communication tools and usually fall into one of these categories: (1) customer or sales newsletters, (2) employee newsletters, or (3) membership newsletters. Newsletters are a combination of *news* (valuable information) and a *letter* (using friendly, personal tone).

Customer or Sales Newsletters

A customer newsletter is prepared for customers and potential customers to help market your products and services as well as build goodwill for your organization. The purposes of a customer or sales newsletter include the following:

- Increase sales to existing customers and clients
- Sell more high-profit products
- Sell new products
- Maintain the products' reputation
- Resell a product by explaining its features and capabilities
- Keep customer satisfaction and goodwill
- Announce customer appreciation sessions or events

A newsletter is usually not viewed as "junk mail" and is therefore more apt to be read.

Employee Newsletters

An employee newsletter is prepared for all employees in an organization. An employee newsletter can have a number of purposes, for example, to:

- Announce dates, times, and places for upcoming events and meetings
- Explain changes in policies or procedures
- Announce changes in management or staff
- Recognize special contributions by employees
- Welcome new employees
- Report on changes in benefits packages
- Answer frequently asked questions
- Share health and fitness tips
- Announce any training or workshop available to employees

Membership Newsletters

Today most trade and professional associations, societies, nonprofit organizations, and so forth, publish a newsletter as a communications tool (see Figure 15-5). A membership newsletter can also have a variety of purposes, for example, to:

- Get current members to renew their memberships
- Attract new members
- Report on new services or products
- Ensure that members understand the benefits of membership
- Report on the election of organization officers
- Announce meetings or other benefits to members
- Promote attendance at upcoming events
- Share information or tips that will help the members
- Recognize members who have contributed to the organization

FIGURE 15-5 This is a basic newsletter (printed front and back) to keep members informed of activities of the organization. (Courtesy of Danville Area Community College Education Association.)

DACCEA
VOICE

September 14, <YEAR>

The Voice is a newsletter published periodically to communicate items of interest to DACCEA members and other interested parties.

Local Government Health Plan

Attached is a fact sheet direct from IEA about the local government health plan and the requirement for all employees to participate. We'll keep you posted on any additional information that comes to us.

Association Officers

Congratulations to our newly elected DACCEA officers:

President................Tom Solon
V. President ....Fred Payne
Secretary ....Connie Schroeder
Treasurer...........Steve Downing
Reg. Council Rep.....Lynn Moody
Alt. Reg. Rep ......Carolyn Jensen

Please contact any of the officers with questions, concerns, ideas, etc., you may have.

Brown Bag Lunch With Dr. Jacobs

Your Social Committee is providing an opportunity for all faculty members to meet and talk with our new president, Dr. Alice Jacobs. Come join your colleagues for a brown bag lunch (or purchase something at Eurest). This event is scheduled for:

> **Brown Bag Lunch**
> **Wednesday, September 29**
> **Lincoln Hall**
> **Cooper Penny Room**
> **All DACCEA Members Welcome**
> **Special Guest: Dr. Jacobs**

Drop in anytime between 11 a.m. and 1 p.m. Stay as long as you can. Drinks and cookies will be provided by DACCEA.... *Continued on back*

Introduce yourself to Dr. Jacobs so that she will know what a great faculty we are, and that we are extremely interested in working together to keep DACC one of the best community colleges in Illinois.

Be an Active Member of Your Association

It's not too late to be an active member. Look over the list of committees and call or e-mail one of the officers to volunteer.

Social
Constitution
Bargaining
Grievance
The Voice (newsletter)
Contract Language
Communication
Public Relations
Insurance
Mentoring (for new members)
PAC (Political Action Committee)

September Association Meeting

Mark your calendar

> DACCEA Meeting
> Thursday, September 23
> Tech Center Room 139
> 2:30 — 3:20 p.m.

The Constitution Committee has been working and will have some proposed bylaws to present to the

association members. The agenda will also include an update on several other pertinent items of interest to the membership.

District 507 Board Meeting

The September Board Meeting is Tuesday evening, September 28. This will be Dr. Jacobs' first meeting, so let's have a big faculty representation there. Your presence is always welcomed whether or not you have signed up to attend.

If you have signed up and find you cannot attend, please notify Connie Schroeder as soon as you can. It would be extremely helpful if you could find a substitute or trade places with another association member.

Treasurer's Report

You will be receiving information from Steve Downing, our Treasurer, in the next two or three weeks about membership dues. Payroll deduction will again be an option.

Future Issues of *The Voice*

Please send items, articles, facts, etc., that you believe are worthy of including in future issues of *The Voice*. Forward them to any of the DACCEA officers.

Preparing a Newsletter

The first step in putting a newsletter together is to determine who your audience is and what your purpose is. You want people to read your newsletter carefully rather than throw it out with barely a glance. The newsletters people read contain useful information presented in appropriate and appealing ways. Readers are attracted by content and design that are targeted to their needs. Successful newsletters keep two things in mind:

- The interests of the reader
- The goals of the newsletter

Guidelines for Preparing a Newsletter

The guidelines on the next page will help you prepare your newsletter.

1. Project a Professional Image

Make the front page eye-catching. Most readers will go to the front page first and, at this point, form their first impression of the newsletter. Have at least three articles on the front page.

2. Use a Nameplate

Prepare a **nameplate** to be located in the same place on each edition of the newsletter. The nameplate contains (1) the name of the newsletter, (2) the name of the organization producing or sponsoring the newsletter, and (3) any graphic or logo associated with the nameplate.

Nameplates are usually located across the top of page 1, or they run vertically along the left or right side of page 1. Sometimes the nameplate is mistakenly referred to as the masthead. (A **masthead** contains editorial information about the newsletter, including the name and address of the sponsoring organization, name of the editor, circulation, frequency of publication, volume number, and so on.)

3. Use Headlines

Use a **headline** (title) for each article. Use larger type than body text for the headline. This makes the newsletter appear easy to read.

4. Use Columns

Use at least two columns so that the publication looks like a newsletter at first glance. Three even-width columns are also effective, as are mixed-width columns (two uneven columns—one that is one-third of the page, and the other two-thirds of the page).

5. Use Graphics to Add Interest

Graphics may be good-quality photos, clip art, or pullquotes. A **pullquote** is a quote that is used in the article and copied and enlarged to catch the reader's attention. The pullquote is often set off by being placed in a four-sided box or by using a rule above and below it. A different font from the body text is usually used.

6. Leave Adequate White Space

Solid text looks boring and is hard to read. **White space** is the blank space where nothing is printed.

7. Use an Easy-to-Read Type Size and Font

Graphic artists recommend that you use no more than three different fonts in your newsletter (one for articles, one for headlines, and one for captions). Be sure that the type size is large enough to be read easily. If the print is too small, most readers will discard your newsletter—unread.

8. Use a Consistent Format

Put regular features such as "Message from the President" or "Dates to Remember" in the same place in every issue so that readers will know where to look for them.

9. Allow Plenty of Time

Allow more time than you think it will take to prepare a newsletter in order to meet your deadline.

With page layout software such as Adobe PageMaker and QuarkXPress, it is easy to prepare a professional-looking newsletter and print a camera-ready copy for the printer, or you may send a disk to an outside printing company. These software programs have templates for newsletters, or you can create your own template so that all issues of your newsletter will have a consistent look.

Dos for Your Newsletter

Readers like to see these things in a newsletter:

- Who, what, where, when information
- Why and how information, if appropriate
- Short articles
- Bulleted lists
- Good visuals (graphics, charts, tables)
- Interesting, relevant topics
- Calendars (dates to remember)
- Helpful hints for saving money or time
- Attractive layout
- Accurate information
- Error-free text (no spelling and grammar errors)

SUMMARY

Writing letters to lawmakers is an effective way to share your ideas and knowledge with those who are responsible for passing laws. The two types of lawmaker letters are (1) legislative letters and (2) service letters. A letter to the editor of a publication expresses your thoughts on a topic that has been published. If the original information is wrong, you have a moral obligation to provide the correct information. Be certain that your information is accurate. Reputable publishers will not publish libelous or anonymous information. A news release (also called a *press release)* should be written in a journalistic style, with the most important information given first. Newsletters are prepared and distributed to a group of people who have similar interests, such as employees or members of an organization, customers or clients, or prospective customers or clients. A newsletter is usually prepared in two or three columns. The same look or design is used in all issues so that readers instantly recognize what the publication is.

Name _____ Date _____

WHAT'S WRONG WITH THESE?

1. News release: Tom Henkens, president of Valmont, announced today that the company will move its head-quarters to Dallas, Texas.

   _____

   _____

2. Letter to Lawmaker:

   Dear Mr. Lawmaker:

   As a citizen and a taxpayer, I want you to raise the taxes on alcohol.

   Sincerely,

   _____

   _____

   _____

   _____

   _____

LETTERS TO LAWMAKERS

3. Look up the names and addresses of the lawmakers who represent you. Pick an issue that is of interest to you, and write (preferably type) a letter to the appropriate lawmaker. Remember to write to your state lawmakers about state issues and to your federal lawmakers about national laws and issues. Do a little research on the topic you choose by reading articles in newspapers and periodicals. In addition to current topics in the news, here is a list of some possible ideas for your letter:

   a. Grandparents' rights
   b. Welfare to work programs
   c. School shootings
   d. E-commerce
   e. Homeless people
   f. Juvenile delinquents
   g. Patient rights
   h. Legal limit of blood alcohol content
   i. Graduated drivers' licenses
   j. Social Security
   k. The court system
   l. Public aid
   m. Aid to dependent children
   n. State lotteries
   o. Undocumented immigrants (illegal aliens)
   p. Violence and sex on television
   q. The prison system
   r. The death penalty
   s. Public and private school financing
   t. Drugs and drug abuse
   u. Drunk driving
   v. Gun control
   w. Missing and/or abused children
   x. Interstate speed limits
   y. The space program
   z. Medical care and/or Medicare

Name _____ Date _____

LETTERS TO THE NEWS MEDIA

4. **Letter to the editor.** Ten years ago your city replaced (using local tax dollars) four blocks of a street in the downtown area with a landscaped mall. Now there is a proposal before the city to tear out the mall and replace it (using local tax dollars) with a street to provide on-the-street parking. Drivers currently may park in garages within one block of the mall area, as well as on some side streets. On a few busy days each year, the parking garages are full. Write (preferably type) a letter to the editor of your local newspaper telling why you are for or against the proposal to replace the mall with a street.

5. **Letter to the editor.** Pick a current topic in your community and write (preferably type) a letter to the editor of your local newspaper expressing your opinion. To get some ideas for topics, read the editorial page for a few days to find out what is current.

6. **Writing a news release.** For the first time, your college is planning to offer an introduction to business class over the Internet. The online class will provide three semester hours of credit and will cost $100. Students should call the registration office at 555-3985 to register. Additional information is available at the Website: <introtobusiness@college.edu>. Assume that you are the virtual learning director on your campus. Write (preferably type) the news release.

7. **Writing a news release.** Your local symphony orchestra has received an unexpected gift of $50,000 from an anonymous donor to be used as needed. Assume that you are the advertising director of the orchestra, and write (preferably type) the news release.

COLLABORATIVE WRITING

Writing a Newsletter *Work with two other students. Each of you should write an article for a newsletter for new students who will register next term. Each article should be about the same length. One article will be about the college bookstore, one will be about how to register for classes, and one will be about your school's library. As a group, design a nameplate (title) for your newsletter and place the articles in an appropriate sequence. If possible, use a graphic with each article. Start each article with a title.*

PROOFREADING EXERCISE

Proofread the following letter to the editor. *Mark errors with proofreaders' marks.*

Editor:

The 566th Air Force Band of the Peoria Air Nartional Guard under the direction of Bryan Miller gave us a grate evening full of wonderful entertainment at Schlarman High School recentley. They truly presented a grate selecktsion of music.

Quiet a few local musicians and a mavelous singer, Molly Nixon from Danville, did an excellent job. It was a great way to spent an evening enjoying free entertainent.

All the musicians and entertaiment was wonderful. And as usual, Dave Schroeder did a great job in emceeing and playing with the band. Thanks to all to of you. We need to suppot these activities better than we do.

Sara Towne

Search the Internet for Lawmaker Addresses and for Newsletter Information
a. Go to the Internet and search for the mailing addresses of your federal lawmakers. Write the addresses of your two state senators and your representative on a separate sheet of paper. Two sites at the time of publication of this book were:
<nwf.org/nwf/action/reps.html> and <lcweb.loc.gov/global/legislative/congress.html>.
b. Go to the Internet and key in the URL<http://thomas.loc.gov/>. This site will give you legislative information. Review the current legislation, the congressional record, and committee information. Write a short memo (preferably type) to your instructor describing two interesting things you found.
c. Go to the Internet and use the search engine <www.mamma.com> and search for actual newsletters. Write a memo or send an e-mail (whichever your instructor prefers) to your instructor telling the name of a site you found that you thought was interesting and why you liked it. If requested, print the information you found on the Internet.

NOTES

Writing Meeting Reports

Chapter 15 presented the basic principles that you need to write letters to public officials and to those in the media services. You also studied

- Newsletters and
- News releases.

In Chapter 16 the topics that will be emphasized are those that will give you a good foundation on which to build your meeting reports. Meetings are a major part of our world today. In order for meetings to be handled efficiently, certain documents must precede and follow the meeting. You will study the documents that relate to each of the topics below, for example

- Meeting notices
- Agendas and minutes
- Parliamentary procedure, and
- Committee work as well as team work.

Objectives

After completing this chapter, you should be able to:

- Prepare a meeting notice.
- Prepare a meeting agenda.
- Understand the difference between a formal and an informal meeting.
- Write minutes of a meeting.

PURPOSE OF MEETINGS

Thousands of meetings take place every day in the United States, and office meetings occupy more than one-third of an American manager's working day. These statistics tell us that meetings are an important segment of business communications. Today there is an increased emphasis on teamwork, problem solving, and involving all stakeholders in reaching business decisions that are productive and profitable. **Stakeholders** are the people who have a vested interest in the outcome.

A **meeting** is a gathering of two or more people for a common purpose. Meetings should lead to good decisions based on the combined intelligence of the members of the group. If all team members share in the decision, they are more apt to support the decision. Unfortunately, meetings can be a waste of time and unproductive, leaving the participants feeling frustrated. Unsatisfactory meetings are usually a result of poor planning.

The specific purpose of most meetings is (1) communicating information, (2) solving problems, or (3) generating ideas.

Communicating Information

A meeting to communicate information to the participants could include introducing and explaining a new product or service or policy. The purpose of the meeting could also be to train the participants to use new software and equipment.

Solving Problems

Many organizations don't have *problems;* they have *opportunities.* Regardless of the terminology used, the method is the same. A technique called **brainstorming** is an excellent way to gather as many ideas as possible in a timely manner. The process of brainstorming involves each participant contributing any idea that pops into his or her head. All ideas are recorded without any judgment about their value or practicality. The next step after brainstorming is to evaluate the suggestions and discuss the feasibility of the best suggestions.

Generating Ideas

We live in a world of fierce competition. There is a constant need to generate new ideas that will result in newer and better products and services at lower prices. Technology also affects the way we do business. Many organizations have groups (teams or committees) that meet on a regular basis for the sole purpose of generating ideas that will keep them competitive. Both positive and negative feedback from customers and clients provides input for generating new ideas. Brainstorming is another way of generating new ideas.

MEETING NOTICES

Meetings may be called on short notice, depending on the urgency and the number of attendees and their accessibility; or they may be set well in advance to stimulate attendance and to allow preparation time.

In organizations that have electronic calendaring systems, the calendaring software can quickly search electronic appointment calendars and find and list times when all people who need to attend the meeting are available.

Attendees may be notified in advance of the meeting in writing or via e-mail. For especially important meetings, a notice may be followed by a reminder a few days before the meeting.

The meeting notice and reminder should contain:

- Day and date of the meeting.
- Time of the meeting.
- The place where the meeting will be held.
- Purpose of the meeting or an agenda.
- Any other applicable information, such as materials to bring.

Notices and reminders may be in the form of:

- An announcement.
- A flier.
- A letter.
- A memo.
- A postcard.
- E-mail and calendaring system.

A reply card or a reservation slip may be enclosed with the meeting notice.

Notifying large numbers of people individually by telephone is time-consuming and provides no guarantee that everyone receives identical information, even if each person is reached. Some organizations have a voice mail system that permits the same voice mail message to be recorded once and forwarded to each person who needs the information. Here is a sample meeting notice:

16-2—Meeting Attendance Is Important
Why would you need to know how many people are planning to attend a meeting?

DATE: November 18, \<YEAR\>
MEMO TO: All Relocation Division and Commercial-Investment Division Personnel
FROM: Ann Faught
SUBJECT: Teamwork Effort to Capture Relocation Business

A joint meeting of the Relocation Division and the Commercial-Investment Division will be held on Friday, November 22, at 3 p.m., in Conference Room C on the fifth floor.

The purpose of the meeting is to discuss a teamwork approach to our goal of capturing a sizable share of the relocation market in the St. Louis area.

Please review the enclosed list of major corporate accounts to be contacted after this meeting, and be prepared to share your ideas for developing this business.

rah

Enclosure

MEETING AGENDA

Advance planning organizes a meeting and helps it run smoothly. The written "plan" for a meeting is called an *agenda*.

 An **agenda** is a program, or a list of the items of business in the order they are to be discussed at a meeting. This list may also include (1) the name of the person responsible for that agenda item and (2) the approximate amount of time to be spent discussing each item.

✳ A typical agenda for a formal meeting includes some or all of the following items:

1. Call to order
2. Roll call
3. Approval or amendment of the agenda
4. Approval of minutes
5. Reading of correspondence
6. Treasurer's report
7. Officers' reports
8. Committee reports (each committee may be listed)
9. Old or unfinished business (specific items may be listed)
10. New business (specific items may be listed)
11. Program and/or speaker, if applicable
12. Announcements
13. Adjournment

An agenda for a more informal meeting would include some or all of the following, not necessarily in this order:

1. Call to order
2. Information items (usually one-way communications such as announcements)
3. Discussion items (topics that need the attention and participation of the entire group)
4. Decision items (topics that require a judgment or an action during the meeting)
5. Adjournment

Providing an agenda will help make any meeting more productive, especially if the agenda is sent out in advance. Including specific items of business on the agenda gives the attendees time to prepare for the discussion. The secretary of an organization is usually responsible for preparing the agenda after consulting with the chairperson. For an informal meeting, the facilitator usually prepares the agenda. An agenda for a board meeting is illustrated in Figure 16-1.

16-3—Meeting Notification *What is the major disadvantage of notifying people about a meeting via a voice mail message?*

Agenda

Illinois Business Education Association
Crowne Plaza Hotel, Springfield, Illinois
Governor's Room
February 18, <YEAR>
6 p.m.

I. Call to Order ....Clora Mae Baker

II. Secretary's Report ....Donna Peterson

III. Treasurer's Report ....Cathie Bishop

IV. Convention/Conference Reports
    A. IACTE Convention/IBEA Sessions ....Cathy Carruthers
    B. Fall Conference ....Cathy Carruthers
    C. Fall Conference (ISBE-Sponsored Sessions) ....N. Dale Snow
    D. Fall Conference Registration Report ....Gayle Appel
    E. Fall Conference Financial Report ....Cathie Bishop

V. Membership
    Membership Report ....John Majernik

VI. Membership Development
    A. Plans/Activities ....J. Norman Anderson/Linda Branch
    B. Affiliate Rebates ....J. Norman Anderson/Linda Branch

VII. Committee Reports
    A. Audit ....Kathleen Anderson
    B. Awards ....Diane David/Julie Knutson
    C. Budget ....Cathie Bishop
    D. Commercial Exhibits ....Jim Bane/Tina Dierkes
    E. Community College Articulation ....Tammy Kessler
    F. Conference Photographer ....Roger Luft
    G. Council of Affiliates ....Pat Gerdes
    H. Educational Exhibits ....Ruth Ann Gaither
    I. Handbook ....Kathleen Anderson
    J. Historian ....Marilyn Walter
    K. IBEA Media
        1. IBEA Home Page ....Linda Hefferin
        2. IBEA Reports ....Marilyn Walter
    L. Illinois Curriculum Council ....Margaret Erthal
    M. ISBE Representative ....Roger Uhe

*Go to Student
CD-ROM
Activity 16-1.*

February 18, <YEAR> Agenda   Page 2

    N. Nominating ....Jim Tarr
    O. Public Information ....James Price
    P. Public Relations ....Clyde W. Cooper, Sr.
    Q. Publications ....Margaret Erthal
    R. Scholarship ....Beth Cuyler
    S. Special Projects ....Marcy Satterwhite/Gaylene Cain
        1. Summer Workshops
    T. Student Organizations ....Melissa Payne
    U. Student Representative ....Melissa Payne
    V. Conference Technology ....N. Dale Snow/Jim Tarr

VIII. Other Reports
    A. Executive Director ....Kathleen Anderson
    B. NCBEA Representative ....Ethel Holladay
    C. IACTE ....Karen Riddell
    D. IBTEC ....Margaret Erthal

IX. President's Report ....Clora Mae Baker

X. Old Business
    A. Who's Who Awards ....Kathleen Anderson
    B. Bulk Mailing Permit ....Marilyn Walter
    C. IACTE Bylaws Revision ....Clora Mae Baker

XI. New Business
    A. Registration Fees for Retired Members ....Clora Mae Baker
    B. Graduate Credit for Fall IBEA Conference ....Clora Mae Baker
    C. Home Page ....Linda Hefferin
    D. Katie School of Insurance ....Kathleen Anderson
    E. Paid Advertising for IBEA Reports ....Marilyn Walter

XII. Announcements/Information Items
    A. House of Delegates ....Clora Mae Baker
    B. Spring/Summer Board Meeting Date ....Clora Mae Baker
    C. Affiliate Meetings/Visits ....Clora Mae Baker
    D. Other
        1. NBEA
        2. ISBE

XIII. Adjournment ....Clora Mae Baker

FIGURE 16-1 An agenda may be quite detailed. (Courtesy of Illinois Business Education Association.)

TRADITIONAL MEETINGS

Face-to-face oral communication among groups of people is essential to certain phases of business. Meetings can range from formal to very informal.

Formal Meetings

Professional organizations, public bodies (e.g., city council), and boards of directors of public and private organizations have formal meetings at regular intervals. The group's elected officers conduct these meetings. The major officers are:

- President or chairperson (responsible for conducting the meeting).
- Vice president or vice chairperson (large organizations frequently have a first and second vice president).
- Recording secretary (responsible for minutes).
- Corresponding secretary (responsible for sending and receiving correspondence on behalf of the organization).
- Treasurer (responsible for the money and for paying bills).

 Formal meetings follow strict parliamentary procedure, which is a set of rules for conducting meetings. Parliamentary procedure ensures that everyone can have input, but the majority rules. An excellent reference book for parliamentary procedure is *Robert's Rules of Order*, Revised Edition.

Corporations may hire professional registered parliamentarians for stockholders' meetings and other meetings where it is important for legal reasons to ensure that strict parliamentary procedure be followed.

Informal Meetings

Informal meetings follow a discussion format, with a *facilitator* (or cofacilitators) managing the meeting process rather than controlling it. An effective facilitator should be neutral and objective and ensure that all members have an opportunity to present ideas. The facilitator keeps the discussion on target by being an active listener so that he or she can restate, clarify, and summarize the ideas being discussed during the meeting.

Decisions may be reached by consensus or by majority rule. **Consensus** means that all members of the group agree to support a decision even if they might not completely agree with the decision. A **majority rule** means that if an agreed-upon percentage of the members vote for the decision, the decision stands.

Team meetings and committee meetings frequently follow the format of an informal meeting.

ELECTRONIC MEETINGS

With today's technology, face-to-face meetings can be held without it being necessary for participants from different parts of the country or the world to travel to a central location.

Videoconferencing

Videoconferencing requires all participants to go to a facility at their location that has specialized equipment and satellite links for interactive video and audio transmission. Many schools conduct classes using a similar approach called *distance learning.* A teacher teaches students located at several remote sites. The students can interact with the teacher and with students at each of the other locations.

An alternative to traditional videoconferencing is *desktop videoconferencing.* This process is much less expensive than traditional videoconferencing because it uses personal computers and telephone lines. With the appropriate and compatible hardware and software on each participant's computer, audio, video, and data can be transmitted. The quality is not as good as a dedicated videoconferencing system, but the cost is much less.

E-Mail Meetings

An e-mail meeting is conducted by sending an e-mail to all persons participating in the meeting and asking them to respond to the meeting organizer by a deadline. This allows ideas to be gathered and shared with other participants without taking the time to physically meet.

Internet Meetings

An Internet meeting, sometimes referred to as a *virtual meeting,* is rapidly gaining popularity as more and more businesses have Internet access. In a virtual meeting, no one has to leave his or her office to participate. In this system of electronic collaboration, everyone sees everyone else's message as soon as it is sent. Discussion boards provide an opportunity for each participant to share ideas, ask questions, and respond to other participants' comments. Educational institutions that offer online courses frequently use a discussion board format to replace classroom discussion.

MINUTES OF MEETINGS

The recording secretary in a formal meeting or the facilitator or a recorder (sometimes called a *notetaker*) in an informal meeting takes notes during the meeting. A type of report, called *minutes*, is prepared after the meeting.

Taking Minutes

The Open Public Meetings Act applies to most meetings held by governing bodies of public agencies. This act *requires* public bodies to keep minutes of all meetings, including open and closed meetings. The purpose of keeping minutes is (1) to ensure that public bodies keep accurate records of their proceedings for their own protection and (2) to provide a record for court, if needed.

 Minutes are an official written record of the business that was conducted at a meeting. Minutes should be a *summary* of the meeting rather than a verbatim report.

16-2:
NOTIFYING THE MEDIA
Ken sent notices for a special public library board meeting next week but forgot to notify the media. Is this acceptable?

Minutes are important, even for an informal meeting, to:

- Prevent any misunderstanding of what took place.
- Have written documentation of the results of the meeting.
- Keep absentees and other interested parties informed of what occurred.

A recorder or recording secretary should:

- Sit near the presiding officer or facilitator.
- Listen for key ideas.
- Take good notes.
- Ask for clarification as necessary during the meeting.

Secretaries or recorders sometimes tape-record meetings or take notes on a laptop computer during the meeting.

The minutes should be prepared as soon after the meeting as possible, while the proceedings are still fresh in the recorder's mind. Depending on the practice of the organization, minutes may be very brief or several pages long.

Organizing Minutes

 Minutes should be *objective* and *concise* and should be written *in the past tense.* The top of the first page of minutes should give the identifying information: *who, what, where, when, why,* and *how.* This information should be followed by a summary of agenda items in *chronological order* (the order in which business was conducted).

Put each item of business in a separate paragraph. To locate items quickly, use one of the following formats:

- Marginal headings (see Figure 16-3 for an example of this format)
- Side headings (headings on a separate line above the text)
- Paragraph headings (see "Proofreading Exercise" in the Worksheet for this chapter for an example of this format)

In formal and some informal meetings, decisions and policies are made through *motions,* a component of parliamentary procedure. Some organizations require that motions be presented in writing to the secretary or recorder. The appropriate sequence is:

1. A person introduces an idea by saying "I move that . . ."
2. Another person endorses the motion by saying "I second the motion."
3. The president or chairperson then asks whether there is discussion. Discussion allows any person who so desires to express his or her views.
4. Motion is voted on.

If the chairperson believes that the discussion is concluded, he or she can repeat the motion and ask for the vote. When someone in the group wants the discussion to end and is ready to vote, he or she says, "I call for the question." This will stop the discussion, and the group will vote.

If the group is not ready to vote on a motion, the motion may be:

- Postponed until a future date—cannot be discussed until the specified date.
- Postponed indefinitely—a nice way of killing the motion.
- Tabled ("lay on the table")—delays action on the motion until later in the meeting or at a future meeting (whenever someone moves to remove the motion from the table).

When reporting motions in minutes, be sure to include:

- The specifics of each motion made, including any amendments.
- The names of both the person who made the motion and the person who seconded it, if appropriate.
- The action taken (whether the motion passed or failed).

Details of the discussion do not need to be included in the minutes.

Voting is done on the basis of one vote per person except at stockholders' meetings, where voting is usually on the basis of one vote per share of stock owned.

Distributing Minutes

The practice of an organization may be to mail the minutes prior to the next meeting, distribute them at the next meeting, and/or read them at the next meeting. Meeting time is saved if the minutes are mailed to members prior to the meeting. This procedure also permits the secretary to highlight on each person's copy the item(s) for which he or she has responsibility.

Sometimes minutes are sent as an attachment to an e-mail message or included in the organization's newsletter.

Correcting Minutes

When it is necessary to make a correction on minutes that have already been distributed or read, draw a line through the error, preferably with a red pen, and write the correction above it. If several lines need to be corrected, draw a line through each incorrect line, make the note "See page . . .," and type the correction on a separate sheet with the appropriate page number.

The entire set of minutes should never be retyped, because of the danger of making additional errors.

An agenda that was mailed prior to a zoning commission meeting is shown in Figure 16-2. The minutes of the meeting are shown in Figure 16-3.

16-5—Recording a Meeting *Why would a secretary or recorder tape-record a meeting?*

Go to Student CD-ROM Activity 16-2.

FIGURE 16-2 Preparing an agenda such as this one will help make a meeting more productive. When possible, list the name of the person responsible for each part of the agenda.

Agenda

City of Albuquerque
Zoning Commission Monthly Meeting

Room 532—City Council Building
Thursday, October 15, <YEAR>
7:30 p.m.

Call to Order .... Richard Trower

Roll Call .... Rick Esposito

Secretary's Report .... Rick Esposito

Committee Reports:

    Mayor's Advisory Review Committee .... Pam Raymond

Old Business:

    Etto Corporation Townhouse .... Steve Woodyard

New Business:

    Rezoning Petition .... Alworth Development Company

Announcements .... Richard Trower

Adjournment .... Richard Trower

---

Minutes
City of Albuquerque
Zoning Commission Monthly Meeting

Room 532—City Council Building
Thursday, October 15, <YEAR>
7:30 p.m.

marginal headings

Presiding:	Richard Trower, Chairperson

Present:

Tom Andrews	John Nash
Barbara Brogdon	Pam Raymond
Glen Davis	Brian Thompson
Lynda May	Carol Willis

Absent:	Randall Matthews	Adam Darzynikus

Call to Order: The regular monthly meeting of the Albuquerque Zoning commission was held on Thursday, October 15,<YEAR>, in Room 532 in the Municipal Administration Building. The meeting was called to order by Richard Trower, Chairperson, at 7:30 p.m.

Secretary's Report: The minutes of the September 17, <YEAR>, meeting were approved as read.

Committee Reports: Pam Raymond, Chairperson of the Mayor's Advisory Review Committee, reported that she had conveyed to the mayor the wishes of the Zoning Commission that a traffic signal be placed at the Intersection of Poplar Avenue and Kirby Parkway.

Old Business: Etto Corporation submitted a request for final approval of the building plans for a 15-unit townhouse project at 1722 Riverdale Road. Lynda May questioned whether the Albuquerque Design Review Committee had approved the landscaping plans. Richard Trower reported that the committee had approved the plans. Steve Woodyard, the developer, presented blueprints and reviewed the completed plans. After some discussion, John Nash moved for final approval. Carol Willis seconded. The motion was approved unanimously.

New Business: Alworth Development Company submitted an application for rezoning of 22 acres of the southwest corner of Mt. Moriah Extended and Ridgeway Boulevard from RTH (Townhouse) to GO (General Office). At the request of Barbara Brogdon, this application was tabled until the next regular meeting to allow the members time to study the proposal.

Announcements: The next meeting will be November 18, <YEAR>, at 7:30 p.m.

Adjournment: The meeting was adjourned at 9 p.m.

Respectfully submitted,

Rick Esposito

Rick Esposito, Secretary
City of Albuquerque

FIGURE 16-3 Minutes serve as a written record of the business conducted at a meeting. The marginal headings shown here make it easy to locate information quickly.

Format for Formal Minutes Checksheet

Do your minutes include the following?

	Yes	No	N/A
Name of the group	❏	❏	❏
Day, date, time of meeting	❏	❏	❏
Location of the meeting	❏	❏	❏
Time the meeting was called to order	❏	❏	❏
Name of presiding person (chairperson, president, or facilitator)	❏	❏	❏
Name of the recorder or the recording secretary	❏	❏	❏
Names of those present and absent	❏	❏	❏
Announcements	❏	❏	❏
Disposition of previous minutes	❏	❏	❏
Record of the meeting in chronological order	❏	❏	❏
Summary of topics covered	❏	❏	❏
Motions	❏	❏	❏
Exact wording of the motion	❏	❏	❏
Name of person who made the motion	❏	❏	❏
Name of person who seconded the motion	❏	❏	❏
Action taken on motion (passed, failed, or postponed)	❏	❏	❏
Conclusions of discussions	❏	❏	❏
Time meeting was adjourned	❏	❏	❏
Date and time of next meeting	❏	❏	❏
Closing of "Respectfully submitted"	❏	❏	❏
Typed name and signature of person preparing minutes	❏	❏	❏

Guidelines for format

	Yes	No	N/A
Heading should include:	❏	❏	❏
Name of group (all caps and bold; centered)	❏	❏	❏
Day, Date, Time (initial caps, centered)	❏	❏	❏
Location of meeting (initial caps, centered)	❏	❏	❏
Margins minimum of 1 inch should be on all sides	❏	❏	❏
Opening paragraph should include:	❏	❏	❏
Time meeting began	❏	❏	❏
Who called meeting to order	❏	❏	❏
Body of minutes should include:	❏	❏	❏
Adequate side or paragraph headings	❏	❏	❏
What business was conducted	❏	❏	❏
What actions were taken	❏	❏	❏
Last paragraph should include:	❏	❏	❏
Date and time of next meeting	❏	❏	❏
Time of adjournment	❏	❏	❏
Signature line	❏	❏	❏

SUMMARY

Meetings are an important element in business communications. Effective, productive meetings result from good planning and preparation, which include preparing and sending accurate meeting notices prior to a meeting. Agendas should be prepared and distributed before a meeting so that the participants will know what business needs to be accomplished at the meeting. During the meeting the secretary or recorder takes notes in order to prepare a report called *minutes of the meeting.* These minutes are a legal requirement at some meetings; they serve as a summary of any meeting and include what was discussed and any action taken.

Name _____ Date _____

WHAT'S WRONG WITH THESE?

1. What's wrong with this meeting notice?

_____

PREPARING MEETING CORRESPONDENCE

Using separate sheets of paper, plan and prepare (preferably type) clear, concise solutions.

> **Delta Kappa Gamma Meeting**
>
> Brunch
>
> 9 to 11 a.m.
>
> $10 per person
>
> Bring a nonperishable food item for the Food Pantry
>
> Turtle Run Resort
>
> 12 Liberty Lane
>
> Danville, Kentucky 40422
>
> **R.S.V.P. 555-8733**

2. As employee benefits coordinator for your firm, prepare (preferably type) a memo to the Management Bargaining Team scheduling a meeting two weeks from today at 4 p.m. in the East Conference Room. Representatives from three insurance companies will present proposals. Ask each team member to bring the salary and fringe benefit surveys distributed at the last meeting.

3. The following is a list of items of business (in no particular order) to be discussed at the Wednesday, May 16, morning board meeting of the Life Underwriters. The meeting will be held at 7 a.m. Arrange the items in the proper order and prepare an agenda for the meeting. The president is Andy Fuseo, the secretary is Dorothy Robinson, and the treasurer is Toni Schultz. Attendance is maintained because members are dropped from the board if they have more than two unexcused absences a year. The meeting will be held in the Cavalier Room at the Lincoln Inn, 936 Gilbert Street, Cedar Falls, Iowa 50613.

- Membership committee report (John Mohr is chairperson).
- The president will appoint a nominations committee to prepare a slate of officers for next year.
- Public service committee report (Jay McHugh is chairperson).
- A proposal to have a booth at the Mature Expo was discussed last month but no decision was made. It should be discussed again.
- Public relations committee report (Susie Stephenson is chairperson).
- At the last meeting the president read a letter from the United Way asking for volunteers to help with the campaign. The president needs to get more volunteers.
- Program committee report (Ted Latoz is chairperson).
- Sue Laury, Director of Roselawn Fitness Center, will speak on "Staying Fit."
- Legislation committee report (Janet Rogalski is chairperson).
- Secretary's report.
- Treasurer's report.

Name _____ Date _____

PREPARING MEETING CORRESPONDENCE *(continued)*

4. Prepare (preferably type) an agenda for the meeting described in the Collaborative Activity that might have been prepared and mailed to the members prior to the meeting.

COLLABORATIVE ACTIVITY: PREPARING AN AGENDA

Work with one or two classmates to complete Problem 4. Organize the following notes and prepare (preferably type) the minutes of the meeting described in the notes.

Background: You are secretary of the administrative board of the local Boy Scout Council. The purpose of this board is to oversee the council's programs, make recommendations for activities and equipment purchases, and serve as a public relations group for the council. There are nine members on the board, which meets four times a year. The following notes were made during the January 8 meeting.

NOTES: Minutes from last meeting (October 9) approved as read. Chairperson Andrew Juliano called the meeting to order at 12:30 p.m. in the boardroom at the council office. The following members were present: Michael Truax, Don Norenburg, Gary Thor, Phil Smith, Angela Garcia, Rose DeMayo, Van Burnett, Ed Brock, and you. Meeting adjourned 1:30 p.m. Phil Smith suggested awarding perfect attendance certificates to scouts at end of each quarter rather than once a year. Several members felt this was a good idea and would be an excellent motivational technique to help scouts develop the habit of being dependable.

Van Burnett gave an update on the annual Scout-O-Rama. Since the last meeting, he has received survey cards from 25 Cub and Boy Scout units expressing an interest in participating. Angela Garcia suggested date be changed from last Wednesday in February to last Wednesday in March because of past problems with bad weather in February which reduced attendance. A vote was taken and the motion passed. After a lengthy discussion of pros and cons, the change was presented as a motion by Ed Brock and seconded by Gary Thor. Next meeting will be April 3 at 1 p.m.

Gary Thor, chairperson of Advancement Committee, reported that he felt the council should recruit more volunteer specialists to assist units with advancement in the more difficult areas. Gary distributed a list of areas needing advancement assistance and some statistics showing the need. After discussion a motion was made by Michael Truax and seconded by Rose DeMayo to adopt this recommendation and forward it to the council executive for implementation. A vote was taken and the motion passed. The treasurer's report, by Rose DeMayo, was placed on file for audit. She indicated there is $2770 cash currently on hand.

Name _____   Date _____

PROOFREADING EXERCISE

Mark the errors in the following set of minutes:

Technology Team
Minutes of April 12, \<YEAR\>, Meeting

Attendance. The Technology Team meting was called to order at l0 a.m. on April 12, \<YEAR\>, by Mike Summers, Chairperson. Members present was Jane Wong, Rich Pate, Fred Payne, Janet Redenbaugh, Merilyn Shepherd, Sharon Stoerger, Jeff Williams, and Naomi Yonke.

Old Business. The team reveiwed the bids submitted fro digital cameras. Jane Wong will contact the to lowest bidder to obtain information on telephoto capabilities.

New Business. The team review a request to change e-mail systems. Jeff Williams will bring information about several e-mail system to the next meetng.

Adjournment. The meeting was adjourned at 11:30 a.m. The next meeting is schedule for May 15 in the Laura Lee Room.

Respectfully submitted,

Sharon Stoerger, Secretary

Search the Web for Information on Parliamentary Procedure

Connect to the Internet and search for parliamentary procedure to learn more about it. Possible sites:

        \<http://www.psychiatry.ubc.ca/dept/rulesord/principles\>
        \<http://www.robertsrules.com\>
        \<http://www.parliamentarians.org/\>

Look at the following Websites to get more information about meetings. If your instructor asks you to, print the information.

        \<http://www.advantagemgmt.com/resource/meetings\>
        \<http://www.csclub.uwaterloo.ca/u/lkmorlan/ScoutDocs/0022-Taking_Minutes.html\>

NOTES

Chapter 17

Writing Memo Reports

You learned how to prepare a meeting notice, an agenda, the minutes of a meeting, and you studied electronic meeting formats in Chapter 16. Chapter 17 presents:

- Memo reports.

- Collaborative reports.

The flow of correct and usable information within an organization is vital to effective decision making. The reports you write often serve as a basis for:

- Making business decisions.

- Evaluating *your* contributions to the organization and your ability to communicate your ideas in writing.

Report-writing skills, therefore, are very important to your success in business.

Depending upon the complexity and length of the information, you may write a long formal report or the shorter memo report. A memo report is a combination of a memo (see Chapter 7) and the formal report.

Objectives

After completing this chapter, you should be able to:

- Identify the elements of reports.
- Write memo reports.
- Write collaboratively.

FORMAL BUSINESS REPORTS

The formal report is appropriate for reports that organizations send outside their offices. You can also use a formal report internally when the importance or the length makes the more informal memo report inappropriate.

Format

A formal business report demands thoroughly *documented, objective, and detailed preparation.* It is longer than a memo report and usually includes the following parts:

- Title page
- Letter or memo of transmittal
- Table of contents
- Abstract or synopsis
- Introduction
- Body or text of several pages including
    Side and paragraph headings
    Tables and/or figures
- Conclusions
- Recommendations
- Appendix
- Bibliography

Formal reports are usually single-spaced to save paper and duplicating costs. Formal reports prepared for publishing should be double-spaced for ease of editing.

A common type of formal report is the research report.

Research Reports

A **research report** presents facts and findings as a result of research, presents the writer's evaluation of the facts and findings, and presents a recommendation or conclusion. Before writing a report, you may need to do some extensive research to collect data. When using another person's material—either directly quoted or paraphrased—you must give the source of the information. Three acceptable styles for listing your sources are:

- Citations (shown with the excerpted material).
- Endnotes (compiled in a list at the end of the report).
- Footnotes (listed at the bottom of the page containing the excerpt).

Check a current reference manual for the proper format for each of these.

 Data that references existing research is secondary research. Data collected from surveys, questionnaires, and interviews is primary research.

Plagiarism occurs when a person uses another's work without giving credit. Plagiarizing another's work is not only unethical and unprofessional but also illegal and could cost you your job.

MEMO REPORTS

In the business world, the memo report is the most popular form for routine reports within an organization.

 A memo report is a combination of an *interoffice memo* and a *formal report.* It uses a memo heading *(TO, FROM, DATE, SUBJECT),* but the body, which is usually two to five pages long, is organized like the body of a formal report and may have side headings.

See Figure 17-1 for an example of a memo report outline.

MEMORANDUM

MEMO TO: All Employees

FROM: Marilyn Satterwhite and Elizabeth Kerbey

DATE: March 30, <YEAR>

SUBJECT: Organization and Content of Memo Reports

Use memo reports to communicate facts, ideas, statistics, and trends within an organization. Memo reports are routine reports arranged with a memo heading and side headings in the body of the report. These reports are usually two to five pages in length. They should begin with an introductory paragraph such as this one.

Summary or Recommendation. This section includes a concise summary of what the report is about or recommendations based on the results of the findings.

Background and/or Facts. This section gives any facts or background necessary to fully understand the report.

Findings. This section reports the results of any investigation, experiment, survey, study, and so on. It could include tables or graphs to help the reader understand the results.

Conclusions. This section interprets the results of the research.

pm

FIGURE 17-1 This is a typical format and arrangement for the popular memo report. Many organizations have a set format for periodic reports.

You can use memo reports to:

- Answer a request for information.
- Report progress.
- Make recommendations.
- State facts.
- Communicate ideas.
- Send statistical data.
- Explain trends within an organization.

Businesses rely heavily on internal communications to make decisions—information presented in an organized memo report makes decision making easier.

A memo report is usually informal, giving facts and recommendations in the first person ("I suggest . . .") and *written in conversational language and style.* The trend is definitely away from the stiff, formal writing style that characterized business reports of the past.

Classifying Memo Reports

Typical memo reports are:

- Progress or status reports.
- Periodic reports.
- Informational reports.

Progress or Status Reports

Some internal communications are simple progress or status reports written on *fill-in forms* and sent as needed or required to those who need the information. Others are fairly *brief narrative reports.* These narrative reports may be:

- Responses to requests for complex information.
- Ideas
- Explanations.
- Simple recommendations.

Longer, more involved progress or status reports may also contain recommendations supported by financial data or operating results.

Periodic Reports

Periodic reports are routine correspondence prepared at regular time intervals—daily, weekly, monthly, quarterly, or annually. *Sales reports* and *financial reports* are among the most common periodic reports prepared in business organizations. A monthly sales report appears in Figure 17-2.

Periodic reports are often prepared on *preprinted forms,* which have blank spaces in which to record information. The forms may also be electronic files into which the report writer inserts the needed information. The use of forms reduces the likelihood that essential information will be omitted, and the predetermined format reduces the time required to prepare the report.

17-1:

PROOFREAD ALL NUMBERS CAREFULLY

An excerpt from a progress report: "We are 51 percent finished with the project." In actuality, the project was only 15 percent completed. Watch those transpositions!

MEMORANDUM

TO: Shannon Glazer

FROM: Jessica Delgado *JD*

DATE: August 30, <YEAR>

SUBJECT: Monthly Sales Report for August

August's ticket sales increased 5.78 percent over last year's August figures. We sold 9472 seats.

Our advertising efforts and the recent season opener contributed to the increase in sales. We will continue our advertising campaign. A complete accounting report will be released at the end of the season.

el

FIGURE 17-2 A periodic report is one of the most common types of business reports.

Reports may also be prepared according to a *standardized outline* to ensure uniformity. Sales reports, credit reports, audit reports, and many legal reports follow a standardized format.

Informational Reports

Most business reports are simple, straightforward factual presentations. Their purpose is to communicate information—facts, ideas, statistics, or trends—in a direct manner. For an informational report, you will:

- Gather facts, figures, and data.
- Organize the information.
- Interpret and present the organized information objectively.
- Make recommendations, if asked.

Data retrieved from a computer database can help you prepare informational reports quickly. Although the computer may provide the data, you must interpret the data. You have responsibility for:

- Evaluating results.
- Reaching conclusions.
- Recommending possible solutions to a problem.

Go to Student CD-ROM Activity 17-1.

You may be able to avoid having to retype data by:

1. Providing statistical information printed directly from the computer file and attaching a simple memo transmittal form.
2. Electronically copying the data to create a new document, and then building the memo report format and your remarks around the data.

Communicating Statistical Data

Tables, charts, and graphs can help your reader understand statistical data. An appropriate introductory statement in the text should precede a table or graph, as in the memo report in Figure 17-3. All tables and graphs should have adequate captions and labels to answer the relevant *who, what, where, when, why,* and *how* questions.

MEMORANDUM

TO: Shannon Glazer

FROM: Jessica Delgado *JD*

DATE: December 30, <YEAR>

SUBJECT: Season Ticket Sales Totals

Season ticket sales for this year increased 7.69 percent over last year. This year we sold 43,288 tickets, as compared with last year's total of 40,195. This represents an increase of 3093, which will certainly boost our operating budget as we begin the new season.

The ticket sales results appear below:

TICKET SALES Comparison of Current Year and Last Year				
Month	**Current**	**Last Year**	**Increase**	**Percentage Increase**
August	9,472	8,954	518	5.78
September	10,561	10,159	402	3.95
October	11,678	10,084	1,594	15.8
November	11,577	10,998	579	5.26
Totals	43,288	40,195	3,093	7.69

The combination of our league championship and second-place finish in last year's play-off had a positive effect on ticket sales.

The ticket sales campaign has officially ended. I hope you are as proud of the results as we are in the Marketing Department.

el

FIGURE 17-3 The statistical material in this memo report appears in a table for easier reading.

Tables

Statistical material in a memo report should be displayed in a table with the material logically arranged in rows (horizontally) and columns (vertically) for quick, easy reading. A title, a subtitle, and column headings should be used to identify the material in the table. Rules (lines) can be added above and below the column headings and at the bottom to give the table a more professional look.

Charts and Graphs

With computer software, you can easily convert data into graphic form. A *line graph* or *bar graph* depicts changes over a period of time. A *pie graph* shows the parts or percentages of the whole. By using integrated software, you can easily insert these graphs at the appropriate place in your report.

Handling a Large Quantity of Information

Although your memo report should contain enough facts to fully inform your reader, too much documentation in the report body can distract from your point. If you have a large quantity of reference material, consider putting most or all of it in a supplement (an appendix or an attachment) to your memo. This allows the reader to scan the supplement for supporting evidence or documentation, and it allows you to focus on the most essential facts. Do not overwhelm the reader by putting all data or statistics within the body of your memo.

Making Recommendations

If you have been asked to make a recommendation, make it the *main point* of your memo. Also, consider whether you should mention alternatives to your recommendation, and check to see whether you should describe specifically how to carry out your proposal.

Including not only your recommendation but also possible alternatives will make your memo report complete—by telling the reader what he or she has asked for and by offering your ideas and suggestions.

Gathering Information

Because a memo report often must be produced quickly, information gathering is frequently more casual and less rigorous than for a longer, formal report that is sent outside the organization. If you are asked to collect data for an informal memo report, be as thorough and factual as your limited time allows.

Suppose you received from your employer the memo shown in Figure 17-4. How would you go about gathering data for the report? Trace the following steps to learn how the project might progress.

Go to Student CD-ROM Activity 17-2.

17-1—Gathering Accurate Data *Analyze this: Allison is responsible for gathering data for a memo report. She was asked to conduct telephone interviews to get consumer opinions. She ran out of time and decided to use her own opinions for some of the data. Do you think this will help the report or distort the report?*

Sandstone Square Townhouses, Inc.

TO: Terry Stevens

FROM: Allen Williams *aw*

DATE: March 10, <YEAR>

SUBJECT: Property Management Study

Because of the increasing costs of salaries, benefits, maintenance, equipment, and supplies, I am wondering whether contracting with a commercial property management firm would be a wiser choice for Sandstone Square.

Will you please investigate the major property management firms in the Boston area and compare their fees with our current operational expenses.

I suggest also that you (1) look at several complexes managed by these firms to examine the interior and exterior conditions and (2) survey the tenants to find out whether they are satisfied with the quality of management.

If you find that by contracting with one of these firms we can realize substantial savings while maintaining our high standards, please present your recommendations to me as soon as you have gathered and analyzed the information.

os

FIGURE 17-4 This request memo will launch an informal study and generate the memo report shown in Figure 17-5.

Steps for Preparing a Memo Report on Property Management Study

1. First, read the request carefully to make sure you know exactly what information Mr. Williams needs. (Since his memo is clearly written and you understand what you are to do, you need not telephone him for further explanation.)

2. Check company files to find out the yearly costs of salaries, benefits, maintenance, equipment, and supplies for Sandstone Square Townhouses, Inc.

3. Next, look in the Yellow Pages and begin telephoning property management firms. Get general information about their services and an estimate of their fee for managing Sandstone Square Townhouses, Inc.

4. Study this information and narrow the choices to four firms that are well known for dependability and that gave comparable estimates.

5. Set up appointments with representatives from the four firms to meet with you to look at Sandstone; discuss contract terms and negotiate an annual fee.

6. Visit two of the complexes managed by each of the four firms. Use the visits to view firsthand and judge the condition of the buildings and grounds and the interior of a few of the units. During your visits, talk with some of the tenants to determine whether they are pleased with the management.

7. Analyze these data and compare cost and service.

8. Select the firm you believe will provide the best management at the lowest cost.

9. To confirm your decision, visit two more complexes managed by the firm you have selected.

10. Draw conclusions and make a recommendation to Mr. Williams, based on your research and the comparisons you have made.

11. Organize the information you have gathered, your recommendations, and your conclusions into a memo report to Mr. Williams.

Organizing Memo Reports

One of the most common and effective techniques of memo organization is to *itemize the information.* A report that contains complex facts and ideas will be easier to read if items are (1) separated into paragraphs, (2) numbered, or (3) preceded by side headings. This technique will also help you to write concisely and to organize carefully.

No rigid rules govern the content and organization of interoffice memos that function as reports. The memo report should follow the form best suited to its particular function.

In our example of the memo report for Mr. Williams, the next step after information gathering would be to determine the best way to present your findings. Remember that he expects your report to be factual and reliable. To accomplish this, you would:

- Present the facts with absolute fairness and accuracy.
- Be careful not to mix your opinions with the facts you report.
- Reserve your comments for your conclusions and recommendations.

The results of your work are transmitted in the memo report in Figure 17-5. It is well done from two points of view:

Sandstone Square Townhouses, Inc.

TO: Allen Williams

FROM: Terry Stevens ^{TS}

DATE: March 29, <YEAR>

SUBJECT: Property Management Study

As you requested, I have investigated the feasibility of engaging the services of a property management firm to provide total management services for Sandstone Square Townhouses, Inc.

Recommendation

To save Sandstone Square Townhouses, Inc., approximately $9000 a year in property management expenses, I recommend that we contract with Garner Management, Inc., on a year-to-year basis.

Findings

1. According to the College Bureau of Economic Research, Garner Management, Inc., manages more commercial and residential space than does any other property firm in the Boston area.

2. The large volume of business that Garner has built during the past 12 years enables it to execute management contracts at lower rates than those of its competitors. Garner bid 7 percent of gross rental revenues, whereas the other three property management firms considered bid 8 percent.

3. The 7 percent rate is guaranteed for a minimum of two years. We would maintain the right to renew or terminate the contract at the end of the first year. If we renew the contract, the rate could be renegotiated at the end of the second year.

4. A survey of four Garner-managed complexes showed three to be in excellent interior and exterior condition and to have generally satisfied tenants. One, mainly because of the economic area in which it is located, had less satisfied tenants but was in good condition.

FIGURE 17-5 Note the content and organization of this memo report, which was written in response to the memo request in Figure 17-4.

Allen Williams   2   March 29, <YEAR>

5. Garner would provide the following:

    a. Salaries and benefits for a resident manager and two assistant resident managers.
    b. Rental expenses on the resident manager's furnished townhouse.
    c. All maintenance—interior, exterior, and landscaping—through its service contracts.
    d. All equipment and supplies.

Cost Breakdown

The following is a comparison of the current cost of managing Sandstone Square Townhouses, Inc., with the estimated cost of contracting with Garner to provide this service.

Current Operating Cost

Annual salary, furnished apartment, and other benefits for resident manager	$22,000
Annual salaries for two assistant resident managers	32,000
Annual salary and benefits for one maintenance employee	19,000
Contracted repair work	15,000
Maintenance equipment and supplies	13,000
Miscellaneous costs	3,000
Total Expenses for <YEAR>	$104,000

Projected Operating Cost

Project Expenses for <YEAR>	$110,000
Estimated Annual Cost of Garner Contract Services	$101,000
Projected Savings	$9,000

Conclusions

1. Total responsibility for property management—including payroll records, hiring and firing, and purchasing equipment and supplies—would rest with Garner.

2. Contracting with Garner would save about $9,000 next year, while maintaining a high quality of management.

os

5 *(Continued)*

1. The information is presented in an orderly, easy-to-read fashion (note the side headings, for example).
2. The report represents something extra because you not only make the recommendation Mr. Williams has asked for, but you also take the time to present the facts clearly and show him a concise but complete comparison.

In writing reports, as in other phases of a job, remember to <mark>do a little more than is required.</mark> You and those around you will benefit from your extra effort to produce a comprehensive, well-written report.

COLLABORATIVE REPORTS

In your career you may have an opportunity to work with others collaboratively on a memo report. Writing collaboratively helps to divide the workload and capitalizes on the talents of several people who are working toward a common goal. To help the work go smoothly, consider the following strategies:

- Determine the purpose of the report.
- Distribute the writing tasks.
- Rewrite collaboratively.
- Assign the final editing.
- Proofread collaboratively.

Determine the Purpose of the Report

Knowing your purpose for any report is vital, but it is especially crucial when several people participate. Having a common goal will keep all the participants focused and on target. At this point you may also decide on the overall format that the document will take. Depending on the length of the assignment, you may wish to establish some basic group guidelines.

Assign the Writing Tasks

During this phase, decide who is to collect, organize, and interpret the data. Subteam or individual assignments may emerge from this session. You may assign someone to collect data, someone to organize the data, someone to write the first draft, and so on. Or, you may choose to work in one group. However you distribute the workload, it is essential to establish deadlines or event time lines.

Some computer word processing programs have the capability of work group writing. These programs maintain all previous editing marks so that one individual can see what another has added or deleted.

Rewrite Collaboratively

Once the individual rough drafts are ready, the group should look at the document together. Going through the entire document as a group helps maintain consistency, for the report represents various writing styles. This procedure also allows all participants equal input into the final document. In addition, each participant should realize his or her *individual* responsibility to be sure that the final document satisfies the original purpose.

Assign the Final Editing

Compiling the drafts into one final document can be accomplished more easily if only one or two people are involved. One or two people can complete the final editing more quickly than a large group can. If the members of the group agree, edited copies can be circulated and each person can initial his or her approval. After obtaining all approvals, print a final copy.

Proofread Collaboratively

If possible, the group should meet one last time to proofread the document. This way, burden for a "perfect" copy does not lie with any individual. And, several pairs of eyes are better than one. Any memo report worth a group's time is worth being correct.

PRESENTING THE REPORT

You may be asked to do a presentation of your memo report. You can prepare an outline, much like your report. An introduction, a body, and a summary will provide the basis for your oral presentation. Many people become nervous at the mention of a presentation. Nervousness is expected; try not to let it overwhelm you. Being well prepared to give your speech, accompanied by some appropriate visual aids, will give you the confidence you need to do an effective presentation.

SUMMARY

Reports serve as a basis for vital business decision making. The formal report is appropriate for reports sent outside the organization. Memo reports are the most popular form for routine reports sent within an organization. Statistical data within a memo report is best illustrated using tables, charts, and graphs. The most common and effective technique for organizing a memo report is to itemize the information.

Many organizations use teams or committees to collaboratively write lengthy documents such as memo reports. You may also be asked to present your report to other decision makers. If you are asked to do this, prepare an introduction, body, and summary for your speech and use appropriate visual aids.

Name _____ Date _____

WHAT'S WRONG WITH THESE?

Indicate on the lines provided what is wrong with each of the following memo report excerpts:

1. In my opinion, you should hire three new workers to cover the extra work.

    _____

2. Attached heretofore are the projected statistical, comprehensive enumerations.

    _____

3. Heading for a memo report:

    TO: Baily Clark
    FROM: Cameron Drew
    SUBJECT: Available Figures for February

    _____

4. The returns for this month are 35, 63, 22, 87, 22. Last month's returns were 34, 23, 44, 51,14.

    _____

    _____

5. We are very sorry to inform you that it will not be feasible for us to change to a staffing service.

    _____

    _____

WRITING EXERCISES

6. Rewrite the following introductory paragraph for a memo report concerning movie re-releases.

There have been huge successes with the re-release of three films. The re-release of three Worldwide films three months ago was in the test markets of New York, Boston, and Atlanta. We thought that we were in an era of "nostalgia" fever. We were right. Because of revenues as evidenced by the gross receipts from these films during the past two months.

_____

_____

_____

_____

Name _____ Date _____

WRITING EXERCISES *(continued)*

7. Write a memo report.

You are the assistant warehouse manager for Poly Plastics, Inc. The main office and the warehouse for your company are located in Los Angeles, California. About two years ago, Poly opened its first branch office, a sales office in New York, from which four full-time sales representatives sell Poly products on the East Coast. These four men and women have developed annual sales on the East Coast of approximately $3.56 million—a growth of about $3 million in about two years. In the same period, Poly's West Coast business has grown from about $12.2 million to $17.6 million. To meet the tremendous increase in demand for its products, Poly expanded its manufacturing facilities last year, but its warehouse space has remained the same.

Everyone in the company (including you and your boss, Tom Chang, warehouse manager) is aware of the obvious need for more warehouse space. In addition, everyone agrees that Poly should lease a new warehouse—but where? Most staff assume that Poly will lease another warehouse in the Los Angeles area, but you are convinced that this is not the best solution.

Having studied the problem carefully, you are ready to recommend that Poly lease a warehouse in New Jersey. Among your reasons are the following: The Los Angeles warehouse is spacious enough to handle all of Poly's West Coast business for many years. Although business has grown in recent years, company analysts agree that sales on the West Coast have peaked; they do not expect West Coast sales to increase substantially during the next ten years. Future growth will come from New York, Pennsylvania, Massachusetts, and Connecticut. A warehouse in the New Jersey area would be able to handle orders for these states faster than a Los Angeles warehouse could handle orders; in addition, shipping would be cheaper from a New Jersey warehouse. Since the space available in the present Los Angeles warehouse would be sufficient to take care of all West Coast business, the New Jersey warehouse could then take care of all East Coast business.

Through a real estate broker, you have found suitable warehouses in three New Jersey towns—Trenton, Somerville, and Secaucus. Each site provides more than 200,000 square feet and is available for long-term leasing at a reasonable rent. You plan to enclose with your memo to Mr. Chang a description, supplied by the real estate broker, of the three warehouses.

After preparing a report plan on the lines below, write your memo report to Tom Chang on a separate sheet of paper.

_____

_____

_____

_____

_____

_____

_____

_____

Name _____ Date _____

_____

_____

_____

_____

COLLABORATIVE ACTIVITY

Compiling Survey Results In groups of three, write five questions about a topic that interests your group. Survey all your class members. Compile the results into a memo report addressed to your instructor from your group. Possible topics could be favorite movies, TV shows, musical groups, occupational goals, hobbies, and so on. Include a table or chart to show the statistical information.

PROOFREADING EXERCISE

Proofread the following statistical report excerpt. Mark errors on the table with proofreaders' marks.

Original data: Title of table: Section Quarterly Report, Section A 1,569 for Jan., 1,126 for Feb., and 2,654 for Mar. Section B 2,578 for Jan., 1,859 for Feb., and 8,764 for Mar. Section C has 7,463 for Jan., 10,811 for Feb., and 5,783 for Mar.

Report data:

Section Bi-Quartrly Report			
	JAN	Feb	MAR
Section A	1,569	1,116	2,456
Section b	2,578	1,589	8764
section C	7,453	10,811	5,783

Search for Information on Nonverbal Communication
Search the Internet for information about body language or nonverbal communication that is appropriate to use in oral presentations. Prepare a list of tips and techniques for effective oral communication and/or presentations.

NOTES

Chapter 18

Writing Directions, Instructions, and Abstracts

Chapter 17 emphasized the writing of various types of reports. You practiced

- Writing memo reports, and

- Formatting various types of tables and charts for your reports.

Did you ever feel as if you would like to get off the Information Superhighway and drive down a quiet country road? Others feel the same way. It is important, therefore, to be able to give information in a concise, accurate form.

Objectives

After completing this chapter, you should be able to:
- Write directions.
- Write instructions.
- Write abstracts and executive summaries.

WRITING DIRECTIONS AND INSTRUCTIONS

Although some people use the terms *instructions* and *directions* interchangeably, for purposes of this discussion, **instructions** tell *how to do a task* and **directions** tell *how to get somewhere.* Instructions and directions are similar, but because there are differences between them, we will discuss them in separate sections of this chapter.

Format

The **format** (arrangement, spacing, and indentions) of a document determines whether that document looks easy to read and understand or looks complicated and difficult to understand.

 Written instructions and directions seem clearer and more concise if they are prepared in a format that is visually clear and easy to follow. To make directions and instructions visually clear, use a listing format with adequate white space, headings, and indentions.

Here are two examples of the same instructions showing how format can influence clarity:

CONFUSING FORMAT:

To automatically insert the path and document name at the end of your Word document, put your cursor in the location where you want the name to appear. Drop the insert menu and choose field, document information, and file name. To include the path with the document name choose options, field specific switches, and Add to Field. Choose "OK twice."

CLEARER FORMAT:

Insert Path and File Name at End of Word Document:

1. Click insertion point in document where Path and File Name appear.
2. Drop the Insert menu.
3. Choose Field.
4. Choose Document information.
5. Choose File name.
6. Choose Options.
7. Click on "Field-Specific Switches."
8. Choose Add field.
9. Choose "OK" twice.

The amount of detail and explanation you use will depend on the background of the person for whom you are writing the instructions. **Visuals** (pictures or sketches) of steps in a procedure are extremely helpful because they allow readers to *see* what they are to do. In this situation, the old saying "A picture is worth a thousand words" really is true.

18-1—Analyzing Instructions Is the instruction "Turn left" a sentence or a phrase?

Writing Directions

Directions tell how to get from one place to another, whether it is just down the hall, across town, or across the country.

Nothing is more frustrating than having directions to your destination and then getting lost because the directions were not clear or accurate.

Keep these guidelines in mind when writing directions:

1. Use a listing format, not paragraphs.
2. Use concise phrases (or short sentences, if appropriate).
3. Put each new direction on a separate line.
4. Give the directions in sequence.
5. Give both compass direction (north, south, east, and west) and right or left information.
6. When listing exits from interstate highways, give both the name of the exit and the exit number. Specify the compass direction if there is a choice of directions (e.g., Neil Street south—Exit 51A).
7. Be specific with distances and time (how many blocks, miles, minutes).
8. Give exact addresses, suite numbers, room numbers, and so on.
9. When describing how many flights of stairs, remember that each set of steps is a flight. To get from one floor to another in a building may be two or even three flights of stairs.
10. Be accurate with descriptions of traffic signs. A stop *light* (traffic signal) and a stop *sign* are not the same thing.

If the person you are writing the directions for is from another culture, you may need to explain the terminology you are using. For example, in Europe the first floor of a building is called the *ground floor* and the floor above it is called the *first floor* (the first floor above ground level). In the United States in most public buildings the ground level is the first floor and the floor above that is the second floor. What we call a *subway* may be called the *underground*, the *tube*, or the *metro* in other countries. We take an *elevator* to get to different floors in a building, but the term in some countries is *lift* instead of elevator.

Most people today are **visual learners.** This means that they grasp information most easily and quickly when they can *see* it. Therefore, visual learners appreciate a map as well as written directions. You can use a light-colored highlighter to mark a route on a map. When drawing a map, remember that the top of a map is north and should be labeled as such.

All labeling on a map should be printed the same direction (vertically, horizontally, or at the same angle). Indicate whether the map is or is not to scale. If part of the map has been omitted, use a jagged line to indicate that fact. This helps keep everything in proportion.

Be sure that the print is big enough to read. People sometimes reduce a big map but forget that the text is also reduced along with the map (sometimes the text is so small that it is impossible to read).

The most difficult directions to write are to a place you know very well. You can get there without even thinking about it, but it is so easy to leave out a detail

18-1:

GIVING DIRECTIONS

John invited several colleagues to his farm to make apple cider and enjoy a potluck supper. Most of his colleagues had never been to his farm. The directions said to turn right at the old Texaco station onto a gravel road. The old Texaco station was closed, and all identifying signs were gone. The road was blacktop for the first quarter mile and then became a gravel road. The number of miles between turns was not given on the directions. The people who had never been to John's farm did not make the turn because they did not see the Texaco station and the road was blacktop, not gravel.

Go to Student CD-ROM Activity 18-1.

SUCCEED!

18-2—Writing Procedures *Why would writing down the procedure make you more productive and show that you are competent?*

that will make your directions incorrect. If possible, you should try to actually make the trip following the directions you wrote to be sure that they are correct and complete.

Writing Instructions

Before you can write instructions, you need to understand how to do what it is you are trying to make clear. You may write instructions for yourself, or you may write instructions for someone else to use.

Instructions for Yourself

Many employees write instruction manuals for their own jobs. These manuals are often referred to as *office procedures manuals*. Written instructions are especially valuable if there are certain tasks you do or documents you produce on an occasional basis. When too much time elapses between each occurrence for you to remember the procedure, writing down the procedure for later reference will make you more productive and show that you are competent.

Most employers or supervisors do not mind explaining something in detail once. After that, they expect you to remember it or have notes of your own to refer to. Having instructions written down in a procedures manual is also very helpful for another employee who needs to complete the task or a temporary employee who must complete the task if you are out of the office.

Instructions for Others

When writing instructions for others, consider the following:

1. **How familiar the reader will be with the process.** For example, instructions for operating a VCR would probably need to be more detailed for a person who seldom used a VCR than they would be for a young adult who is very comfortable with technology. Likewise, instructions on how to copy files from the desktop to a disk would need to be more detailed for someone who rarely performs this procedure on a computer.

2. **How much detail should be included.** For example, instructions for resetting the time on a clock or setting an alarm do not need to include details about how the clock is made—only how to reset the time and set the alarm. Instructions for adding a watermark to a document do not need to include information on why this feature is important or the pros and cons of using a watermark.

If you are writing instructions for a large audience and you do not know the audience members, it is best to assume that your readers know nothing about the process. Be careful, however, not to include unnecessary information.

Follow these guidelines when writing instructions:

1. **Use a descriptive title.** Identify the purpose of the instructions by giving them a descriptive title. If necessary, use an introductory paragraph that explains what will be accomplished by completing the steps and/or why the instructions should be followed. List any materials that are required.

2. **Number and list each step on a separate line in correct order.**
   Numbering the items implies that the instructions should be completed in the order in which they are listed. Put each step on a separate line instead of putting the instructions in paragraph format. The separate-line setup is much easier to follow.

3. **Use phrases or concise sentences.** Start each instruction with an action verb (e.g., *Click, Choose, Do, Press, Type, Mix*).

4. **Limit each step to one item.** Instructions are much easier to follow if the reader can read one step, complete it, and then check the list for the next step. If two things need to be completed at the same time, put both of them in the same numbered item.

5. **Group instructions under side headings.** If there are numerous steps, use some side headings to group the instructions. Each group of instructions should have no more than ten steps.

6. **Interrupt instructions.** You may put "notes" in instructions letting the reader know what will happen if the step has been performed correctly. Include any warnings about safety issues that could cause injury or damage. Set interrupting instructions off from regular text in some way. Possibilities include putting them in bold, in all-capital letters, in a different font, in italics, or in a box.

7. **Write instructions for completing a form.** Give both the name and number of the form. Supply a sample of a form that has been completed correctly.

8. **Check the accuracy of the instructions.** Have someone who is not familiar with the process follow your instructions to find out whether they are accurate, complete, and clear. Then, revise the instructions if necessary and have another person try to follow the revised version.

9. **Identify and date the document.** At the end of the instructions supply the document name and the date. This is especially important when instructions are revised or updated. With this information at the end of the instructions, you can quickly determine which is the most recent version.

Use words that will be clear to the user—not industry jargon. A good example of this is the message "Hit any key to continue" that we frequently see on computer screens. *Hit* means "striking an object with a blow." Actually, you only need to *press* (not *hit*) any key to continue.

WRITING AN ABSTRACT

Because of the information overload phenomenon everyone is experiencing today, the ability to read a report or publication and summarize the relevant points is an extremely valuable skill. Many executives or supervisors ask for condensed versions of documents because they simply don't have time to read complete reports or publications. Reading summaries of publications, research, and reports makes it possible for the professionals, senior-level executives, and others to keep up to date on current information. Many newsletters

18-2:

*GIVING COMPLETE
INSTRUCTIONS*

Marietta had to be absent from work on Wednesday, but she knew that on her desk that morning would be a very important document that would be edited by her employer and would need to be corrected on disk and sent out by noon. Marietta left detailed instructions for the temp (temporary worker) about whom to get to sign the document, whom to mail it to, etc. The one detail she left out, however, was the name of the file or on which disk the file could be found.

**Go to Student
CD-ROM
Activity 18-2.**

and journals provide abstracts of published articles that are of interest to their subscribers.

Many libraries, particularly college and university libraries, subscribe to one or more services that provide abstracts of articles and research in a variety of fields.

 An **abstract** is a brief or condensed version of a report or publication. The purpose of an abstract is to

- Save the reader time.
- Give the reader a summary or condensed version.
- Give enough information so that the reader can decide whether to read the entire article or report.

Abstracts are generally one of two types:

1. **Descriptive abstracts.** A descriptive abstract is like an expanded table of contents in sentence form. It tells you *what is covered* in the article or publication.
2. **Informative Abstracts.** An informative abstract *summarizes the entire report or publication* by presenting an overview of the facts.

Here is an example of both types of abstracts using the same article:

DESCRIPTIVE ABSTRACT:
This report discussed the advantages of voice mail for a small organization.

INFORMATIVE ABSTRACT:
Voice mail improves communication because a message can be left 24 hours a day, no caller receives a busy signal, and messages can be retrieved from anywhere in the world.

An **executive summary** is used in the business world and is a kind of informative abstract. Other terms sometimes used for an abstract are *overview, synopsis, brief, digest, highlights,* or *abridgment.* An executive summary is a short, concise version of the full report and contains only relevant information. An executive summary should contain enough information that an executive could make a decision without reading the entire report.

Before writing an abstract or executive summary, do the following:

1. Make a photocopy of the original document.
2. Underline or highlight the important points (the key points).
3. Check the opening and closing paragraphs closely for main ideas.
4. Look for the purpose and scope of the document.
5. Look for the methods used if research or an experiment is involved.
6. Look for results obtained or findings.
7. Look for conclusions.
8. Look for recommendations.

18-3—Taking Notes
How is taking notes from a textbook or speech similar to writing an abstract?

 The length of an abstract can range from one paragraph to a page or two. The generally accepted guideline is that the length *of an abstract or executive summary should be no more than 10 percent of the length of the original document.*

When writing an abstract or executive summary, follow these tips:

1. **For accuracy, use the same terminology the author used.** In this case, plagiarism is *not* a problem.

2. **Summarize the original work.** Write so that the abstract is concise and clear but complete. Omit or condense lengthy examples, tables, and details. Do *not* include anything in the abstract that is not in the original document.

3. **Write the summary as an independent document.** Do not refer the reader to the report or publication itself or to any figures or tables that appear in the document. Write the summary as though the reader will not have an opportunity to read the whole document.

4. **Use a standard report format.** Use complete sentences. If you are using a bulleted format, phrases may be acceptable for the bulleted items.

5. **Use side headings, if appropriate.** Side headings help the reader quickly understand the information.

6. **Edit and condense the abstract.**

Give a complete citation for the publication so that the person reading the abstract can obtain the complete document, if desired. A citation includes the name of the publication, name of the article, name of the author, publication date, publishing company, and page number(s).

Figure 18-1 displays an article written by Carolyn Grady, and Figure 18-2 is an abstract of the article.

FIGURE 18-1 This article by Carolyn Grady discusses the principles of effective communication.

Carolyn Grady of Oshkosh Office Systems, Inc., Oshkosh, Wisconsin, has this to say about effective communication:

Effective communication within any organization is critical to its success. Just like a successful marriage, an organization needs to find ways to ensure that it has in place an open, two-way communication network. Simply put, management must deliver a unified message as to organizational goals and direction, and employees need to be encouraged to give their views on conditions and concerns preventing them from performing their job responsibilities.

A top priority of management in organizations of all sizes should be making sure that everyone gets the straight story. Regardless of whether an organization is spread out geographically or housed at one location, typically not everyone receives a message at the same time or in the same way. Organizations are made up of men and women from all walks of life, each interpreting what the message is and reacting to it differently. Great effort needs to be made to ensure the message is clear and consistent. Organizations use lots of different ways to communicate— from companywide memos, publications, and formal meetings to e-mail, teleconferencing, and videos. The size and complexity of the organization in most cases dictate the practicality of the vehicle used.

Although communicating effectively from the top down is a challenge, it is even more difficult to make sure employees have the opportunity to voice their concerns. Large and small organizations alike can employ several different methods to make this happen. Utilizing opinion surveys so that all employees have an opportunity to convey their thoughts and ideas can generate positive results. The results of these surveys must be measured and tracked. Management must demonstrate a true sincerity in reporting back the results and making the necessary changes indicated. Without follow-up, the use of opinion surveys within an organization will be criticized and over time will not be successful. In addition, all organizations must encourage an open door policy. This policy encourages employees who have concerns to go to whatever level of management they feel is necessary to voice their concerns without retribution. These types of upward communication allow employees to feel that their opinions are valued and respected.

Although having an effective communication network in place is critical for a successful organization, making sure employees have the proper skills to communicate, in and outside the organization, is just as vital. In my opinion, the most important communication skill any employee can have is good listening. Now this may sound rather simplistic, but it should not be underestimated. A good listener is one who clarifies what has been communicated and asks questions when confused. As a former insurance agent and now responsible for managing

---

customer relationships for a medium-size business, I know the value of good listening. It is my responsibility to listen to my clients' concerns, ask key questions to evaluate the situation, and take the appropriate actions necessary to make sure things are done to correct the situation and take care of their needs. Without good listening skills, I could not do my job thoroughly.

In addition, employees need to be able to write and speak effectively. Getting ideas down on paper, professionally and concisely, is mandatory to being successful in the workplace. Your written words are a reflection of you and your organization. Writing a letter or any other form of written communication needs to be done properly. If not, your message will not be taken seriously and you risk the chance of being misunderstood. Speaking clearly and properly is also necessary to good communicating.

These skills are probably no different from those required for good communication years ago. Although the need for these basic skills has not changed, what has changed is the vehicle in which we use them today. Changes in technology have provided us with instant communication. Mailing a letter has been replaced with instant e-mail, and the keyboard and printer have eliminated the typewriter and reduced our handwriting skills. An emergency meeting can be called quickly via conference calling. Cellular phones and pagers are widely used. Voice mail allows us to no longer have to take a handwritten message and to rarely find a live voice at the other end of the phone line. And last, organizations can hold companywide meetings around the world via teleconferencing.

Global communications, language barriers, and foreign customs are growing factors we need to address as our world gets smaller. More than ever before, we need to sharpen our basic communication skills. In the future, it will be the organizations that demand this and utilize the newest technology to ensure they have well-informed employees who will reap the benefit of success for their investment.

(Source: Carolyn Grady, Oshkosh Office Systems, Inc., Oshkosh, Wisconsin, May 29, 2000. Ms. Grady was with Allstate Insurance Company for 15 years as an insurance agent. She and her husband Scott manage Oshkosh Office Systems, Inc. which they purchased in 1998.)

FIGURE 18-1 *(Continued)*

Effective communication is critical to an organization's success.

A top priority of management in any size organization should be making sure everyone gets the "straight story." Organizations use companywide memos, publications, and formal meetings as well as e-mail, teleconferencing, and videos to communicate.

All organizations must encourage open, two-way communication between all levels of employees.

Successful organizations make sure that employees have the proper skills to communicate in and outside the organization. The most important communication skill is good listening. Employees also need to be able to write and speak clearly and properly. Your words are a reflection of you and your organization.

Changes in technology have provided instant communication. As our world gets smaller, we need to sharpen our basic communication skills.

FIGURE 18-2 An informative abstract of the article by Carolyn Grady.

Today technology is available to help with abstracting. Some word processing programs have an "AutoSummarize" or "abstracting" feature that highlights and prints the main points of an article.

SUMMARY

An important part of written communication today is the ability to give clear directions and instructions. A listing format is the best way to present this information.

An abstract or an executive summary is a brief summary of an entire report. An abstract can be an informative summary or a descriptive summary. The summary may be from one paragraph to one or two pages but should not be more than 10 percent of the length of the entire report. You can use side headings to help the reader quickly understand the information.

Name _____ Date _____

WHAT'S WRONG WITH THESE?

1. Directions to post office: Go on Logan Avenue to Fairchild Street and turn. Drive to Hazel Street (you will pass three or four stop lights) and turn. The post office is on your left side.

   _____
   _____
   _____
   _____
   _____
   _____
   _____

2. Directions to football stadium in neighboring city: Take I-74 to Champaign and take the second exit. Drive to Florida Avenue and turn. Follow this street until you see the football stadium. Park in the parking lot.

   _____
   _____
   _____
   _____
   _____
   _____
   _____

WRITING EXERCISES

3. Write directions. Assume that you have invited a speaker to your class to talk about the importance of writing in the business world. This speaker knows how to get to the front entrance of your school. Write directions to your classroom, starting with where to park and ending up in your classroom.

   _____
   _____
   _____
   _____
   _____
   _____

4. Write instructions. Steps for folding a fitted bed sheet are given on the next page. Rewrite the instructions in a listing format following the guidelines in the chapter. Use separate paper for your instructions.

Name _____ Date _____

WRITING EXERCISES *(continued)*

To fold a fitted bed sheet if you are right-handed, simply follow these instructions. Turn the fitted sheet inside out and place one hand in each of two adjacent corners. Bring your right hand over to meet your left, and fold the corner in your right hand over the corner in your left hand. The sheet corner on top will be right-side out.

Reach down and pick up the corner that is adjacent to the one that was in your right hand; fold it onto your left hand, on top of the other two corners; this third corner will be inside out. Bring the fourth corner up, and fold it over the others so that it is right-side out.

Carefully lay the sheet on a flat surface, such as a bed or a table used for folding laundry. Adjust it into a rough square shape with one rounded corner where all four elasticized corners are layered together. Fold two sides toward the center, so the square is folded into thirds and you have a rectangle with straight sides; the elastic will now be hidden. Finally, fold the rectangle into the shape that fits best on your shelf or in your cupboard.

5. Write instructions. Write instructions for folding a letter for a No. 10 envelope. Use separate paper for your instructions.

6. Read the following summarized paragraph written by Shirleen Hackmann and write an informative abstract. (Source: Marilyn Satterwhite and Judith Olson-Sutton, *Business Communication at Work,* Glencoe/McGraw-Hill, Columbus, Ohio, 2000, p. 447.)

   > What are some of the challenges of communicating effectively within organizations? Challenges include the fast pace at which issues arise and decisions are made for treating them proactively. This brings to the forefront the importance of communication in delegating new tasks with additional responsibility. You must be able to communicate with people or the mission will be impossible to accomplish and the opportunity to gain the trust and respect of those with whom you work will be lost.

   _____

   _____

   _____

   _____

   _____

   _____

COLLABORATIVE WRITING

Writing Instructions With another team member, write complete instructions on how to tie shoe laces. Assume that the person reading the instructions has never tied a shoe before. Write a draft and then type it for submission to your instructor if requested or to share with your classmates.

Name _____ Date _____

PROOFREADING EXERCISE

Mark the errors in the following abstract using proofreaders' marks.

Computer work involves inputing, proccessing, and out-putting infarmation. Most information is input through the keyboard attach to a computer. Information is processed through the use of hardwar and softwear. Integrated soft-ware is the most popular software in offices today. Integrated software include word processing, spreadsheet, database, graphics and/or presentation packages. The most popular form of output are hard copy with disks not far behind. This article give several examples of ways too input, process, and output information.

Search the Internet for Abstract Guides
Connect to the Internet and look at these Websites. Print the information if asked to do so by your instructor.
<http://www.gmu.edu/departments/writingcenter/handouts/abstract.html>
<http://www-nss.oit.umass.edu/buscomm/absumm.html>
<http://myrin.ursinus.edu/help/resrch_guides/annotate.htm>

PART 4

Employment Communications

How do you get a job or find a better job?

It's a "job" to get a job! You need more than formal education, previous experience, and availability to get you on a payroll. You need to prepare a résumé and put into action a plan for securing employment. Even the best-qualified people need to know the techniques of getting a job.

Every business writer should be able to produce a professional document using the principles of good writing that you studied in Chapters 1 through 18. The techniques that you learned in Part 1 gave you the basic foundations of good writing. In Part 2 you learned specific approaches and techniques to write several different types of documents, such as e-mail messages, inquiries, order and acknowledgment messages, credit and collection messages, persuasive messages, and goodwill messages. In Part 3 you concentrated on the various meeting and memo reports, and you studied and practiced writing instructions and directions.

Part 4 continues to build your business writing skills, but concentrates on employment communications such as résumés, application letters, and other employment-related documents.

Job hunting is hard work—it takes just as much effort and skill as actually doing the job once you've been hired. You can make your job search easier if you take the time to do some careful planning and preparation.

You can't prepare a professional-looking résumé and a letter of application in an hour or two. Your personal "marketing campaign" takes time, research, careful planning, and analysis.

The main thing is to sell a product—yourself—to a customer—the prospective employer. Your résumé and letter of application should, therefore, be planned as carefully and strategically as a marketing campaign.

The goal in Part 4 is to help you prepare a résumé, complete an application form, prepare for an interview, and write thank-you and follow-up letters, letters accepting and refusing job offers, and resignation letters. Appendix B will help you prepare for an interview and give you some helpful tips for successful interviewing.

Statistics show that most of you will change careers several times and change jobs even more times in your working life. You will use the information in this part many times as you seek a new or a better job.

The following chapters will start you on the path toward a successful career:

Chapter 19 Preparing Résumés and Employment Applications

Chapter 20 Writing Application Letters and Other Employment Documents

Preparing Résumés and Employment Applications

You have studied various approaches to good business writing and have developed your skills in proofreading and editing. Now, you are ready to put your skills into the real world practice of finding a job or seeking a new position or an entirely new career. What will it take to make you successful in these endeavors? You already know most of the answer to that question. Now is the time to learn the rest. Chapter 19 presents information that will help you prepare an appropriate résumé. You will study the various formats that you may select and learn the reasons why one format may be better than or more appropriate than another one.

Objectives

After completing this chapter, you should be able to:

- Determine what employment skills you have.
- Identify three types of résumés.
- Prepare a résumé and a summary of qualifications and accomplishments.
- Complete an application form.

TODAY'S WORKPLACE

The only thing certain in today's workplace is change. We live and work in a global economy in which technological advances take place constantly. The traditional layers of management are gone as organizations look for ways to become more productive at less cost. To succeed in the job market, you need to be flexible and willing to learn new things so that you can adapt to the inevitable changes.

Let's start your "marketing campaign" to sell yourself to an employer by taking an inventory of your skills.

WHAT SKILLS DO YOU HAVE TO OFFER?

Before you can sell your ability and experience to an employer, you must identify your best traits, aptitudes, and skills. Try to get a complete and objective picture of yourself as an applicant by evaluating your qualifications as though they belonged to someone else.

The first step is to take an inventory of yourself:

- Your experience
- Your education
- Your personal qualities
- Your special interests and abilities

Jot down everything you can think of relating to:

- Part-time, temporary, and even volunteer work (include job duties).
- Subjects you excelled in as a student.
- What you learned in your courses and workshops.
- School and community activities.
- Hobbies and interests.
- Memberships and leadership roles in professional and service organizations.
- Awards, achievements, and honors.

Writing down these items (in any order) will help you think about what you have to offer a prospective employer. It will also give you clues about the kind of work you should be looking for.

Take the selling points you have and make the best of them by emphasizing them positively.

Assignment: To help you take inventory of yourself, complete the inventory in the section "Analyzing the Job Market and Yourself" in the worksheet at the end of this chapter.

WHAT DOES AN EMPLOYER WANT?

 No employer will give you a job because you need a job. You must keep the emphasis on *what you can do for the employer.*

According to employers, the top six areas that are vital to job success are:

1. Communication skills (write and speak effectively using proper grammar and correct spelling).
2. Good work habits (being organized).
3. Concern for productivity (doing it right the first time).
4. Dependability (being on time every day and meeting deadlines).
5. Ability to read job-related information and then apply it.
6. Teamwork (includes respect and politeness toward everyone).

If you believe that you do not have enough skills, employers suggest that you take the following actions to make yourself more employable:

- Take business and technical courses to keep up with new technology.
- Keep your computer skills up to date.
- Acquire business experience, perhaps through summer, part-time, and/or temporary jobs.
- Improve your communication skills.
- Enroll in a work-study program or internship through your school.
- Define your career goals.
- Improve your knowledge of business and how it works.
- Be flexible in the types of work you will consider.
- Be willing to relocate, travel, or work variable hours.
- Meet the requirements for entry-level jobs.
- Have a strong academic background.

PREPARING A RÉSUMÉ

Now that you have completed the first step in the employment process—analyzing yourself—you're ready to take the next step: preparing a written summary of your background. This summary is your résumé.

 Always prepare your résumé *before* you write your application letter. The application letter should not repeat details in the résumé but should interpret them in terms of the job.

19-1—Check Your Understanding of Terms *What is a biography?*

Putting your résumé together should help you organize your thoughts about yourself and see yourself realistically in relation to the job you want. Begin by rearranging the notes you've made into categories. Then pick out the key points (a résumé is a *summary*, not a biography) and present them in a way that will give an employer a truthful and persuasive picture of (1) who you are and (2) what you can do. A good résumé must be tailored to suit your background as well as the specific type of job you are applying for.

The résumé is probably your most helpful job-hunting tool because it focuses attention on your strong points and can be left behind as your representative. Think of the résumé as your sales promotion piece.

Dozens of books, pamphlets, and articles have been written on how to prepare a résumé, and they all have different approaches. Likewise, all human resources managers are different and have their own likes and dislikes concerning résumés. Consequently, there is no "right" format for a résumé. Remember, the fact that the employer is looking at your résumé means that you are in competition with many others.

 The more professional your résumé, the better your chances are to be selected for an interview. Quality is critical in *every* aspect. Your résumé is *you*—on paper.

The suggestions in this section—based on the likes and dislikes of many employers—will help you prepare an effective résumé that will make a favorable impression on most prospective employers. First, let's examine the blocks of information that most résumés contain: heading, career or job objective or summary, experience, education, additional information, and references.

The Heading

Begin with your identification:

- Your full name.
- Complete mailing address (both permanent and temporary, if applicable).
- Telephone number (including area code).

These items should stand out at the top of the page. Be sure that the telephone number is one where messages will be taken during business hours. Do not type a heading such as *DATA SHEET* or *RÉSUMÉ* (it will be obvious).

Job or Career Objective or Summary

You can incorporate your career goals in one of three ways: (1) a job or career objective, (2) a summary, or (3) in your letter of application (instead of on the résumé).

 A general *job or career objective* stating the type of work desired works best for job seekers who have limited work experience. A *summary* of skills and accomplishments that match the employers' needs works best for the job seeker who has work experience.

Job or Career Objective

The **career objective** is a concise statement indicating the type of job you are looking for and reflecting your goals for the next three to five years. Avoid stating a job objective in the following ways:

> Position as sales associate with eventual goal to become president of the organization. (That's a bit presumptuous!)

> An interesting job with a challenging opportunity. (This is too general; everyone wants a challenging opportunity.)

> A job working with people. (This is also too general; practically every job requires working with people.)

19-2—Writing Career Objectives *When would you list a specific job as your career objective? When would you list a type or category of jobs?*

Better ways to express a job objective include the following:

Medical office assistant in health services environment.

Customer service position in the travel industry.

Web master for a medium-sized organization.

You can change the job objective on each résumé to fit the particular position you are applying for. This kind of adjustment is easy with word processing.

Summary

A summary (instead of a career or job objective) is used most often by people who have work experience. Summarize three or four of your skills that match the prospective employer's needs.

Omission of Job Objective or Summary

A résumé does not have to contain a job objective or summary. Instead, this information can be included in the letter of application that you mail with your résumé.

Experience

Work experience is usually the key part of a résumé. Begin with your current or most recent job, and work backward to your first job.

List All Pertinent Work Experience

Give the organization name and complete mailing address, and list your job responsibilities and accomplishments.

Emphasize what you have accomplished. List part-time jobs such as baby-sitting, delivering newspapers, mowing lawns, retail sales, stocking shelves, fast-food service, and waiting on tables. If your paid work experience is limited, list volunteer work you have done. Work experience doesn't have to be paid to be valuable to a prospective employer.

Remember, *you learn something of value from every job*. Let's look at some examples of beginning jobs:

- A baby-sitter is wholly responsible for the life of a helpless human being.
- A newspaper delivery route offers good training in meeting a schedule whatever the weather, in managing other people's (the newspaper's) money, and in selling.
- Mowing lawns means caring for other people's property, running an expensive machine, and being reliable in your service.
- A salesclerk gives customer service, operates a cash register, and handles money.
- A person stocking shelves has to keep records, work with inventories, and follow directions.
- People who work in the food service industry write orders, run a cash register, and make change.

19-1:
PROOFREAD CAREFULLY
Sally's résumé contained this statement in the summary: "Proven ability to track down and correct erors."

All these jobs offer experience in meeting the public and dealing with people.

If you have lots of work experience, you can omit the less important part-time jobs.

Give Concise but Complete Facts

Include the following facts for *each* job:

1. Position held.
2. Name of supervisor.
3. Organization name.
4. Complete mailing address.
5. Brief description of your duties.
6. Starting and ending dates (month and year).

If you have gaps in your work history, you may

- Give only the beginning year and ending year of employment.
- Give the length of employment (e.g., 2 years or 4 years).
- Use a skills or functional résumé.

Emphasize previous job duties that pertain to the job for which you are applying (even though they may not have been your primary job responsibilities). Present your job duties in the best possible light.

WEAK: "Did some filing."

IMPROVED: "Filing and retrieving correspondence and customer orders for Sales Department."

Start with *action* verbs that describe your job responsibilities. Here are some examples:

analyzed	implemented	planned
conducted	improved	prepared
coordinated	increased	produced
created	initiated	reorganized
developed	maintained	saved
established	managed	sold
expanded	operated	supervised
handled	organized	trained

Education

Begin with your current or most recent education and work backward to high school. If you have a degree or diploma from college, you may omit your high school education. List the following information about your education:

1. Names of schools.
2. Complete mailing addresses.
3. Degrees earned.
4. Majors and minors.
5. Dates attended (optional).
6. Year(s) graduated (include this information if it is recent).

19-2:
PROOFREAD DATES CAREFULLY
Jose listed his work experience dates as 1891–1998.

If you have not completed a degree, list what you have completed, such as a one-year certificate for software support specialist or 18 semester hours in business. If your grade point average is B or better, you may wish to include it.

If education is your main selling point, use a subheading called *Educational Highlights* and list the following:

1. Courses (a few major courses with the most important ones first).
2. Skills (such as typing speed, letter composition, records management, ability to operate special equipment, customer service).
3. Knowledge (such as software programs and programming languages).
4. Specialized training (such as seminars, workshops, and special courses).

List these items in the order of importance to a prospective employer, with the most impressive first.

Additional Information

If you think it will help your qualifications for a job, develop a category on your résumé to include any other information that you consider a selling point, such as:

- Leadership.
- Leisure activities (your interests and hobbies that are job related).
- Special honors and accomplishments (scholarships and other awards).
- Military service and current status.
- Membership in professional and service organizations.

If you've been out of school for more than a few years, don't include extracurricular activities—list only honors and awards.

Personal Details

Do not include a picture of yourself or personal details such as age, weight, height, marital status, dependents, health, and Social Security number. If you are female and have young children, do not include that information on your résumé. Many recruiting firms recommend omitting any reference to your age—especially if you are over 39 years old.

Signature and Date Line

Some employers like the personalized touch of a handwritten date and signature at the end of a résumé, as illustrated in Figure 19-1. If you wish to provide a place to date and sign your résumé, type a line with the word *Date* under it and a second line (either under or to the right of the date line) with the word *Signature* under it.

References

Ask permission before naming any person as a reference. Since you want to list only people who will give you a favorable recommendation, ask for permission

Amy J. Delphi

319 Blue Street	Montezuma, Indiana 47862	(317) 555-2417

Career Objective
An administrative assistant position with opportunity for advancement Montezuma Community College, Montezuma, Indiana 47862.

Education
Associate of Applied Science degree, Administrative Assistant and Desktop Publishing majors (May 2000)

Educational Highlights

Office Skills	Computer Skills
Typing—60 wpm	Microsoft Office
Transcription	Word
Records Management	Excel
Centrex Phone System	Access
Correspondence	PowerPoint
Design fliers	PageMaker
Work independently	WordPerfect

Experience
Secretary, part-time, Kelly Temporary Services, 2 Towne Center, Danville, IL 61832   (June 1999 to present)
Duties: type correspondence, file, answer phone and take messages, take inventory, type purchase orders, use microfilm machine including changing film cartridges, and ordering film for files. Arrange and display products on the selling floor.
          Supervisor: Adrian Hinkle, Agent
          Telephone: 317-555-0418

Work-study student, part-time, Montezuma Community College, Montezuma, IN 47862   (August 1998 to May 1999)
Duties: check out mechanical and electrical tools to students, keep records of tools, answer phone, type, file, write correspondence.
          Supervisor: Nancy McDonald, Tool Room Supervisor
          Telephone: 317-555-9643

Activities and Honors
Montezuma Community College Dean's List, Fall 1999
MCC's Cross Country and Track team,
          varsity letter winner, 1998-2000

References
Available upon request

_____   _____
(signature)   (date)

FIGURE 19-1 The signature line and the date line personalize the résumé. Some employers like these optional additions.

in this way: "Do you feel you know me well enough that I could use your name as a reference?" That gives people a tactful way to decline if they can't honestly give you a good recommendation.

When listing references, follow these suggestions:

1. Give three to five references (maximum of one character reference), putting them in list form for easier reading.

2. Use a courtesy title *(Mr., Miss, Ms., Mrs., Dr.,* and so on) before each name.

3. Follow the name with the person's job title *(Manager, Accounting and Collection Department; Professor of English; Sales Manager; Word Processing Supervisor).*

4. Give a complete mailing address (business rather than home address) for each reference.

5. Give a telephone number (including the area code) for each reference. Many employers would rather telephone than write to a reference. The employer saves time and can also tell a lot from the person's tone of voice as he or she describes you.

 Include both school and job references. Name as references only people who know you well enough to report on your work habits and on the quality of work you do in school or on the job.

References may be included as part of the résumé or on a separate sheet of paper.

References as Part of the Résumé
List your references in an easy-to-read arrangement as the last block of information on the résumé.

References on a Separate Page
Instead of listing references, many résumés include a statement at the end of the résumé: "References available on request." This may be necessary if you wish to limit your résumé to one page. If you choose this option, you should prepare a separate sheet with the heading "References for (your name)."

Now that we have examined the basic categories of information for your résumé, let's look at some other aspects of writing and preparing the finished product.

What to Include and What to Omit
Borrow a trick from the professionals who write advertisements and sales letters. Have you ever seen an ad for wood siding for a house that points out that it will have to be painted every four years? It's unlikely. These professionals avoid the negative; you should do the same in your résumé. If your typing speed is good or your grade point average is high, include the information. If not, don't mention it.

 You get to pick and choose the information that goes on your résumé. Obviously, you will include only your positive selling points.

A statement such as "Federal law prohibits discrimination because of race, color, religion, age, sex, marital status, disability, or national origin" is on most

19-5—Selecting References *What message does it send to an employer if you are a recent graduate and do not list any of your instructors as a reference?*

employment forms, and these forms have no questions about this information. However, no law prohibits *you* from including this information on your résumé. As a general rule, omit any information that gives your race, religion, political preference, salary, or reasons for changing jobs. However, if you believe that any of this information could be an asset to you in securing a particular job, include it.

Go to Student CD-ROM Activity 19-1.

Stressing the Qualifications Most Important to the Job

Remember that a human resources manager reads résumés the way you read a newspaper article—you start at the beginning and you read until you lose interest. After the heading and job or career objective, put the category (education or experience) that is your stronger selling point for the job you want.

Writing Style

 Think of your résumé as an *organized summary in outline form* highlighting facts (not opinions or interpretations) about your abilities and your training. These facts should be tabulated—listed in columns, *not* explained in sentences and paragraphs.

Use only words and phrases, and eliminate the use of the word *I*. For example, you would write, "Responsible for setting up and maintaining central filing system for regional office" rather than "I was responsible for . . ."

Format and Appearance

Your résumé is probably the first glimpse a prospective employer has of you and how you do things. Make it attractive, uncluttered, neat, and correct.

Paper

Use good-quality (20-pound) 8½- by 11-inch paper. Never use an organization's letterhead; plain white paper is the most common, but some people use a buff color and a few people use a pastel color for attention. The envelope should match the paper used for the résumé in weight, finish, and color.

White Space

Leave sufficient white space around and between columns so that all information stands out and is easy to find and read. Center all the headings, or use all side headings. Arrange all the data on one page if you can do so without crowding. If you need to include more details than will fit on one page, arrange the information attractively on two sheets (use only one side of the paper). The heading on the second page should have your name at the left margin and Page 2 at the right margin.

Length and Accuracy

Your résumé should be as long as necessary to do the job effectively—but no longer. Proofread it very carefully for typing errors, misspelled words, and inaccurate details such as dates, ZIP Codes, and phone numbers.

A prospective employer will consider your résumé a sample of your best work; it must be perfect.

Types of Résumés

Three popular styles for the arrangement of data in a résumé are (1) chronological, (2) skills or functional, and (3) combination.

Chronological Résumé

This style gives information in reverse chronological order with dates. A chronological résumé is the easiest to write and prepare and works best for people with a steady employment background. Human resources people like this style best because they don't have to hunt for any information. The résumés in Figure 19-2 and Figure 19-3 illustrate this style.

David S. Douglas
3166 Logan Terrace
Glasgow, Kentucky 42141
606-555-8826

CAREER OBJECTIVE
Position in motel/restaurant management with opportunity for advancement.

EXPERIENCE

6/98—present **Mando's Italian Food,** 4023 Summer Avenue, Glasgow, KY 42141. Duties: Worked as cook six nights a week (about 45 hours a week). Responsible for closing restaurant Mondays through Thursdays.

7/9—5/98 **Red Apple Inn,** 611 Madison Avenue, Glasgow, KY 42141 Duties: Worked as waiter (about 25 hours a week) while attending State Technical Institute.

6/94—5/96 **U.S. Army,** Fort Polk, LA 71459. Attained rank of sergeant. Supervised training for 500 personnel. Received Honorable Discharge and Good Conduct Medal.

9/93—5/94 **Oscar's Grocery,** 4070 Willow Street, Neon, KY 41840. Duties: Did general grocery duties including stocking shelves, arranging displays, and serving customers.

EDUCATION

9/96—/98 **State Technical Institute,** Glasgow, KY 42141. Received Associate of Science degree in Motel/Restaurant Management.

9/91—6/94 **Memorial High School,** Neon, KY 41840. Graduated in top 15 percent of class.

ACTIVITIES

ROTC officer at State (two years). Photographer for college yearbook. President of high school senior class. Captain of high school basketball team.

REFERENCES

Mr. James P. Lucchesi   Ms. Lena Jensen
Owner, Mando's Italian Food   Manager, Red Apple Inn
4023 Summer Avenue   611 Madison Avenue
Glasgow, KY 42141   Glasgow, KY 42141
606-555-8361   606-555-4492

Mr. William B. Champion, Division Head
General-Vocational Technologies
State Technical Institute
Glasgow, KY 42141
606-555-4468

FIGURE 19-2 This résumé illustrates a chronological style. David Douglas stresses his work experience by listing it first.

Skills or Functional Résumé

This style highlights skills and qualifications. Because it does not include dates or places of employment, it is convenient for an applicant who wants to avoid mentioning breaks in employment or frequent job changes. This style also works well for the person who is shifting career focus and wants to emphasize skills rather than job titles.

Combination Résumé

This style combines aspects of the chronological and the skills or functional résumé. The experience block is divided into two sections: (1) job skills and qualifications followed by (2) dates and places of employment. This style is especially effective when you've had several jobs with similar job duties, because it allows you to eliminate repetition and to prepare a more concise résumé. This style is illustrated in Figure 19-4.

19-6—Defining Terms *What does* chronological *mean?*

Katie M. Trosper
121 South Bowman
Danville, IL 61832
217-555-1687

OBJECTIVE   An Administrative Assistant position with opportunity for advancement

EDUCATION: Danville Area Community College, Associate of Applied Science
degree, Administrative Assistant major, May 2000

EDUCATIONAL   *Computer Skills*   *Office Skills*
HIGHLIGHTS   Microsoft Office 2000   Typing—56 wpm
                    Adobe PageMaker 6.5   Accounting
                    WordPerfect 2000   Machine Dictation
                    Lotus 1-2-3   10-key calculator
                    Internet/E-mail   Communication Skills

                    Management Skills
                    Supervisory Training
                    Interpersonal Relations
                    Principles of Management

WORK   Office Assistant
EXPERIENCE   Danville Area Community College, 2000 E. Main Street, Danville, IL 61832
11/98 — 5/00   217-555-8847 Viv Dudley, Supervisor
                            Duties: Filed, answered phone, distributed mail, composed
                            letters and memos, worked independently, typed, photocopied,
                            operated fax machine

10/97 — 1/98   Office Support
                    Pro Staff Temporary Services, 13739 Omega Drive, Dallas, TX 75244
                    972-555-4400 Marnie McCuistion, Supervisor
                            Duties: Customer service, filed, answered phones, directed
                            calls, retrieved documents, documented payroll hours in
                            books, typed, photocopied, operated fax machine

2/96 — 12/96   Waitress
                    Pizza Inn, 3003 North Galloway, Mesquite, TX 75150
                    972-555-7861 Dawn Nelson, Supervisor
                            Duties: Customer service, answered phones, took orders,
                            prepared food, operated cash register

9/92 — 3/95   Shift Manager and Waitress
                    Pizza Hut, 3585 North Vermilion Street, Danville, IL 61832
                    217-555-1006 Abe Pezeshki, Supervisor
                            Duties: Customer service, answered phones, took orders,
                            prepared food, operated cash register, made deposits, completed
                            books for day ending, managed staff of five employees

REFERENCES   Available upon request.

FIGURE 19-3 Katie Trosper has prepared two résumés. The chronological style is shown here, and the combination style in Figure 19-4.

Katie M. Trosper
121 South Bowman
Danville, IL 61832
217-555-1687

OBJECTIVE   An Administrative Assistant position with opportunity for
             advancement

QUALIFICATIONS
             Computer Skills: Windows   Microsoft Office Suite 2000
                                 Internet/E-mail   (Word, Access, Excel, PowerPoint)
                                 WordPerfect 2000
                                 Adobe PageMaker 6.5
                                 Lotus 1-2-3
                     • Set up merge files
                     • Created databases
                     • Created spreadsheets
                     • Created PowerPoint Presentations
                     • Designed publications

             Organizational Skills:
                     • Set up filing system on disks
                     • Responsible for distributing paychecks to companies

             Customer Service Skills:
                     • Communicated daily with public and consistently projected
                       a positive company image
                     • Dealt well with customers via telephone and fax

             Secretarial Skills:
                     • Maintained and updated employee records
                     • Answered phones and took messages

EXPERIENCE   Office Assistant, Danville Area Community College
             2000 East Main Street, Danville, IL 61832
             11/98 to 5/00

             Office Support, Pro Staff Temporary Services
             13739 Omega Drive, Dallas, TX 75244
             10/97 to 1/98

EDUCATION   Danville Area Community College, 2000 East Main Street,
             Danville, IL 61832, Associate of Applied Science degree,
             Administrative Assistant Personnel major, May 2000.

REFERENCES   Available upon request.

FIGURE 19-4 A combination résumé. A true skills or functional résumé would not list places of employment.

Scannable or Electronic Résumés

At the time this book was published, 30 to 50 percent of medium- to large-sized organizations and employment search firms scanned résumés and stored them in databases. When an opening occurs, the résumés are electronically searched for key words pertinent to the job opening. Key words include items such as job titles, degrees, majors, work habits, job duties, and computer skills. The résumés that contain the key words are electronically selected from the database for further review.

 Computers do not read résumés the same way human beings do. When you prepare a résumé that will be scanned, use *nouns* rather than action verbs, because the key words used for searching scannable résumés are nouns. Avoid lines, underlining, shading, graphics, and decorative typefaces. Avoid colored paper. Use 10- to 14-point Times Roman, Helvetica, or Arial typeface. Use plenty of white space.

Today it is common practice for organizations to ask that a résumé be faxed or e-mailed so that they will receive it quickly.

SUMMARY OF QUALIFICATIONS AND ACCOMPLISHMENTS

Although you will use your résumé primarily when applying for a job, you may also use it when you are seeking a promotion or asking for a raise or when you need a biographical sketch of yourself (to give to someone who will introduce you or nominate you for an award, for instance). For these reasons, it is important to keep your résumé up to date even when you're not looking for a job.

You may wish to prepare a summary of qualifications and accomplishments that includes the following information about you:

- Achievements
- Responsibilities
- Accomplishments
- Any additional pertinent training or education

You might use this report to help verify your productivity when you ask for a salary increase or seek a promotion or an interdepartmental transfer with your current employer.

COMPLETING THE EMPLOYMENT APPLICATION FORM

Even though you have a résumé, almost all prospective employers will ask you to complete an *application form* for employment. An application form seeks information by listing various statements to which you are to respond. The answers can give the prospective employer basic information about your skills and experience, for example. From this information and the way you respond to the statements, the employer can interpret it and learn other things about you.

Why do organizations use application forms?

- The form asks for the exact data the employer needs.
- The interviewer may use it as a guide for interviewing you.
- Information is listed in the same order for all applicants.

Interpreting Your Responses

By having you complete an application form, a prospective employer can get information about your education and experience. In addition, the prospective employer can get other information without your realizing it. The way you complete the application form answers the following hidden questions:

1. How well can you follow written directions?
2. How accurately can you complete a task?
3. How good are you with detail?
4. Are your work habits neat or sloppy?

Completing the Basic Information Statements

The best preparation for completing an employment application is to know what kinds of "information statements or questions" you will be asked.

Application forms can be one page or several pages long, but all application forms ask for these basic categories of information:

1. **Personal:** Your name and mailing address and your phone number during business hours.
2. **Education:** Dates and the levels of education you have completed, and names and addresses of schools.
3. **Experience:** Places and dates of previous employment. A category for volunteer experience now appears on many applications.
4. **References:** Names, addresses, and phone numbers of at least three people who can recommend you.
5. **Signature:** To verify that the information you have given is accurate to the best of your knowledge.

Some applications ask essay-type questions, which are really intended to test your ability to communicate in writing and your spelling, punctuation, grammar, and proofreading skills.

You will usually be asked to fill out an application when you apply in person for a job. Remember the motto "Be prepared." Follow these suggestions:

1. **Take with you (in writing) all the information you will need.** You will make a poor impression if you can't remember a phone number, date, or ZIP Code. *Never* write "see résumé" across an application; fill out the form completely.
2. **Read completely through the form *before* you start to fill it out.** This will help you answer the questions correctly. Once you have completed the application, reread the directions and recheck all information for accuracy.
3. **Take two working pens.** These two pens should have black ink. Take an ink eraser. A pencil can smudge and fade in time. Write legibly—most employers won't consider an application they can't read.
4. **Carry a pocket dictionary.** A spelling error could mean an automatic rejection when you apply for an office position.
5. **Follow directions.** If the instructions say "print," don't write in cursive style. Put nothing in sections marked "Do Not Write Below This Line," "Office Use," and "Not to Be Completed by Applicant."
6. **Answer all questions.** If the information does not apply to you, put "N/A" (not applicable) or draw a line in the blank to show that you have read the question. If your answer to a question will reflect negatively on you, leave that question blank and discuss it in the interview.

Go to Student CD-ROM Activity 19-2.

19-7—Being Prepared *Why should you take two pens when you go for an interview?*

If there is a place to include "other business skills" or "comments," put *something* there to sell yourself. Never leave this section blank.

7. **Avoid listing the salary you expect.** If this question is asked, answer with "open." This question can best be answered during the interview. You might eliminate your chance for an interview if your figure is out of line with current salary guidelines.

8. **Give positive reasons for leaving previous jobs.** When this information is requested, give reasons such as "better job opportunity," "career advancement," or "return to school." Answers such as "work too hard," "didn't like boss," or "hours too long" may reflect negatively on you and should be avoided.

Remember that you start applying for the job the minute you walk in the door. It is just as important to make a favorable impression on the receptionist as on the interviewer. More often than you realize, employers ask that office personnel "screen" applicants and share their impressions. These impressions may include:

- Your dress and appearance
- Manners
- Ability to convey a good first impression
- The way you carry yourself (posture and self-confidence)

The receptionist's reaction may determine whether you get an interview. Follow these suggestions to make a positive professional impression:

1. Be polite and courteous. Don't act bored and impatient.
2. Ask for only one copy of the application.
3. Have adequate supplies and information with you to complete the form.
4. Avoid asking unnecessary or obvious questions. If you must ask questions, make notes as you fill out the application so that you need to interrupt the receptionist only once.

Remember that an application form becomes part of your permanent employment record if you are hired.

SUMMARY

Getting a job requires the preparation of written documents. The first step is to list the skills and qualifications you have to offer to an employer in exchange for the paycheck you will receive. Preparing a professional résumé that will highlight your education and experience is the next step. A résumé can be prepared in one of three formats: chronological, skills or functional, or combination. Your résumé is your "sales promotion piece." A summary of qualifications and accomplishments is used when you are asking for a raise or being considered for an award or a departmental transfer.

Application forms seek basic information that gives the prospective employer insight about your skills, experience, education, and the like. Complete applications carefully and truthfully.

Name _____ Date _____

WHAT'S WRONG WITH THIS?

1. Your friend Juan asks you to look at his résumé. Please mark any changes you would make to it.

RESUME

555-28909
Juan Rodriquez
287 Orange Street
Cincinnati

Career Objective: Any job you have.

Education: Middlefork High School. Attended 1996-1999
Suffolk Community College. Attended 1999

References: Curt Huffman
Suffolk Community College
318-555-326

Tom Hainline, family friend
Cincinnati, OH

Experience: Bouncer at Sam's Bar and Grill

Wal Mart

McDonald's—sanitation engineer

Yard work for neighbors

ANALYZING THE JOB MARKET AND YOURSELF

Answer the following questions, but do not hand them in. Instead, keep them for your own reference when you study the job market, analyze your personal traits and abilities in reference to a prospective job, and assemble some "evidence" that you may use in the employment communications you will write.

2. Self-analysis
   a. What vocation do you plan to enter? (If you have not yet decided on one vocational goal, list two or three vocational choices.)

Name _____ Date _____

ANALYZING THE JOB MARKET AND YOURSELF *(continued)*

_____

_____

_____

b. List two or more specific jobs that could help you realize one of the vocational choices you listed in Problem 2a and that might be appropriate for you when you are ready to look for a job.

_____

_____

c. List several duties that a person holding one of the jobs you listed in Problem 2b would be expected to perform.

_____

_____

_____

_____

d. List several organizations in your community (or in other communities in which you would like to live and work) that employ persons in the job you described in Problem 2c.

_____

_____

_____

_____

e. In the left-hand column below, list your personal traits (not physical features) that could help you in carrying out the job duties you listed in Problem 2c. Use concrete adjectives such as *dependable, neat, cheerful,* and *tactful.* In the right column, opposite each trait listed, record any evidence you can think of to show that you have the trait. Here are some examples to get you started:

Punctual.   **Get to class on time and turn in assigned work when it is due.**

Intelligent and industrious.   **Have record of good grades along with participation in out-of-class leadership activities.**

Dependable.   **Have excellent attendance record and complete assignments on time.**

_____   _____

_____   _____

Name _____ Date _____

f. In the column to the left, list your abilities (things you can do well) that could help you in carrying out the job duties. Be specific—for instance, "Writing computer programs in COBOL," "Preparing financial statements," or "Composing effective business letters." In the column to the right, opposite each ability listed, jot down any evidence you can think of to show that you have that ability. For example:

Can merge documents in Word.
Can create fliers and brochures.

Have keyed and merged data source files with main document files to prepare letters, envelopes, and mailing labels.
Have created and designed publications in my desktop publishing class.

_____   _____

_____   _____

_____   _____

_____   _____

_____   _____

_____   _____

_____   _____

_____   _____

_____   _____

WRITING YOUR RÉSUMÉ AND COMPLETING AN EMPLOYMENT APPLICATION

3. Select a format (chronological, skills or functional, or combination) and prepare your résumé for the job you want. Make it an attractive, easy-reference summary of your qualifications. Assume that you have successfully completed any courses you are enrolled in.

4. Using the résumé you prepared in Problem 3, arrange the material in a different résumé format. For example, if you prepared a chronological résumé, use the same information to prepare a skills résumé.

5. Complete the application form on page 376. Include part-time jobs and summer employment. Type the data or write in longhand (using a pen with black ink); in either case do it neatly, carefully, and correctly—as though you were actually applying for a job.

Name _____ Date _____

Employment Application

PERSONAL DATA	Name (Last, First, MI)		Present Phone # (include area code)			
	Present Address (street, city, state, zip)	Check one Seeking	F/T or		P/T employment	
		Check one	U.S. Citizen		Permanent Resident	
			Student Visa			
	Career Interests:					
	Job Related/Special Skills (computer languages):					

EDUCATION	High School/College Attended:	Degree	Graduation Date	Major/G.P.A.
	College course Highlights, Awards, Honors, etc.			

Employment	Dates Mo./Yr.	Employer Name & Address	Title/Description	Wages or Salary	Reason for Leaving
	From				
	To				
	From				
	To				

References	Give names and addresses of 3 personal or professional references (not relatives)			
	Name	Address	Relationship	Telephone
	1.			
	2.			
	3.			

PLEASE READ AND SIGN THE FOLLOWING: I understand that my employment will be subject to complete verification of all information on the application and that false answers or statements will be sufficient grounds for immediate discharge. I further understand that employment will not be for a fixed term and will depend upon work performance of a continuing high standard. I consent to taking a pre-employment physical examination as may be required by this company, and further agree that the contents of this application form as well as the report of any such examination may be used by the company in whatever manner it may wish.

Applicant's Signature _____ Date _____

Name (Last, First, MI)

Name _____ Date _____

COLLABORATIVE WRITING

Evaluating Application Forms Work with two or three classmates and evaluate and rank the four application forms below and on pages 378 to 380 for the administrative assistant position. Write a memo to your instructor giving your ranking and explaining why you ranked them as you did.

Employment Application

PERSONAL DATA	Name (Last, First, MI) *Brown, Chris*		Present Phone # (include area code)		
	Present Address (street, city, state, zip)		Check one Seeking	F/T or	P/T employment
			Check one	U.S. Citizen	
				Student Visa	Permanent Resident
	Career Interests:				
	Job Related/Special Skills (computer languages):				

EDUCATION	High School/College Attended:	Degree	Graduation Date	Major/G.P.A.
	College course Highlights, Awards, Honors, etc.			

Employment	Dates Mo./Yr.	Employer Name & Address	Title/Description	Wages or Salary	Reason for Leaving
	From				
	To				
	From				
	To				

References	Give names and addresses of 3 personal or professional references (not relatives)			
	Name	Address	Relationship	Telephone
	1.			
	2.			
	3.			

see resume

PLEASE READ AND SIGN THE FOLLOWING: I understand that my employment will be subject to complete verification of all information on the application and that false answers or statements will be sufficient grounds for immediate discharge. I further understand that employment will not be for a fixed term and will depend upon work performance of a continuing high standard. I consent to taking a pre-employment physical examination as may be required by this company, and further agree that the contents of this application form as well as the report of any such examination may be used by the company in whatever manner it may wish.

Applicant's Signature _____ Date _____

Name _____ Date _____

COLLABORATIVE WRITING *(continued)*

Employment Application

PERSONAL DATA

Name (Last, First, MI)	Present Phone # (include area code)
Sanford, Diane L	217-555-7774

Present Address (street, city, state, zip)	Check one Seeking		F/T or	P/T employment
601 E. Young Street Hoopeston, IL 60942		X		

	Check one		U.S. Citizen	
		X	Student Visa	Permanent Resident

Career Interests:

Office Assistant and Customer Service

Job Related/Special Skills (computer languages):

Keyboarding 60 wpm, Windows 98, Microsoft Office, Adobe Pagemaker

EDUCATION

High School/College Attended:	Degree	Graduation Date	Major/G.P.A.
Danville Area Community College	A.A.S.	May 2001	Adm. Asst. 4.0
Shiloh High School	Diploma	May 1999	College Prep 4.0

College course Highlights, Awards, Honors, etc.

President's List – 3 semesters, Honors List – 4 semesters
Perfect Attendance Awards, Student Worker Recognition

Employment

Dates Mo./Yr.	Employer Name & Address	Title/Description	Wages or Salary	Reason for Leaving
From 5/2000 To present	Danville Area Com College Danville, IL 61832	student secretary	6.00	N/A
From 5/1998 To present	Paris First Bank Paris, IL	teller	7.00	N/A

References

Give names and addresses of 3 personal or professional references (not relatives)

Name	Address	Relationship	Telephone
1. Diane Strong	DACC, 2000 E. Main, Danville	Supervisor	217-555-8731
2. Merilyn Sheperd	DACC, 2000 E. Main, Danville	Instructor	217-555-8824
3. Merle Clark	Paris First Bank, Paris, IL	Manager	217-555-6330

PLEASE READ AND SIGN THE FOLLOWING: I understand that my employment will be subject to complete verification of all information on the application and that false answers or statements will be sufficient grounds for immediate discharge. I further understand that employment will not be for a fixed term and will depend upon work performance of a continuing high standard. I consent to taking a pre-employment physical examination as may be required by this company, and further agree that the contents of this application form as well as the report of any such examination may be used by the company in whatever manner it may wish.

Applicant's Signature Diane Sanford   Date May 1, 2001

Name _____ Date _____

Employment Application

<table>
<tr><td rowspan="5">PERSONAL DATA</td><td colspan="2">Name (Last, First, MI)
Green, Mary A.</td><td colspan="3">Present Phone # (include area code)</td></tr>
<tr><td colspan="2" rowspan="2">Present Address (street, city, state, zip)
361 N. Chicago Ave
Rossville</td><td>Check one
Seeking</td><td>X F/T or</td><td>P/T employment</td></tr>
<tr><td>Check one</td><td>✓ U.S. Citizen</td><td></td></tr>
<tr><td colspan="2">Career Interests:

Office Assistant and Customer Service</td><td>✓ Student</td><td>X Visa</td><td>Permanent Resident</td></tr>
</table>

	Name (Last, First, MI)	Present Phone # (include area code)		
	Green, Mary A.			

PERSONAL DATA

Name (Last, First, MI): Green, Mary A.

Present Phone # (include area code):

Present Address (street, city, state, zip): 361 N. Chicago Ave, Rossville

Check one Seeking: X F/T or ___ P/T employment

Check one: ✓ U.S. Citizen / ✓ Student / X Visa / ___ Permanent Resident

Career Interests:

Office Assistant and Customer Service

Job Related/Special Skills (computer languages):

Xerox, telephone, postage meter

EDUCATION

High School/College Attended:	Degree	Graduation Date	Major/G.P.A.
DACC	none	?	Business?
Rossville	passed	5/99	not sure

College course Highlights, Awards, Honors, etc.

typing, Windows, software courses

Employment

Dates Mo./Yr.	Employer Name & Address	Title/Description	Wages or Salary	Reason for Leaving
From 2/95 To present	Country Store Rossville, IL	waitress	tips	—
From 3/96 To 4/98	Corner Tap Rossville	bartender	?	fired

References

Give names and addresses of 3 personal or professional references (not relatives)

Name	Address	Relationship	Telephone
1. Samantha Lee	Rossville	housewife	748-5555
2. Father John David	Hoopeston	minister	331-5206
3. Joe LaBounty	Rossville	supervisor	748-3489

PLEASE READ AND SIGN THE FOLLOWING: I understand that my employment will be subject to complete verification of all information on the application and that false answers or statements will be sufficient grounds for immediate discharge. I further understand that employment will not be for a fixed term and will depend upon work performance of a continuing high standard. I consent to taking a pre-employment physical examination as may be required by this company, and further agree that the contents of this application form as well as the report of any such examination may be used by the company in whatever manner it may wish.

Applicant's Signature _Mary Green_ _____ Date _____

Name _____ Date _____

COLLABORATIVE WRITING *(continued)*

Employment Application

PERSONAL DATA	**Name (Last, First, MI)** Susie "Dimples" Edington	**Present Phone # (include area code)** none

Present Address (street, city, state, zip) Catlin, Illinois	Check one Seeking	F/T or		P/T employment
	Check one	U.S. Citizen		
		Student Visa		Permanent Resident

Career Interests:
I'm interested in any job you have.
I need to work!

Job Related/Special Skills (computer languages):
watching TV

EDUCATION	High School/College Attended:	Degree	Graduation Date	Major/G.P.A.
	~~Catlin~~ Catlin High		yes	passed

College course Highlights, Awards, Honors, etc.

Employment	Dates Mo./Yr.	Employer Name & Address	Title/Description		Wages or Salary	Reason for Leaving
	From 8/95	Truck Stop	waitress		?	Quit
	To 7/98	Catlin	served food			
	From 8/98	Quick 6	clerk		?	Quit
	To 10/99	Indianola		conven. mart		Quit

Give names and addresses of 3 personal or professional references (not relatives)

References	Name	Address	Relationship	Telephone
1.	Sam Edington	~~Catlin~~ Catlin	husband	none
2.	Connie Light	Royal	friend	none
3.	Loni White	Ogden	friend	none

PLEASE READ AND SIGN THE FOLLOWING: I understand that my employment will be subject to complete verification of all information on the application and that false answers or statements will be sufficient grounds for immediate discharge. I further understand that employment will not be for a fixed term and will depend upon work performance of a continuing high standard. I consent to taking a pre-employment physical examination as may be required by this company, and further agree that the contents of this application form as well as the report of any such examination may be used by the company in whatever manner it may wish.

Applicant's Signature _____ Date _____

Name _____ Date _____

PROOFREADING EXERCISE

Use proofreaders' marks to indicate the errors in the section of a résumé shown below. The first set of duties is for a current job, and the next set is for a former. Hint: Watch verb tense.

Duties: type documents, filed, photocopied, ansser phone,

take and deliver messages, record payments, distribute

mail, prepare monthly newsletter, order and maintain sup-

plies, make and confirm appointmeents, prioritized job

orders, and other office duties with minimun supervision.

Duties customer service, prepare databases, prepare

monthly sales reports, operated cash register, scheduled

staff meetings, make travel arrangements, prepare annual

report four division, and handling correspondence with

authors and marketing staff.

Search the Internet for Information on Résumés
Connect to the Internet and go to one of the following two sites. Read the tips for preparing a résumé.
<www.rpi.edu/dept/llc/writecenter/web/text/resume.html>
<www.umn.edu/ohr/ecep/resume
To learn more about electronic résumés, connect to the Internet and go to this Website:

NOTES

Chapter 20

Writing Application Letters and Other Employment Documents

Chapters 19 and 20 emphasize the employment process by:
- Discussing the self-inventory analysis and the various types of résumés.
- Presenting the application package along with the types of employment letters usually written in job situations.

After completing this chapter, you should be able to:
- Identify two types of application letters.
- Write an effective application letter.
- Write a postinterview thank-you letter.
- Write a resignation letter.
- Write other types of employment letters.

A résumé without a cover letter is like a cake without icing. Even the best-written résumé has a mass-produced look because of the format. A cover letter is the feature that will make an employer want to read your résumé. *A résumé should never be mailed without a cover letter,* which we call a **letter of application.** Many employers will not even look at a résumé if it comes without a cover letter.

PREPARING TO WRITE YOUR APPLICATION LETTER

An application letter may be the most important letter you will ever write, because it may determine the course of your life—at least for a time. An application letter is not like a letter of transmittal (see Chapter 7); it is your personal sales letter and should be written according to the steps used in writing a sales promotion letter (see Chapter 12).

 The purpose of an application letter is to get an interview; the purpose of the interview is to get an offer for a job that you hope will lead to a satisfying and successful career.

Yes, an application letter that will get you an interview is difficult to write. You will need to spend considerable time planning, writing, and rewriting your application letter before it is ready to mail.

Never copy a letter that someone else has written or that you find in a textbook. Human resources people will probably recognize it, just as you recognize a movie that you have seen or a book you have read. You may not remember all the details of the movie or book, but you remember enough to know that you have seen it or read it before. You don't want to run the risk that a prospective employer will "recognize" your letter as one that sounds unusually familiar. You should not even copy sentences word for word from model application letters.

Plan and write *your own letter* in your own style. To be successful for *you*, an application letter should reflect *your* personality, and *your* attitude toward life and work.

Prepare a Mailing List of Prospective Employers

When you write your application letter, make a list of prospective employers who should receive the letter.

One way to obtain names of prospective employers for your mailing list is to find organizations that have employees who do the kind of work you plan to do. You can get names of these organizations by checking with current employees, your teachers, placement offices, the local Chamber of Commerce, the Yellow Pages of your phone book, the Internet, and so on. You can then write an application (called a *prospecting or cold contact application)* to the organizations at which you feel you could be happy working. The purpose of the prospecting application is to interest the human resources people in your qualifications so that they will ask you to schedule an interview.

One of the most effective ways to obtain names for your list is to locate organizations that are advertising suitable job openings. You can then write an application letter (called an *invited application*) to each prospective employer for a job that you know is open and for which you are qualified. You can readily find out about such job openings through:

- Help-wanted ads in newspapers, magazines, and trade journals.
- Job postings on the Internet.
- School placement or career services.
- Public or private employment agencies.
- Relatives, friends, or acquaintances who tell you about vacancies.

Study the Organization and the Job

You must understand both the organization and the job for which you apply before you can tell an employer how your personality, training, and experience make you a good choice—ideally *the* choice—for that job. Learn any information you can about what products or services the organization offers, how many employees it has, whether it is publicly or privately owned, and so on. Many organizations today have a Website that contains this information. The more you know about the organization and the job requirements, the more interesting and convincing you can make your application letter.

Go to Student CD-ROM Activity 20-1.

Determine What You Can Do for the Organization

To gain attention and interest, write about doing something for your reader. Don't start your letter with *I*, and avoid overusing *I* and *my* throughout your letter. Just as a sales person must consider the customer's needs, you should consider your qualifications in terms of what the employer requires for a particular job. Only then can you give the employer practical reasons for buying your services.

 Remember that you are competing with many other people who are also trying to sell their services. If your application is to stand out from the others, it must highlight the specific qualifications that would make you a valuable employee.

Every reply to an advertisement for a word processing position will probably mention the applicant's ability to type. To make your letter stand out, find out what kind of documents are prepared and then determine what you can offer. You might learn, for example, that preparing reports that contain statistics is part of the job. If this is a requirement for which you are prepared, be specific in your reply.

WEAK: can type

IMPROVED: can arrange statistical material in tables, charts, and graphs and type technical reports rapidly and accurately.

Decide on the Central Selling Point

In the letter you may mention all your important qualifications for the job, but you can't stress them all. Ask yourself these questions:

- Of all my qualifications, which one would be most important in the job for which I am applying?
- Which one of my qualifications will appeal most to this employer?

Your most important qualification may be your experience in similar work, your ability to get along well with people, your college training, or a special skill, such as the ability to operate a computer and keyboard rapidly. This most important qualification becomes your *central selling point,* around which you build your letter.

Make a Plan for the Letter

Remember, the purpose of your application letter is to get an interview. Your letter has to convince the prospective employer of your excellent qualifications and must persuade the employer to talk with you before filling the job.

Plan the content of your letter in the following order:

- Attract the employer's favorable attention and interest.
- Convince the employer that you have the qualifications to do an outstanding job.
- Persuade him or her to invite you for an interview.

WRITING YOUR APPLICATION LETTER

To interest the employer in you as an applicant and to obtain an invitation for an interview, aim to accomplish the following four purposes in your letter.

Four Purposes of an Application Letter

1. Show the Employer That You Can Write a Superior Business Letter

An application letter should:

- Be an original letter (do not copy a sample letter).
- Address a named individual (unless you are replying to a blind ad).
- Be printed on good-quality plain paper (see the discussion of format and appearance in Appendix A, "Formatting").
- Be centered on the page (left and right margins equal, and top and bottom margins equal).
- Use a modified-block style (since letterhead is not used, this style makes the letter look more balanced on the page).
- Have the appropriate parts (see Appendix A, "Formatting").
- Pass the six tests of effective correspondence (see Chapter 1).
- Have accurate grammar, punctuation, spelling, and an appropriate font.
- Be signed in black ink.
- Omit reference initials (you should type the letter yourself).
- Include an enclosure notation (your résumé is enclosed).

2. Show the Employer That You Understand the Requirements of the Job

If you are answering an advertisement, read it thoroughly and know exactly what it tells you about the job advertised and the qualifications wanted. If you are not answering an ad or if the ad does not give details, determine the job requirements by applying what you have learned in school, at work, or in talking with people who have done similar work. For example, if you are applying for a job as a salesperson, think of all the duties a salesperson usually performs—calling on customers, making sales presentations, demonstrating products, handling telephone calls, writing orders, working with coworkers and a supervisor, and the like—and the abilities and personality traits that are necessary to handle these duties successfully.

3. Show the Employer That You Are Qualified for the Job

Your qualifications are the heart of an application. The employer wants someone who can do the work that needs to be done and do it well. Explain in detail how your background, personality, training, and experience will help you do the job well. If you are answering an advertisement, be sure to give all information requested and show that you have every requirement suggested in the ad. Cover all the requirements in the letter itself; don't depend on the résumé to take the place of a thorough application letter.

> Explain your qualifications in specific terms.
>
> **POOR:** "I can do accounting work."
>
> **IMPROVED:** "I can do payroll, keep the records either manually or on a computer, prepare quarterly reports, and . . ."

Toward the end of the message, call attention to the résumé enclosed.

4. Show the Employer That You Want to Serve the Organization

 Keep the emphasis in your application letter on *what you can do* for the organization. Do *not* talk about what the organization can do for you and your career.

Be sincere and enthusiastic when you talk about working, serving, and cooperating. Use the "you" attitude. A writer interested only in getting something for his or her own benefit is quickly eliminated from the applicant pool. You certainly won't sound as though you are interested in providing service to the organization if your letter is filled with questions about salary, raises, vacations, pension plans, sick leave, and overtime pay. Leave these matters for the interview.

Desirable Features of an Application Letter

Perhaps the best way to be sure that an application letter accomplishes all four objectives is to develop it in three parts:

Go to Student CD-ROM Activity 20-2.

20-1:
PROOFREAD CAREFULLY
Sentence from application letter: "*Enclosed is my résumé with additional information about my qualifications for you to overlook.*"

20-3—Using Appropriate Objectives "*I am looking for a job where I can use my education and skills to advance in my career.*" *What's wrong with this sentence from an application letter?*

1. An interesting opening that will get the employer's attention.
2. A convincing presentation of your qualifications.
3. A strong closing with a request for action.

AN INTERESTING OPENING

Your opening must attract favorable attention and get the employer interested enough in your qualifications to read on. Four ways to get the reader's attention are discussed in the next sections. Use the first method if you are writing an invited application for an advertised job. Use the second, third, or fourth method if you are writing a prospecting application for an unadvertised job.

Opening for Invited Application Letter

If a job has been advertised, you will send an *invited* application.

Tell How You Learned About the Vacancy

Here is an opening written by an applicant who learned of a job opportunity from a college placement office:

> Your posting in the Lake Land College Placement Office indicates that you are looking for a top-flight sales representative who can also give outstanding field demonstrations with FonFriend portable phones.

This applicant heard about a job opportunity from a teacher:

> Miss Ellen Wachs, director of the School of Medical Records Administration at Maryland College, brought to my attention your need for an assistant administrator in your medical records department. Miss Wachs is confident that my college preparation and my experience in the medical records department of Giles County Hospital will enable me to meet all the requirements of this job.

Opening for Prospecting Application Letter

If a job has not been advertised, you will send a *prospecting* application. Possible ways to open these letters are: (1) summarize your qualifications for a specific kind of job, (2) refer to the organization's reputation, progress, or policies, or (3) express support for the kind of work in which the organization engages.

Summarize Your Qualifications for a Specific Kind of Job

Try to narrow down, as much as possible, the kind of work you would like to do for the organization, for example:

> As an employee in your purchasing department, I could put my accounting and computer knowledge to work for you. I would also enjoy working with your clients and promoting goodwill with other organizations both in the office and by phone.

Here's another example of an opening that summarizes the writer's qualifications:

> With my college background, accounting and selling experience,
> and ability to get along with people, I believe that I could success-
> fully sell Eastman Kodak products.

Refer to the Organization's Reputation, Progress, or Policies

Because employers receive so many "formula-like" letters, your letter will stand out if it indicates that you've done a little research on the organization.

> The recent expansion of Colgate-Palmolive's facilities, as reported in
> *The Daily News,* suggests that there might be openings for adminis-
> trative assistants.

Here is another example of this type of opening:

> Congratulations on your No.1 rating by *City Magazine.* As a recent
> SSCC graduate with a major in desktop publishing, I would like to
> contribute to the continued growth and success of the Randolph
> County School System.

Express Support for the Kind of Work in Which the Organization Engages

This type of opening allows you to show the organization that you share its area of commitment.

> Retailing means, to me, the challenge of meeting people and selling
> them on a product, an idea, a principle, or a goal.

WRITING A CONVINCING PRESENTATION

If your letter is to be convincing, the presentation of your qualifications must be related to the work to be done and must be backed up by evidence.

Avoid vague, unconvincing statements such as:

"I have a good personality."

"I am intelligent."

"I am dependable."

"I am interested in working with people."

You can portray your personal traits more convincingly by *presenting the evidence* and letting the reader draw his or her conclusions. Notice how this applicant uses previous work experience to tell the employer he is a hard worker:

> After delivering newspapers several mornings a week while in
> high school, I'm not afraid of the long hours of work that always
> occur during rush periods. Hard work doesn't bother me either,
> since I enjoyed three busy summers assisting my father on con-
> struction jobs.

1. Interpret Your Training in Terms of the Work to Be Done

The courses you take and the school activities you participate in are not nearly as important to an employer as the lessons you learn from these experiences. In your letter, instead of listing courses and extracurricular activities (these will be on your résumé), try to highlight ways in which you can do a better job for the organization because of something you learned in school. Notice how the successful application letters in this chapter (Figures 20-1 to 20-4) and the following excerpts relate qualifications and work experience to the work to be done.

546 McKinnley Street
Utica, MS 39175
March 15, <YEAR>

Ms. Carol Craig
Marketing Director
Mettam Safety Supply Co.
P.O. Box 854
Utica, MS 39175

Dear Ms. Craig:

Mettam Safety Supply Co. is a leading company in supplying safety equipment. David Wyatt, career services director at Utica Junior College, told me you have a marketing assistant position open.

At Utica Junior College, we did numerous marketing projects. Our class compiled a newsletter that informed students about the marketing program. I researched and wrote a section on financial aid for the newsletter. I also participated in a campaign to get current students to register for next term before the current semester was over. I really enjoyed creating and conducting the survey and calculating the results.

In my direct marketing class, I put together direct mail pieces using Microsoft Publisher and analyzed direct mail pieces from other companies. It was a pleasant experience and very interesting. With these skills I know I could make a contribution to your marketing department.

Enclosed is my résumé. Please review it and call me at 983-555-9879 to set up an interview time. If I'm not home, please leave a message on the answering machine and I will return your call.

Sincerely,

Dave Bomar

Dave Bomar

Enclosure

FIGURE 20-1 The writer of this application letter relates his school experience to the job for which he is applying.

February 22, <YEAR>

Mr. Marty Brown
Human Resources Manager
Anderson Temporary Services
123 East Main Street
Danville, IL 61832

Dear Mr. Brown:

Please consider me an applicant for the administrative assistant position you advertised in the February 20 *Commercial News*.

The courses that I have completed at Danville Area Community College have furthered my skills in the administrative assistant and management fields. I am dependable and am driven to complete any tasks to the best of my ability. Anderson Temporary Services is rated No. 4 in the nation of temporary services, and I am sure I would be an asset to your company. Through my course work at the college, I have gained knowledge and experience in working with the Microsoft Office Suite software programs. My previous experience has thoroughly prepared me for a job in this field.

Enclosed is my résumé with additional information about my qualifications. I am requesting an interview to discuss my skills with you. My phone number is 217-555-1687. If there is no answer, please leave a message, and I will return your call promptly. I look forward to hearing from you soon.

Sincerely,

Katie Trosper

Katie Trosper
121 North Gilbert
Danville, IL 61832

Enclosure

FIGURE 20-2 This application letter shows confidence and highlights the writer's skills and work ethic. Katie's résumé, which she mailed with this application letter, appears in Chapter 19 (see Figure 19-4).

27894 North 8780 East Road
Newton Centre, MA 02159
July 8, <YEAR>

Mrs. Verna Quick
Human Resources Specialist
Madison Medical Center
3783 East Prospect Boulevard
Newton Centre, MA 02159

Dear Mrs. Quick:

During a recent review of the employment opportunities presented in the *Newton Centre Gazette*, I read with interest your advertisement for a medical transcriptionist.

At this point in my career, I offer a prospective employer many positive qualities, including a track record of successful achievements, a strong work ethic, and excellent communication skills. In return, I am seeking a position with a progressive establishment such as Madison Medical Center where I can make a very valuable contribution.

Enclosed is a résumé detailing my skills and credentials. I believe that my education and experience are well suited to your current organizational needs.

I would appreciate the opportunity to discuss this position. Please call me at my home number (378-555-9964) to schedule an interview. You may leave a message on my answering machine if I am not home. I look forward to hearing from you soon.

Sincerely,

Janice Johnson

Janice Johnson

Enclosure

754 Citrus Drive
Dade City, FL 33525
April 21, <YEAR>

Mr. Robert Ingrum
Human Resources Manager
DOMAR Marketing
965 Michigan Avenue
Dade City, FL 33525

Dear Mr. Ingrum:

Are you looking for an energetic and very creative staff member for your office? Do you want a person who can do more than a fair share to help your office? How about a person who is looking for a career?

Well, I am interested in a desktop publishing position in your organization. Given the opportunity to apply the skills I have learned while going to school for my desktop publishing degree, I feel I would be a great asset to your office by being creative, being energetic, and doing my job as a career rather than just for a paycheck. I am a very hard worker and have a strong work ethic.

Enclosed is my résumé which will show you that I have the ability and the skills needed to make a valuable contribution to your organization. Please call me for an interview to answer any questions you may have, and to further discuss how my qualifications fit your needs. I can be reached at 356-555-7589 Monday through Friday after 4 p.m. If no one answers, please leave a message on my answering machine.

Sincerely,

Maria Martinez

Maria Martinez

Enclosure

The following excerpts also relate qualifications and work experience to the work to be done:

APPLICANT FOR FIELD REPRESENTATIVE FOR TIMELY CLOTHES, INC.:

My college courses in clothing construction and design and in sales techniques have given me a fairly broad knowledge of the makeup of men's and women's fashions and many pointers about selling that I could put to good use for Timely.

In my basic college courses—including psychology, humanities, social science, and public speaking—I gained a broader understanding of human behavior and learned to "think on my feet" and win people to my point of view.

APPLICANT FOR A JOB IN RETAILING:

Among other extracurricular activities, I worked on the advertising staff of the college newspaper and had the opportunity to meet and talk with most of the merchants in Weston. Through this experience I learned about business problems and about what the public expects of a retail store.

Because I have held several part-time jobs and have participated in many outside activities while in college, I have learned the value of budgeting my time and getting important things done first. This knowledge should be helpful in your busy office.

2. Adapt Your Work Experience to Job Requirements

In the application letter, discuss your work experience in terms of what you have learned from it. The employer is interested in how your previous jobs prepared you to do good work for his or her organization. Use the application letters in this chapter and the following excerpts to help you adapt your work experience to the job for which you are applying.

APPLICANT FOR JOB AS SALES REPRESENTATIVE:

As a successful book sales representative for Lawrence Publishing Company, I have learned to get along with people in the most difficult selling situation—in the customer's home. This job also taught me time management, which is very important to a salesperson working outside an office.

APPLICANT FOR ASSISTANT IN THE PURCHASING DEPARTMENT OF A MAJOR MANUFACTURER:

I am familiar with purchasing terms and the overall structure of a manufacturing firm. Working as an assistant in the purchasing department of Bohn Aluminum Corporation also gave me a good background in buying policies and practices. This experience would enable me to process your orders quickly and accurately.

USING A STRONG CLOSING

Close your application letter with a specific request for action—usually that the employer name a time for a meeting with you about the job—and give the reader a good reason for inviting you for an interview.

20-2:
CHECK WORD MEANINGS AND SPELLING
Sentence on an application letter: "I am a rabid typist and a winner of the Gregg Typting Award."

POOR CLOSING: As you can see on my résumé, I will graduate on August 20. (Doesn't ask for an interview.)

STRONG CLOSING: The references listed on the enclosed résumé will be glad to confirm that I can meet the high requirements of word processing specialist for United American Bank. Please call me any day after 3 p.m. at 701-555-4932, or write to me at the above address to tell me when it would be convenient for you to talk with me.

STRONG CLOSING: I can start work for Midwest Logistics Corporation after my graduation on August 20. I would like to have an appointment to meet and talk with you at your convenience. Please call me at 392-555-4951; if you will leave a message on the answering machine, I will return your call promptly.

When you apply for a job far from your home, you must make it easy for the organization to reach you. Although some organizations will pay your travel expenses if they wish to interview you, others, particularly small companies, cannot afford to do so. Possible closings include:

A PHONE INTERVIEW

I will phone you on February 2 to set up a meeting or telephone interview at your convenience.

YOU WILL BE IN EMPLOYER'S AREA

I'll be in the Houston area from February 20 to February 25. I'll telephone you on February 2 to find out whether we might set up a meeting, at your convenience, during that week.

THEIR REPRESENTATIVE LOCATED IN YOUR AREA

Since you have an office in nearby Plainsville, I could meet with a representative from your organization in that office to discuss how my skills and abilities meet the needs of your organization. Please call me any day before 10 a.m. at 317-555-3379 to set up a mutually convenient time.

THEIR REPRESENTATIVE TRAVELING IN YOUR AREA

Do you have a representative who will be in this area in the near future? I could arrange for a place for us to meet to discuss my qualifications for the marketing position. I can be reached at 834-555-8874; please leave a message and I will return your call promptly.

In the successful applications in Figures 20-1 to 20-4 and in the excerpts above, each applicant asks for an interview.

GIVING YOUR LETTER A FINAL CHECK

When you have completed an application letter, ask yourself the questions in the checklist on page 394 to decide whether it is the best letter you can write.

20-4—Using a Message System *If a prospective employer tries to reach you by phone three or four times and gets no answer, what will he or she do? What could you do to prevent the prospective employer from getting no answer?*

Checklist for Contents of Application Letter

1. Does the letter show that I know how to apply the principles of writing effective business letters? (e.g., exhibiting the "you" attitude, using the word *I* sparingly).. ☐ ☐

2. Does my opening paragraph gain the reader's favorable attention?............. ☐ ☐

3. Does my opening paragraph indicate my interest in a particular job or organization?... ☐ ☐

4. If the name of a newspaper is mentioned in the opening paragraph, did I put the name in italics?... ☐ ☐

5. Does the letter make clear that I understand the requirements of the job?... ☐ ☐

6. Does the letter emphasize that I have the personality, training, and experience to fill the job?.. ☐ ☐

7. Have I eliminated information that is on my résumé?............................ ☐ ☐

8. Does my letter emphasize what I can do for the employer rather than talking about what I want? .... ☐ ☐

9. Do I mention that my résumé is enclosed?....................................... ☐ ☐

10. Do I ask for specific action (an interview) in the closing paragraph— and motivate the employer to give the reply I want? .... ☐ ☐

11. Is the letter concise and no longer than one page? .... ☐ ☐

12. Is the letter free of spelling, grammatical, and punctuation errors?............. ☐ ☐

13. Have I read the letter from an employer's perspective? (projected an image of a person I would like to interview if I were the employer)............. ☐ ☐

14. Do I have an enclosure notation at the end of the letter? .... ☐ ☐

15. Did I omit reference initials? .... ☐ ☐

16. Have I signed the letter in black ink?... ☐ ☐

17. Have I planned the mailing so the letter and my résumé will arrive on a Tuesday, Wednesday, or Thursday?... ☐ ☐

Once you've determined that you have written the best letter you can, proofread it several times for errors in spelling, grammar, and other areas. Then mail your letter so it will *arrive on a Tuesday, Wednesday,* or *Thursday.* On Mondays, most organizations are busy getting the week's work started and going through a heavy volume of mail. On Fridays, they are busy trying to finish up the week's work.

PREPARING FOR THE INTERVIEW

Turn to Appendix C, "Interviewing for a Job," for information on how to prepare for your interview and some typical interview questions you can expect to be asked. The quality of your letter of application and résumé will determine whether you get an interview.

Few people are hired at the first interview. The employer usually narrows the field down to a few applicants and then makes a decision and phones the top applicant to offer the job to him or her. The employer may call in the top two or three applicants for a second interview before making the final selection.

WRITING THANK-YOU AND FOLLOW-UP LETTERS

You can help keep your image in the interviewer's mind if you continue to show interest in the job after the interview has been concluded. An effective postinterview strategy involves the preparation of a thank-you letter.

Postinterview Thank-You Letters

Within 24 hours after the interview, write a short but courteous thank-you letter expressing appreciation for the interview and your continued interest in the job. You can compose such a letter and store it in the computer, adjusting it as appropriate to each situation by adding a sentence or two of specific comments about the organization.

 A thank-you letter is always welcome, and it serves two purposes: (1) as a written record of your good manners and (2) as a demonstration of your ability to communicate.

A thank-you letter also gives you an opportunity to reemphasize one of your selling points or mention one that didn't come up during the interview. Even if you applied to a local firm, send a letter rather than interrupt your interviewer with a phone call.

Sending this letter will give you a decided advantage over the other applicants. Very few applicants send postinterview thank-you letters. Since your purpose is to keep the interviewer from forgetting you, be sure to mail the letter promptly after the interview.

Remember the two most important characteristics of thank-you letters. Make certain your letter is:

- Courteous
- Correct

Katie Trosper sent the following thank-you letter after her interview with a human resources manager (her application letter to Mr. Brown is shown in Figure 20-2).

20-5—First Impressions *What message does a prospective employer get when your application letter has a spelling error and/or a sentence fragment?*

Dear Mr. Brown:

Thank you for talking with me about the job in your Customer Service Department. The tour of your facilities was very interesting, and I was especially impressed by the time you spent with me as a prospective employee.

I am still very much interested in the position as office assistant; you can reach me at my home telephone, 217-555-1687.

Sincerely,

Write a similar thank-you letter if you have been told that your application will be kept on file for consideration when a job opening fits your qualifications.

Follow-Up Letters

If you hear nothing within a reasonable time (usually two weeks) after writing your thank-you letter, you may write a follow-up letter. Often you can make this follow-up more effective by providing additional information, such as a change of address, graduation from school, or completion of a temporary job.

Sometimes a follow-up letter will spark a response when you have had no reply to an application sent several weeks earlier and you think that the employer has overlooked it. In this letter you should mention the following:

- The date of the previous application.
- The job for which you applied.
- Your continued interest in the job.

You may summarize and give additional information about your major qualifications, but you do not need to enclose a second copy of your résumé.

Other Thank-You Letters

When you accept a job, you have several thank-you letters to write.

- Did someone tell you about the job opening?
- Did someone give a favorable reference or in any other way help you to get the job?
- Did someone write you a note congratulating you and wishing you success in the new job?

All these people deserve simple, sincere messages of appreciation (see Chapter 14). You may be applying for a job again someday, and these people will be more willing to help you the next time if you let them know you appreciated their help this time.

REQUESTING AND SENDING INFORMATION ABOUT JOB APPLICANTS

Employers are very concerned about hiring the right person for the job. In addition to interviewing you, they will request information from your references.

Requesting Information About Job Applicants

When an employer writes to one of the references given on a résumé to ask for information about the applicant, the letter follows the form of a direct inquiry (see Chapter 8). The employer should mark the inquiry *Confidential* and ask questions that will obtain the facts and opinions that he or she needs. Many times a form letter is sent.

Sending Information About Job Applicants

The person who answers a request for information about an applicant should also mark the response *Confidential*. The reply should consist of *facts that will give an accurate picture of the applicant* rather than a biased recommendation. Opinions should be clearly separated from facts. For example:

> **OPINION:** "Mary Kester will make an excellent accountant for you."

> **FACT:** "Mary Kester did superior work as an accountant in my office."

> **OPINION:** "Mary Kester will be dependable and be at work every day."

> **FACT:** "Mary Kester was dependable and her attendance was excellent during the time she worked here."

If the recommendation is positive, use the direct approach. If the recommendation is negative, you should verify only that the applicant was an employee and give the dates of employment. To avoid the possibility of a lawsuit, no other information should be provided. Organizations have been sued by applicants who claim they lost a job because of a bad reference.

When replying to a request for information about a job applicant:

1. Answer promptly (before the position is filled by another applicant).
2. Answer honestly (your letter is important because it could affect a person's career and an organization's opinion of you).

ACCEPTING AND REFUSING JOB OFFERS

If you receive a job offer by mail, write an acceptance or a refusal as soon as you can. If you accept, say so in a short, enthusiastic letter. Notice the happy—not gushy—tone of Katie Trosper's acceptance:

Dear Mr. Brown:

I am happy to accept the administrative assistant job with Anderson Temporary Services. Thank you for choosing me. The job, as you described it, seems both interesting and challenging to me. As you suggested, I'll report at 9 a.m. on Monday, June 6. I am looking forward to the challenge of office work at Anderson Temporary Services.

Sincerely,

20-6—
Recommendations
Will your attendance record at school have any influence on a recommendation for you from one of your instructors?

If you decide to decline the job offer, say no so graciously that you leave the door open for future employment with the organization. Someday you may have contact with the people or the organization, or you may even wish to reapply.

NOTIFYING AN APPLICANT OF APPOINTMENT OR REJECTION

Just as a job applicant should show courtesy by sending a postinterview thank-you letter, the organization should show courtesy when notifying each candidate of his or her selection or rejection. The selected applicant is usually notified by phone. Candidates not selected will have a much better impression of the organization if they receive a reply. Many organizations send a card or letter to let the unsuccessful applicants know that the position has been filled. These messages can be prepared, stored on a computer, and then individualized by typing the name, address, and salutation for each letter. An example is shown here; notice how the bad-news approach is used:

> Dear Miss Swenson:
>
> Thank you for submitting your résumé in response to our recent newspaper advertisement. Although you have excellent qualifications for employment, another applicant was selected. We will keep your résumé in our active files for one year and call you if opportunities arise for an individual with your background.
>
> Good luck with your employment search.
>
> Sincerely,

Just as most applicants never get around to sending the postinterview thank-you letter, many organizations fail to notify the unsuccessful applicants. It is, however, just plain common courtesy to send these letters.

RESIGNING FROM A JOB

When you decide to change jobs, you will need to prepare a letter of resignation. You should always notify your supervisor or employer in writing, even if you communicate your decision orally. You should give at least two weeks' notice; higher-level positions and some civil service systems require more than two weeks' notice.

 Even though you may be angry or dissatisfied when you resign, avoid the temptation to write an emotionally charged

letter; this letter will become a permanent part of your personnel file. Keep in mind the old saying: "Don't burn your bridges behind you."

When you need a reference from this employer in the future, the people who knew you best may be gone. The person contacted for a reference may have only your personnel file as a source of information. The reason you give for leaving should be one you can live with for the rest of your career. And remember, you never know when a former supervisor or colleague will show up at your current place of employment.

A typical plan for a resignation letter is:

1. Tell your plans for the position you have accepted (assuming you took another job).
2. State in a positive way that you are resigning, and give the effective date.
3. Offer to train a replacement, if appropriate.
4. State your reason for leaving, unless it is obvious or negative.
5. Tell how you've benefited in terms of experience.
6. Use a goodwill closing.

The following resignation letter can be adapted to fit many situations:

Dear Mr. Luzader:

As we discussed yesterday, I have accepted a position with Federal Express Corporation. I plan to leave Phoenix on November 15 to begin my new job. Please accept my resignation from First Commercial Bank effective November 8. I will be available for the next two weeks to train a replacement.

During the three years I have worked here, I have appreciated the help you have given me and the business we have been able to cultivate. It has been a pleasure to work with you and the staff.

Sincerely,

Ending your resignation letter on a pleasant note will help leave a favorable image of you in your personnel file.

SUMMARY

Before writing your letter of application, you need to find some prospective employers, study the organizations and the jobs, decide what you can offer to the different organizations, and pick a *central selling point* for your letter. An application letter should not repeat the information given on a résumé; it should interpret the information on a résumé and present *evidence* of your qualifications for the job. Your letter of application should also show the employer that (1) you can write a superior business letter, (2) you understand the requirements of this job, (3) you are qualified for the job, and (4) you can make a contribution as an employee of the organization.

Other employment letters that you may write include a postinterview thank-you, requests for recommendations, acceptance or refusal of job offers, and resignation from a job when it is time to make a career move.

Name _____ Date _____

WHAT'S WRONG WITH THIS?

Read the letter of application in Problem 1 carefully for spelling, format, and content errors.

> **Wanted immediately:** Office person with good telephone skills and familiar with payroll, bookkeeping, Lotus 123, WordPerfect. Send résumé to Human Resources Manager, Driscoll Corp., 750 Commercial Drive, Dallas.

1. *The Daily News* ran the want ad shown at the right. **The following letter was sent in reply to the ad. Read and evaluate the letter. Circle the spelling errors and list the other errors on a separate sheet of paper.**

Jan. 4, <YEAR>
Humane Resources Manager
Driscall Corp.
75 Commercail Drive
Dallas

Dear Gentlemen:

You wouldn't be intereasted in hiring a person with no expereince, wood you? May I trouble you to take a few minutes of your valuable time to read my letter? I was bourne in Houston but just moved too Dallas. I have took some college curses and I am a very very inerjetick person.

I will male you a reseme if you are intrested. I am looking for a job with a pleasant atmosfere because I am a "people person" and I love to talk to people on the telephone.

I really think I would like working for you cooperation and I really do need a job. I can start imediately but I have a Doctor appt. that I wood need off for on on december 11.

Yours Very Truly

Susie "Dimples" Smith

Susie "Dimples" Smith

WRITING SITUATIONS

Plan and prepare the following two letters thoughtfully and edit them carefully. Make them your very best—models that you can adapt quickly to actual situations when you have limited time to write and mail employment letters. Type each letter on plain paper.

2. **Invited application letter.** Clip an ad from a newspaper or a magazine or print a job opening from the Internet about a job you would like to have. If you do not find an ad, write one for a job you would like to have.

Name _____ Date _____

WRITING SITUATIONS *(continued)*

Prepare an application letter in response to the ad. Hand in the ad with your letter. Refer to the application letters in the chapter for ideas, but *do not copy them*. Address the letter to the appropriate person in the organization if you can find out his or her name and official title or position. Otherwise, address it to the human resources director of the organization. Assume that you will enclose your résumé.

3. **Prospecting application letter.** Choose an organization you would like to work for, and prepare a letter of application. Assume that you will enclose your résumé. Refer to the letters of application in this chapter for ideas, but *do not copy them*.

WRITING OTHER EMPLOYMENT COMMUNICATIONS

4. **Postinterview thank-you letter.** Assume that you wrote the application letter to Mr. Brown in Figure 20-2 and that you interviewed yesterday for a position as administrative assistant. Although you were told that you made a good impression and that you would hear more later, you received no job offer. Write the letter of appreciation to be sent to Mr. Marty Brown, the human resources manager, the day following the interview.

5. **Follow-up letter.** It's been four weeks, and you have not heard from Mr. Brown. You decide to write a follow-up letter. Tell him that since your interview you moved to a new address less than five minutes from the office of Anderson Temporary Services and you are available immediately for full-time work.

6. **Letter requesting a recommendation.** Assume that during your interview with Mr. Brown (Problem 4), he asked you for a letter of recommendation from a former instructor or employer. Write the necessary request letter asking that the recommendation be sent directly to Marty Brown, Human Resources Manager, Anderson Temporary Services, 123 East Main Street, Danville, IL 61832.

7. **Recommendation letter.** Assume that you are the former instructor or employer receiving the letter in Problem 6. Write the letter of recommendation about the applicant. Give some serious thought to what you

Name _____   Date _____

can honestly say in the recommendation. Suggestion: Write the letter of recommendation using information about yourself. That is, put yourself in the role of applicant.

8. **Letter acknowledging a job offer.** Mr. Brown offers the applicant (you) the job. Write a letter thanking him for the offer. Indicate that you will let him know within two weeks whether you will accept or reject the offer.

9. **Letter declining a job offer.** Write a letter to Mr. Brown declining the job offer you received in Problem 8. You may assume any reason or reasons you wish for declining the job offer.

10. **Thank-you letter.** Now assume that you accepted the job offer from Mr. Brown. You have heard that the person you gave as a reference recommended you highly. This recommendation was a strong factor in the decision to offer you the job. Write a letter to the person who wrote the recommendation in Problem 7, thanking him or her for helping you.

COLLABORATIVE WRITING

Analyzing and Evaluating Application Letters Work with one or two classmates to analyze two application letters received for a position in your organization (see page 404). Assume that you are employed in the human resources department of your organization and you are asked to analyze these two letters. Do you think they are original letters? Write your responses on the lines below.

_____

_____

_____

_____

_____

_____

_____

_____

_____

_____

_____

_____

_____

_____

Name _____ Date _____

COLLABORATIVE WRITING *(continued)*

June 4, <YEAR>
Mr. Mel Ward, President
XYZ State Bank
4 Towne Center
Catlin, IA 50021

Dear Mr. Ward:

XYZ State Bank has always been loyal to its customers. As a customer, I would like to return some of that loyalty as an employee of the bank. I am very familiar with the employees and the customers and am sure I would be accepted.

During my 22 completed credit hours at college, I learned how to complete such financial statements as capital statements, income statements, balance sheets, work sheets, and schedules of accounts. I have also learned the methods for determining depreciation, such as sum-of-the-years digits, straight-line method, and units of production method. I can compute interest with the 60-day, 6 percent method. I adapt to new situations and people very easily.

I have enclosed a copy of my résumé, which will tell you my other qualifications and experience.

I would really like to be employed by the XYZ State Bank. I would like to be considered for the next job opening available in my field of study. Please call me after 3:30 p.m. at 555-2638.

Sincerely,

Applicant A

Applicant A

Enclosure

June 4, <YEAR>

Mr. Mel Ward, President
XYZ State Bank
4 Towne Center
Catlin, IA 50021

Dear Mr. Ward:

XYZ State Bank has always been a warm and friendly place to do our business. As a customer, I would like to return some of my gratitude for making me feel so comfortable in your bank. Since Catlin is such a small town, I am familiar with the employees and they know me.

In my two years at Des Moines Area Community College, I have completed 42 credit hours, I have learned how to work with balance sheets, work with numbers and properly work with different invoices, such as the 2 percent n/30 for the discounts. I would like to try new situations and meet new people.

Enclosed is a copy of my résumé; it will tell you more about me and my qualifications.

I would like to be considered for the opening at the bank in my field of study. Please call me after 2 p.m. at 555-9230.

Sincerely,

Applicant B

Applicant B

Enclosure

Name _____   Date _____

PROOFREADING EXERCISE

Use proofreaders' marks to indicate the errors in this thank-you letter:

> Dear Charlotte:
>
> Thank-you for taking the time to interview me for the
>
> Office Assisdant position. The position is just what Ive
>
> been looking for and I'm eager too provide your any adi-
>
> tional information about my skills and qalifications.
>
> My three year's expereince at Solo Corporation have given
>
> me valueable experience that I can bring to your company.
>
> I look forward to hear from you.
>
> Sincerely,

Search the Internet for Job Information

1. **Connect to the Internet and go to the Website <www.careermag.com> and read several of the articles about job seeking skills, careers, and employment that interest you.**
2. **Connect to the Iinternet and go to the Website< http://www1.kaplan.com> and choose "Careers." Then choose "Résumés and Cover Letters" and read several of the articles about résumés and cover letters that interest you.**

NOTES

Formatting

FORMATTING MEMOS

Memo formats vary from organization to organization. A standardized format for all organizations isn't necessary because memos are internal—they are distributed within an organization. Memos should be efficient and save typing time; therefore, the format is simple. Most organizations prefer to use 8½- by 11-inch paper so that all correspondence will be the same size and less apt to become lost in the files.

Memo Formats

Most organizations now use plain paper memos because it is too difficult and time-consuming to align printed memo forms with printed text from a computer. To prepare a memo the easiest and fastest way on plain paper, follow these guidelines and refer to Figure A-1.

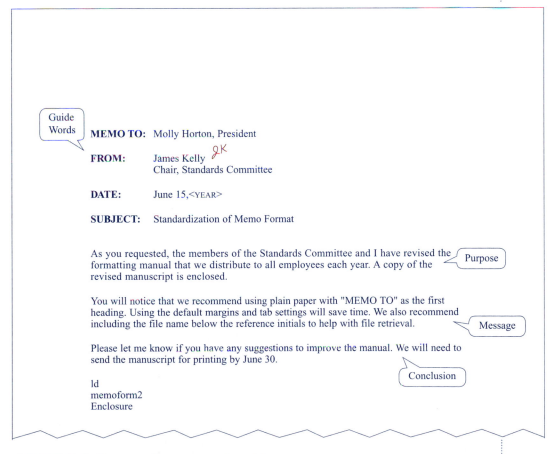

FIGURE A-1 The parts of a memo typed on plain paper.

- Use default word processing program side margins (1 to 1 ¼ inches).
- Leave a 2-inch top margin for most memos. However, you may use a top margin of as little as 1 inch if doing so will eliminate the need for a continuation page. It is usually easier to leave the default word processing program top and bottom margins (usually 1 inch); then press the Enter key to leave the desired first-page top margin.
- If you are using plain paper, you may key *INTEROFFICE MEMO-RANDUM* or *MEMORANDUM* or *MEMO* 1 inch from the top of the page.
- Double-space and block the heading guide words *(TO, FROM, DATE, SUBJECT)* in bold all-capital letters at the left margin. Use *MEMO TO* instead of *TO* if you do not type *INTEROFFICE MEM-ORANDUM* or *MEMORANDUM* at the top of the page.
- Type a colon after each guide word.
- Tab after the colon following each guide word so that names, date, and subject will block-align at least two spaces after the longest guide word. You may be able to use the default tabs, or you may find it necessary to set a tab two to three spaces after the longest guide word.
- Using capital and lowercase letters, type the addressee's name, sender's name, date, and subject. (Be sure to type each guide word followed by a colon; tab, and then type the name, date, or subject—do not type all the guide words first.)
- You may use additional guide words in your heading; for example, *COPIES TO*.

Although most companies have abandoned the use of paper memo forms with the printed words *MEMO TO, FROM,* and so on, with space for typing, some companies use memo paper for internal communications. The paper may have the company name and/or department and the words *Memo* or *Memorandum* or *Interoffice Memorandum* at the top. The sender then types the memo in the same way as on plain paper or may use a macro or stored strokes to insert *TO, FROM,* and so on.

In companies that do not have a standard memorandum format, word processing program templates offer an easy way to create a professional-looking memo. These templates may be modified to meet the organization's needs.

Memos are now commonly distributed as attachments to e-mail. Remember to avoid including confidential material in memos that will be attached to e-mail messages.

Parts of a Memo

A memo has two parts: (1) the heading and (2) the body.

Heading

The heading of all memos should contain the following minimum information:

MEMO TO: (Use only *TO* if the word *MEMORANDUM* appears at the top.)

FROM:

DATE: (Some organizations insert the date first.)

SUBJECT:

Using *MEMO TO* eliminates the need to type *Memorandum* at the top of the paper; however, some companies use paper already printed with *Memo* or *Memorandum*. You may wish to create a heading macro with your word processing software to eliminate repetitive keying.

If the organization has several divisions or has offices in more than one location, the memo forms may include additional guide words such as:

DIVISION: OR **DEPARTMENT:**

LOCATION OR **FLOOR:** OR **BRANCH:**

PHONE: OR **EXTENSION:**

Each organization tailors its heading to fit its structure and style. You can easily store the heading information in your computer and retrieve it without retyping each time you prepare a memo.

Titles in Headings

Omit courtesy titles *(Mrs., Ms., Miss, Mr.,* etc.) in memo headings. Use business titles *(Vice President, Sales Manager,* etc.) when:

1. The addressee has several titles, and this particular memo pertains to the responsibilities associated with only one of them.
2. The name of the addressee is the same as, or could easily be confused with, that of another employee.
3. The writer wishes to show respect to a superior.
4. The writer wishes to ensure prompt and accurate delivery of the memo.

Addressee

Interoffice memos may go to:

- An individual.
- Several individuals.
- A division or department.
- All personnel.

If a memo is going to two or three people, try to type all the names on the same line. If all names will not fit on the same line, the heading may look better if you list the names at the end of the memo (the heading should not take up more than half of the page). First, type *See Distribution Below* or *Distribution* on the *MEMO TO* line. Then, after the reference initials or whatever comes last on your page, double-space and type *Distribution:*, and list the names of the recipients in alphabetical order. (A few organizations may list the names by rank.) You may find it necessary to arrange the names in two or more columns.

When you have made copies for all recipients, place a check mark on each copy next to the name of the person who is to receive that copy. The memo in Figure A-2 is the copy intended for C. Donaldson (see page 411).

INTEROFFICE MEMORANDUM

TO: Distribution

FROM: Meryl L. Timpson

DATE: April 23, <YEAR>

SUBJECT: Part-time Employment and Early Retirement for Nonprofessional Staff

Please give me your suggestions about ways to encourage part-time employment or early retirement for approximately 700 of our full-time nonprofessional staff. Our professional staff is adequate, but the number of nonprofessional employees in relation to occupancy rates is very high and costly to operations.

These are some of the key points discussed in the executive staff meeting last Friday:

- We are experiencing declining occupancy rates in our three facilities, as are other hospitals in San Antonio and throughout the nation.

- Year to date through March, we had an average 74.3 occupancy rate, distributed as follows:

Central Region	78.8 percent
North Region	76.8 percent
West Region	72.9 percent
South Region	68.6 percent

- These rates fell into the 80th percentile in years past, and we project that they will decrease even further by the end of the fiscal year.

- Some of the major factors contributing to fewer hospital admissions and shorter stays include changes in Medicare reimbursements, increasing trends toward insurance copayments, wellness programs, and outpatient clinics.

In order to avoid layoffs next year, we are urging employees to voluntarily change to part-time status or to take early retirement. Currently, 11 percent of our 4700-member workforce is classified as part-time, and we need to double that figure. Another 200 workers are eligible for early retirement options.

FIGURE A-2 This memo illustrates one proper format for a two-page memorandum. The continuation page is shown on page 411.

Distribution   2   April 23, <YEAR>

Please give me your immediate feedback as to how we can achieve these necessary
goals through attrition instead of layoffs.

MLT

MLT
ckr
attrit.25b

Distribution:

L. Benning
P. Crandell
C. Donaldson
✓ R. Fisher
J. Lindsey
R. McIntyre
H. Zimmerman

FIGURE A-2 *(Continued)*

The Writer
The writer does not use a courtesy title but may include a business title, department, location, and/or phone number for identification purposes and to facili-
tate a response.

The Date
Type the date in full—it is best not to abbreviate or express the date in figures.
A complete date is as necessary to a memo as it is to a letter, to prevent misinter-
pretation.

> The business translation of *6/9/04* is *June 9, 2004*.

> The military or European translation of *6/9/04* is *September 6, 2004*.

If you use a memo template or the automatic "Insert Date" feature of your
word processing software, you may find it necessary to change the defaults in
order to insert the proper date format.

The Subject Line
The subject line serves as the title of your message and as an aid in filing the
memo for future reference. When writing a subject line, remember to:

- Use a concise phrase (not a complete sentence) that tells the reader what the message is about.
- Be specific. (For example, do not use *Sales Information* on all memos written from the Sales Department.)
- Capitalize the important words.
- Not use a period at the end of the subject line.

The Body

This section of the memo contains the message. Some general guidelines for preparing this section are:

- Leave one or two blank lines between the heading and the body.
- Single-space the text and double-space between paragraphs.
- Use block paragraphs.

Most memo writers prefer to initial or sign their names next to the typed *FROM* line. Others prefer to have their names or initials typed at the bottom of the memo, with space to initial or sign. With this style, type the name four lines below the message, starting at the center, or align it at the left margin.

Type the reference lines starting on the second line below the end of the message at the left margin in the following order:

- Reference initials (the initials of the person who typed the document).
- File name notation, if required. (It is good practice to include this notation, the name under which the document will be stored on a disk, for later retrieval of the document.)
- Enclosure or attachment notation. An enclosure notation indicates that the sender has included another item, such as a pamphlet, form, booklet, flier, or other printed material. An attachment notation indicates that an item will be physically attached to the memo with a staple or paper clip.
- Copy notation. Use *c,* or *cc* (abbreviations that indicate *copy to*), or *Copy to* or *Copies to* followed by a colon when a copy of the memo is sent to a third party who has an interest in the subject of the memo.

See additional illustrations of reference initials, enclosure notations, and copy notations later in this appendix in the section "Formatting Business Letters."

Continuation Pages

If your memo requires more than one page, use the same color and weight of paper for the second and succeeding pages. Keep the same left and right margins as on the first page. The second and succeeding pages should have a heading positioned about ½ to 1 inch from the top of each page. Use your word processing software's "header" feature to type a heading that includes:

- Name of addressee (the person who will receive the memo).
- Page number.
- Date (same as on the first page).

Choose one of two styles:

1. Type the heading on one line horizontally across the page:

Distribution   2   August 14, <YEAR>

2. Type the heading vertically on three lines:

Mr. Lloyd Caviness
Page 2
August 14, <YEAR>

You may wish to press the Enter key one or two times after the date in your header to allow extra space between the header and the body of your second page. Be sure that the header applies only to the second and succeeding pages— check your software guidelines to determine how to prevent the header from appearing on the first page.

If a paragraph of your memo continues from one page to the next, be sure that at least *two lines* (not sentences) of the paragraph appear at the bottom of a page and at least two lines (or one line and part of a second line) of the paragraph appear at the top of the next page. Word processing programs have a feature that will automatically prevent the occurrence of a single line of text at the top or bottom of a page (called *widows* and *orphans*).

The Signature

A handwritten signature or initials make the memo authentic. The writer should sign the memo by one of these methods:

- By writing his or her initials after the keyed name in the *FROM:* line. (See Figure A-1.)
- By signing his or her name at the bottom of the memo just above the keyed initials or name, as illustrated in Figure A-2.

FORMATTING MEMO REPORTS

Memo reports are routine reports arranged with a memo heading. The body, usually two to five pages long, is organized like the body of a formal report and may have side headings. A typical memo report is shown in Figure A-3.

MEMO TO: All Employees

FROM: Janet Sanzone

DATE: July 16, <YEAR>

SUBJECT: Memo Reports

Today the memo report is a popular way to communicate detailed information to other employees within an organization.

DEFINITION AND PARTS

A memo report is a cross between a memo and a formal report. The memo report has two main parts:

1. A heading like a memo with *TO, FROM, DATE,* and *SUBJECT* as the minimum items.
2. The body containing the information with side headings to help organize the material.

LENGTH

Most memo reports range from two to five pages in length—longer than a memo but shorter than a formal report. The second and succeeding pages of a memo report need a heading that contains the same information as the continuation pages of memos and letters. The heading on the continuation pages includes the following information: who the document is going to, the page number, and the same date that appears on page 1 of the memo report.

SIDE HEADINGS

The use of side headings distinguishes a memo report from a memo. Side headings may include the same parts found in a formal report, such as *Summary, Recommendations, Background, Findings, Conclusions.* Other categories could include these: *Cost* or *Financial Information, Project* (by name), *Status,* or any other applicable category.

FORMAT

In the business world, memo reports are usually single-spaced with one blank line between paragraphs. One or two blank lines appear between the heading of the memo report and the body. The side headings are keyed on separate lines with one blank line above and below each heading.

br

FIGURE A-3 A memo report.

Follow these general guidelines for formatting memo reports:
- Complete all heading elements of the memo as usual. Use the report title for the subject.
- Leave one or two blank lines between the heading and the body of the report.
- Single-space the paragraphs; double-space between paragraphs.
- For continuation pages, use the same color and weight of paper as used on the first page. Keep the same left and right margins as on the

first page. Format the heading on the continuation pages the same as for a regular memo.

Itemize the information. A report that contains complex facts and ideas will be easier to read if items are (1) separated into paragraphs, (2) numbered, (3) bulleted, or (4) preceded by side headings.

FORMATTING E-MAIL

E-mail system templates provide *To, From, Subject* or *Re,* and *cc* lines, much like the ones on a simplified memo. Although e-mail is considered an informal means of communication, you should still make sure that it is correct and complete.

Addressee

- Insert the recipient's e-mail address exactly as written.
- Do not change the spacing, punctuation, symbols, or capitalization of an e-mail address.

Date and Sender

Both the date and the registered e-mail user's name are automatically entered.

Subject Line

- Use a concise, specific phrase (not a complete sentence) that tells the reader what the message is about. A descriptive subject line will help the recipient determine importance.
- Cover only one topic in each e-mail.
- Capitalize important words.
- Do not use a period at the end of the subject line.

Body

- Keep e-mail messages brief. Consider writing a memo attachment for longer messages.
- Use short paragraphs; single-space the text and double-space between paragraphs.
- Do not indent the first line of each paragraph. (Use block paragraphs.)
- Do not use all-capital letters in your e-mail messages; use uppercase and lowercase letters.
- You may omit salutations; however, you might like to give your e-mail messages a friendlier opening by typing the addressee's name at the beginning of your message.
- You may omit closing lines. Some writers believe, however, that a typed or automatic signature at the end of an e-mail adds a nice touch.
- Remember to include all attachments.

Remember these additional points when writing e-mail:

- Never send confidential information via e-mail.
- Use *smileys* (or *emoticons*) sparingly and only when you are certain that they will not offend the recipient. These symbols suggest facial expressions and may appear in informal e-mails to express feelings. See Figure A-4 for examples of smileys.
- Use abbreviations sparingly in business e-mail. Figure A-5 shows a few common e-mail abbreviations.
- Proofread carefully—follow standard grammar, spelling, punctuation, and capitalization rules.

:-(	Angry	:-]	Sarcastic smirk
:'-(	Crying	:-@	Screaming
:-D	Laughing	:-O	Shocked
:-(	Sad	8-)	Wide-eyed look
:-)	Smiling	;-)	Winking

FIGURE A-4 Smileys or emoticons face sideways.

BTW	by the way
IMHO	in my humble opinion
GMTA	great minds think alike
J/K	just kidding
BRB	be right back
BAK	back at the keyboard
LOL	laughing out loud
ROTFL	rolling on the floor with laughter

FIGURE A-5 E-mail abbreviations.

FORMATTING BUSINESS LETTERS

Letter Format and Letter Styles

The appearance of your letter is the first impression your reader has of you and the organization you represent. You want that impression to be a positive one, so it is important to format your letter correctly and to use a correct letter style.

 The **format** of a business letter refers to the horizontal positioning of the parts of a business letter—heading, opening, body, and closing. **Style** is the arrangement of these four parts into a block, a modified-block, or a simplified letter style.

How your letter is placed on the page also will make an impression on the reader. Your letter will look balanced and the reader will be more likely to react positively if the left and right margins as well as the top and bottom margins are equal.

Word processing templates offer an easy way to create nicely formatted letters. Such templates may be modified to meet an organization's needs.

Parts of a Business Letter

The four parts of a business letter, in order, are the heading, opening, body, and closing.

The Heading

The heading contains either a letterhead or a return address and a date line. Optional features include reference notations and personal or confidential notations.

Letterhead or Return Address

Most businesses use stationery with a printed letterhead for the first page of a business letter. These letterheads provide the company name, address, telephone number, fax number, e-mail address, company logo, and sometimes a Website address. Therefore, the date line is the only part of the heading you need to provide. Leave at least $\frac{1}{2}$-inch space between the letterhead and the date line.

For a personal-business letter that you write on plain paper instead of letterhead, you will need a return address. Start about 2 inches from the top of the paper, or center the page vertically if your letter is one page. Type your street address as the first line and your city, state, and ZIP Code as the second line. Never put your name or that of your organization in the heading.

304 East Cunningham Street
Tifton, GA 31794

If you wish to provide your telephone number, you may add it as the third line under the city, state, and ZIP Code.

Another way to handle your return address is to type it below your typed name in the closing:

Sincerely,

Larry Allison

Larry Allison
304 East Street
Tifton, GA 31794

Date Line

On letterhead stationery, place the date about 2 inches from the top of the page, or at least ½ inch below the letterhead.

When a return address is typed at the top of plain paper, type the date immediately below the return address as follows:

> 4083 Robinson Street
> Abilene, TX 79601
> September 10, <YEAR>

OR

> 4083 Robinson Street
> Abilene, TX 79601
> 725-555-3234
> September 10, <YEAR>

If the return address appears under the signature, type the date about 2 inches from the top of the paper. The date line should be on one line and should contain:

- The name of the month, spelled in full.
- The day of the month, in digits.
- The year, written as four digits.

Always spell out the month and include all four digits for the year. Using all digits can lead to misinterpretation:

> The business translation of *6/9/04* is *June 9, 2004.*

> The military or European translation of *6/9/04* is *September 6, 2004.*

Date Styles   The following examples of date styles show the date August 28 in both business style and military or European style:

> **BUSINESS STYLE:** August 28, 2004
> Month Day, Year (requires comma)

> **MILITARY STYLE:** 28 August 2004
> Day Month Year (no comma)

Personal and Confidential Notations

Type these optional notations on the second line below the date, at the left margin and in bold all-capital letters.

Reference Notations

Place a reference notation (which is optional) such as *In reply to: . . .* or *When replying, refer to: . . .* on the second line below the date or below the *Personal* or *Confidential* notation, whichever comes last.

Another way to include a reference notation is to type it in a subject line, such as:

SUBJECT: Policy 93829

The Opening

The purpose of an opening is to direct a letter to its destination and to greet the reader. It includes an inside address, a salutation (unless you are using the simplified letter style), and (optionally) an attention line.

Inside Address

Begin the inside address at the left margin on the fourth line below the date or below any notation that follows the date. (The simplified style of letter, however, follows different spacing. See Figure A-8 on page 432.

The inside address includes the:

- Name of the addressee.
- Job title of the addressee (if applicable).
- Name of the addressee's organization (when available).
- Street address or post office box number.
- City, state, and ZIP Code.

Name of Addressee   When writing the name of the addressee, follow these rules:

- Write the addressee's name exactly as he or she writes it, and spell it correctly.
- If you know the correct courtesy title *(Mr., Mrs., Miss, Ms.)*, use it with the name.
- If you are unsure of the addressee's gender *(Terry, Chris, Gerry)*, omit the courtesy title.
- If you do not know the name of a specific individual, you may use a job title *(Sales Manager)* or department name *(Sales Department)* as the addressee. Repeat the title or department name in the salutation.
- When addressing a letter to a doctor, use the abbreviation *Dr.* for the courtesy title, and do not use double titles. *(Dr.* and *M.D.* mean the same thing.)

CORRECT: Dr. Sara E. Briggs   OR   Sara E. Briggs, M.D.

INCORRECT: Dr. Sara E. Briggs, M.D.

Both of the correct forms use the salutation *Dear Dr. Briggs.*

Job Title of Addressee   Follow these rules concerning job titles:

- Use the addressee's job title *(Personnel Manager, Sales Manager, Maintenance Superintendent)* when you know it.
- Type the title on a separate line under the addressee's name. If the title is long, break it into two lines but indent the second line two or three spaces.

> Mrs. Sue Valdez
> Office Manager and
>   Personnel Administrator

If the title is very short, you may type a comma and the title on the same line as the name or the department name.

> Mr. L. B. Pei, Manager
> Rawlins Corporation
>
> **OR**
>
> Ms. Saundra Lawson
> Chair, Sales Division

Street Address   Type house numbers and building numbers on a separate line preceding the city, state, and ZIP Code. Express these numbers in figures, except for *One*, and do not use a prefix such as *No.* or a symbol such as *#*.

> **CORRECT:**   One Carriage Lane
> **INCORRECT:** 1 Carriage Lane
>
> **CORRECT:**   2 Carriage Lane
> **INCORRECT:** Two Carriage Lane
>
> **CORRECT:**   520 Dawn Street
> **INCORRECT:** #520 Dawn Street   **OR**   No. 520 Dawn Street

For street names, follow these guidelines:

- Write out words such as *North, South, West,* and *Southeast* when they are used before a street name.

> 9896 North Hunter's Way

- If a compass point comes after a street name, follow these examples:

> 9896 Hunter's Way, NW (abbreviate section designations)
>
> 9083 Hunter's Way North (spell out *North, South, East,* and *West* and omit the comma)

- If the street name is a number, spell out numbers up to and including ten; use figures for numbers above ten.

> **CORRECT:**   7430 Seventh Street
> **INCORRECT:** 7430 7th Street

```
CORRECT:    606 14th Avenue
INCORRECT:  606 Fourteenth Avenue
```

- Write *street, avenue,* and similar designations in full.

Post Office Box   A post office box number may replace the street address:

```
Mr. Randy Felgenhauer
P.O. Box 852   OR   Post Office Box 852
Albion, MI 49224
```

If you have both a street address and a post office box number, use the box number for regular U.S. Postal Service (USPS) deliveries and the street address for express mail. If you type both addresses on the envelope, the postal service will deliver to the designation on the line preceding the city, state, and ZIP Code.

Other carriers, such as Federal Express (FedEx) and United Parcel Service (UPS), *require a street address.* The USPS owns post office boxes and is the only delivery service that can use them.

City, State, and ZIP Code   Type the city, state, and ZIP Code on one line, immediately below the street or post office box address.

```
Columbus, OH 45227-9999
```

Do not abbreviate the name of a city unless it is customarily abbreviated. For example, write *St. Louis* and *St. Paul* (abbreviate the word *Saint*). Spell out *Fort Myers* and *Mount Pleasant.*

Treat the state name as follows:

- Use the two-letter state abbreviations (in capital letters with no periods and with no space between them) recommended by the USPS, or write the name of the state in full. See the list of the states and Canadian provinces and their corresponding two-letter abbreviations in Appendix C. Use the two-letter abbreviations only with ZIP Codes in addresses; they are not considered correct abbreviations in other written material.
- Leave one space (use no punctuation) between the state and ZIP Code.

```
CORRECT:    Cleveland, OH 44100-1718   OR
            Cleveland, Ohio 44100-1718

INCORRECT:  Cleveland, Oh. 44100-1718   OR
            Cleveland, OH. 44100-1718
```

All addresses should have a five-digit ZIP Code. The USPS recommends the use of the nine-digit ZIP Code (ZIP + 4) whenever possible. The additional four digits make it possible for the mail to be sorted by electronic equipment according to the delivery route. Use a hyphen to separate the two parts of the ZIP Code as shown in the previous example.

Attention Line

The attention line, an optional part of a business letter opening, is no longer frequently used. Its purpose is to alert the letter recipient that this is a business matter that someone other than the person named may respond to. The trend now is to type the name of the person, title, or department above the company name instead of using an attention line.

If you use an attention line, however, you have two options. First, you may place the attention line as the first line of the inside address. This location works well if you are using window envelopes or electronically copying the inside address to create the envelope address.

Attention: Manager
Starr Motor Company
9869 Linley Court
Boston, MA 29680

The attention line arrangement used in the past is not suitable if your computer will automatically format your envelope by copying the inside address of your letter. If you prefer this arrangement, however, follow these guidelines:

- Type the attention line on the second line below the inside address, and leave one blank line above the salutation.
- Type in all-capital letters or in initial cap and lowercase letters:

    ATTN: SALES DEPARTMENT   OR   Attention: Sales Department

- Use a colon after the word *Attention*.
- Use the salutation *Ladies and Gentlemen*: OR *Dear (Organization Name):* because a letter with an attention line is considered to be addressed to the *organization* rather than to the *person, title,* or *department* named in the attention line.

Ace Industries
1022 Tremont Parkway
Columbus, OH 43215

Attention: Purchasing Department

Ladies and Gentlemen:

It is always preferable to address your letter directly to an individual, thereby eliminating the need for an attention line.

Salutation

The salutation greets the reader and helps set the tone of the letter. If you use the simplified style of letter, omit the salutation. When typing salutations for business letters:

- Type the salutation on the second line below the inside address (or attention line if used), at the left margin.
- Type a colon after the salutation unless you are using open punctuation (no comma after the complimentary closing).
- Leave one blank line below the salutation.
- Abbreviate the titles *Mr., Mrs., Ms.,* and *Dr.,* but spell out titles such as *Major, Professor,* and *Reverend.*
- Capitalize the first word and any noun or title in a salutation: *My dear Miss Marsh, Dear Father Tedrick, Dear Senator Taylor.*

Determining the salutation can sometimes be difficult. An important concern is avoiding sexist language. Remember, however, that the salutation must agree with the addressee named in the inside address. Some guidelines for each type of addressee follow:

- **Individual.** In the salutation for an individual, such as Mr. Jeff Winland, use a courtesy title and last name: *Dear Mr. Winland.* If you are on a first-name basis with Mr. Winland, use *Dear Jeff.*
- **Individual—gender or title preference unknown.** If you don't know the addressee's gender, drop the courtesy title and use the full name— *Dear Gerry Fulton.* Do the same if you don't know a woman's marital status and/or preference for the courtesy title *Miss, Mrs.,* or *Ms.—Dear Ann Garcia.*
- **Organization, department, or box number (as you might find in a blind ad in the newspaper).** The salutation should be *Ladies and Gentlemen.* If the group is composed entirely of women, use the salutation *Ladies.* Likewise, address a group of men as *Gentlemen.* Never put *Dear* in front of these salutations. An alternative is to repeat in the salutation the organization or department name used in the inside address: *Dear General Motors, Dear Consumer Relations Department.* Another alternative is to use the simplified letter style, which omits the salutation entirely.
- **Job title.** A letter that gives a job title as addressee uses the same title in the salutation: *Dear Personnel Manager.*

When you send a form letter, it is often impossible to know the gender and title preference of each addressee. A salutation such as *Dear Customer, Dear Friend,* or *Dear Parents* is a friendly alternative to using both first and last names in the salutation. Note that the use of the salutations *Dear Sir* and *Dear Madam,* now considered sexist, is rapidly declining in business correspondence.

Salutations that start letters in a friendly, conversational way are growing in popularity. These "dearless" salutations have been used for some time in sales promotion letters but are now being used in other informal business letters. Among the unusual salutations are the greetings:

Good morning, Mr. Wilson
Hello, Mrs. Tabels
Happy Holidays, Ms. Skoog

A letter may also start right out with the message. The reader's name is then inserted in the first sentence.

Miss Margaret D. Ryan
One South Michigan Street
Adrian, MI 49221

Thank you, Miss Ryan, for your suggestions, which will help us to serve you more efficiently.

The Body

The body of the letter contains the writer's thoughts. It consists of the message and, optionally, a subject line.

Subject Line

A subject line precedes the message and tells the reader in one glance what the letter is about. Although it is an optional part of a letter, its use is increasing and is very helpful for both reader and writer. Type a subject line:

- One blank line above the message and leave one blank line below the salutation.
- In all-capital letters or in initial capital and lowercase letters.
- With or without the word *Subject* (see, for example, Figure A-7).
- Centered, at the left margin, or indented, depending on the letter style.

Dear Mr. Douglas:

Subject: Revision of City Sales Tax

Dear Miss Mooney:

SERVICE CALLS ON WEEKENDS

Message

In general, begin typing the message on the second line below the subject line. When typing the message:

- Single-space each paragraph.
- Double-space between paragraphs.
- Block all paragraphs in a block or simplified style letter.
- Either block or indent the first line of each paragraph ½ inch in a modified-block style letter.

Paragraphs that are too long are not easy or inviting to read. Follow these general rules:

- Limit your first and last paragraphs to no more than four lines.
- Make all other paragraphs no more than eight lines.

The Closing

The closing in a business letter typically includes a complimentary closing phrase, the writer's name and title, and reference initials. It may also include the typed name of the organization, a file name notation, an enclosure notation, a mailing notation, a copy notation, and a postscript.

Complimentary Closing

The complimentary closing is a parting phrase that indicates the end of the message. It is typed:

- One blank line below the last line of the message.
- At the left margin in block style letters.
- At the horizontal center point in modified-block style letters.
- With only the first word capitalized.
- With a comma following the closing unless you are using open punctuation.

The tone of the complimentary closing should match that of the salutation. If you have greeted your reader with *Dear Marcy,* you will probably close with *Sincerely.* Some typical closings follow:

Sincerely,
Sincerely yours,
Cordially,
Cordially yours,

Formal closings such as *Very truly yours* and *Respectfully yours* are used rarely. Omit the complimentary closing in the simplified letter style.

Writer's Name and Title

Leave three blank lines for the handwritten signature, and type the writer's name. The writer's title or department can be placed on the same line with the writer's name or on a separate line, depending on which location will make the lines most nearly the same length. See the following examples:

Sincerely yours,

Art Troglia

Art Troglia, President

Cordially,

Eleanor Turner

Eleanor E. Turner
Reservations Manager

Sincerely,

Alice Wernig

Ms. Alice Wernig

Sincerely,

Elizabeth Weaver, Ph.D.

Elizabeth L. Weaver, Ph.D.

Sincerely,

Grace Stevenson

Ms. Grace Stevenson

Sincerely,

Catherine Smith

Mrs. Catherine Smith

Sincerely,

Lynn Winkle

Mr. Lynn Winkle

Courtesy Title in Signature Lines   A man does not use a courtesy title *(Mr.)* preceding his handwritten or his typed signature unless his name could also be a woman's name. A woman who wants to specify her courtesy title preference *(Miss, Mrs.,* or *Ms.)* should include the courtesy title in either the handwritten or the typewritten signature.

Several correct forms of signature lines, along with the appropriate courtesy titles, are shown at the left.

Reference Initials

The easiest and most popular style for reference initials is to provide the typist's initials alone in small letters. If the writer or signer prefers to show his or her initials, type them first, and then type the initials of the typist. The writer's initials may also be used when the writer is not the signer of the letter. Usually, type reference initials:

- At the left margin.
- One blank line below the last line in the signature section.
- With a forward slash between the writer's and typist's initials.
- In all-lowercase letters or in all-capital letters.

Some popular reference-initial styles are:

    jwc (typist's initials only)
    MVL/EF (writer and typist)
    sme/prg (writer and typist)
    GCBrown/sn (writer and typist— writer's name not
        provided in signature block)
    mls/06/quote (typist's initials, identification of disk, and
        document name)

Organization Name

Some business organizations include a company signature in the closing to indicate that the organization—not the writer—is legally responsible for the message. If the organization name is used, type it in all-capital letters on the second line below the complimentary closing phrase.

Sincerely,

ALLSTATE DRILLING COMPANY

Jan Carson, President

xx

File Name Notation

It is good practice to include the name under which the document will be stored on a disk, for later retrieval of the document. Type this notation on the line below the reference initials. An alternative location for the file name notation is in a reference notation.

bk
kalden938

OR

When replying, refer to: aikman85 (in reference notation)

Enclosure Notation

An enclosure is anything included in the envelope with the letter. Position the enclosure notation:

- At the left margin.
- On the line below the reference initials or file name.

The notation helps the writer remember to include the enclosures and tells the reader that enclosures should have been sent. If there is more than one enclosure, you may indicate the number. When the material is actually attached to the letter, some writers use the word *Attachment* instead of *Enclosure*.

Enclosure	Enclosures 2
Check enclosed	Enclosures:
2 Enc.	1. Catalog
	2. Reply card

Delivery Notation

If you want to indicate that the letter was sent in a special way, use a delivery notation on the line below the reference initials (or below the file name notation or enclosure notation). Some possible delivery notations are:

> By Federal Express
> By messenger
> By fax

Copy Notation

If you want the addressee of the letter to know that you are sending a copy to someone, type a copy notation one line below the enclosure notation (if used) or below the reference initials. Make notations in one of the following ways:

> c: Jamie Harris
> Copy to: Jamie Harris
> cc: Jamie Harris
>
> cc: Catherine Cobb
>   Gerald Hawley
>   Lucinda Bates

If you do not want the addressee to know that you are sending a copy to one or more other persons, type a blind copy notation *(bc, Blind copy to,* or *bcc)* on copies of the letter. Place the notation on the second line below the last item in the letter. Since the original letter should not show the blind copy notations, print the original letter before adding the blind copy notation to the copies.

Postscript

Some writers use a postscript to give emphasis to an important idea that has been deliberately withheld from the body of the letter.

Limit postscripts to occasions when you wish to take advantage of their attention-getting qualities. Some recipients may view the use of a postscript to express an afterthought as poor planning and organization. Type a postscript:

- At the left margin on the second line below the last typed line.
- Type *PS.* or *PS:* and leave one or two spaces before the first word of the postscript (or omit the abbreviation *PS).*

The following are accepted postscript styles:

> mls
> Enclosure
>
> PS. Mail the card today!
>
> eeb/dm
> hawkins29a
>
> For your complimentary copy, just call 1-800-555-4289.

Continuation Pages

If a letter takes more than one page, print each page after the letterhead page on plain paper that matches the letterhead paper. Use the same margins as on the first page of the letter. Use your word processing software's "header" feature to type a heading that begins ½ to 1 inch from the top of the page and consists of:

1. The name of the addressee.
2. The page number.
3. The date that appears on the first page.

Leave one or two blank lines below the last line of the continuation-page heading. (You may need to add a blank line at the bottom of your header.) The following are two acceptable styles:

Mr. Randal Wilkey
Page 2
August 28, <YEAR>

Mrs. Rita Haggerty   2   May 3, <YEAR>

In typing continuation pages, follow these guidelines:

1. Carry at least two lines of the body of the letter to the second page; do not type only the closing of the letter on the second page.
2. If a paragraph is divided at the end of a page, leave at least two lines at the bottom of the first page, and carry at least two lines to the top of the second page. Do not divide a paragraph containing fewer than four lines. Word processing programs have a feature that will automatically prevent the occurrence of a single line of text at the top or bottom or a page (called *widows* and *orphans*).
3. Never divide the last word on a page.
4. Be sure that the header applies only to the second and succeeding pages—check your software guidelines to determine how to prevent the header from appearing on the first page.

Business Letter Styles

When selecting a letter style, consider the design of your organization's letterhead as well as the image you want to convey. Three popular letter styles today are *modified-block, block,* and *simplified.*

Modified-Block Style

In the *modified-block style,* the date line, complimentary closing, company signature, and the writer's identification begin at the horizontal center of the page. Other lines begin at the left margin. In a variation on this style, the first line of each paragraph is indented.

Figure A-6 illustrates the *modified-block style.*

NET TECHNOLOGY CORPORATION

8866 Saturn Lane
Chicago, IL 60603-8866
Phone: 903-555-2898
Website: netcorp.com

April 9, <YEAR>

Mrs. Heather Mitchell
Birnbaum Corporation
59 Littlefield Road
Crockett, VA 22401

Dear Mrs. Mitchell:

The modified-block letter style is a very popular letter style used in business today.

In this letter style, the date line, complimentary closing, company name, and writer's signature and title begin at the horizontal center. All other lines begin at the left margin (unless you wish to indent the paragraphs). The enclosed sample letter shows indented paragraphs.

The modified-block style usually uses standard or mixed punctuation. This means that a colon follows the salutation and a comma follows the complimentary closing, as illustrated in this letter.

Please return the enclosed reply card if you would like to receive one of our Training Department's booklets on letter formats.

The enclosure notation below shows an acceptable style for specifying the items that you enclose.

Sincerely,

NET TECHNOLOGY CORPORATION

Dennis R. Landry
Business Manager

drl/ism
modblock
Enclosures:
1. Letter
2. Reply Card

FIGURE A-6 A modified-block style letter.

Block Style

In the *block style,* which is illustrated in Figure A-7, all lines begin at the left margin.

PROFESSIONAL IMAGES CONSULTING

890 Bay Area Drive
San Francisco, CA 93797
Phone: 213-555-9111
Website: pic.coms

February 15, <YEAR>

Mr. Larry Johnson
Johnson & Turner
206 Hillsboro Avenue
Dallas, TX 76645

Dear Mr. Johnson

Subject: Block Letter Style

All lines begin at the left margin with a block style letter, as you see here. The primary appeal is the time you save compared with the modified-block style.

This letter also illustrates the open style of punctuation, which means that no punctuation is used after the salutation and complimentary closing.

When you need a subject line, you may use the format shown here. You may also omit the word *Subject* or type the entire line in capital letters. Since the subject line is considered part of the body, leave one blank line above and below the salutation. The subject line begins at the left margin.

This style has a neat, streamlined appearance, as you can see, and looks very up to date. It eliminates many extra keyboarding strokes and motions and, therefore, helps to increase letter production rates.

The copy notation below shows an acceptable style for indicating that copies of this letter are going to two persons.

Sincerely

Mary L. Carson

Mary L. Carson
Public Relations Director

lk
blockletter4
c: Ralph Barnes
     Peter Lawrence

FIGURE A-7 A block style letter.

Simplified Style

The *simplified style,* illustrated in Figure A-8, includes these features:

- All lines begin at the left margin.
- A subject line replaces the salutation.

- The complimentary closing is omitted.
- The writer's identification is typed in all-capital letters on one line.
- Open punctuation is always used.

Business Office Technology Corporation

6363 Spencer Street / Cedar Falls, IA 50613 / Phone: 319-555-9999 / Fax: 319-555-8888

September 3, <YEAR>

Ms. Carolyn Short
Short & Associates
2525 Memory Lane
Newark, NJ 19628

SIMPLIFIED LETTER STYLE

All lines begin at the left margin in a simplified letter style, as you see here. This style is becoming more popular because:

- It is quick and easy to format.
- The writer does not need to determine a salutation or appropriate closing lines.

Instead of a salutation, type a subject line in all-capital letters. Omit the complimentary closing and type the writer's identification (name and job title) in all-capital letters on one line. Always use open punctuation.

Notice the line spacing after the date (five blank lines), before and after the subject line (two blank lines), and before the closing (four blank lines).

G. R. BROWN, DIRECTOR, TECHNOLOGY DIVISION

pts
simpli3

FIGURE A-8 A simplified style letter.

Punctuation Styles

The two punctuation styles commonly used today are *standard* and *open*.

- **Standard punctuation** (also called *mixed punctuation)* calls for a colon after the salutation and a comma after the complimentary closing.
- **Open punctuation** requires no punctuation after the salutation and the complimentary closing.

Addressing Envelopes

Most business letters are mailed in No. 10 envelopes (9 ½ by 4 ⅛ inches); some correspondence requires No. 6 ¾ envelopes (6 ½ by 3 ⅝ inches). See a correctly addressed No. 10 envelope in Figure A-9.

You can easily generate envelopes using your word processing program envelope feature. The software may also allow you to insert the USPS POSTNET bar code, if required by your organization. When addressing an envelope, follow these guidelines:

- Single-space the address regardless of the number of lines.
- Position the address on the lower half of the envelope and start all lines near the center.
- Type the address with capital and lowercase letters with appropriate punctuation. *Note*: You may also type the mailing address in all-capital letters with no punctuation.
- Always place the city, state, and ZIP Code on one line and use the same rules as for inside addresses.
- Never type anything below the city, state, and ZIP Code on the envelope. Using ZIP + 4 allows automatic sorting in the order the mail is delivered on the route.
- To accommodate automatic sorting equipment, allow at least ½-inch margins on each side of the address block and a ⅝-inch margin below the address block.
- Type special mailing notations *(AIRMAIL, CERTIFIED,* or *REGISTERED),* if any, in all-capital letters below the stamp or postage meter insignia.
- Type recipient notations *(PERSONAL, HOLD FOR ARRIVAL,* or *CONFIDENTIAL),* if any, on the third line below the return address.
- Type an attention line, if used, as the first line of the mailing address.

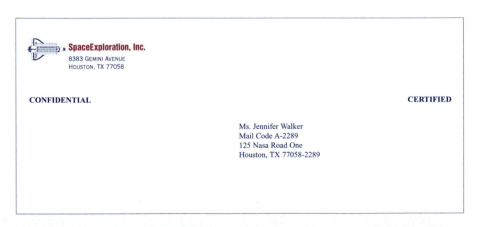

FIGURE A-9 Correctly addressed No. 10 envelope. Type notations such as *Confidential* or *Personal* on the third line below the return address. Mailing notations such as *CERTIFIED* and *REGISTERED* go below the bottom edge of the stamp or postage meter insignia.

Folding Letters

- When folding a letter for a *No. 10 envelope,* fold the bottom third of the letter up and then fold the top third down to within $\frac{3}{8}$ inch of the first crease, and insert the last crease into the envelope first.
- When folding a letter for a *No. 6 ¾ envelope,* bring the bottom half up to within $\frac{3}{8}$ inch of the top, and then crease. Next fold the right third toward the left and crease, fold the left third toward the right and crease to within $\frac{3}{8}$ inch of the crease just made, and insert the last crease into the envelope first.

Figure A-10 shows the correct way to fold letters for both large and small envelopes.

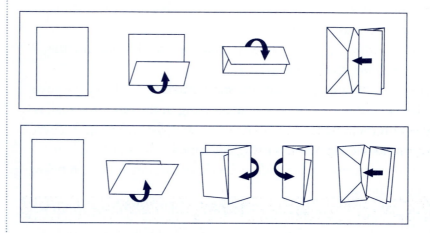

FIGURE A-10 Folding letters for different-size envelopes.

Interviewing for a Job

The objective of the résumé and the letter of application you have prepared (see Chapters 19 and 20) is to persuade the prospective employer to interview you.

 During a job interview you need to convince the interviewer(s) that you have the skills and abilities to do the job and make a positive contribution as an employee. You must sell yourself, just as a salesperson would sell a product or service. The objective of a job interview is to get a job offer.

Remember, it isn't always the best-qualified person who gets the job; it's the person who does the best job of interviewing for the job.

TYPES OF INTERVIEWS

Prospective employers and human resources people may use one of several types of interviews when talking with job applicants. Some of the more common types of interviews are:

Screening Interview

A **screening interview** is most often used by medium- to large-sized organizations that have human resources departments. The purpose of this interview is to determine whether you have the qualifications for the job. If you do, you will then be scheduled for a second interview with the person(s) for whom you would be working.

Campus Interview

A **campus interview** is held on your college campus and arranged through your career services or placement office. These interviews are usually conducted by large organizations or new companies needing a number of employees (part-time or full-time). A campus interview may be a screening interview. The next interview may be held at the company, or a job offer may be made as a result of the campus interview.

Panel or Team Interview

Many companies have begun to use panel or team interviews in an attempt to make the best hiring decision possible. Everyone on the panel has input before a decision is made. The panel can range in number of members from two to ten people. The panel members usually take turns asking questions and everyone takes notes. If you are interviewed by a panel, focus your attention on the person asking the question.

Serial or Corporate Ladder Interview

This interview is similar to the panel interview, but each person on the panel speaks with the applicant separately. This type of interview could take several hours. Each interviewer is likely to ask different interview questions depending on how he or she will work with the person hired. After the interview, these people meet to discuss and evaluate the interview.

Simultaneous Group Interview

With a **simultaneous group interview,** several candidates are interviewed at the same time. The purpose of this interview is to see how candidates relate to and interact with each other. Are they genuinely friendly to each other? Do they support or help each other as the interview progresses? Or do they seem to be competing with the other candidates and always trying to outshine the other candidates? This type of interview is used when several people may be hired and where it is important for employees to work together as a team. The Walt Disney Company uses this technique when hiring interns for its theme parks.

Stress Interview

A **stress interview** will test your behavior and emotional control under pressure. These interviews may be used if the job is very fast-paced and you will be under pressure and stress much of the time. The purpose is to see how you would handle irate, unreasonable customers and clients. Typical techniques used in the stress interview are:

>   Firing questions at you rapidly
>   Long periods of silence after an answer
>   Criticizing and/or questioning your answers
>   Putting you on the defensive

Unstructured Interview

An unstructured interview may have one question: "Tell me about yourself." You will be expected to give a "speech" about yourself. This question does not call for a "This is my life history" approach. Instead, keep the emphasis on your qualifications for the job and talk about what you can do for the organization.

An unstructured interview may have *no* questions; this type is a conversation. It is your job to work into the conversation information about your skills and qualifications for the job. These two types of unstructured interviews are more apt to be used by a person who has little or no training in human resources and/or little experience in interviewing. An unstructured interview will show how good your oral communication skills are.

Virtual Interview

To save time and travel expenses, some companies conduct interviews through videoconferencing technology. The videoconference can be taped, with the applicant's permission, and played again by the interviewer(s) when deciding which applicant(s) to invite for an on-site, personal interview.

PREPARING FOR THE INTERVIEW

In getting ready for an employment interview, you are preparing for one of the most important meetings you will ever have. Employers know that the key to success in their organizations is to match the available jobs with the best-suited applicants.

Do Your Research

Do your homework about the organization with which you will be interviewing. The worst question you can ask is, "So what do you do here at your organization?" You should research and know the following information about the organization *before* the interview:

- Services and/or products
- Location of corporate office and other facilities, if applicable
- Divisions and subsidiaries
- Date business was established
- Privately or publicly owned
- Approximate number of employees
- New products or services
- Names of competitors
- Any other information you can find

The following sources are excellent places to get this information:

The Website for the organization
Your career services or placement office
Chamber of Commerce
Library—public or school

During an interview, interviewers will sometimes ask "Tell me what you know about our organization" to see whether you've done your homework.

 Knowing about the organization demonstrates your interest and your enthusiasm for the job. With this knowledge, you will be able to talk intelligently to the interviewer and tell how your experience and qualifications match the organization's needs. You can also point out how you can make an immediate contribution to the organization.

Prepare a Portfolio

Put together a portfolio with examples of the skills you have to offer to an employer. The portfolio should have the following items:

- Title page
- Your résumé
- Application letter
- List of references
- Copies of diplomas, certificates, awards
- Letters of recommendation, favorable reviews
- Writing samples
- Software skills examples
- Class projects, team projects

Put the items between clear plastic sheets in a three-ring binder so that you can easily insert and remove them depending on the job requirements and the company. Use the portfolio to help prove that you have specific skills.

Understand Requirements for Interviews

A successful interview requires:

- Using good speaking skills—correct grammar and pronunciation.
- Showing knowledge of the organization's products and services, background, and competitors.
- Sending effective nonverbal messages—through eye contact, voice, attitude, naturalness, interest, appearance, handshake, posture, mannerisms, promptness, and so on.
- Anticipating questions the interviewer is likely to ask.
- Preparing questions to ask the interviewer.
- Projecting a "people" personality, maturity, and a serious work ethic.

Anticipate Interview Questions

An interview is like a test in school. If you study for the test, you will usually get a much higher grade. If you prepare for an interview and practice, you will generally do a much better job of selling yourself.

Frequently Asked Interview Questions

Look back at your analysis of what you have to offer and what you want. Be prepared to answer questions such as:

1. Why do you want this job?
2. What would you contribute to our organization?
3. Why did you leave your last job?
4. What are your strong points? Weaknesses?
5. How have your education and experience helped prepare you for this job?
6. What would your former supervisors or teachers say about you?
7. Do you prefer to work independently or as part of a team?
8. How do you get along with coworkers?
9. Where do you see yourself five or ten years from now?
10. Why do you think you are the best candidate for this job?

Behavioral Interview Questions

In recent years, human resources people have been using a method called *behavioral-based interviewing.* The idea behind this method is that a person's past behavior is a good predictor of future behavior. Behavioral-based interview questions ask for specific examples, including details, of how you handled specific situations. Sample questions might include:

1. Tell me about an irate customer you had and how you handled the situation.
2. Tell me about a problem you had with a coworker or classmate and how you handled it.
3. Tell me about a time when you failed to meet a deadline. What things did you fail to do? What happened? What did you learn from the situation?
4. Describe for me a time when you worked on a team and one of the team members was not doing his or her share of the work. What did you do?
5. What is the biggest mistake you ever made?
6. Tell me the details of the last time you gave extraordinary customer service.

 Remember that every interview question is a way of asking "Why should I hire you?" Keep the emphasis on *what you can do* for the organization—not what you want out of the job.

DURING THE INTERVIEW

In addition to the way you answer interview questions, you make a positive or a negative impression on the interviewer in these ways:

Interviewer Turn-Offs

Some behavior or traits that make an unfavorable impression on an interviewer are:

Wandering—inability to focus on relevant information. The interviewer's time is valuable, and he or she hopes that you would use your time effectively if you were an employee. Stick to the question or subject and provide informative, related, and concise answers.

Compulsive talking—rambling, won't stop talking, is unable to listen. Compulsive talking is the "kiss of death" in an interview situation.

Nervousness—wringing hands, touching face, scratching, jingling coins, fidgeting, toe tapping, and so on.

Boredom—mind is obviously not on the interviewer, does not hear the question or pay attention enough to understand, or stares out the window. Shows no enthusiasm.

Noncommunicativeness—quiet to the point of being unable or unwilling to communicate or interact with the interviewer. This trait is just as deadly as compulsive talking.

Unprofessional actions—bringing children or friends with you, having your cell phone ring during the interview (leave your cell phone in your car or at home), using profanity during an interview.

Poor first impression—inappropriate dress, surly attitude, no smile, poor hygiene, body odor, too much makeup, bizarre hairstyle, too much perfume or aftershave.

Interviewer Turn-Ons

Some behavior or traits that favorably impress an interviewer are:

Friendliness—pleasant person to be around, shows sense of humor, obviously enjoys people.

Preparedness—has taken the time to learn what products the organization makes or what services it offers, when it was established, how big it is, how many people work there, how many locations there are, and so on.

Sincerity—genuinely interested in the organization, the position, in getting along with fellow workers, and in making a contribution to the organization.

Good work ethic—arrives early, works hard, doesn't mind putting in overtime (paid or unpaid) to get the job done. A person with this trait would be cheerful and grateful to have the job.

Pride in quality of work—believes in doing the job right the first time and doing everything possible to please the customer.

UNDERSTANDING THE INTERVIEW PROCESS

If you've had limited experience as a participant in job interviews, it will help you to understand some of the techniques a typical interviewer may use and why he or she may ask certain questions.

Building Rapport

Usually an interviewer will begin by making small talk to break the ice and help you overcome your initial nervousness. This is the time for you to relax, be pleasant, and show the interviewer that you are an enjoyable person to be around. Be careful, however, not to be too casual—be friendly but professional.

Expect to shake hands (a firm handshake, please) at the beginning of the interview. Never smoke during an interview, even if the interviewer offers you a cigarette.

Opening Statements

After a few minutes of small talk, the interviewer will explain in a businesslike fashion that the purpose of the interview is to determine whether there is a match between you and the available job. He or she will also provide you with a brief overview of the organization and describe the job and its requirements.

At this stage the interviewer likely is watching you to judge your:

- Appearance and dress (conservative hairstyle, business attire—no jeans or party dresses, minimal jewelry).
- Signs of nervousness (see Figure B-1).

FIGURE B-1 Social cues.

Body Language	Specific Traits
Openness	Unbuttoned coat or jacket, upturned hands, uncrossed legs
Defensiveness	Crossed arms and/or clenched fists
Suspicion	Avoiding eye contact, sideways glances
Readiness	Sitting close to edge of chair, arms spaced on table
Need for reassurance	Rubbing hands, hand to throat
Frustration	Short breaths, wringing hands
Confidence	Lack of hand-to-face gestures; slow, deliberate speech; occasional relaxed smile
Nervousness	Clearing throat, heavy breathing, fidgeting
Boredom	Doodling, tapping foot, staring into space
Rejection	Body shifting, rubbing eye, ear, or nose
Self-control	Erect posture, locked ankles
Impatience	Drumming fingers, filling in words for interviewer

- Willingness to interact and react appropriately.

If there's a pause in the conversation, and you've done your homework on the organization, this is a good time to make an appropriate comment or ask an intelligent question. Be careful not to interrupt or to talk too fast.

The Heart of the Interview

The interviewer will now begin asking two basic types of questions:

1. Open-ended questions to discover information.
2. Closed-ended questions to obtain specific facts.

Open-ended questions are general inquiries designed to get you to speak and provide information. The purpose is to see how well you organize and express your thoughts, how well you communicate orally, and whether your views are consistent with the image of the company.

Closed-ended questions require a yes or no answer or are fill-in-the-blank types of inquiries. Think about the type of organization and the image it wants to project before you answer. Some thought and preparation can help you avoid making opinionated statements that are in direct conflict with the philosophy of the organization.

Watch for subtle questions that may test your level of awareness about the organization and its products or services. For example, imagine you are interviewing with a soft drink company and the interviewer asks you, "Would you like a cup of coffee or a soft drink?" Naturally, no matter how fond you are of coffee, you'd want to pick the soft drink—stating by brand name one of the company's products. Concentration and quick thinking can give you an added advantage in such a situation.

Your Questions

You will be asked near the end of the interview whether you have any questions. You should always have three or four questions written down. Be sure that you listened carefully during the interview so that you don't ask something that has already been answered. It is perfectly acceptable to take notes during an interview.

Good questions are related to the job and the company. Some examples are:

- How will my performance be evaluated, and how often?
- What are the opportunities for advancement?
- Describe the type of person who does best in your company.
- Why is this position open?

Poor questions are related to "what's in it for me." Some examples are:

- How much vacation do I get?
- How soon can I get a raise?
- When will I be promoted?

Salary and benefits should be discussed after a job offer is made.

Closing the Interview

When the interview ends, the interviewer will usually present a plan of action. A specific plan is a good sign that you are being considered.

Wait and watch for the "Anything else?" question. This is a technique the interviewer uses to give the candidate an opportunity to sell himself or herself. Some applicants who are not paying close attention will be eager to gather up their things and will miss this opportunity. Others won't be expecting the question and will not know how to answer. Be prepared to make, and maybe even rehearse, a very strong closing statement, such as: "I can see that the two computer classes I took would be very beneficial to me in this position. I'm glad I took my business teacher's advice and became computer literate."

When the interview is concluded, stand, smile, and give a firm handshake and a thank-you for the interviewer's time.

AFTER THE INTERVIEW

Immediately after the interview, make notes about the interview and any questions you had not prepared for. It is a good idea to keep a list of interview questions so that you can practice them before the next interview.

Write a thank-you letter to the people who interviewed you and mail it the same day if possible (see Chapter 20).

Few people are hired at the first interview. The employer usually narrows the field down to a few applicants, checks references, and then makes a decision and phones the top applicant to offer the job to him or her. The employer may call in the top two or three applicants for a second interview before making the final selection.

Grammar

The ability to use the English language competently is an enviable skill in the business world. A goal of every business executive is to speak and write clearly, coherently, and effectively. The words you use in conversation, in the office, and in business letters must be well chosen so as to convey your meaning accurately. You therefore need to know which word to use—and when and why.

Studying and practicing the rules of grammar will help you to make fewer errors in your writing—and to recognize and correct your errors *before* you mail a letter or submit a report.

When you put together even two words that make a complete thought, you have formed a sentence. *I work* expresses a complete thought. The subject is *I* and the predicate is *work*. Every sentence must have a subject and a predicate. The subject must contain a noun or a pronoun. The predicate must contain a verb.

PARTS OF SPEECH

Words classified according to use in the sentence are called **parts of speech.** The parts of speech are nouns, pronouns, verbs, adjectives, adverbs, prepositions, conjunctions, and interjections.

G-1. Nouns

A noun is the name of a person *(Vanessa)*, place *(Baltimore)*, object *(mountain)*, idea *(beauty)*, quality *(courage)*, or activity *(surfing)*.

Nouns may be proper *(Rodney)* or common *(book)*, concrete *(tree)* or abstract *(freedom)*, or collective *(family)*.

The *gender* of a noun may be masculine *(boy)*, feminine *(woman)*, common *(child)*, or neuter *(piano)*.

G-1-a. Plurals of Nouns. The **number** of a noun indicates whether it is singular or plural. To form the plurals of *most* nouns, follow these rules:

1. Add *s* to the singular *(order, orders; decision, decisions; price, prices)*.
2. Add *es* to a singular that ends in *s* (or an *s* sound), *sh, ch, x,* or *z* *(business, businesses; loss, losses; church, churches; tax, taxes)*.
3. Change *y* to *i* and add *es* for words ending in *y* preceded by a consonant *(company, companies; copy, copies)*.
4. Add only *s* for words ending in *y* preceded by a vowel *(Tuesday, Tuesdays; attorney, attorneys)*.

5. Add only *s* for words ending in *o* preceded by a vowel *(ratio, ratios; video, videos; studio, studios; patio, patios)*.

6. Add *es* to some nouns ending in *o* preceded by a consonant *(hero, heroes; tomato, tomatoes)*. Add *s* to others *(memo, memos; photo, photos)*.

7. Add *s* to the singular of most nouns that end in *f, fe,* or *ff (belief, beliefs; brief, briefs; proof, proofs; plaintiff, plaintiffs)*. For other nouns, change the final *f* or *fe* to *v* and add *es (half, halves; self, selves; wife, wives)*.

8. A few plurals are formed irregularly *(foot, feet; child, children; woman, women)*. If you are not sure of a plural form, consult a dictionary.

9. For a hyphenated or a two-word compound noun, change the chief word of the compound into a plural form *(account receivable, accounts receivable; brother-in-law, brothers-in-law)*. If a compound does not contain a noun, form the plural on the last element of the compound *(trade-in, trade-ins)*. Compounds written as one word usually form the plural at the end *(letterhead, letterheads)*. If the compound is composed of a noun and a preposition, change the noun (not the preposition) to the plural *(passerby, passersby)*.

10. Add *s* to most proper nouns *(Buzan, Buzans; Romano, Romanos; Gary, Garys)*. But add *es* to a proper noun ending in *s* (or an *s* sound), *sh, ch, x,* or *z (James, Jameses)*.

11. Form plurals of personal titles as follows: the *Misses Shelton* (formal usage) or the *Miss Sheltons* (ordinary usage).

12. Some nouns have the same form in the singular and the plural *(Japanese; deer; corps; series)*.

13. Certain nouns are always singular *(athletics; economics; mathematics; news)*.

14. Certain nouns are always plural *(credentials; goods; proceeds; statistics; earnings)*.

15. For plurals of words from other languages that have been incorporated into the English language, consult a dictionary *(analysis, analyses; parenthesis, parentheses; criterion, criteria)*. Some of these words have both a foreign and an English plural; in fact, the dictionary may show that there is a difference in the meaning of each plural form.

16. Add *s* to form the plurals of most abbreviations *(Dr., Drs.; no., nos.; apt., apts.)*. The abbreviations of many units of weight and measure, however, are the same in both the singular and the plural—*oz* for both *ounce* and *ounces; ft* for both *foot* and *feet)*. A few single-letter abbreviations form the plural by doubling the same letter *(p.* and *pp.* for *page* and *pages; f.* and *ff.* for *following page* and *following pages)*. Form the plurals of capital letters, abbreviations ending with capital

letters, and figures by adding *s (Ph.D.s, 3s, Rs)* unless the omission of the apostrophe would cause misreading *(A's, I's, U's)*. The plurals of words referred to as words are formed by adding *s* or *es* unless the plural form would be likely to be misread or would be unfamiliar *(ands, dos, don'ts,* but *which's* and *or's).* Add an apostrophe plus *s* to form the plural of uncapitalized letters and uncapitalized abbreviations with internal periods *(i's, c.o.d.'s).*

G-1-b. Possessives of Nouns

1. Add an apostrophe and *s* to form the possessive of most singular nouns *(woman's coat; manager's office; assistant's desk).*

2. For singular nouns that end in *s,* be guided by pronunciation. If a new syllable is formed and is easily pronounced, add an apostrophe plus *s (Charles's vacation).* If adding the apostrophe and *s* makes the word hard to pronounce, add only the apostrophe *(Ms. Jennings' idea; Jesus' teachings).*

3. Add only an apostrophe to regularly formed plurals *(employees' vacations; ladies' suits; presidents' portraits).*

4. Add an apostrophe and *s* to irregularly formed plurals *(men's shirts; children's toys).*

5. Add an apostrophe and *s* to the final member of a compound noun *(her mother-in-law's car; the editor in chief's responsibilities; the secretary-treasurer's report).* It is usually preferable to rewrite a sentence to avoid the plural possessive of a compound noun *(the decision of all the editors in chief* is better than *all the editors in chief's decision).*

6. To indicate joint ownership of two or more nouns, form the possessive on the final noun *(MacLaren and MacLaren's clients).* But if separate ownership is meant, make each noun possessive *(the secretary's and the treasurer's reports).*

7. To indicate the possessive of a singular abbreviation, add an apostrophe and *s (the HMO's office; Mr. Hugh Miller Sr.'s resignation);* of a plural abbreviation, add only an apostrophe *(the M.D.s' diagnoses).*

8. Restrict the use of the possessive to persons and animals. Do not use the possessive form to refer to inanimate things; use an *of* phrase *(the format of the letter; the provisions of the will).* Some exceptions are expressions of time and measurements *(today's market; two weeks' vacation; an hour's work)* and personification *(the company's assets).*

G-2. Pronouns

A pronoun is used in place of a noun to avoid repetition.

> The chairperson has studied the recommendations and agrees with *them.*

G-2-a. A pronoun must agree with its **antecedent** (the word for which the pronoun stands) in number, person, and gender.

> One of the men left *his* keys on the desk.

G-2-b. Demonstrative pronouns *(this, that, these, those)* should refer clearly to a specific antecedent. Do not use *this* or *that* to refer to the thought of an entire sentence.

> **VAGUE:** Four people in our word processing department were absent yesterday. *This* accounts for the backlog today.

> **CLEAR:** Four people in our word processing department were absent yesterday. Their absences account for the backlog today.

G-2-c. Relative pronouns *(who, whom)* do not agree in case with their antecedents. Their grammatical function in the sentence determines the case. A relative pronoun usually introduces a clause. To determine the correct case of the pronoun, rearrange the clause in the order of subject, verb, object. Disregard any parenthetical clauses. Use *who* when *he, she, I,* or *we* could be substituted; use *whom* when *him, her, them,* or *us* could be substituted.

> She is the one whom I believe the committee will choose. (Disregard the parenthetical clause *I believe,* and the normal order of the clause is *the committee will choose whom.* The subject is *committee,* the verb is *will choose,* and the object is *whom.)*

G-2-d. Compound personal pronouns *(yourself, myself,* and so on) have two uses. They may be used to emphasize a noun or pronoun already expressed. They may reflect the action of the verb upon the subject. Do not use a compound personal pronoun in place of a personal pronoun.

> He told me that himself. (Emphasis)

> She gave herself time to get to the airport. (Reflexive)

G-3. Verbs

A verb states a condition (linking verb—*is, was*) or expresses action *(run, sailed).* A sentence must contain a verb to be complete. When the complete verb is a group of words, it is called a *verb phrase.* A verb phrase has one principal verb and one auxiliary verb (the auxiliary may include more than one word). The common auxiliary verbs are forms of the verbs *to be* and *to have.*

> Marcie *works.* Marcie *has been working.* (Auxiliary: *has been)*

G-3-a. Verb Tenses. The tense of a verb tells when the action of the verb takes place.

The children play. (Present)

The children played. (Past)

The children will play. (Future)

The children have played. (Present perfect)

The children had played. (Past perfect)

The children will have played. (Future perfect)

1. The tense of the verb in a dependent clause must agree with the tense of the verb in the principal (independent) clause unless the subordinate clause expresses a general truth.

   We *thought* (past) you *would see* (past form of *will see)* the video tomorrow.

   Carmen *saw* (past) a movie that the industry *does* (present) not recommend for children. (General truth)

2. In a sequence, all the verbs should be in the same tense unless any expresses a general truth.

   I *went* to the university, *registered* for five courses, and *returned* home at about 2 p.m.

3. Do not use the present tense for past events.

   He *came* to me and *said,* "I can explain the error."

   NOT: He comes to me and says . . .

G-3-b. Agreement of Verb With Subject. A verb must agree with its subject in person and number.

   Three sales *representatives* complete *their* new-product training today.

1. Singular subjects connected by *either . . . or, neither . . . nor* require singular verbs.

   Either a refund or a credit memorandum is acceptable.

2. When *either . . . or, neither . . . nor* connects subjects differing in number, the verb should agree with that part of the subject that is nearer to the verb.

   Neither the retailers nor the wholesaler is liable.

   Neither the wholesaler nor the retailers are liable.

3. When such expressions as *together with, as well as,* or *including* separate the subject and the verb, the verb agrees in number with the real subject.

> The *catalog*, together with the special sales brochures, *is* ready.

4. When the subject is a collective noun that names a group or unit acting as a whole, use a singular verb.

> The organization *is* liberal in its promotion policies.

But when the members of the group or unit are considered to be acting separately, use a plural verb.

> The committee *were* still discussing the issue.

> A group of programmers *are* arriving from 12 different countries.

5. The indefinite pronouns *each, every, neither, one, another,* and *much* are always singular. When they are used as subjects or adjectives modifying subjects, use singular verbs.

> Every person *is* eligible.

> Each of us *has* a responsibility.

6. The indefinite pronouns *both, few, many, others,* and *several* are always plural. When they are used as subjects or adjectives modifying subjects, use plural verbs.

> Both offices *were* open today.

7. When a pronoun is used as the subject to indicate quantity *(some, all, none, any, more, most)* or when a fraction or portion is the subject *(part, one-half),* use a singular verb when a singular sense is meant and a plural verb when a plural sense is meant. The object of the prepositional phrase used with the subject usually indicates whether the subject is plural or singular.

> None of the catalogs *were* shipped today.

> All of the event *was* televised.

> One-half of the students *were* absent.

> One-tenth of the population *are* Orientals. **(EXCEPTION)**

8. When the subject is *a number* followed by a prepositional phrase, the verb must be plural. When the subject is *the number,* the verb must be singular.

> A number of students *are* going to Europe.

> The number of complaints *is* not surprising.

9. Normally, treat organizational names as singular. If you wish to emphasize the individuals in the organization, however, you may make the name plural.

> Boyle, Rickman and Associates *has* opened new offices.
>
> **OR**
>
> Boyle, Rickman and Associates *have* opened *their* new offices.

10. When the subject is a group of words, such as a slogan, a title, or a quotation, use a singular verb.

> *Sell the sizzle not the steak* is a well-known saying in the restaurant industry.

G-3-c. Verbal Nouns. Participles ending in *ing* are often used as nouns and are called **gerunds**. A pronoun modifying a gerund should be in the possessive form.

> I shall appreciate *your* sending the check promptly.

G-4. Adjectives

An adjective describes or limits a noun or a pronoun. An adjective construction may be a single word, two or more unrelated words, a compound, a phrase, or a clause. It may either precede or follow the noun or pronoun.

> We need *five new portable* dictating machines.
>
> The office administrator *for whom we advertised* is hard to find.
>
> Liz, *dressed in a gray flannel suit,* was the first guest to arrive.
>
> The *loss-of-income* provision is explained below.

An adjective may be modified only by an adverb, not by another adjective.

> Jonathan is *extremely* (adverb) *agile* (adjective).

G-4-a. Comparison of Adjectives. To express different degrees or qualities, descriptive adjectives may be compared in three forms: positive, comparative (two things compared), and superlative (three or more things compared).

> Shep's grades are *high*. (Positive)
>
> Shep's grades are *higher* than mine. (Comparative)
>
> Shep's grades are the *highest* in the class. (Superlative)

To form the comparative and superlative degrees, follow these rules.

1. To form the comparative of most adjectives, add *er* to the positive: *tall, taller*. To form the superlative, add *est* to the positive: *tall, tallest*.

2. For irregular adjectives, change the form of the word completely (*good, better, best*).

3. For adjectives of two syllables, form the comparative by adding *er* or the word *more* or *less* to the positive, and form the superlative by adding *est* or the word *most* or *least* to the positive: *likely, likelier, likeliest;* OR likely, less likely (or *more likely*), least likely (or *most likely*). Compare adjectives of three or more syllables by adding *more* or *most, less* or *least (more* efficient, *most* efficient).

4. Some adjectives state qualities that cannot be compared (*complete, correct, level, round, perfect, unique*). However, these words may be modified by *more nearly* (or *less nearly*) and similar adverbs to suggest an approach to the absolute.

5. The word *other* or *else* must be used in comparing a person or a thing with other members of the group to which it belongs.

> Our new model is selling better than any *other* model we have developed.

> Our new model is more efficient than anyone *else's* model.

G-4-b. Compound Adjectives.
A compound adjective is made up of two or more words used together as a single thought to modify a noun.

A compound adjective should be hyphenated when it precedes the noun if the compound:

1. Is a two-word one-thought modifier (*long-range* goals).

> EXCEPTION: Very commonly used compounds are not hyphenated: *high school* teachers; *real estate* agent.

2. Is a phrase of three or more words (*up-to-date* report).
3. Is a number combined with a noun (*fourteen-day* period).
4. Has coequal modifiers (*labor-management* relations).
5. Includes irregularly formed comparatives and superlatives (*better-selling* items; *worst-looking* letter).
6. Combines *well* with a participle (*well-educated* executive).

A compound adjective that follows the noun should also be hyphenated when it:

1. Is a *well* compound that retains its one-thought meaning (*well-read, well-to-do;* BUT NOT: *well known, well managed*).
2. Is made up of an adjective or a noun followed by a noun to which *ed* has been added (*high-priced, left-handed*).
3. Is a noun or an adjective followed by a participle (*time-consuming, factory-installed, strange-looking, ill-advised*).
4. Is formed by joining a noun with an adjective (*fire-resistant, tax-exempt*).

Consult a dictionary for compounds composed of common prefixes and suffixes *(audiovisual, postscript, preaddressed, interoffice, mid-July, businesslike)*.

Do not hyphenate most foreign phrases used as compound modifiers *(per capita consumption, ad hoc ruling, ex officio member)*.

Do not hyphenate a two-word proper noun used as an adjective *(Latin American conference, Western Union telegram, Supreme Court decision)*.

Consult a reference manual for compound adjectives commonly used without hyphens *(real estate, income tax, social security, life insurance, word processing)*.

G-5. Adverbs

An adverb explains, describes, or limits a verb, an adjective, or another adverb.

> Does this machine work *efficiently?* (Modifies verb)

> It is *very* efficient. (Modifies adjective)

> We drove *quite* carefully on the ice. (Modifies adverb)

G-5-a. Place an adverb as close as possible to the word it modifies. Its position may alter the meaning of the sentence.

> He met her *only* today.

> He met *only* her today.

> *Only* he met her today.

G-5-b. Verbs of the senses *(look, taste, feel, smell, and so on)* and linking verbs (forms of *be, become, seem, and appear)* are usually followed by an adjective that describes the subject.

> The meat smells *bad*. (Adjective, modifies *meat)*

> He looked *happy*. (Adjective, modifies *He)*

> I feel *bad*. (Adjective, modifies *I)*

But to describe the action of the verb, use an adverb.

> She looked *happily* at him. (Adverb, modifies *looked)*

> He felt *carefully* for his key. (Adverb, modifies *felt)*

G-5-c. Do not use adverbs that are negative in meaning with negatives.

> Anne *scarcely* had time to finish the report.

> **NOT:** Anne *hadn't scarcely* time to finish the report.

G-6. *Prepositions*

A preposition is a word used to connect a noun or a pronoun with some other word in the sentence.

> Jorge asked *about* the current financial condition *of* the store.

G-6-a. The noun or pronoun following a preposition is called the **object of the preposition.** A preposition and its object, called a **prepositional phrase,** may be used as a noun, an adjective, or an adverb. The object of a preposition must be in the objective case.

> Trisha sat between *him* and *me*.

G-6-b. Do not use superfluous prepositions.

> Where has he gone?

> **NOT:** Where has he gone *to?*

G-6-c. Do not omit necessary prepositions.

> Alex is interested *in* and excited *about* the trip.

> **NOT:** Alex is interested and excited about the trip.

G-6-d. Certain words are always followed by certain prepositions.

> Noah is angry *about* the mix-up. (Angry *about* or *at* something.)

> Noah is angry *with* me. (Angry *with* a person.)

If you are unsure, look up the word in a dictionary or a reference manual.

G-6-e. Ending a sentence with a preposition is acceptable for emphasis. Short questions often end with prepositions.

> These are the questions I want answers *to.*

> Which files are you finished *with?*

G-7. *Conjunctions*

A **conjunction** is a word or phrase that connects words, phrases, or clauses.

G-7-a. A conjunction may be coordinating or subordinating. A **coordinating conjunction** connects words, phrases, or clauses of equal grammatical construction. A **subordinating conjunction** connects dependent clauses to the main, or independent, clause.

We have received ten applications, *and* more are still coming in. (Coordinating)

We have not received the desk, *although* we ordered it six weeks ago. (Subordinating)

G-7-b. **Correlative conjunctions** are a type of coordinating conjunctions used in pairs to connect two or more words, phrases, or clauses. They should immediately precede the words, phrases, or clauses that they connect, which should be parallel in form.

You may order *either* now *or* when our sales representative calls.

NOT: You may *either* order now or when our sales representative calls. (Note that *now* and *when* are in parallel form; both are adverbs.)

G-7-c. Do not use prepositions such as *without, except,* and *like* to introduce a subordinate clause.

The package looks *as though* someone has tampered with it.

NOT: The package looks *like* someone has tampered with it.

G-8. Interjections

An **interjection** is a word that shows emotion. Interjections are found in sales and advertising copy. Use interjections sparingly in business writing.

Wow! What a view!

USING WORDS IN SENTENCES

To convey your meaning successfully in letters or in conversation requires expertness in putting words together. A successful letter is composed of strong, well-constructed sentences and paragraphs.

G-9. Kinds of Sentences

A sentence must contain a subject and a verb (predicate) and must express a complete thought. A **simple sentence** contains a subject and a predicate—one independent clause. A **compound sentence** contains two or more independent clauses. A **complex sentence** contains one independent clause and at least one dependent clause in either the subject or the predicate. A **compound-complex sentence** contains two or more independent clauses and one or more dependent clauses.

SIMPLE: The vice president left yesterday and will return on Thursday. (This simple sentence contains two verbs joined by the conjunction *and*. A simple sentence may also contain two or more subjects joined by conjunctions.)

COMPOUND: The survey has been completed, and the results will be available in a few days.

COMPLEX: Results of the survey, which has just been completed, will be announced tomorrow.

COMPOUND-COMPLEX: Our Chromex model aroused much interest, and we believe it will appeal to a new market because its price is lower than that of any other model.

G-10. Sentence Fragments

A group of words that does not express a complete thought is not a sentence. Occasionally such an incomplete thought may stand alone for emphasis. Experienced writers sometimes use this device—but sparingly. In business correspondence, this technique is generally limited to sales writing.

South Padre Island. *The* place to spend your vacation this summer.

Please check these figures carefully and return them to me as soon as you have finished.

NOT: Please check these figures carefully. Returning them to me as soon as you have finished.

G-11. Run-On Sentences

A sentence containing two or more complete thoughts loosely strung together without proper punctuation is called a **run-on** sentence. The remedy for this sentence error is either to place each complete thought in a separate sentence or to retain the several thoughts in a single sentence by the use of proper subordination and punctuation.

RUN-ON: The meeting had to be canceled and the chairperson asked me to notify each of you and she regrets any inconvenience this cancellation may have caused you.

BETTER: The chairperson asked me to notify you that the meeting had to be canceled. She regrets any inconvenience this cancellation may have caused you.

G-12. Sentence Length

The length of the sentences in any written message is an important factor in catching and holding the reader's interest. Avoid monotony by varying sentence length. However, very long sentences are suitable for business letters only if they are used sparingly and if they are carefully constructed.

In letter writing, as in cooking, too much of anything is not good. Avoid too many short words, too many short sentences, too many long words, too many long sentences. Avoid also too many similar sounds or too many sentences of similar construction.

G-13. Sentence Rhythm

To achieve good sentence rhythm, learn to place words carefully in the sentence. Vary the length and emphasis of the sentences. Use—but do not overuse—intentional repetition of sounds, words, and phrases.

Cultivate an ear for the sound of a sentence. Read your sentences aloud, emphasizing the important words. If the sentences sound awkward, fragmented, or involved, rewrite them until they are pleasing to listen to.

G-14. Parallel Construction

To achieve sentence clarity, use similar grammatical structures in phrases, clauses, and listings to express similar ideas. For example, use the same parts of speech in a sequence.

> **NOT PARALLEL:** The supervisor encouraged us to give a higher level of service, to improve customer relations, and making fewer errors and higher profits.

> **PARALLEL:** The supervisor encouraged us to give a higher level of service, to improve customer relations, and to make fewer errors and higher profits.

CONSTRUCTING PARAGRAPHS

Combining sentences into paragraphs requires an understanding of the work a paragraph should do in any written message. A **paragraph** is composed of one or more sentences that together make a single point or relate to one aspect of a central theme.

G-15. Topic Sentence

A paragraph should usually contain a topic sentence that summarizes the main idea of the paragraph. The topic sentence is usually at the beginning of the paragraph, but it may be at the end or in the body of the paragraph. In business letters made up of short paragraphs, the topic sentence may be only implied.

G-16. Transition

One paragraph should lead naturally into the next, to guide the reader from one central thought or point to the next. To achieve this continuity, use transitional words or phrases, such as *however, therefore, for example, in addition, as a result.*

G-17. Paragraph Length

A paragraph may be of any length as long as it treats only one point or one aspect of the central thought. Business communications, particularly sales and advertising letters, tend to have fairly short paragraphs so as to keep the reader's interest. Technical communications often contain longer paragraphs.

G-18. Paragraph Rhythm

Like sentences, paragraphs should be pleasing to the ear when read aloud. Avoid a succession of very long or very short paragraphs. Vary the placement of the topic sentence. Avoid starting successive paragraphs in the same manner, such as with a participial phrase.

G-19. Unity, Coherence, and Emphasis

In addition to applying the fundamentals of grammar, a good business writer will be sure to observe the principles of unity, coherence, and emphasis.

G-19-a. To secure *unity*, include only relevant material and exclude all that is irrelevant. Ask yourself, "Is this word, this sentence, this paragraph, essential to the development of my main thought?"

G-19-b. **Coherence** is the result of an orderly presentation of your message. Main points should follow each other in logical order. To achieve coherence, you should plan your message carefully before you begin to write.

1. One enemy of coherence in the sentence is the misplaced modifier. Be sure to place every modifier where it clearly modifies the word it is intended to explain or qualify. Put phrases as close as possible to the words they modify. Placement of participial and infinitive phrases needs special care in order to avoid the dangling modifier with its often ludicrous distortion of meaning.

   After examining the encyclopedias in your home, you may return them if you are not completely satisfied.

   NOT: After being examined in your home, you may return the encyclopedias if not completely satisfied.

2. Another enemy of coherence is unclear antecedents. Be sure that every pronoun has a clear antecedent.

   John told Sam that *Sam* won the prize.

   NOT: John told Sam that *he* won the prize.

G-19-c. **Emphasis** means giving the important points in your message special prominence to show the reader that the points are important. Ways to achieve emphasis include:

1. **Position.** Put the important word, phrase, or clause at the beginning or the end of a sentence, of a paragraph, or of the whole message.

2. **Proportion.** The most important point in the message should usually occupy the most space. Don't clutter a letter with trivial details.

3. **Repetition.** You gain impact by careful use of the same construction. Like all good things, do not overdo intentional repetition.

   > By using the new vocabulary builder, *you will discover how* to find the right word and *how* to avoid hackneyed words. *You will discover how* to increase your word power and *how* to put that power to profitable use.

4. **Balance.** You gain emphasis by balancing words, phrases, clauses, or sentences. But don't strain for this effect or your writing will sound forced.

   > The more words you know, the better you can express your ideas.

CAUTION: If you heed the following warnings, you will not weaken the emphasis in your messages:

1. Avoid generalizations and other vague expressions.

   > POOR: As a rule, we ordinarily make an exception for such circumstances as yours.

   > BETTER: Your circumstances merit our making an exception.

2. Use active constructions instead of passive constructions.

   > WEAK: Your check must be mailed to us immediately in order to avoid legal action.

   > STRONGER: To avoid legal action, you must mail your check to us immediately.

3. Eliminate general, unemphatic sentence openings.

   > POOR: There are several new features planned for our next issue.

   > BETTER: Among the new features in our next issue will be . . .

   > OR: Featured in our next issue will be . . .

4. Watch the placement of transitional expressions. They are usually more effective after, rather than before, an important word, phrase, or clause.

   > If you have a particular problem, however, please write to me about it.

PUNCTUATION

P-1. Period

The period is used at the end of a declarative sentence (one that makes a statement) and at the end of an imperative sentence (one that gives a command).

> This organization employs half a million people. (Declarative)

> Take these books to the library. (Imperative)

P-2. Question Mark

The question mark is used at the end of an interrogative sentence (one that asks a question). Even if the question is part of a declarative statement, the question mark is used. Even though a question does not form a complete thought, it may be set off if it logically follows the preceding sentence.

> How should we introduce our new product? On a television show?
> At a press conference?

Do not use a question mark at the end of a courteous request; use a period.

> Will you please send us your latest price list.

P-3. Exclamation Point

Use an exclamation point at the end of an exclamatory sentence to indicate strong feeling, surprise, or enthusiasm. An exclamatory sentence is seldom appropriate in business messages except in sales and advertising letters.

> Yes! You can save $100 today only!

P-4. Comma

A comma indicates a short break in thought within a sentence. Used properly, a comma ensures clarity by conveying the writer's exact meaning. Do not use commas, however, in a sentence simply because a speaker might normally pause. Rather, use commas according to well-established rules. For a fuller discussion of comma usage, consult a handbook of English grammar and usage.

P-4-a. Separate the principal clauses of a compound sentence by placing a comma before a coordinating conjunction *(and, but, or, nor)*.

> We will install a new computer, and we will then hire a computer
> programmer.

P-4-b. Set off nonessential elements by commas. A nonessential element is not necessary to complete the meaning of the sentence.

The annual report, *which we publish in April,* shows our financial condition. (Nonessential)

P-4-c. Do not use commas to set off an essential element, that is, one that limits the meaning of the sentence.

The bank cannot honor checks *that are improperly signed.* (Essential)

P-4-d. Use a comma after introductory participial and infinitive phrases. (Avoid overuse of this construction in letters.)

Having committed ourselves to this plan, we are not backing down now. (Participial)

To do the job right, you must have the right tools. (Infinitive)

Use a comma after an introductory dependent clause.

Since this assignment is due tomorrow, I must finish it tonight.

Use a comma after an introductory prepositional phrase unless the phrase is very short or very closely connected to what follows.

In the five years following our merger with Dynamo Sales Corporation, our sales increased 50 percent.

P-4-e. Use a comma after an introductory inverted phrase or clause.

Because the check was improperly signed, the bank did not honor it.

P-4-f. Set off parenthetical (or interrupting) words, phrases, and clauses by commas.

We, *like all unions,* must protect the interests of our members. (Interrupting phrase)

We cannot, *as you will agree,* make such an exception. (Interrupting clause)

P-4-g. Set off transitional words, phrases, and clauses by commas.

We must, *therefore,* change our plans.

Therefore, we must change our plans.

P-4-h. Set off appositives by commas. An appositive has the same meaning as the word or phrase it follows.

Heather Frazee, *the new manager,* telephoned today.

P-4-i. Use a comma to set off a direct quotation from the rest of the sentence.

> The speaker said, "I agree with your recommendation."

P-4-j. Use a comma before and after such expressions as *for example, that is, namely,* when they introduce explanatory words or phrases.

> Homonyms, *that is,* words that sound alike, are often confused.

P-4-k. Use a comma preceding *such as* only when it introduces a nonessential expression. When *such as* introduces an essential expression, do not use a comma.

> Order all stationery, *such as* letterhead, second sheets, memorandum forms, as well as envelopes, from A.R. Taylor Stationers. (Nonessential)

> An office *such as* this is every executive's dream. (Essential)

P-4-l. Separate items in a series by commas. If *and* or *or* connects each member of a series, do not use a comma. If a comma appears within any item of a series, use a semicolon to separate the items.

> We refinished the chairs, desks, and tables.

> Attending last week's conference in Williamsburg were David Rice, marketing director; Vicki Fuentos, advertising manager; and John Holmes, sales promotion manager.

P-4-m. Use a comma before and after *etc.* (unless it closes the sentence).

> The cabinet containing file folders, labels, tablets, etc., is in the next room.

P-4-n. Separate two or more adjectives modifying the same noun by commas if each alone modifies the noun *(simple, well-designed letterhead)*. But if the first adjective modifies the combination of the noun and the second adjective, do not use the comma *(fireproof metal container)*.

P-4-o. Indicate by a comma the omission of a word or words in a parallel construction.

> Model 101 will be available June 1; Model 109, July 1.

P-4-p. Separate repeated words by commas to make the sentence easier to read.

> The fire spread very, very quickly.

P-4-q. Use a comma to prevent misreading a sentence.

> Soon after, the strike ended.

P-4-r. Use a comma to separate thousands, millions, and so on, in numbers of five or more digits, except years, page numbers, addresses, telephone numbers, serial numbers, temperatures, and decimal amounts.

P-4-s. Separate consecutive unrelated numbers by a comma.

> In 1996, 15 new plants were built.

P-4-t. Separate by commas the parts of a date and of an address.

> We made our April *21, 2004,* deadline.

> Send the contract to *3412 Lincoln Avenue, Riverside, California,* with a copy to my office.

P-4-u. Set off by commas the name of a state when it follows the name of the city.

> Our restaurant in Decatur, *Alabama,* burned last week.

P-4-v. A comma follows the complimentary closing of a letter unless open punctuation is used throughout.

P-5. Dash

Use a dash to indicate a stronger break in thought than a comma shows. The word or phrase enclosed in dashes is grammatically separate from the sentence and not necessary to the meaning.

P-5-a. Use dashes to set off a parenthetical expression or an appositive that already contains commas.

> All large appliances—microwave ovens, ranges, refrigerators, washers, dryers—will be drastically reduced this weekend.

P-5-b. Use dashes to separate a summarizing word from a preceding enumeration.

> M.A., M.S., M.B.A.—all are graduate degrees.

P-5-c. Do not use other punctuation with a dash. When an expression set off by dashes ends a sentence, omit the closing dash and use the appropriate sentence-end punctuation.

> See our dealer in your area—today!

P-6. Semicolon

The semicolon indicates a stronger break in thought than the comma.

P-6-a. Separate the principal clauses of a compound sentence by a semicolon when no connective is used.

> We sent the meeting notices yesterday; today we prepared the agenda.

P-6-b. When a transitional expression (such as *consequently, therefore, however)* connects the principal clauses of a compound sentence, use a semicolon.

> Budget requests arrived late; *therefore,* the preparation of the final budget was delayed.

P-6-c. When either of the principal clauses in a compound sentence contains one or more commas, use a semicolon to separate the clauses if using a comma before the conjunction would cause the sentence to be misread.

> We ordered letterhead stationery, envelopes, file folders, and file guides; but plain paper, carbon paper, and file folders were delivered to us instead. (The semicolon is necessary to prevent misreading.)

P-6-d. When *for example, that is, namely,* or a similar transitional expression links two independent clauses or introduces words, phrases, or clauses that are added almost as afterthoughts, use a semicolon before the expression and a comma after it.

> Amy K. Shelby is a leader in many professional organizations; *for example,* she is president of the National Administrative Assistants' Association, a member of the board of directors of the Medical Assistants' Association, and program chairperson of the Business and Professional Women's Club.

P-7. Colon

The colon has the following uses:

P-7-a. A colon introduces an explanation or an amplification following an independent clause.

> The organization has one objective: to satisfy its customers.

P-7-b. A colon introduces a formal listing or an enumeration.

> David's qualifications are these: honesty, dependability, and sincerity.

P-7-c. If the list or enumeration grammatically completes the sentence, omit the colon.

> David's qualifications are honesty, dependability, and sincerity.

P-7-d. A colon introduces a quotation of more than one sentence.

> Dr. Truemper said: "The fate of Velasco's chemical discharges will be determined by the judge. There are, however, two possible alternatives to the procedure now used."

P-7-e. A colon follows the salutation in a business letter unless open punctuation is used.

P-7-f. A colon separates hours and minutes *(11:15 a.m.)*.

P-7-g. A colon separates the main title of a work from the subtitle *(Customer Service: Skills and Concepts for Success)*.

P-8. Parentheses

Within a sentence parentheses set off explanatory words, phrases, and clauses that are not essential to the meaning of the sentence. Do not use punctuation preceding an opening parenthesis, but use the appropriate punctuation after the closing parenthesis. If the material enclosed in parentheses requires a question mark or an exclamation point, that punctuation should precede the closing parenthesis.

> Sales have increased (about 20 percent) despite the weather.

> He expected to stop overnight in Chicago (or was it Detroit?).

Parentheses also have the following uses:

P-8-a. To give references and directions.

> Insert key at A (see Operating Manual, page 10).

P-8-b. To verify a spelled-out number in legal material.

> The sum of Fifteen Hundred Dollars ($1500) . . .

P-8-c. To enclose figures and letters of enumerated items that do not begin on separate lines.

The reasons are these: (1) rising labor costs, (2) inadequate space, and (3) shortage of personnel.

P-8-d. To indicate subordinate values in an outline.

   1. Operating procedure

      a. Open switch A.

         (1) Hold switch A open and turn valve B.

            (a) Check flow at nozzle C.

P-9. Brackets

Brackets are seldom used in business letters but are sometimes required in formal reports (1) to enclose material in a quotation that was not in the original; (2) to enclose *sic,* which indicates an error in the original quoted material; (3) to enclose material within a parenthesized statement.

P-10. Quotation Marks

Use quotation marks to set off direct quotations. Set off by single quotation marks a quotation within a quotation.

P-10-a. Consecutive quoted paragraphs each begin with quotation marks, but only the final paragraph closes with quotation marks.

P-10-b. Place the comma and period inside closing quotation marks. Place the colon and the semicolon outside closing quotation marks. A question mark or an exclamation point precedes closing quotation marks only if the quoted material is in the form of a question or an exclamation.

P-10-c. Use quotation marks to enclose titles of chapters, parts, sections, etc., within books; titles of speeches, articles, essays, poems, short musical compositions; and slogans and mottoes.

P-10-d. Do *not* use quotation marks for names of books, newspapers, and magazines. Usually capitalize the main words of such titles, and italicize or underline the complete titles; or type the titles in all-capital letters.

P-11. Apostrophe

Use the apostrophe to form the possessive of nouns (see G-1-b). The apostrophe also has the following uses:

P-11-a. To indicate a missing letter or missing letters in a contraction *(can't, wouldn't).*

P-11-b. To form the plurals of letters, figures, and symbols, if the omission of the apostrophe would cause misreading (see G-1-a-16).

P-11-c. To indicate the omission of the first part of a date *(class of '06)*.

P-11-d. As a single quotation mark.

CAPITALIZATION

Capitalize parts of business letters as follows:

C-1. Each word of the inside address and the envelope address, including main words of titles of persons.

C-2. The main words in subject and attention lines (or use all-capital letters).

C-3. The first word of the salutation, plus titles.

C-4. The first word of the complimentary closing.

C-5. Main words of titles following the writer's name.

Capitalize the first word of:

C-6. A sentence or a group of words used as a sentence. *(Sales have skyrocketed. No wonder we need help.)*

C-7. Items in an outline.

C-8. Separate-line itemizations.

C-9. A direct quotation. (Howard W. Newton said, "People forget how fast you did a job—but they remember how well you did it.")

C-10. Lines of poetry.

C-11. An explanatory statement following a colon if it is a complete sentence that states a formal rule or principle or requires special emphasis. (He made this point: *Build your speech to a climax.)*

C-12. An independent question within a sentence. (The question is, *How much would such a procedure save us?)*

Capitalize the first word and the main words of:

C-13. Titles and subtitles of publications, musical compositions, motion pictures, plays, paintings, sculpture *(Sports Illustrated; Official Airline Guide; "A Midsummer Night's Dream")*.

C-14. Titles of speeches, lectures, addresses. (The title of his speech was *"How to Double Your Income."*)

Capitalize the following:

C-15. Proper nouns—names of particular persons, places, and things—and proper adjectives derived from them *(Jefferson, Jeffersonian; Latin America, Latin American; Discovery II)*.

C-16. Words that are used in place of proper names *(the Lone Star State)*.

C-17. Common nouns when substituted for specific proper nouns *(the Territory,* meaning "Indian Territory"; *the Zone,* for "Canal Zone")*.

C-18. Exact titles of courses of study. (He enrolled in *Accounting II* and *Business Communication.*)

C-19. Titles of persons—business, professional, military, religious, honorary, academic, family—when preceding the name *(President James Kusyk; Lieutenant Beatty; Judge Watts; Cousin George)*.

C-20. Titles following a name only if they refer to high government officials *(Frank Bates, Associate Justice; but Priscilla Cartmell, mayor of Cordova)*.

C-21. Official names of organizations, such as associations, bureaus, clubs, commissions, companies, conventions, departments *(National Sales Executives Association; Dallas Chamber of Commerce)*.

C-22. Names of governments and subdivisions of government, whether international, national, state, or local *(Commonwealth of Australia; the Supreme Court; the Port of New York Authority)*.

C-23. Common nouns substituted for a specific organization or for a government agency *(the Association; the Council; the Department; the Commission; but our company; that department)*.

C-24. Names of streets, buildings *(Broadway; Chrysler Building)*.

C-25. Religious names and pronouns referring to the Deity *(the Bible; the Heavenly Father; First Baptist Church)*.

C-26. Military services, branches, and divisions *(the Navy; the Armed Forces; the 101st Airborne; the Seventh Regiment)*.

C-27. Trademarks, brand names, names of commercial products, proprietary names, and market grades. Manufacturers and advertisers often capitalize the common noun following the trade name *(Xerox; Dictaphone; Coca-Cola, Coke; Midas Mufflers)*.

C-28. The word *State* only when it follows the name of the state or is part of an imaginative name *(New York State; Volunteer State;* but *state of New York);* and the word *States* only when it stands for *United States.*

C-29. A particular geographic area *(Great Plains; the Far East; the West Coast; to visit the South;* but *southern agriculture; drive south two miles; southern Illinois)*.

C-30. Days of the week, months, holidays.

C-31. Personifications *("O Truth, where art thou?")*.

C-32. Races, peoples, languages *(French; Asians; Spanish;* but *blacks* and *whites)*.

C-33. Historical events and documents *(Vietnam War; Declaration of Independence)*.

C-34. Nouns followed by a number referring to parts, divisions, or sequence *(Column 2; Volume II; Room 17; Car 16788;* but *page 15; paragraph 3)*.

C-35. Certain important words in legal documents such as the name of the document, references to parties, special provisions, and spelled-out amounts of money may appear in initial capitals or all capitals *(WHEREAS, RESOLVED, THIS AGREEMENT, Notary, SELLER, WITNESS)*.

C-36. Emphasized words in sales and advertising material (Don't miss *our End-of-the-Year Sale!)*.

Do *not* capitalize the following:

C-37. Names derived from proper nouns but no longer identified with them *(diesel engine; india ink; manila envelope)*. If in doubt, consult a dictionary or reference manual.

C-38. The word *the* unless it is part of an official name *(the Denver Post; the First National Bank;* but *The New York Times)*.

C-39. The word *the* when the name is used as a modifier. (I find *the New York Times* foreign news complete and informative.)

C-40. The word *city* unless it is part of a name *(Kansas City; Sioux City)*.

C-41. *Ex, former, late* preceding titles *(former* President Ford, the *late* Senator Mann)*.

C-42. Names of subjects of study. (I enjoy *psychology* more than I do *history.)*

C-43. The words *federal, government, nation, union,* and *commonwealth* in ordinary business writing. Capitalize these words when they are part of an official name. Capitalize *union* and *commonwealth* only when they refer to a specific government.

NUMBERS

In business correspondence, numbers are more often expressed in figures than in words, both for clarity and for quick reference. The following rules reflect acceptable business practice.

Use words to express the following:

N-1. Exact numbers up to and including ten *(seven* sales).

N-2. Indefinite numbers *(several* thousand; *few* hundred).

N-3. Ages unless expressed in exact years, months, and days. (He has a *twelve-year-old* son; he is *12 years, 5 months, 11 days old.)*

N-4. A number at the beginning of a sentence. Or, better, rewrite the sentence. *(Seventy-five* applications arrived today. **OR:** We received 75 applications today.)

N-5. Approximate designations of time. (The meeting will begin *about eleven o'clock.)* But use figures if exact time is given with *a.m.* or *p.m.* (Our hours are from *8:30 a.m. to 4 p.m. daily.)* Use words also to express periods of time except in discount and credit terms and interest periods *(for the last fifteen years; a 60-day note; 2% 10 days, net 30 days)*.

N-6. Ordinals, except dates and street numbers (our *eighth* anniversary).

N-7. Fractions used alone *(one-third* of the coupons).

N-8. Numbers in legal documents, usually followed by the amount in figures in parentheses.

N-9. Political and military divisions; sessions of Congress *(Thirty-first Regiment; Ninety-first Congress; Thirty-third Congressional District)*.

Use figures for the following:

N-10. Numbers above ten when used alone *(450 miles)*.

N-11. Exact amounts of money, no matter how large (an increase of *$55,000,000)*. For very large amounts the word *millions* or *billions* may be used with figures *($55 million or 55 million dollars)*; be consistent within a piece of writing. In a series, repeat the dollar sign before each amount *($10 to $15 deductions)*. Do not use the decimal point or zeros with whole-dollar amounts *($6; $250)*; do use them in tabulations if any of the amounts include cents. Do not use the symbol ¢ except in such technical material as price lists.

N-12. Population figures unless indefinite. (More than *50,000 people* visited the festival; but we expect *several hundred thousand* next year.)

N-13. Mixed numbers, including stock quotations (an average of *5½* errors per page; IBM closed at *31⅛)*.

N-14. Numbers in a series of related items *(5 local men, 15 from Nashville, and 20 from neighboring states)*.

N-15. One of two adjacent related numbers. As a rule, spell the first unless the second would be shorter *(three 10-unit buildings, 125 six-page brochures)*.

N-16. Measurements. Express in figures unless the expression lacks technical significance. (Delivery within a *20-mile* radius is free. **BUT** It's about a *twenty-mile* trip to the coast.)

N-17. Ratios, proportions, and percentages (outnumbered *3 to 1; 22 percent)*.

N-18. House numbers over one, street names over ten, and all ZIP Code numbers *(77 West 34th Street, Los Angeles, California 90017)*.

N-19. Highway numbers, pier and track numbers, page numbers, policy and other serial numbers *(Route 75; Pier 88; WA 5-7770)*.

N-20. Dates *(March 5, 1986;* your order of *May 15;* shipped on the *7th of June)*.

N-21. Decimal amounts (savings of *0.812 mills;* an increase of *12.3 per day)*.

N-22. Votes (defeated by *a vote of 12 to 5)*.

Appendix C   471

N-23. References to parts of publications *(Figure 17; Chapter 23; Plate VI; Table 41).*

N-24. Statistical material, including ages, time, and so on.

ABBREVIATIONS

Abbreviate the following:

A-1. These titles when used with personal names: *Dr., Mr., Messrs.* (plural of *Mr.* and pronounced "messers"), *Mrs., Mme.* (short for *Madame*), *Ms.* (pronounced "mizz"), and *Mses.* or *Mss.* (plural form of *Ms.*). The plural of *Mme.* may either be spelled out *(Mesdames,* pronounced "may-dahm") or abbreviated *(Mmes.).* The titles *Miss* and *Misses* are not abbreviations.

A-2. These titles following personal names: *Esq., Jr., Sr.;* also, academic and honorary degrees such as *M.D., O.D., Ed.D.* (used when *Dr.* does not precede the name).

A-3. Names of government agencies, without periods *(FCC for Federal Communications Commission).*

A-4. Names of well-known business organizations, labor unions, societies, and associations. When these abbreviations consist of all-capital initials, they are typed without periods or spaces *(IBM, AT&T, AFL-CIO, NAACP, YMCA).*

A-5. *B.C.* and *A.D.* in dates *(350 B.C.; A.D. 440).*

A-6. *a.m.* and *p.m.* designations of time *(6:15 a.m.).*

A-7. *No.* for *number* preceding a figure *(No. 189).*

A-8. Common business terms, according to usage in a particular field *(c.o.d.; f.o.b.; e.o.m.).* Such terms are often capitalized, without periods *(COD, FOB, EOM).*

Do not abbreviate the following except as indicated:

A-9. Personal, professional, religious, and military titles when used with a surname only *(Professor Jensen; Vice President Maxon).* When both first name and last name are used, the title may be abbreviated in business correspondence but not in formal usage *(Lt. Col. Robert E. Morris).* **EXCEPTION:** The title *Doctor* is usually abbreviated *Dr.*

A-10. Any part of the name of a business firm unless the abbreviated form appears in the firm's letterhead or other official usage *(Hammond Steel Corporation; Marz Brothers Inc.).*

A-11. *Honorable* and *Reverend* except in addresses, lists, and notices. And, except in these usages, use *The* preceding the title.

A-12. Names of days and months, except in columnar work if space is limited.

A-13. Geographical names—cities, counties, countries—except for states and possessions of the United States, which may be abbreviated in lists, addresses, and tabulations, according to the forms recommended by the United States Postal Service.

A-14. Units of measure except in invoices, lists, and tabulations. Be consistent in using abbreviations in a particular piece of work *(15 inches,* or *15 in,* or *15")*.

A-15. Note that no periods are used in the following: ordinals *(5th);* letters referring to a person or a thing *(Mr. X);* radio and TV station letters and broadcasting systems *(WMCA; CBS)*; mathematical symbols *(tan)*; chemical symbols *(NaCl);* and such symbols as *IOU, SOS,* which are not abbreviations.

Abbreviations: States and Territories of the United States

Alabama	AL	Kansas	KS	Northern Mariana Islands	MP
Alaska	AK	Kentucky	KY	Ohio	OH
American Samoa	AS	Louisiana	LA	Oklahoma	OK
Arizona	AZ	Maine	ME	Oregon	OR
Arkansas	AR	Marshall Islands	MH	Palau	PW
California	CA	Maryland	MD	Pennsylvania	PA
Colorado	CO	Massachusetts	MA	Puerto Rico	PR
Connecticut	CT	Michigan	MI	Rhode Island	RI
Delaware	DE	Minnesota	MN	South Carolina	SC
District of Columbia	DC	Mississippi	MS	South Dakota	SD
Federated States of		Missouri	MO	Tennessee	TN
Micronesia	FM	Montana	MT	Texas	TX
Florida	FL	Nebraska	NE	Utah	UT
Georgia	GA	Nevada	NV	Vermont	VT
Guam	GU	New Hampshire	NH	Virgin Islands	VI
Hawaii	HI	New Jersey	NJ	Virginia	VA
Idaho	ID	New Mexico	NM	Washington	WA
Illinois	IL	New York	NY	West Virginia	WV
Indiana	IN	North Carolina	NC	Wisconsin	WI
Iowa	IA	North Dakota	ND	Wyoming	WY

Abbreviations: Canadian Provinces

Alberta	AB	Nova Scotia	NS
British Columbia	BC	Ontario	ON
Manitoba	MB	Prince Edward Island	PE
New Brunswick	NB	Quebec	QC
Newfoundland	NF	Saskatchewan	SK
Northwest Territories	NT	Yukon Territory	YT

DIVIDING WORDS

Whenever possible, avoid dividing a word at the end of a line. If a word must be divided, insert a hyphen at the point of division, according to the following generally accepted rules.

Divide a word:

D-1. Only if it is more than one syllable and more than five letters and can be divided so that more than a two-letter syllable is carried over. Divide between syllables. If unsure of syllabication, consult a dictionary *(knowl-edge,* **NOT:** *know-ledge; prod-uct,* **NOT:** *pro-duct; passed,* **NOT:** *pas-sed; strength,* **NOT:** *streng-th).*

D-2. By retaining a single-vowel syllable preceding the hyphen *(cata-log).*

D-3. Between two one-vowel syllables *(situ-ation).*

D-4. After a prefix or before a suffix rather than within the root word *(inter-national;* **NOT:** *interna-tional.)* Avoid divisions that could confuse a reader.

D-5. Between double consonants not ending a root word *(begin-ning),* and following other double consonants *(bluff-ing).*

D-6. Before a suffix that has three or more letters *(compensa-tion).*

D-7. Preferably, only between the elements of a compound word *(air-conditioning).*

D-8. Avoid dividing the following: proper nouns; titles with proper names; abbreviations; contractions; numbers, including dates and street addresses.

Do not divide a word:

D-9. At the ends of more than two consecutive lines.

D-10. If it is the last word on a page.

SPELLING

Here are three simple suggestions to help you produce letters free from mis-spellings: (1) check each word carefully; (2) when in doubt, consult a dictionary; (3) keep an up-to-date list of your personal spelling demons and memorize the correct spelling of each word on your list. To correct some of your own spelling problems, study the following words that many businesspeople find troublesome.

Words Frequently Misspelled in Business Communications

absence	cancellation	debtor	finally	noticeable	receive
accommodate	capital	decide	formerly	occasion	recognize
accompanying	career	deductible	freight	occurrence	recommend
accumulate	casualty	defendant	further	offering	referred
achievement	circumstances	definitely	government	omission	requirement
acknowledgment	collateral	dependent	grateful	omitted	responsibility
adequate	commercial	depreciation	guarantee	opportunity	restaurant
advertisement	commitment	desirable	incidentally	ordinary	salary
advice	committee	develop	independent	overdue	satisfactorily
advisory	comparable	disappear	interest	pamphlet	separate
affidavit	competent	disappoint	itinerary	parallel	sincerely
all right	competitor	discrepancy	its	partial	stationery
analysis	complement	dissatisfied	judgment	particular	statistics
announcement	concede	economical	liaison	permanent	succeed
apologize	conceivable	effect	library	permitted	successful
apparently	concurred	eligible	license	personal	superintendent
appearance	confidential	eliminate	lose	personnel	supervisor
appropriate	congratulate	embarrass	magazine	practically	temporary
approximately	conscience	emphasize	maintenance	precede	their
associate	conscious	employee	management	preliminary	there
attendance	consistent	envelope	material	principal	thorough
authorize	continuous	especially	memorandum	principle	transferred
believe	convenience	exceed	merchandise	privilege	typing
beneficial	cooperative	excellent	miscellaneous	proceed	unfortunately
benefited	corporation	except	mortgage	professor	unnecessary
brochure	correspondence	exercise	necessary	quantity	usually
business	correspondents	existence	negligible	questionnaire	vendor
calendar	counsel	expense	negotiate	quite	warehouse
campaign	creditor	experience	ninety	receipt	yield

PROOFREADERS' MARKS

Using proofreaders' marks when editing and proofreading helps writers make necessary changes quickly and correctly. Study the following list, and refer to it until you have memorized the symbols.

Revision	Edited Draft	Final Copy
Delete stroke	qual*l*ity	quality
Delete word	~~very~~ **OR** ~~very~~	
Change	~~letter~~ *document*	document
Let it stand	~~however~~	however
Transpose	ta*ht*	that
Move as shown	to the reader (aid)	to aid the reader
Insert word	a *timely* ∧ fashion	a timely fashion
Insert space	all∧right	all right
Close up space	key board	keyboard
Insert period	sentence○	sentence.
Insert comma	clause∧	clause,
Underscore	<u>Proofreading</u>	<u>Proofreading</u>
Boldface type	important	**important**
Italic type	caution	*caution*
Hyphenate	9 by 12 inch envelope	9- by 12-inch envelope
Spell out	(Ave.)	Avenue
Capitalize	council	Council
Lowercase	Monthly	monthly
Begin new paragraph	¶ He agreed	
No new paragraph	NO¶ To accomplish this	
Align horizontally	Thomas arrived at	Thomas arrived at
Align vertically	Thomas arrived at the office early to finish the report.	Thomas arrived at the office early to finish the report.
Move left	[library	library
Move right	university]	university
Center	]preface[	preface
Single-space	Thomas arrived at the office early	Thomas arrived at the office early
Double-space	Thomas arrived at the office early	Thomas arrived at the office early

Index

Photo Credits

Notes

Notes

Notes

Notes